Investing Online For Dummies,® 3rd Ed

D0567803

Getting Started

1. **Know your starting point.** Determine your net worth by using an online worksheet at E-Analytics (www.e-analytics.com).

2. **Understand how much you can invest.** Use the online calculators at FinanCenter (www.financenter.com).

3. **Determine your risk-tolerance level.** At the Bank of America home page (www.bankofamerica.com), click the Personal Finance drop-down list and select Investments. Next, click Tools ☞ My Investor Profile and complete the online forms to discover how much risk you can take.

4. **Allocate your assets.** ThirdAge (www.thirdage.com/features/money/allocator) provides helpful suggestions about the types of investments that are right for you.

Analyzing Investments

1. **Check out the economic landscape.** For economic data, use free online sources such as the GSA Government Information Locator (www.gsa.gov) and Federal Reserve Web sites (www.bog.frb.fed.us/otherfrb.htm).

2. **Use mutual fund and stock screens.** Web sites such as MS Money Central (moneycentral.msn.com) and Quicken.com (www.quicken.com) offer online tools to help you screen investment candidates.

3. **Read the mutual fund's prospectus.** Internet sources for mutual fund prospectuses include the Mutual Fund Educational Alliance (www.mfea.com) and Find a Fund (www.findafund.com).

4. **Analyze the company's annual report.** Online sources of company annual reports include Company Sleuth (www.companysleuth.com), EDGAR (www.sec.gov), and the Public Registrars Annual Report Service (www.prars.com).

5. **Do your homework.** Charles Schwab (www.schwab.com) can assist you with your investment analysis. From the home page, click Investments ☞ Stock Analyzer. For fundamental data, price history, and comparisons, enter the ticker symbol of the stock you are researching.

6. **Find out what the experts are saying about your investment selection.** Go to Thomson Investors Network (www.thomsoninvest.net), click Earnings, and enter the ticker symbol of the stock you are investigating. You get a company snapshot, an estimated earnings profile, and news about any recent earnings revisions.

7. **Understand the tax implications of your investment selections.** For information about tax-exempt mutual funds and municipal bonds, refer to online sources such as Quote.com (www.quote.com) and CBS MarketWatch (www.cbsmarketwatch.com). At the CBS MarketWatch home page, click Mutual Funds.

For Dummies®: Bestselling Book Series for Beginners

Investing Online For Dummies,® 3rd Edition

Cheat Sheet

Buying Investments

- **If possible, minimize fees.** See Mutual Funds Interactive (www.interactive.com) for a listing of no-load funds.
- **Buy shares directly from the company.** For a listing of companies that sell stock directly to the public, see Net Stock Direct (www.netstockdirect.com).
- **Maximize your returns with dividend reinvestment programs (DRIPs).** StockPower (www.stockpower.com) offers StockClick, a product that enables investors to enroll in a direct stock-purchase plan, purchase, and sell stocks online.
- **Pay the lowest brokerages fees available by trading online.** For a listing of online brokerages and their services, see Cyberinvest (www.cyberinvest.com). For a ranking of electronic brokerages, see Gomez Advisors (www.gomezadvisors.com).

Monitoring Investments

- **Use online portfolio management tools.** Check out the X-ray feature of the portfolio management program at Morningstar.com (www.morningstar.com) to make certain you don't have "stock overlap." To keep up on what's happening with your portfolio on a daily basis, use MoneyNet (www.moneynet.com) and find out how much you've gained or lost today and since you purchased your investment.
- **Keep current.** Have the news sent to your e-mailbox from such online sources as the *Wall Street Journal* (www.wsj.com), CNNfn Briefings (www.cnnfn.com) and *The Economist* (www.economist.com).
- **Watch for new investment opportunities.** Join a mailing list, an investment chat group, or search for new opportunities using such online sources as Alert IPO! (www.ostman.com/alert-ipo) and IPO Scan (www.iposcan.com).

Selling Investments

- **Know when to hold and when to fold.** Beginning investors can gain valuable insights from such sources as Investorguide (www.investorguide.com) and the Investor FAQ (www.invest-faq.com).
- **Minimize your trading.** If you can't resist trading online, join a free simulation such as Virtual Stock Exchange (www.virtualstockexchange.com).

IDG BOOKS WORLDWIDE

For Dummies®: *Bestselling Book Series for Beginners*

TM

References for the Rest of Us!®

BESTSELLING BOOK SERIES

Are you intimidated and confused by computers? Do you find that traditional manuals are overloaded with technical details you'll never use? Do your friends and family always call you to fix simple problems on their PCs? Then the ...*For Dummies*® computer book series from IDG Books Worldwide is for you.

...*For Dummies* books are written for those frustrated computer users who know they aren't really dumb but find that PC hardware, software, and indeed the unique vocabulary of computing make them feel helpless. ...*For Dummies* books use a lighthearted approach, a down-to-earth style, and even cartoons and humorous icons to dispel computer novices' fears and build their confidence. Lighthearted but not lightweight, these books are a perfect survival guide for anyone forced to use a computer.

Already, millions of satisfied readers agree. They have made ...*For Dummies* books the #1 introductory level computer book series and have written asking for more. So, if you're looking for the most fun and easy way to learn about computers, look to ...*For Dummies* books to give you a helping hand.

IDG BOOKS WORLDWIDE

1/99

Investing Online
FOR
DUMMIES®
3RD EDITION

by Kathleen Sindell, Ph.D.

Foreword by Charles R. Schwab
Chairman, The Charles Schwab Corporation

IDG
BOOKS
WORLDWIDE

IDG Books Worldwide, Inc.
An International Data Group Company

Foster City, CA ◆ Chicago, IL ◆ Indianapolis, IN ◆ New York, NY

Investing Online For Dummies,® 3rd Edition

Published by
IDG Books Worldwide, Inc.
An International Data Group Company
919 E. Hillsdale Blvd.
Suite 400
Foster City, CA 94404
www.idgbooks.com (IDG Books Worldwide Web Site)
www.dummies.com (Dummies Press Web Site)

Library of Congress Control Number: 00-103655

ISBN: 0-7645-0725-7

Printed in the United States of America

10 9 8 7 6 5 4 3 2 1

3O/RT/QZ/QQ/IN

Distributed in the United States by IDG Books Worldwide, Inc.

Distributed by CDG Books Canada Inc. for Canada; by Transworld Publishers Limited in the United Kingdom; by IDG Norge Books for Norway; by IDG Sweden Books for Sweden; by IDG Books Australia Publishing Corporation Pty. Ltd. for Australia and New Zealand; by TransQuest Publishers Pte Ltd. for Singapore, Malaysia, Thailand, Indonesia, and Hong Kong; by Gotop Information Inc. for Taiwan; by ICG Muse, Inc. for Japan; by Intersoft for South Africa; by Eyrolles for France; by International Thomson Publishing for Germany, Austria and Switzerland; by Distribuidora Cuspide for Argentina; by LR International for Brazil; by Galileo Libros for Chile; by Ediciones ZETA S.C.R. Ltda. for Peru; by WS Computer Publishing Corporation, Inc., for the Philippines; by Contemporanea de Ediciones for Venezuela; by Express Computer Distributors for the Caribbean and West Indies; by Micronesia Media Distributor, Inc. for Micronesia; by Chips Computadoras S.A. de C.V. for Mexico; by Editorial Norma de Panama S.A. for Panama; by American Bookshops for Finland.

For general information on IDG Books Worldwide's books in the U.S., please call our Consumer Customer Service department at 800-762-2974. For reseller information, including discounts and premium sales, please call our Reseller Customer Service department at 800-434-3422.

For information on where to purchase IDG Books Worldwide's books outside the U.S., please contact our International Sales department at 317-572-3993 or fax 317-572-4002.

For consumer information on foreign language translations, please contact our Customer Service department at 1-800-434-3422, fax 317-572-4002, or e-mail rights@idgbooks.com.

For information on licensing foreign or domestic rights, please phone +1-650-653-7098.

For sales inquiries and special prices for bulk quantities, please contact our Order Services department at 800-434-3422 or write to the address above.

For information on using IDG Books Worldwide's books in the classroom or for ordering examination copies, please contact our Educational Sales department at 800-434-2086 or fax 317-572-4005.

For press review copies, author interviews, or other publicity information, please contact our Public Relations department at 650-653-7000 or fax 650-653-7500.

For authorization to photocopy items for corporate, personal, or educational use, please contact Copyright Clearance Center, 222 Rosewood Drive, Danvers, MA 01923, or fax 978-750-4470.

About the Author

Kathleen Sindell is an expert on electronic commerce and an adjunct faculty member at the Johns Hopkins University MBA program. She is the author of numerous popular, academic, and professional books, articles, and Web sites. A dynamic consultant, speaker, writer, and scholar, Dr. Sindell is regularly tapped as an e-commerce expert on CNNfn, The Nightly Business Report, and at popular online and print outlets. She is the founder of a firm that provides consulting and authoritative publications about management, finance, and real estate in the e-commerce environment. She and her colleagues work with organizations to deliver effective business solutions for new ways of conducting business and managing finances in the emerging electronic environment. She is the former Associate Director of the Financial Management and Commercial Real Estate Programs for the University of Maryland, University College Graduate School of Management & Technology.

Dr. Sindell is the author of the *Unofficial Guide to Buying a Home Online* (IDG Books Worldwide, Inc., 2000) and *A Hands-On Guide to Mortgage Banking Internet Sites*, a separate directory published by *Mortgage Banking Magazine* (1999, 1998, 1997). She is the author of *The Handbook of Real Estate Lending* (McGraw-Hill Professional Publishing, 1996), and edited a book titled the *Essentials of Financial Management Kit* (Dryden Press, 1993).

Dr. Sindell developed the *Lending Solutions Decision Support Program* to identify, assess, monitor, and mitigate the credit quality of real estate loans. This software application is based on her hands-on experience as a Real Estate Vice President for American Savings & Loan and as the Construction Lending Services Manager for Perpetual Federal Savings Bank.

Dr. Sindell has taught more than 25 graduate-level courses in financial management; she lectures for the New York Institute of Finance; and she is a well-known speaker at regional and national conferences, where she addresses the development of online customer loyalty, online investing and mortgage lending topics, and electronic customer relationship management issues.

She received her BA in Business from Antioch University, an MBA in Finance from the California State University at San Jose, and a PhD in Administration and Management from Walden University, Institute for Advanced Studies.

ABOUT IDG BOOKS WORLDWIDE

Welcome to the world of IDG Books Worldwide.

IDG Books Worldwide, Inc., is a subsidiary of International Data Group, the world's largest publisher of computer-related information and the leading global provider of information services on information technology. IDG was founded more than 30 years ago by Patrick J. McGovern and now employs more than 9,000 people worldwide. IDG publishes more than 290 computer publications in over 75 countries. More than 90 million people read one or more IDG publications each month.

Launched in 1990, IDG Books Worldwide is today the #1 publisher of best-selling computer books in the United States. We are proud to have received eight awards from the Computer Press Association in recognition of editorial excellence and three from Computer Currents' First Annual Readers' Choice Awards. Our best-selling *...For Dummies®* series has more than 50 million copies in print with translations in 31 languages. IDG Books Worldwide, through a joint venture with IDG's Hi-Tech Beijing, became the first U.S. publisher to publish a computer book in the People's Republic of China. In record time, IDG Books Worldwide has become the first choice for millions of readers around the world who want to learn how to better manage their businesses.

Our mission is simple: Every one of our books is designed to bring extra value and skill-building instructions to the reader. Our books are written by experts who understand and care about our readers. The knowledge base of our editorial staff comes from years of experience in publishing, education, and journalism — experience we use to produce books to carry us into the new millennium. In short, we care about books, so we attract the best people. We devote special attention to details such as audience, interior design, use of icons, and illustrations. And because we use an efficient process of authoring, editing, and desktop publishing our books electronically, we can spend more time ensuring superior content and less time on the technicalities of making books.

You can count on our commitment to deliver high-quality books at competitive prices on topics you want to read about. At IDG Books Worldwide, we continue in the IDG tradition of delivering quality for more than 30 years. You'll find no better book on a subject than one from IDG Books Worldwide.

John Kilcullen
John Kilcullen
Chairman and CEO
IDG Books Worldwide, Inc.

Eighth Annual Computer Press Awards ≥1992

WINNER

Ninth Annual Computer Press Awards ≥1993

WINNER

Tenth Annual Computer Press Awards ≥1994

Eleventh Annual Computer Press Awards ≥1995

Dedication

My gratitude to my husband, Ivan Sindell, for his advice and encouragement.

Author's Acknowledgments

Investing Online For Dummies, 3rd Edition, represents my desire to help people take control of their finances by accessing quality online information. This book was made possible through the teamwork and dedication of many people. My thanks to Laura Moss, acquisitions editor, for her enthusiasm for this work. Thanks to John Pont, possibly the best development editor ever. My appreciation to my literary agent, Carole McClendon, and to all the folks at Waterside Productions for their support. Many thanks to Maridee Ennis, Carmen Krikorian, Jamie Smith, and all the other talented people at IDG Books Worldwide, for all their efforts in producing this book and the accompanying CD-ROM. And a special thanks to Joe Harper for his thorough technical review.

I deeply appreciate my editorial assistant, Reuven Goren, who coordinated copyright permissions, verified Web sites, and coordinated all the multiple tasks necessary to deliver this book on time.

A very special thank you to my brother-in-law, Gerald Sindell, for his profound counsel on everything relating to the business of publishing.

And finally, my thanks to the folks who put investing information online for the public. Because of them, online investing has gone mainstream.

Publisher's Acknowledgments

We're proud of this book; please register your comments through our IDG Books Worldwide Online Registration Form located at `http://my2cents.dummies.com`.

Some of the people who helped bring this book to market include the following:

Acquisitions, Editorial, and Media Development

Project Editor: John W. Pont

Associate Acquisitions Editor: Laura Moss

Proof Editor: Teresa Artman

Technical Editor: Joe Harper, CFP

Permissions Editor: Carmen Krikorian

Associate Media Development Specialist: Jamie Smith

Editorial Manager: Constance Carlisle

Media Development Manager: Heather Heath Dismore

Editorial Assistant: Candace Nicholson, Sarah Shupert

Production

Project Coordinator: Maridee Ennis

Layout and Graphics: Amy Adrian, Joe J. Bucki, Barry Offringa, Tracy K. Oliver, Jill Piscitelli, Julie Trippetti

Proofreaders: Laura Bowman, Toni Settle, York Production Services, Inc.

Indexer: York Production Services, Inc.

Special Help:
Craig Poeppelman

General and Administrative

IDG Books Worldwide, Inc.: John Kilcullen, CEO

IDG Books Technology Publishing Group: Richard Swadley, Senior Vice President and Publisher; Walter R. Bruce III, Vice President and Publisher; Joseph Wikert, Vice President and Publisher; Mary Bednarek, Vice President and Director, Product Development; Andy Cummings, Publishing Director, General User Group; Mary C. Corder, Editorial Director; Barry Pruett, Publishing Director

IDG Books Consumer Publishing Group: Roland Elgey, Senior Vice President and Publisher; Kathleen A. Welton, Vice President and Publisher; Kevin Thornton, Acquisitions Manager; Kristin A. Cocks, Editorial Director

IDG Books Internet Publishing Group: Brenda McLaughlin, Senior Vice President and Publisher; Sofia Marchant, Online Marketing Manager

IDG Books Production for Branded Press: Debbie Stailey, Director of Production; Cindy L. Phipps, Manager of Project Coordination, Production Proofreading, and Indexing; Tony Augsburger, Manager of Prepress, Reprints, and Systems; Shelley Lea, Supervisor of Graphics and Design; Debbie J. Gates, Production Systems Specialist; Steve Arany, Associate Automation Supervisor; Robert Springer, Supervisor of Proofreading; Trudy Coler, Page Layout Manager; Kathie Schutte, Senior Page Layout Supervisor; Janet Seib, Associate Page Layout Supervisor; Michael Sullivan, Production Supervisor

Packaging and Book Design: Patty Page, Manager, Promotions Marketing

◆

The publisher would like to give special thanks to Patrick J. McGovern,
without whom this book would not have been possible.

◆

Contents at a Glance

Cartoons at a Glance

By Rich Tennant

The 5th Wave — By Rich Tennant

"IT HAPPENED AROUND THE TIME WE SUBSCRIBED TO AN ON-LINE SERVICE."

page 9

The 5th Wave — By Rich Tennant

I DON'T KNOW - MY SPREADSHEET TELLS ME WE SHOULD BASE OUR OVERHEAD BUDGET ON SALES FIGURES RATHER THAN FIXED, MY PLOT CHART INDICATES WE SHOULD ESCALATE OUR MARKETING THRUST, AND MY PSYCHOANALYSIS PROGRAM TELLS ME I DEPEND TOO MUCH ON OUTSIDE INPUT AND SHOULD TRUST MY INSTINCTS MORE.

page 91

The 5th Wave — By Rich Tennant

NERD-MOMS

Okay young man, it's time to wash your hands, brush your teeth, and defrag your hard disk.

Awwww, Mom.

page 255

The 5th Wave — By Rich Tennant

"HERE'S YOUR PROBLEM. SOME BOZO JAMMED YOUR KEYBOARD WITH A 4-LEAF CLOVER."

page 313

Fax: 978-546-7747
E-mail: richtennant@the5thwave.com
World Wide Web: www.the5thwave.com

Table of Contents

Foreword

• •

*T*he Internet seems made for investing. Along with delivering information, breaking news, and online shopping, the Internet provides some of the best financial tools and resources available. You can learn more about investing, trade online, and track your portfolio. You can also get free up-to-the-minute news, quotes, charts, and research — as much information, if not more, than you'd ever want.

The key, of course, is to use this information effectively. That's where a book like Kathleen Sindell's *Investing Online For Dummies* comes in. It provides clear instructions and ample illustrations so you don't get lost in cyberspace. Now in its third edition, it draws on Dr. Sindell's considerable experience teaching and lecturing to explain the basics as well as the ins-and-outs of online investing for investors of all ages and income levels.

Of course, my favorite website is www.schwab.com. I invite you to visit us online or at one of our more than 360 branches throughout the United States, or through one of our overseas affiliates. At Schwab, our goal is to offer you the technology, information, and help and advice you need to be a well-informed investor. Whether you access your account in person, over the telephone, through the Web, or through our PocketBroker™ wireless service, our Investment Specialists can assist you in managing your trading and accounts. You can enjoy the peace of mind that comes from trading with an acknowledged leader in electronic brokerage.

Charles R. Schwab
Chairman and Co-CEO
Charles Schwab & Co., Inc.

Introduction

● ●

*W*elcome to *Investing Online For Dummies,* 3rd Edition, and the exciting world of online investing. Online investing continues its meteoric rise. At a time when online trading volume surged to an all-time record level of about 500,000 trades per day, the New York Stock Exchange — the so-called "big board" — executed about 312,000 trades per day. Clearly, online investing is going mainstream. Worldwide, thousands of investors are opening online trading accounts. They want to take control of their investments, stop paying full-service commissions, and research and trade securities when it's convenient for them.

Regardless of whether you are a new investor or an experienced trader, this book can guide you to the Internet-based resources that can help you make better, more well-informed investing decisions than ever before. The Internet offers an astounding amount of financial information, and *Investing Online For Dummies,* 3rd Edition, provides clear instructions and ample illustrations so you don't get lost in cyberspace. With the assistance of this book, you can find up-to-the second stock quotes, historical financial data on public companies, professional analyses, educational materials, and more.

In this book, I show you how to get started, what you really need to know, and where to go on the Internet for additional information. You don't need to memorize complex commands or formulas. I describe everything in plain English, and I leave the Wall Street-speak out in the street.

Who Are You?

More than 8 million investors now trade online, and researchers predict that this number will increase at an annualized rate of between 28 and 30 percent to reach 18 million by 2003. Industry analysts predict we'll reach this number even sooner!

These online investors are divided almost equally into four groups:

- ✔ Affluent traders who make about ten trades per year and have a net worth of more than $320,000. (*Net worth* is what you have less what you owe to others.)
- ✔ Young traders who also make about ten trades per year and have a net worth of about $39,000.

- ✔ Middle-class investors who make approximately one trade per year and have a net worth of about $49,000.
- ✔ Affluent investors who make about three trades per year and have a net worth of $362,000.

In writing this book, I assume you want join one of the four groups of online investors, or you already invest online, and you want to maximize your returns. Therefore, you want to

- ✔ Take advantage of all the timely investment information available on the Internet.
- ✔ Get some work done with the Internet. (Online selecting, evaluating, and monitoring of investments can be time-consuming. Online investing really is work.)
- ✔ Partner with the Internet in making your money work harder for you.

About This Book

This book has no hidden agenda. It focuses on commonsense ways to create and build wealth with the Internet.

I've designed *Investing Online For Dummies,* 3rd Edition, for beginning online investors, but it can also benefit experienced investors. Each chapter stands alone and provides all the instructions and information you need for solving an investment problem or making an investment decision.

Most online investors will read this book in chunks, diving in long enough to solve a particular investment problem ('Hmmm, which online brokerages offer wireless trading?') and then putting it aside. However, I have structured the book in such a way that if you want to read it through from beginning to end (even though the book's primary function is as a reference tool), you can do so.

I discuss online investment topics in a logical way, from online investing fundamentals through making your own online stock transactions to purchasing bonds online and directly from the Federal government.

Here's a quick rundown on some of the topics I cover:

- ✔ Building your own online investment information system
- ✔ Using the Internet to simplify your financial planning
- ✔ Selecting the online brokerage that meets your individual needs

✔ Locating Internet resources for the selection of mutual funds

✔ Working with Internet tools for analyzing and selecting stocks and bonds

✔ Using mutual fund and stock online screens to find investment candidates that will help you meet your financial goals

✔ Trading online or going wireless and paying the lowest commissions possible

✔ Keeping track of your portfolio and knowing exactly how your assets are allocated (even the holdings in your mutual funds)

✔ Discovering direct stock purchase and sharebuilder plans that let you become an online investor for as little as $25 a month

✔ Finding out how to take advantage of international opportunities online

Additionally, I offer warnings to help you avoid dangerous or costly traps, and I point out excellent online investment resources. *Investing Online For Dummies,* 3rd Edition, puts you in the driver's seat on the information highway. It provides the Internet knowledge you need to get the edge on investors who rely solely on newspapers and magazines.

How to Use This Book

If you have a question about an online investing topic, just look up that topic in the table of contents at the beginning of the book or in the index at the end of the book. You can get the help you're seeking immediately or find out where to look for expert advice.

Investing has evolved into a specialized field and isn't particularly easy for normal people. Don't feel bad if you have to use the table of contents and the index quite a bit. Luckily, the Internet offers plenty of sites that let you practice before you buy or trade.

If you want to experience electronic trading and are concerned that a mistake may cost you money, try practicing at the Virtual Stock Exchange (www. virtualstockexchange.com). The Virtual Stock Exchange is a free fantasy stock market game. You can compete with tens of thousands of online investors in a realistic stock trading simulation in which you can buy and sell shares of stocks from NYSE, AMEX, and NASDAQ.

If you're new to investing on the Internet, check out the first three chapters in Part I. They give you an overview of the Internet and some important investor tips. To get more familiar with the Internet, try some of the activities that I detail in these chapters.

If you are new to the Internet, I recommend getting a copy of *The Internet For Dummies,* 7th Edition, by John R. Levine, Carol Baroudi, and Margaret Levine Young (IDG Books Worldwide, Inc.). This book is great for anyone who needs help getting started with the Internet. *The Internet For Dummies* can assist you in hooking up with local Internet providers, surfing the Net, downloading free software, and joining mailing lists or user groups.

If you're a new investor, check out Chapter 17, which offers warnings about online frauds, schemes, and deceptions. When you start subscribing to investor newsgroups, mailing lists, or online publications, you're likely to receive e-mail stock tips and investment offers. Treat these messages as you would any telephone cold call. Thoroughly examine the investment and get a second opinion from an independent investment expert you respect before you purchase.

How This Book Is Organized

This book has four parts. Each part stands alone — that is, you can begin reading anywhere and get the information you need for investment decision-making. Or you can read the entire book from cover to cover. The first part of this book lays the groundwork that beginning online investors need. The next three parts focus on how you can navigate the Internet to get the information you want about specific types of investments, online trading, and portfolio tracking.

Here's a quick rundown on the parts of the book and what they contain.

Part I: Online Investing Fundamentals

In Part I, you find out what investor tools are available on the Internet for special interest groups such as children, college students, seniors, and women. The chapters in Part I discuss important investor uses of the Internet: searches for financial topics, electronic mail, newsgroups, and access to databases that until recently were only available to large financial institutions. You also find out how to make your money work harder and how to find an online brokerage that meets your individual needs. You'll clearly see how online investing can fit into your personal financial aspirations.

Part II: Finding the Right Investments

The chapters in Part II show you how to find the right investments. This part of the book describes how you can select, analyze, and purchase mutual funds, stocks, and bonds on the Internet. The chapters in this part of the book cut through the jargon and get to the heart of what investments are (and what they're not). These chapters help you understand rates of return and what mutual funds, stocks, and bonds are all about. They also cover how to research and analyze stocks and bonds online. I point you to many online sources for annual reports, economic data, analyst recommendations, industry standards, and more. You'll discover great online investment analysis tools so you don't have to be a math whiz to determine which investment is best.

Part III: Expanding Your Investment Opportunities

Part III includes a chapter that details how to evaluate international investments. You also find out how to use the Internet to find investment opportunities like initial public offerings (IPOs) and dividend reinvestment plans (DRIPs). This part of the book also covers online portfolio management.

Part IV: The Part of Tens

No more guessing about what to hold and when to fold. Part IV provides handy top-ten lists packed full of ready online references. The chapters in this part cover such essentials as avoiding cyberfraud, knowing when to hold and when to fold, and recognizing buying signals.

Special features

Check out this book's Investing Online Directory, which is bigger and better than ever. The Investing Online Directory includes the latest and greatest investor sites on the Internet.

The Internet is constantly changing. Thousands of new Web pages are added each day. Some sites listed in this directory (and elsewhere in the book) may have changed or gone away due to mergers with larger sites. Some Web sites just vanish for no reason. If a site has moved, you may find a link to the new location. If not, try a search engine (such as AltaVista or Infoseek) to locate the resource you need.

The companion CD-ROM packaged with this book contains a selection of the finest Internet investment software tools and demos available for investors who use PC and Macintosh computers. (Yes, the Mac is back!) You also get Microsoft Internet Explorer 5.0, and a complete Web version of the book's Investing Online Directory. (You don't have to type in the Web addresses of sites you want to visit; just launch your browser program, access the Investing Online Directory on this book's companion CD-ROM, connect to the Internet, and click a site's name.)

What's New

In this third edition of *Investing Online for Dummies,* I describe dozens of the latest and greatest Internet resources available for assisting you in your wealth-building efforts. These Web sites include the newest online investing information, research sources, calculators, spreadsheets, shareware, freeware, and product demonstrations.

The content of *Investing Online For Dummies,* 3rd Edition, is bigger and better than ever, with new chapters and more information on hot topics, such as:

- ✔ New online portfolio management tools that let you know exactly what your mutual funds are holding so you can avoid "stock overlap"
- ✔ Picking a rising star: introducing new online tools for analyzing stocks
- ✔ More online information about fixed-income securities and bonds
- ✔ Increasing profits by selling short
- ✔ Trading in international securities online and without a broker
- ✔ Joining an online brokerage's after-hours club and trading after normal market hours
- ✔ Going from hard-wired to wireless trading
- ✔ The big buy and sell signals

And so much more . . .

Technical Requirements

The following list details the minimum system requirements for connecting to the Internet. This list describes all the computer hardware and software you need:

- ✔ An IBM PC-compatible computer with a minimum of 8MB of RAM, 60MB available hard disk space, a 486 or Pentium processor (Pentium preferred), and Windows 3.*x,* 95/98, NT 4.0 with Service Pack 3 or later, or 2000 operating systems. Or a Macintosh or Mac clone with 16MB of RAM, 60MB available hard disk space, a PowerPC 603 RISC or faster processor, and Mac OS 8, 9, or X operating systems.
- ✔ Any Internet browser (such as Netscape Navigator 4.*x* or Internet Explorer 5.0).
- ✔ A SLIP or PPP Internet connection, with a telephone line modem that runs 28.8 Kbps or faster. You may want to consider a cable modem or DSL direct connection (if available in your area).

Icons Used in This Book

Throughout *Investing Online For Dummies,* 3rd Edition, I use icons to help guide you through all the suggestions, solutions, cautions, and World Wide Web sites. I hope you find that the following icons make your journey through online investment strategies smoother.

This icon indicates an explanation for a nifty little shortcut or time-saver.

This icon points out riskier investment strategies plus other things to watch out for.

The Technical Stuff icon lets you know that some particularly nerdy, technoid information is coming up so that you can skip it if you want. (On the other hand, you may want to read it.)

The Remember highlights information that you should file away for future reference. This is basic information that you'll need to use over and over again.

This icon indicates that the software discussed is also included on this book's companion CD-ROM. The software may be freeware (yours forever), shareware (free to try but to own it you must buy), or a product demonstration. (Note: All the URLs for the Web sites listed in this book are included on the CD ROM for easy access to your favorite Web sites.)

Feedback, Please

I am always interested in your comments, suggestions, or questions. I'd love to hear from you. Please feel free to contact me in care of IDG Books Worldwide, 10475 Crosspoint Blvd., Indianapolis, IN 46256. Better yet, visit my Web site at www.kathleensindell.com, and send me an e-mail message at ksindell@kathleensindell.com.

Part I

Online Investing Fundamentals

The 5th Wave   By Rich Tennant

"IT HAPPENED AROUND THE TIME WE SUBSCRIBED TO AN ON-LINE SERVICE."

In this part . . .

The chapters in this part help you discover why the Internet should be your starting point for researching investments. You find out how to develop your own online investment information system that is geared to your specific requirements. These chapters point you to a variety of online investor resources and data, including numerous Web sites geared primarily to the beginning investor. You also find out how to select an online brokerage that meets your individual needs and you examine the basics of making an online trade.

Chapter 1

Finding Investor Stuff on the Net

● ●

In This Chapter

▶ Making your own online information system

▶ Using search engines

▶ Joining newsgroups

▶ Subscribing to Internet mailing lists

▶ Accessing online databases

▶ Finding Web sites that fit your unique needs

● ●

*T*he Internet has millions of Web pages and is still growing. This information overload has sent some timid investors to full-service brokers, where they pay high commission fees for brokerage services and investment advice. Smart online investors can avoid information overload by developing their own information systems.

This chapter shows how you can take maximum advantage of the Internet's many investment tools, links, and resources. The chapter explains the Internet basics of using search engines, finding investor newsgroups, subscribing to investor mailing lists, accessing online databases, and using Web sites that are tailored to your specific needs to maximize your personal wealth.

Building Your Own Online Information System

Investments provide opportunities to make money in both a *bull* market (that is, an up market) and a *bear* (down) market. No one ever knows for certain whether the market will go up or down, but investors can develop an information system to watch indicators for potential price changes and investment opportunities. This chapter introduces the elements you can use for building an online investment information system that meets your specific needs.

Investment indicators often signal future market trends. For example, changes in bond prices and interest rates often reflect market trends that may affect stock prices. That is, if bond yields decline, investors often rush to purchase stocks, causing stock prices to increase.

Investors need this information to decide whether they should buy, sell, or hold. Gathering, organizing, and saving this information can be time-consuming. However, using your own online information system can make the process more efficient.

Successful investing involves five basic steps:

1. **Identifying new investments**

2. **Analyzing investment candidates**

3. **Purchasing investments**

4. **Monitoring investments**

5. **Selling investments — to reap your rewards**

The following sections summarize the online sources for the information you need for each step. Knowing what type of information you need and where to get it online can help you build your personalized online information system.

Identifying new investments

Before investing, you need to clearly state your financial objectives and know your risk-tolerance level. This information can help you determine your required rate of return. By doing this type of homework, you can determine which categories of financial assets you may want to consider investing in. For example, if you're selecting investments for your Individual Retirement Account (IRA), you don't want to invest in tax-exempt municipal bonds (because being tax-exempt twice doesn't make sense).

Here are some examples of online sources for identifying investment opportunities:

✔ Company profiles describe a firm's organization, products, financial position, chief competitors, and executive management. (See Chapter 11 for details.)

✔ Direct purchase plans show how to purchase stock in a company without paying a broker's commission (see Chapter 15).

✔ Directories of investor sources provide hard-to-find information that is necessary for investment decision-making. (See this book's Investing Online Directory for a listing of sources.)

✔ Dividend reinvestment plans describe how to join dividend reinvestment programs to purchase company stock at a discount and without a broker. (Chapter 15 shows you how to get started.)

✔ Initial public offerings are new opportunities for investor profits (see Chapter 15).

✔ Investing *e-zines* (electronic magazines) provide educational articles and pertinent facts for beginning and experienced investors (see Chapter 2).

✔ Mailing lists provide opinions and investors' insights about investment candidates. (I discuss mailing lists later in this chapter, in the section "Getting Investor Information from Mailing Lists.")

✔ News reports on the Net can provide information about new investment opportunities (see Chapter 11).

✔ Newsgroups are informal, online groups of individuals who share ideas about a common interest. You can find dozens of investment-related newsgroups with topics ranging from specific types of investments to investor strategies. (See "Understanding How Newsgroups Can Help You," later in this chapter.)

✔ Online databases (free and fee-based repositories of information) provide historical stock prices, economic forecasts, and more. (See the section "Using Free and Fee-Based Online Investor Databases," later in this chapter, for examples of what's available.)

✔ Search engines (specialized Internet programs that seek the data you desire) provide you with links to the Web pages that have the investor information you want. (I discuss search engines later in this chapter, in the section, "Setting up Your Basic Investment Search Strategy.")

✔ Stock recommendations from professionals enable you to find out what brokers and analysts are saying about your investment selections (see Chapter 11).

✔ Mutual fund and stock screens for selecting specific securities enable you to sort through thousands of investment candidates in seconds to find not only the right investment but also the best investment available. (I discuss Internet-based stock screens in Chapter 9.)

Analyzing investment prospects

The process of analyzing investment prospects includes examining groups of investments or individual securities. For this task, you need information to forecast the timing and amount of future cash flows of investment candidates.

That is, the price you pay today is based on the future income of the asset. To figure out what the asset will be worth in the future requires some homework, analysis, and good luck. Here are a few examples of online sources for this type of information:

- Company profiles and annual reports often forecast the company's future revenues and earnings. (For more information about finding annual reports online, see Chapter 10. You can find more information about company profiles in Chapter 11.)

- Databases (free and fee-based online sources) provide news, market commentary, historical stock prices, economic forecasts, industry standards, and competitor information. I introduce you to these databases in the section, "Using Free and Fee-Based Online Investor Databases," later in this chapter. (For additional information, see this book's Investing Online Directory for a good overview of what's available for investors.)

- Earnings estimates from brokers and analysts give you forecasts of a company's future earnings (see Chapter 11).

- Industry or business-sector news can frequently indicate whether an industry is in a downward cycle. (See this book's Investing Online Directory for a listing of online investor news, news services, and newsletters.)

- National and economic data can point you toward a particular investment strategy. For example, if the country is going into a recession, you may want to select stocks that provide you with some defense (see Chapter 8).

- News databases offer breaking news that can help you judge whether your stock purchase is a winner or a loser. (Chapter 2 and this book's Investing Online Directory offer a good overview of online news sources.)

- Securities and Exchange Commission (SEC) filings provide you with financial statements from publicly traded companies. These companies are required to file financial statements every 90 days and more often if big events are happening within the firm. More than 7,000 of these filings are now online. (For details, see Chapter 10.)

Purchasing investments

After you decide which investments you want to purchase, you have to decide how you want to purchase them. For example, you must decide whether you want a full-service broker, a deep-discount broker, or an electronic broker. Usually, deep-discount, online brokerages can execute your trades but do not offer any recommendations or advice. (See Chapter 4 for details.)

You may participate in an automatic investment plan (AIP). With your approval, this type of plan deducts a certain amount from your checking account to purchase mutual funds, savings bonds, or other investments. (Chapter 5 provides step-by-step directions for opening an AIP account.)

Monitoring investments

If you have more than one investment, you will likely want a way to monitor and compare their performances to the market and similar investments. Here are a few examples of the information and the software you need to accomplish this objective (see Chapter 16 for more details about online portfolio management):

- ✔ Market monitoring tools are often alerts that you determine. For example, if your stock increases by 25 percent, you may want to consider selling it. You can set up an alert that sends you an e-mail message notifying you that your stock has reached this target.

- ✔ The Internet provides many portfolio management programs that let you know when your investments are in the news.

- ✔ Online portfolio management tools can automatically send you an e-mail message at the end of the day letting you know whether your investments gained or lost value.

- ✔ PC-based portfolio management tools are downloadable software programs that assist you in tracking your investments and record keeping.

- ✔ Your online broker may track your portfolio for you and keep records of your profits and losses.

Selling investments

You need to decide what proportion of your personal wealth you want to invest in specific assets, how long you want to hold those assets, and whether now is a good time to sell those assets to harvest your rewards. To that end, you need information about the following topics:

- ✔ **Asset allocation methodologies:** You need to determine what portion of your portfolio should be invested in mutual funds, stocks, and bonds. (See Chapter 3 to find a strategy that's right for you.)

- ✔ **Capital gains and tax issues:** You must understand how tax issues impact your profits. The Investment FAQ Web site (www.invest-faq.com) provides useful articles about the tax implications of the distributions of mutual funds and the computations of capital gains and tax rates. The Quicken Investor Tax Center (www.quicken.com/taxes/investing) provides online calculations that do the math and assist you in determining your tax liability for holding shares and estimating your capital gains on different stock issues.

✔ **Selling strategies:** Determining when you should harvest your investments requires using specific order execution strategies, mutual fund redemption plans, and analyses. (See Chapters 4, 5, and 16 to explore these topics in more detail.)

Setting up Your Basic Investment Search Strategy

Search engines are commercial enterprises that collect and index Web pages or Web page titles. You can use them to help you sift through all the Web pages out there so you can find the information you need.

Some of these enterprises review the sites they collect, and others provide site information unfiltered and unedited. Some search engines are hierarchical indexes (like Yahoo!) and use subject listings that are similar to the card catalog in a library. Often, you can search hierarchical indexes by *keyword* (a word that sums up or describes the item or concept you are seeking) and by topic.

Knowing how to use a search engine is a basic Internet skill. Currently, more than 600 different search engines exist on the Net. These Internet tools can be divided into two categories: metasearch engines and search engines.

Metasearch engines enable you to enter a single search term to query many individual search engines. This kind of all-in-one shopping is used to match your inquiry to the millions of Web pages on the Internet. Here are some examples of metasearch engines:

✔ **Ask Jeeves** (www.askjeeves.com) is designed for individuals who are new to the Internet. Write your question in plain English to focus your search.

✔ **Dogpile** (www.dogpile.com) is a metasearch engine that searches the Web, Usenet newsgroups, FTP sites (sites for downloading software and data via FTP — the file transfer protocol), weather information, stock quotes, business news, and other news wires. (For more information about Usenet newsgroups, see the section "Understanding How News-groups Can Help You," later in this chapter.) This site also includes a Web catalog.

✔ **SavvySearch** (www.savvysearch.com) uses more than 200 search engines, guides, auctions, Usenet archives, news archives, shareware libraries, and other Web resources. SavvySearch integrates and lists results by relevancy.

✔ **Webcrawler** (`www.metacrawler.com`) works like Dogpile but doesn't search Usenet newsgroups and FTP (file transfer protocol) sites. Search results are not annotated.

Search engines are trustworthy Internet programs that match the words in your query to words on the Internet. Each search engine is a competitive, commercial enterprise with different databases, search programs, and features. Everyone has a favorite search engine. The search engine that is best is the one that works the best for you.

Search engines employ "spiders" or "crawlers" (robot programs) that constantly seek new information on the Internet. These robot programs index and categorize their findings and then let you probe their lists with keywords. The program shows your search results with short descriptions and hyperlinks. Just click the hyperlink and go to the Web page you are seeking.

Here are a few of the more popular search engines on the Net:

✔ **AltaVista** (`altavista.digital.com`) may be the best search engine on the Web. AltaVista has the largest database on the Internet — twice the size of Infoseek. AltaVista recently partnered with LookSmart, which provides it with directory listings. AltaVista and Infoseek have more features than their competitors. As of June 2000, AltaVista had indexed about 35 percent of the Internet's 1 billion Web pages.

✔ **Excite** (`www.excite.com`) enables you to browse many subject categories. It uses a combination of concept (a general idea) and keyword (a specific word in the Web page) searches, so the results are usually pretty good. Excite also offers helpful reviews (editor evaluations of Web sites) and support for various advanced search techniques. Excite was launched in 1995 and soon purchased Magellan (`www.magellan.com`). In November 1996, WebCrawler (`www.webcrawler.com`) was purchased. All three engines are run as separate services. As of June 2000, Excite had indexed about 25 percent of the total pages on the World Wide Web.

✔ **Google** (`www.google.com`) is currently ranked as the search engine with the largest amount of the Internet indexed (about 56 percent). Google has received high praise for providing search results with a high level of relevancy and provides some of its index results to Yahoo! and Netscape Search.

✔ **Infoseek** (`infoseek.go.com`), shown in Figure 1-1, is easy to use and accurate. Results are fast. It also has Web site reviews, company profiles, stock prices, and other investor information for one-stop shopping. My favorite feature is the capability to search the search results. After several iterations, you can reduce the number of responses to the several that you can effortlessly check. For example, if you are beginning your general research on retirement planning, you may search for **"Retirement Planning"** in your first search. This search results in 1,683,130 responses. You can refine your search by entering **Online** and clicking Search These

Results. This search produces 237 responses. If you add **Invest** to the query and click Search These Results, you get 17 responses. You can then print a copy of the search results and begin visiting Web sites.

✔ **Lycos** (www.lycos.com) is a hybrid search engine that searches its subject categories and provides editor reviews and a listing of its top 5 percent of the search results. (By the way, Lycos is Latin for *wolf spider*.)

✔ **Netscape** (www.netscape.com) offers this portal site with search engines and navigation offerings. The Netscape search engine is powered by Excite, but the site gives you the option of using other company search engines.

✔ **Northern Light** (www.northernlight.com) includes about 27 percent of the Internet, as of June 2000. Northern Light is often used by researchers because of its ability to cluster documents by topic. Northern Light offers a set of "special collection" documents that are available for a small fee. Other research results are free.

✔ **Search** (www.search.com) and **Snap** (www.snap.com) are owned and operated by Cnet. Search.com taps into Infoseek for a general database and uses its own database for more subject searches. Snap is a directory supported by Inktomi.

✔ **Yahoo!** (www.yahoo.com) is a popular starting point. This directory search engine includes a vast array of subject directories, categories, and special services such as people search, weekly picks, What's New This Week, Yahoo! Loan Center, Finance Yahoo!, and Real Estate Yahoo!

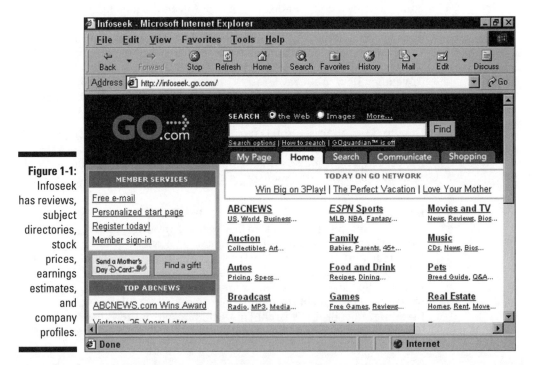

Figure 1-1:
Infoseek has reviews, subject directories, stock prices, earnings estimates, and company profiles.

TIP

Personalized search engines

With more than 1 billion Web pages, your search for investment information is likely to dredge up many articles that are outdated or simply not relevant. One way to increase your treasure-to-trash ratio is to use a personalized search engine. My Yahoo! (my.yahoo.com) allows users to set up profiles for (among other things) specific news topics and a stock portfolio.

The My Excite Channel (my.excite.com) — known as Excite Live in a previous life — includes much of the same personalization features as My Yahoo! The Wall Street Journal Interactive Edition (www.wsj.com), the grand-daddy of all investor information, lets readers build a personalized profile that monitors your news interests, favorite *Wall Street Journal* features, and stock portfolio.

Selecting the best search engine

With more than 1 billion Web pages on the Internet, finding the one page you need can be difficult. Using search engines is often like a crapshoot. Sometimes you win (and you find the Web page you want), and sometimes you lose (you find no relevant Web pages in your search results). If you lose, you have go to another search engine and spend more time researching.

Not all search engines are equal. Some have indexed a large portion of the Internet. Others are just starting or are slow in keeping up with the thousands of new Web pages that are added each day. To be competitive, search engines are always adding new features. Some search engine databases include Usenet, mailing lists, news sources, indexes, directories, Web sites, company profiles, and other information. Other search engines include only a portion of this data.

When you evaluate search engines, see how they match up to the following criteria:

- ✔ **Subject Directory:** Does the search engine enable you to limit searches to specific subject areas? Searches are quicker if the search engine offers a subject directory because the search engine searches only in the topic area that you specify.

- ✔ **Results Ranking:** Does the search engine rate your search results so that you know how likely you are to find what you're looking for? (For example, listings with relevancy ratings of less than 90 percent are usually worthless.)

- ✔ **Web:** Does the search engine look through the World Wide Web for your results?

- ✔ **Usenet:** Does the search engine look through newsgroups for your results?

- ✔ **URL (Uniform Resource Locator):** Does the search engine provide the Internet addresses for your search results? Getting the address can be very helpful; you can save or print the results of your search and then later you can backtrack and get to those difficult-to-find Web sites.

- ✔ **Summary:** Does the search engine provide a short text description of the search results?

- ✔ **Boolean Searches:** Does the search engine allow you to conduct more targeted searches?

Getting great search results

Search engines often bring more results than you're looking for. Here's some helpful advice for getting better results:

- ✔ Don't use just one word for your search. The more words you use to describe what you're looking for, the better.

- ✔ If the search engine has a prepackaged subject database, start your search there. Using one of the prepackaged subject databases can reduce your search time. For example, Lycos has a Stock Find category. Click Stock Find and you see links to mutual funds, an IPO (Initial Public Offering) Corner, money market fund information, and more investor-related links.

- ✔ Use synonyms of the topic you want — for example, Treasury securities, U.S. bonds, savings bonds, and EE bonds.

- ✔ Find out how to use Boolean operators to fine-tune your searches.

For Netscape browser users, here's a quick trick that can shorten your research time: If you are searching for one or two keywords, type them in your browser's location for URL addresses and press Enter. The description to the left will change from Netsite to Go To. The Excite search engine will match your keywords to its database of Web sites and display the results.

The Internet provides many guides for using search engines — for example:

- ✔ **About.com** (websearch.about.com/internet/websearch/msub21.htm) explains how to choose the best general-purpose search engine and offers advanced search technique tips and tricks.

- ✔ **Gelman Library Search Engine Guide** (gwis.circ.gwu.edu/~gelman/websearch) can assist you in learning how to search the Web using search engines. Get a description of what search engines do, types of search engines, basic search techniques, and more.

✔ **Nueva School Library Help** (nuevaschool.org/~debbie/library/ research/adviceengine.html) includes "Choose the Best Search for Your Purposes." This handy guide lists examples of information needs (I need a pinpoint search of a unique word, I have a general keyword and need help refining my strategy, and so on) and the matching search strategy (Alta Vista works best for needle-in-the-haystack searches of unique words, HotBot Super Search's template can help you create a Boolean or phrase search, and so on).

✔ **UC Berkeley Tutorial** (www.lib.berkeley.edu/treachinglib/ guides/internet/findinfo.html) presents "Finding Information on the Internet — A Tutorial," with step-by-step directions on how to get the best search results on the Internet.

✔ **ZDNet** (www.zdnet.com/pccomp/features/fea1096/sub2.html) provides "The Search Is Over," an online publication about how to unlock the secrets of search engines and how to search online like a pro. Look into the basics of Boolean searches to fine-tune your search results.

Portals are another name for search engines. Portals are designed to be the Internet user's first window on the Web. Often, you can personalize portals — for example, so you can get financial news, current portfolio data, and interest rate information before moving on to other Web sites. Examples of portals include Netscape (www.home.netscape.com/index.html), Microsoft Start (home.microsoft.com), and Cnet Snap! (www.snap.com).

Understanding How Newsgroups Can Help You

Newsgroups are discussion forums (or electronic bulletin boards) where individuals post messages for others to read and answer. New newsgroups appear — and old, unused newsgroups disappear — almost daily.

The advantage of these groups is that the opinions of authors are disparate and come from around the world. More than 5,000 publicly accessible newsgroups exist, ranging from serious to silly. Newsgroups support almost all religious ideologies, political points of view, and philosophical beliefs. If you want to know what investors think about a particular investment, a newsgroup is a good place to start. Newsgroup participants aren't necessarily investment professionals but many of them are savvy investors.

Knowing how newsgroups are named can help you determine whether a certain newsgroup may interest you. Newsgroup names typically have two or more parts. The first section of a newsgroup's name is the most general grouping or topic. Here are some examples of different first names:

Section	Description
Alt	Alternative subjects, ranging from the serious (investing and finance) to the weird (occult and alternative lifestyles)
Biz	Business subjects, including commercials
Misc	Miscellaneous topics, from items for sale to finance

Newsgroup names with two sections — for example, `alt.finance` — don't have any subgroups under that major topic. Groups such as `alt.invest.funds` branch into other newsgroups. That is, each component of the name represents a different level in the newsgroup. The last named component is the actual theme of the group. For example, `alt.invest.funds` is about investing in mutual funds.

Subscribing to a newsgroup is very easy. With most browsers, you simply click the name of the newsgroup you want to subscribe to. For details, use your Web browser to check out Beginners Central at Northern Webs (`www.northernwebs.com/bc/index.html`). Discover how to navigate your browser's newsreader, select a newsgroup, and post to newsgroups.

Tired of the same old newsgroups? Find out what's new at netINS's List of Recently Created Newsgroups, located at `www.netins.net/usenet/hyperactive/recent-newsgroups.html`.

Finding the perfect newsgroup

The Internet provides various sources for finding Usenet newsgroups. Here are a few examples:

- **Usenet Info Center Launch Pad** (`sunsite.unc.edu/usenet-i`) uses an excellent search engine that can help you find the right newsgroup. Additional information includes statistics about the number of messages posted per month and the percentage of Usenet sites that carry the group.

- **Infinite Ink Finding News Group** (`www.ii.com/internet`) is a user-friendly site that can assist you in finding the perfect newsgroup.

- **Robot Wisdom Newsgroup Finder** (`www.robotwisdom.com/finder/index.html`) enables you to search by historical period, numbers of articles, and country or state locations. This site uses clickable maps of the U.S. and the world. Responses include the newsgroup name, address, description, charter, and sometimes Frequently Asked Questions (FAQs) if available.

Note: Frequently Asked Questions (FAQs) are lists of the most frequently asked questions about specific topics. Some newsgroups have one or more FAQs. FAQs can have a table of contents and several sections.

Finally, some investor news reading

My favorite newsgroup site is Deja.com (`www.deja.com`), shown in Figure 1-2. This site lists thousands of Usenet newsgroups and provides a sophisticated search engine. You can search categories such as Business/Money and then search subcategories such as Investments. Web pages indicate the name of the newsgroup and the number of articles available.

The best feature of this site is that you can post your questions directly to the newsgroup without a great deal of fuss. You can also search newsgroup articles for keywords. For example, assume that you are thinking about investing in Delta Airlines. As part of your research, you can see what (and when) newsgroup members had something to say about the airline.

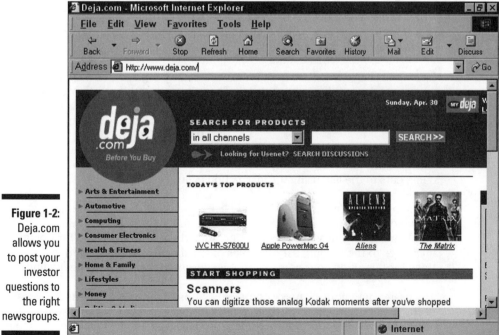

Figure 1-2:
Deja.com allows you to post your investor questions to the right newsgroups.

Another great feature is that you can research the author of the newsgroup article. Deja.com shows how many articles the author has posted and which newsgroup that author is posting to. This data can indicate which newsgroups regularly carry the type of information you're seeking.

Posting the matchless investor question

Newsgroups give you an opportunity to read the opinions of other people who are interested in the same topics as you. Before you ask a question, read the newsgroup's Frequently Asked Questions (FAQs) section to see whether someone has already answered your question. Checking out the FAQs is likely to save you from being *flamed* (receiving a hot, angry message from an experienced newsgroup user) by an old hand who is tired of seeing the same question over and over again. Another good reason to read this file is that FAQs are often the real pearls of newsgroups. Narratives vary from insipid to brilliant.

If you still want to ask a question, you can use your browser's newsreader or the Deja.com Web site. Deja.com provides you with instructions, and *The Internet For Dummies,* 7th Edition, by John R. Levine, Carol Baroudi, and Margaret Levine Young (published by IDG Books Worldwide, Inc.) can show you how to configure your Internet browser's newsreader.

Getting Investor Information from Mailing Lists

Mailing lists are e-mail groups that are started by organizations or individuals who purchase mailing list programs. Then they advertise to others who may be interested in joining a topic-specific discussion group. The advertisement usually provides precise instructions for subscribing to the mailing list.

Mailing list participants exchange e-mail about issues in their subject areas. If someone starts a *thread,* or topic, that you want to comment on, you post your comments to the list, using the instructions you received when you subscribed.

You subscribe to a particular mailing list by sending an e-mail message to the list's moderator. In return, you receive an e-mail message confirming your enrollment. This message typically includes the address you use for posting messages to the mailing list, the rules of the discussion group, and instructions for removing your name — that is, *unsubscribing* — from the mailing list.

To answer questions or make comments, subscribers send an e-mail message to the mailing list address (which differs from the mailing list program's address), and everyone gets a copy of the message. Unlike newsgroups, most lists are moderated so that inappropriate messages aren't sent to the group.

You may find a mailing list while surfing the Net, but they tend to be private. The best source for finding an investor-related mailing list is Liszt, at www.liszt.com. Liszt has more than 90, 000 mailing lists and is growing. Don't despair; the site is searchable. However, the amount of information available about each group varies.

Here are some other directories of mailing lists:

- ✔ **CataList** (www.lsoft.com/lists/listref.html) has only 34,000 mailing lists but is searchable by site, country, and number of list subscribers. (Sometimes knowing how many subscribers will receive your investment question is a good idea.)

- ✔ **Liszt Home Page** (www.liszt.com), shown in Figure 1-3, is an index of listservers (mailing list programs) arranged alphabetically, by description, name, and subject. The site is searchable.

- ✔ **PAML — Publicly Accessible Mailing Lists** (paml.alastra.com) is a smaller, older database of about 7,500 mailing lists.

Mailing lists members receive an average of 30 messages per day. If you just signed up for four mailing lists, you may have more than a hundred messages tomorrow.

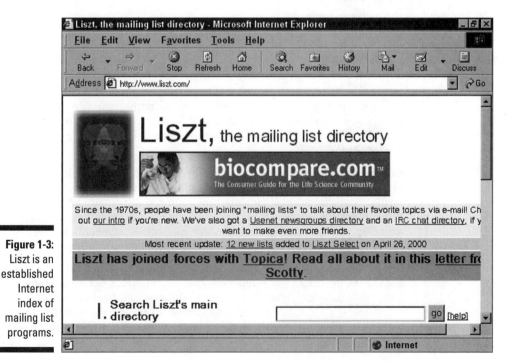

Figure 1-3:
Liszt is an established Internet index of mailing list programs.

Using Free and Fee-Based Online Investor Databases

Online investors have their choice of searching free or fee-based online databases. One advantage of both types of databases is that they are constantly open. That is, you can access them 24 hours a day, 7 days a week.

It's a no-brainer that savvy online investors should start with the free databases. If the information you desire isn't available in the free databases, try fee-based databases. If you carefully select a fee-based database for your well-constructed query, you can often get the information you want without paying big bucks.

Totally free databases

Colleges and universities played a large part in the development of the Internet. These organizations never charge for the knowledge they create. Consequently, many free databases exist online. Here are a few examples of free online databases:

- **Federal Reserve Bank of St Louis** (www.stls.frb.org/research/index.html) provides links to high-quality economic research such as FRED, a historical database of economic and financial statistics. Sign up for the mailing list and be notified about late-breaking data or new publications.

- **GovBot Database** (www.business.gov) has gathered more than 353,000 Web pages from government sites around the country. The database includes economic data collected by government and military organizations.

- **Government Information Locator Service** (www.gsa.gov) includes many U.S. government agency reports in both full-text and abstract forms. Government agencies are now required to provide and maintain publicly accessible databases. To meet this requirement, most federal agencies use the Internet. Sources are cataloged and searchable. This GSA site enables you to search more than one agency at a time.

- **STAT-USA** (www.stat-usa.gov), shown in Figure 1-4, is sponsored by the U.S. Department of Commerce. This site includes economic indicators, statistics, and news. It also offers data about state and local bond rates, foreign exchange rates, and daily economic news. Statistics include interest rates, employment, income, prices, productivity, new construction, and home sales.

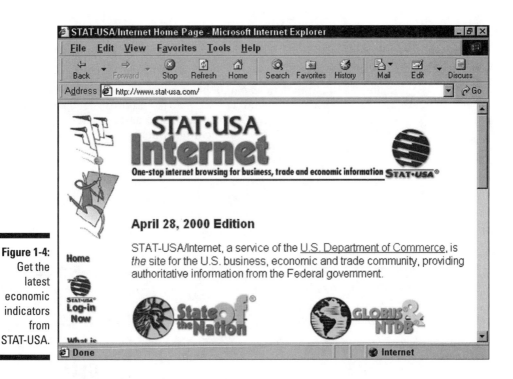

Figure 1-4:
Get the
latest
economic
indicators
from
STAT-USA.

When all else fails — fee-based databases

For specialized investor topics, the only information available may be in an online database that you have to pay for. How each organization charges for database access varies from company to company. Charges can be by query, month, hour, or document. Most firms were designed for large corporate use, and they tend to flounder in their attempts to find equitable ways of charging individuals for private use.

Fee-based databases have several limitations. Often, they use their own search methodologies that require some getting used to, and they can be costly. The fee structure may be geared for corporations and too expensive for individual use. Databases tend to be traditional and may not have that bit of unique information you're seeking.

Here are a few examples of fee-based databases (all price quotes are as of this writing and subject to change, just like everything else on the Internet):

✔ **Lexis-Nexis** (www.lexis-nexis.com) includes information from major regional and national newspaper, news sources, company information, financial information including SEC reports and proxy statements, in addition to other business sources in English and foreign languages. Lexis-Nexis accepts online credit card payments and charges $24 to $69 per day and $49 to $129 per week.

✔ **The Electric Library** (www.elibrary.com), shown in Figure 1-5, has, among other things, many newspapers, periodicals, and journals. You can search by keyword. The Electric Library is a good source for background or academic financial research. Pricing is for unlimited access. Charges for individuals are $9.95 per month and $59.95 for 12 months.

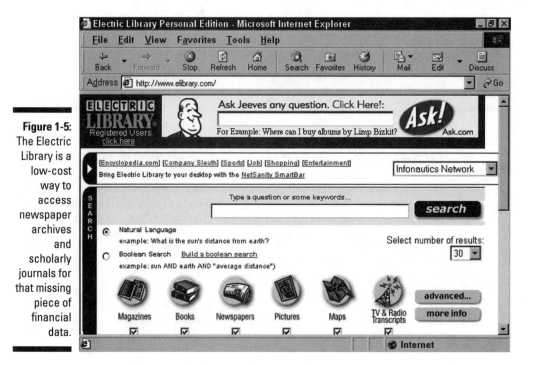

Figure 1-5:
The Electric Library is a low-cost way to access newspaper archives and scholarly journals for that missing piece of financial data.

Getting Online Investor Information Geared to Your Needs

Today, online investors come from the entire spectrum of society. Online investors range from young to old, beginners to professionals, and so on. Each of these groups has specific needs and interests. Many of the individuals in these special interest groups are looking to online communities for answers and information about their special investment needs. Others see communities as a way to make online investing simpler because information is geared to their way of thinking. The Internet provides special Web sites targeted for online investors with specific interests. The following is a sample of what you'll find on the Internet.

Investor Web sites for children

Everyday, we are bombarded with information about the stock market. Turn on the car radio, walk through a hotel lobby, or watch the news on television, and you'll get updated about the stock market whether you want to or not. In a recent Merrill Lynch survey of 512 teenagers between the ages of 12 and 17, about 9 percent who save their money invested in mutual funds or stocks. How can young people invest? Their parent must open a custodial account, because a minor can't make securities transactions without the approval of an account trustee. The Merrill Lynch statistic indicates an interest in investing that is supported by a number of online young investor Web sites.

Here are a few examples of the wide range of online resources that can meet the needs of even the youngest investor:

- **Big Money Adventure** (www.agedwards.com/bma/index.shtml) is a site where you select your guides and adventure based on your age: 2 to 6, 6 to 10, and 10 to adult. Visit the Rainbow Castle, jump into a storybook adventure and learn about investing, or play a stock-picking game and win prizes.

- **Kidstock** (www.kidstock.com) is aimed at teaching children and parents about money and investing. Sponsored by Netstock Direct (www.netstockdirect.com), the Web site also teaches how to buy stock directly from a company that has a direct stock purchase plan (DSP).

- **The Young Investor Web site** (www.younginvestor.com), shown in Figure 1-6, is an interactive community designed for children and parents. Get a hold of the fundamentals of managing money and investing. Don't forget to visit the game room and download a few games on investing.

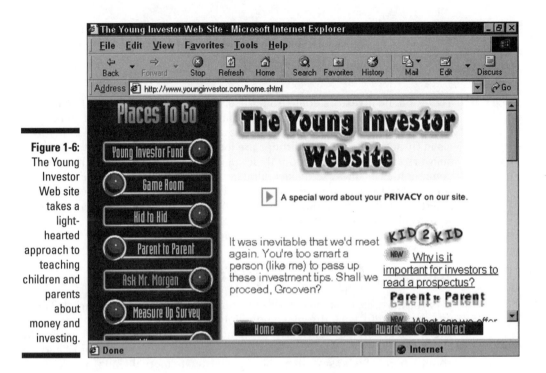

Figure 1-6:
The Young
Investor
Web site
takes a
light-
hearted
approach to
teaching
children and
parents
about
money and
investing.

Web sites for young investors

In a recent NASDQ survey, college-aged individuals (say 18 to 34 years old) account for about 20 percent of all U.S. investors. Online brokerages target these investors as their next revenue source. Many online brokerages understand that college-aged investors don't have a lot to invest now but will likely become substantial investors over time.

Here are a few examples of sites that target this group:

- ✔ **Edustock** (library.thinkquest.org/3088) is an educational Web site designed by high school students for young and old investors. The Web site includes beginning investor tutorials about how to select stocks, company profiles, and a free 20-minute delayed online stock market simulation.

- ✔ **Independent Means** (www.anincomeofherown.com) is a Web site designed for women under 20 (and their over-20 mentors) to find an income of their own. The motto of the Web site is girls, money, and power. Discover articles about money and investing, teen business pages, and more.

- ✔ **Young Investor Monthly** (www.youngmonthly.com) is staffed by a group of young investors aged 15 to 16 years old. Using their knowledge of investing and experience, they bring young investors the information they need in a fun and informative manner.

Other investor special-interest sites

Many financial institutions sponsor special-interest Web sites that provide selected groups with the information they need to be educated investors. These and other specialty Web sites (which are often nonprofit) understand that many investor sites attempt to educate online investors but fail to do so correctly because they don't understand the unique needs, top issues, and interests of the Internet users they serve. The following sections present a sampling of the various special-interest investor Web sites available:

Senior investors

Older investors can turn to the following sites for investment information:

- ✔ **Money & Investing (**www.eldernet.com/money.htm**)** is geared for senior citizens. You access this site from the ElderNet home page, shown in Figure 1-7. ElderNet's Money & Investing site provides tutorials on the basics of investing, mutual funds, stocks, and bonds. Also, it includes sound advice on how to select a financial advisor.

- ✔ **ThirdAge** (www.thirdage.com/money) provides information about investing, money management, and retiring well for adults in their mid-40s through 50s. If you are investing for an early retirement, this Web site can help you.

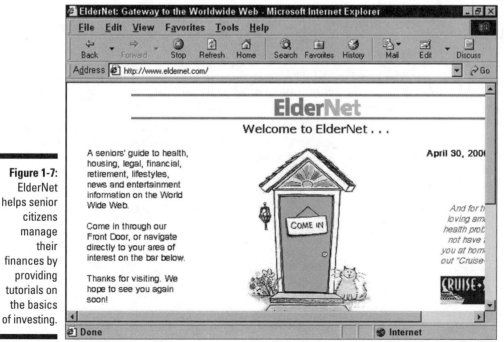

Figure 1-7: ElderNet helps senior citizens manage their finances by providing tutorials on the basics of investing.

Images © Jeff Moores, 1997. Used by permission.

Socially responsible investors

If you have an active social conscience, consider these sites as starting points for your investment research:

- ✔ **SocialFunds.com** (www.socialfunds.com) has more than 1,000 pages of strategic content to help investors make informed decisions regarding socially responsible investing. The Web site provides news, information, research, investment analysis, and financial services.

- ✔ **The Investor Responsibility Research Center** (www.irrc.org) provides research related to corporate governance, social issues, and environmental practices. Get information about corporate benchmarking and environmental indices.

- ✔ **The Social Investment Forum** (www.socialinvest.org) offers comprehensive information, contacts, and resources on socially responsible investing. The Web site includes an online guide, financial services, news, and research.

Minority and women investors

The following sites are representative of Internet investment resources targeted specifically to minority and women investors:

- ✔ **Cassandra's Revenge** (www.cassandrasrevenge.com) is a place for women to talk about money, investing, and personal growth, and to have some serious fun.

- ✔ **Coalition of Black Investors** (www.cobinvest.com) is a national investors group dedicated to being a clearinghouse for information about well-run companies and mutual funds.

- ✔ **The Gay Financial Network** (www.gfn.com) provides free financial news, information, and services. The site also includes articles by featured columnists and a weekly poll.

- ✔ **Wife.org** (www.wife.org) is the Web site of the Women's Institute for Financial Education (WIFE), a nonprofit organization dedicated to financial independence for women.

- ✔ **Women's Wire/Bloomberg** (womenswire.com/money/index.html) targets women who want to take control of their finances and start investing. Other topics include handling credit and debt, and life and money, and money talk.

Chapter 2

No Experience Required: Getting Started with Online Investing

In This Chapter

▶ Discovering how to get a cost-free investor education online

▶ Locating beginner investor and new online investor Web sites, FAQs sources, and glossaries

▶ Getting expert advice and news from online investor news sources, newspapers, magazines, and scholarly journals

▶ Getting investment newsletters automatically sent to your e-mailbox

▶ Investing and earning profits with investment clubs

▶ Practicing what you've discovered with Internet stock simulations

*T*he Internet can assist you in getting the information you need to be a savvy investor. I suggest that you start with one of the many online tutorials for beginning investors. I highlight several helpful online tutorials in this chapter. I also show you the best Web sites for new investors. I continue with directions to online Frequently Asked Questions (FAQs) sources and Internet glossaries to help you with those troublesome investment terms and concepts that the experts use.

This chapter also points out where you can find expert advice and late-breaking financial news from online news organizations, newspapers, and magazines. You discover how you can find scholarly financial journals to research the latest stock-picking methodology that your lunch buddy expounds about daily. I even show you how to get specialized investment newsletters automatically sent to your e-mailbox so that you can stay on top of current events. I often give you prices for various services, as well, but these prices may change, so check the Web site for any updated information.

Finally, this chapter shows you how to practice what you have discovered without losing a dime. First, you can join or start an investment club, which enables you to learn and earn with other folks that are interested in maximizing their investment returns. Second, you can register for one of the many online stock simulation games (some even offer monthly prizes or cash awards).

Getting Smart Online

According to *Money* magazine, the average online investor uses the Internet about 11.6 hours each week. The average time non-online investors spend on the Internet is 8.4 hours per week. This comparison indicates that if you start using the Internet to do your own investing, you won't spend a significantly longer time in front of your computer than other people do.

Connecting to the Internet gives you access to millions of documents, a vast variety of software programs (some of the best are on this book's companion CD-ROM), and high-caliber information that in the not-too-distant past only large financial institutions could access. The World Wide Web provides an easy-to-use interface with which you can access the Internet's many financial resources. With your Web browser, you can acquire an education in investing, frequently avoid costly financial services, and conduct high-grade online research.

Avoiding information overload

When you're just starting out on the Internet, you can easily become overwhelmed by the huge amount of business and finance information that's available. The best way to avoid this information overload is to divide these sources into specific categories. You can add these categories to your browser's bookmark file. (Netscape Communicator calls them bookmarks. In Internet Explorer, they're known as favorites.) For example, this chapter provides information for these bookmark categories:

- ✔ Investment Clubs
- ✔ Investment News and Market Commentary
- ✔ Investment Publications
- ✔ Investment Simulations
- ✔ Investment Tutorials and Training

Bookmarks offer a convenient way to retrieve Web pages. When you find a Web page that you know you'll want to revisit, add it to your Web browser's list of bookmarks (or favorites — both terms mean the same thing). The next time you want to visit that page, you don't have to search for it or remember the series of links you followed to reach the page in the first place. Instead, you can simply select the page from your list of bookmarks, and voilà! You're there.

Your Internet browser has menu commands and icons that enable you to create and organize your bookmarks. For more information about bookmarks, refer to *The Internet For Dummies*, 7th Edition, by Levine, Baroudi, and Young (IDG Books Worldwide, Inc.).

Online investor tutorials

If you are serious about seeing your capital grow at the fastest rate possible, you need to get smart about investing. The Internet provides many online tutorials, courses, and feature articles that can bring you up to speed. Traditional investment bankers and brokerages that are competing for your investment dollar often sponsor these sites.

These Web sites are usually 80 percent content and 20 percent sales pitch. In my opinion, the ratio makes them well worth the annoyance or inconvenience of having to complete a free registration or read an advertising banner. Here are a few examples of these informative sites:

- ✔ **Investing Basics** (www.aaii.com/invbas), shown in Figure 2-1, contains feature articles from the American Association of Individual Investors. Articles show individuals how to start successful investment programs, pick winning investments, evaluate their choices, and more. The articles cost nothing with your free registration. However, higher levels of information require your annual membership ($49).

- ✔ **Investment Basics** (www300.fidelity.com) is a site where Peter Lynch, a successful investor, former fund manager, and author, freely offers his expert advice on such topics as the key things that every investor should know, how to design your investment strategy, and ways to implement your investment plan.

- ✔ **Invest Wisely** (www.sec.gov/consumer/inws.htm) is a feature article for beginning investors from the Securities and Exchange Commission (SEC), a government regulatory agency. The SEC Web site (www.sec.gov) provides this and many other feature articles to inform and protect first-time investors.

- ✔ **Money 101** (www.money.com/money/101) is written by the editors of *Money* magazine and includes 24 interactive courses on managing all your finances. Each online tutorial takes about ten minutes. Lessons include calculators, quizzes, and a library for supplemental materials for online investors who want to dig deeper.

- ✔ **NASD Education** (www.investor.nasd.com)**,** provided by the National Association of Securities Dealers, offers educational materials for investors. Click the Site Map to get an overview of the online training materials provided.

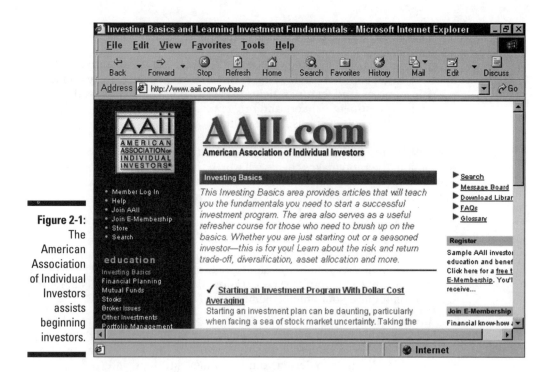

Figure 2-1:
The American Association of Individual Investors assists beginning investors.

Web sites for new investors

You can find many investor news, finance, banking, and investment organizations on the Internet. Competition is high, so they're willing to give away a large amount of high-quality information, downloadable software, and online tools for free. Many of these organizations hope that you become a fan of their great services. For those that charge fees, or those that support themselves, they want to acquire you as a steady paying customer for their products or services.

To see a few examples of investment sites for new investors, check out the following Web pages:

- ✔ **Money Advisor** (www.moneyadvisor.com) provides many free online calculators and links to online government agencies and financial institutions. You may want to consider this site your online financial management tool kit.

- ✔ **MSN MoneyCentral** (moneycentral.msn.com/investor/research/wizards/SRW.asp), shown in Figure 2-2, shows how to research a stock. Discover how to determine whether a company is financially sound, how much investors are willing to pay for the stock, how much investors are likely to pay for the stock in the future, and how it compares to the industry.

✔ **Quicken.com** (`www.quicken.com/investments`) has an extensive investment section that covers stocks, mutual funds, and bonds. A basics section with quick answers and commentary by well-known investment authors is available, in addition to columns that provide daily investment news and features.

FAQs sources

The Internet is continually flooded with *newbies* — that is, inexperienced users. To keep up with the demand for beginner information, experienced online investors have developed Frequently Asked Questions (FAQs) Web sites to avoid answering the same questions over and over again. These Web sites are convenient and can often save you much time and effort (even if you are an experienced investor).

If you're seeking the answer to just one question, use your Web browser's Find function. For example, go to the FAQs Web site you select from the following list of sites. Open your browser's Edit menu and choose the command that finds the words you specify on the currently displayed Web page. (In Netscape Communicator, the command is Find in Page. In Internet Explorer, it's Find (on This Page.)) In the resulting dialog box, enter your keywords and press Enter. Your Internet browser searches the page for the words you entered, which makes your page search more efficient and shortens your research time.

Figure 2-2: MSN MoneyCentral shows how to research a stock.

Overall, the accumulated answers in these FAQs Web sites make a solid personal finance seminar, highlighting the stock market and investing. Here are two of the better FAQs sites available at this time:

- ✔ **The Investment FAQ Homepage (**invest-faq.com**):** Enter your question to search for answers about investment and personal finance questions. Alternatively, you can browse categories for the answers you're seeking. Don't miss the regularly updated *tours* for beginning, intermediate, and experienced investors.

- ✔ **The Syndicate (**www.moneypages.com/syndicate/faq**):** Check out this list of FAQs from investment newsgroups, as shown in Figure 2-3. The Web site is designed to help beginning or experienced investors better understand investing.

Glossaries

As you cruise the Internet, you may encounter Web sites that discuss stocks, online trading, technical analysis, and derivatives. The language may seem arcane and undecipherable. However, the Internet can help. You can find many online glossaries that can assist you in stretching your vocabulary. Here are a few examples:

- ✔ **Investor Words** (www.investorwords.com) has more than 5,000 definitions of financial terms and 15,000 links between related terms. This financial glossary can save you time and effort.

- ✔ **Prudential's Glossary of Terms** (www.prusec.com/glossary/ glos_txt.htm) provides an online glossary for finding the definitions of financial and investment terms. This extensive glossary offers helpful examples of how investment terms are used.

- ✔ **Silicon Investor: Glossary** (www.siliconinvestor.com/misc/ glossary/alist.html) provides a fast and easy way to find out investment terms and concepts. Definitions include links to related online sources.

- ✔ **Yahoo! Financial Glossary** (biz.yahoo.com/f/g/g.html) offers a convenient glossary that includes hyperlinks that define words used in the text. For example, if a definition uses the word *option,* you can click the hyperlink and get the definition of *option.*

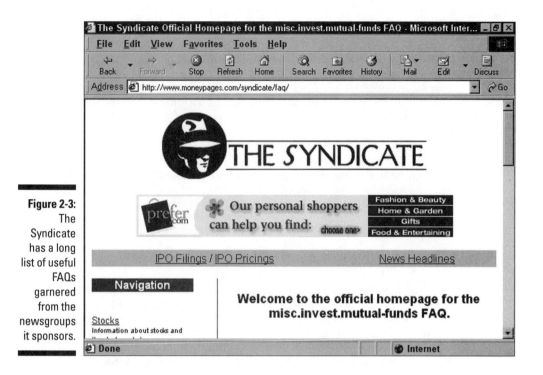

Figure 2-3:
The
Syndicate
has a long
list of useful
FAQs
garnered
from the
newsgroups
it sponsors.

News You Can Use

Savvy investors are knowledgeable investors. By using the Internet, you can easily keep informed about fast-breaking business and investment news, as well as stay in tune to the political and economic environment that affects your investments. Hundreds of business and finance Web sites are available that provide compilations of this data, which means that by using the Internet at any time, on any day, you can discover the following:

- What the experts are saying about the economy
- Changes in industry trends
- What's happening at companies that interest you
- What the experts are saying about your investment candidates
- Forecasts of future earnings
- Historical performance data

Remember, identifying investment candidates doesn't cost you a dime. You can track companies that interest you for several months or several years without being obligated to purchase their mutual funds, stocks, or bonds. The Internet helps you quickly and easily check out how these companies react to a volatile market, what technological changes are affecting their industries, and how shifts in the regional or national economy affect company performance.

This section divides online investment news sources into five categories. The sources listed in this chapter are a selection of the Internet's best offerings for your daily reading. Be certain to look for features that have value to you, such as breaking news, special features, delayed stock quotes, searchable archives, and newsletters.

Large news organizations

This section contains large Internet news organizations and focuses on those that specialize in investment and financial news. I also include international news organizations that may have affiliations with newspapers, magazines, TV stations, or radio stations:

- **Bloomberg Personal Finance** (www.bloomberg.com) is loaded with timely news, data, and analyses of financial markets and businesses. Find data on securities, statistics, indices, and research for free. Access to the member area of the Web site is $49 per year. Additional levels of service are available, including portfolio tracking, online stock quotes, company news, mutual fund information, and at-home delivery of the monthly magazine.

- **CBS MarketWatch** (cbs.marketwatch.com) has many free and fee-based services. The free edition offers delayed stock quotes, feature articles, and breaking news targeted for individual investors. With CBS MarketWatch LIVE, you get real-time equities for $79 per month when you prepay your subscriptions, or $99 on a month-to-month basis, plus exchange fees. CBS MarketWatch provides additional services; for details, see the Web site.

- **CNNfn** (www.cnnfn.com) offers news, articles on investment topics, and professional advice on money management. Major global stock indices, stock quotes, currency rates, commodities, and interest information are also available. The Research Center has links to official company Web sites, a glossary of business terms, general references, and government resources. At your request, free daily news briefings are sent to your e-mailbox.

✔ **Dow Jones** (www.dowjones.com) information technology has been on the Internet forever with a wide variety of products and services designed for individual investors who want to manage their own portfolios and make their own investment decisions. A few examples of its products are *Smart Money* (www.smartmoney.com), CNBC (www.cnbc.com), *Far Eastern Economic Review* (www.feer.com), Barrons Online (www.barrons.com), and the *Wall Street Journal* (www.wsj.com).

✔ **The Laughing Stock Broker**(www.laughingstockbroker.com), which is featured on ABC News (abcnews.go.com), includes business and industry news, market commentary, and personal finance articles. At the ABC News site, you can catch up on the latest investment issues with the Laughing Stock Broker (shown in Figure 2-4), The Street, and S & P's Personal Wealth.

✔ **Reuters MoneyNet** (www.moneynet.com) is sponsored by Reuters and specializes in financial data. MoneyNet is a convenient Web site for quotes, financial and company news, charts, research, and market snapshots. If you're looking for free online portfolio management, check out this site's Portfolio Tracker, one of the better portfolio management programs on the Web.

Figure 2-4:
The Laughing Stock Broker provides humorous investor insights and education.

Newspapers

Many of the nation's daily newspapers now have online editions that provide fast-breaking news. Frequently, these sources offer online portfolio management, delayed quotes, historical stock prices, and other resources:

- ✔ **Financial Times** (www.ft.com) provides the latest headlines, special reports, world and company news, market and industry data, and archives with your free registration.

- ✔ **Investor's Business Daily** (www.investors.com) is a daily newspaper with an online edition that provides facts, figures, and objective news for investors. The online edition has an educational section and a two-week free trial.

- ✔ **The Mercury News** (www.mercurycenter.com/business/) Business Center section presents feature articles and news, a portfolio management program, major indexes, and searchable archives ($1 to $2.95 for the full article).

- ✔ **Newspage** (www.individual.com) lets you customize the daily news abstracts it sends to your e-mailbox for free. With your free registration, you have access to the full-text version of news articles and to the archives.

- ✔ **The New York Times** (www.nytimes.com) Business section provides quotes and charts, an online portfolio function, breaking business and finance news, and information about the most active stocks, gainers, and losers. You can receive the daily Business Web page free by e-mail with The New York Times Direct.

- ✔ **USA Today** (usatoday.com) features a Money section that includes feature investment articles and news, economic and mutual fund information, calculators, and other resources. The Marketplace section includes stock quotes, market indexes, information on industry groups, currency rates, information on options and futures, and other investment information.

- ✔ **The Wall Street Journal** (www.wsj.com), considered the granddaddy of all financial newspapers, is now online and better than ever. Free offers include market alerts automatically sent to your e-mailbox. The online edition includes everything the daily edition has, plus a personal journal that enables you to customize your news and track your portfolio. One excellent feature is the Company Briefing Books, which present company backgrounds, financial overviews, stock charts, company news, and press releases. Links to Zacks Research Reports, SEC filings, and the company's official Web site are also available. You can get two levels of service: free and fee-based ($59 per year for nonsubscribers of the print edition, $29 per year for print edition subscribers).

Magazines

Like newspapers, many business and investment publications have online versions that provide the same news and feature articles that their paper-based counterparts do. Often, these online publications include additional features, such as Web-based tools for calculating your investment returns or tracking your portfolio. Here are a few examples of online magazines that are available:

- ✔ **Barrons Online** (`interactive.wsj.com/barrons`) includes This Week's Barrons, Weekday Extra, Market Lab, and a searchable archive. For a limited time, and with your free registration, you can receive This Week's Barrons at no charge.

- ✔ **Business Week** (`www.businessweek.com`) is free to all subscribers of *Business Week* magazine. Free registrants get a daily briefing, special reports, the searchable archive, banking centers, quotes, and portfolio tracking.

- ✔ **The Economist** (`www.economist.com`) offers a one-year subscription for $125 and includes full access to the online edition, which has the complete contents of the magazine. Subscriptions to the Web edition only are $48 a year and include a searchable archive. When you register, you receive five free retrievals, a downloadable The Economist's World Data Screensaver, and *Politics This Week* and *Business This Week* sent to your e-mailbox.

- ✔ **Forbes** (`www.forbes.com`) is available in an online version. Departments include technology, personal finance, startups, and e-business, in addition to conferences, publications, and the Forbes online toolbox.

- ✔ **Kiplinger Online** (`www.kiplinger.com`) presents news, stock quotes, listings of the top performing funds, mutual fund analyses, online calculators, yield and rate information, retirement advice, Web site recommendations, personal finance information, advice, and a FAQs section.

- ✔ **Money** (`www.money.com/money/`) is the online version of Time Warner's *Money* magazine. With your free registration, you can access market information, stock and fund quotes, and charts. You can also track your portfolio and receive business and finance news.

- ✔ **Mutual Funds Online** (`www.mfmag.com`) requires your free registration for access. Registrants have access to fund family guides and brokers, fund services, a load performance calculator, and related links. Your member subscription ($9 a month) includes performance rankings, profiles, screens, calculators, access to back issues, a weekly e-mail newsletter, and the monthly magazine.

- ✔ **Newsweek Online** (`www.newsweek.com`) includes breaking news from its sister publication, the *Washington Post,* daily updates from *Newsweek,* narrated photo essays, quotes, company look-ups, market data, and personal portfolio tracking.

Scholarly journals

If you really want to check out those newfangled stock analysis methods, you can find lots of scholarly financial journals online. Some articles you can download immediately. Other Web sites only provide abstracts, and you may have to contact the author by telephone, fax, e-mail, or U.S. mail for the complete article. Here's a sampling of the many scholarly financial journals online:

- ✔ **Financial Economics Network** (www.ssrn.com — click FEN at the home page) is directed by Michael C. Jensen, the Jesse Isidor-Straus Professor at the Harvard Business School. You can search for information by topic or author. You can download abstracts published in the last 60 days, and subscribers regularly receive e-mailed abstracts of journal articles and working papers. The site encourages journal readers to communicate with other subscribers concerning their and others' research. Membership fees are $15 for students, $25 for nonstudents, and $50 for professionals. The cost per journal is $5 for students, $10 for nonstudents, and $20 for professionals. A free trial offer is available.

- ✔ **FINweb** (www.finweb.com) is a Web site managed by James R. Garven, the William H. Wright, Jr., Endowed Chair for Financial Services in the Department of Finance at the E. J. Ourso College of Business Administration at Louisiana State University. The site provides Internet sources that have substantive information concerning economics and finance-related topics. FINweb supports electronic publishing and has a long list of links to journals and working papers.

- ✔ **The Journal of Finance** (www.afajof.org/jofihome.shtml) is the journal of the American Finance Association and publishes leasing research across all the major fields of financial research. Nonmembers have access to abstracts. Access to online journal articles is for members only. Annual membership for individuals is $80 and $58 for students.

Electronic newsletters

The Internet offers investors hundreds of newsletters. For your convenience, these newsletters can be sent to your e-mailbox at regular intervals. Many newsletters are free and only require that you provide your name and e-mail address. Others are fee-based and can cost anywhere from a few dollars to several hundred dollars per month.

The quality of these newsletters varies. Higher quality newsletters have educational value. Junk newsletters often promote a stock-picking methodology or recommend that you purchase a particular stock. For example, I recently received a newsletter encouraging me to buy stock in a gold mine in Bolivia. This e-mail is clearly junk e-mail, and I deleted the message immediately.

Sometimes when you visit a Web site or complete a free registration, you may not notice a pre-checked box. If you do not uncheck this box, you will receive a newsletter from the Web site's sponsor after you click the submit button on the free registration form.

Daily newsletters or alerts from the *Wall Street Journal* (www.wsj.com) or Ziff Davis Publications (www.zdnet.com/zdnn) contain breaking news. Weekly, biweekly, or monthly newsletters tend to focus on larger investor issues and are more educational. According to Newsletter Access (described in the following list), more than 2,000 investor newsletters are available. Here are two useful directories that can assist you in finding the newsletters that are right for you:

- ✔ **InvestorGuide** (www.investorguide.com) provides a listing and search function for investment newsletters. You can search for newsletters by name, category, or publisher.

- ✔ **Newsletter Access: Investments** (www.newsletteraccess.com/subject/invest.html), shown in Figure 2-5, has an extensive searchable directory of investment newsletters. If available, information includes newsletter name, description, frequency, subscription price, organization, editor, publisher, address, e-mail, telephone, fax, and Web address.

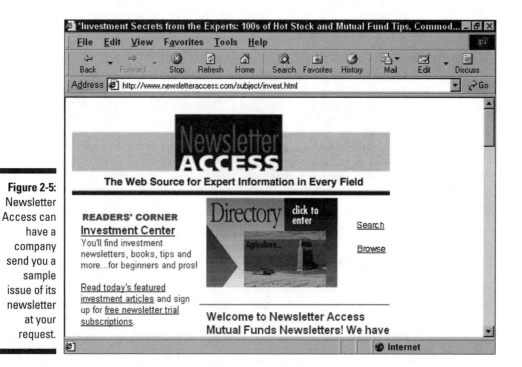

Figure 2-5: Newsletter Access can have a company send you a sample issue of its newsletter at your request.

As you can see from this section, you can get information in several flavors by going to different online sources. Many of these sources publish news as it develops. Trying to stay tuned to all these sources can lead to information overload, so I suggest selecting two or three sources that agree with your personality and lifestyle. For example, if you check your e-mailbox two or three times a day, an investment newsletter with special alert editions may be for you. If you like reading all the daily news at one time, an online news-paper with a clipping service to personalize the news may be your cup of tea.

Practicing with Your New Investment Information

In the not-too-distant past, only large investment firms had access to the high-quality financial information that's available on the Internet. Traditional investment bankers use this financial information to pick investments that look promising and then they charge their clients substantial commissions to buy or sell investments based on those recommendations. Now you can access the same types of information sources and make your own recommen-dations, which makes investing less expensive and enables you to take con-trol of your own portfolio. After all, no one is more concerned about your financial success than you.

Previous sections in this chapter point you to various online resources you can use to find out about companies, industries, the economy, and other areas that investors need to know about. However, at this early stage in your online investing career, you may not feel confident enough to start selecting your own investments. Don't despair! You can practice your new investment strategies in two ways and not risk any of your hard-earned savings. First, if you don't have a clue about how to start investing, you can join an invest-ment club and get some one-on-one advice. Second, you can try out your strategies with one or more online investment simulations.

Join the club! Become a member of an investment club

In an investment club, members pay a monthly amount to be invested. The club makes the investments based on member recommendations. The mem-bers incur a pro-rata share of the gains or losses.

In the past, investment clubs often didn't involve a lot of research. Members of many clubs purchased only safe, conservative stocks, and thus, members made small profits. Over the last five years, however, members of investment clubs have begun taking more risks, resulting in higher profits. Due to this phenomenon, the number of investment clubs is increasing at a tremendous rate. For example, the National Association of Investors Corporation (NAIC) states that its membership has tripled since 1993.

No prerequisites are necessary to join or form an investment club. So investment clubs are great for absolute beginners. Generally, investment clubs have three purposes:

- ✔ Finding out about investing
- ✔ Having fun
- ✔ Making money

You can find many investment clubs online. A good starting place is NAIC Online (`www.better-investing.org`), shown in Figure 2-6. This Web site shows how to join or start an investment club. The goal of NAIC members, and most investment clubs, is to help beginning investors become smart investors — that is, to educate investors in a disciplined approach to successful investing, portfolio management, and wealth building. The people who belong to these investment clubs often believe that finding new Web sites and investments, and meeting new people with the same interests, can be very helpful and profitable.

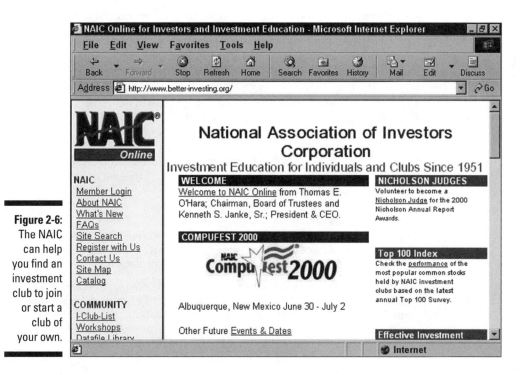

Figure 2-6: The NAIC can help you find an investment club to join or start a club of your own.

Investorama (www.investorama.com) provides an extensive guide to invest-ment club articles. Find out what people are saying about the advantages and limitations of joining an investment club. Investorama also has a directory of investment club Web sites listed by state (www.investorama.com/ directory/Investment_Clubs/Club_Web_Sites). Discover an investment club near your home.

No-cost investment simulations

Investment games enable you to invest in a virtual portfolio so that you can test your new investment strategies or try out new theories without losing any money. It's a great way to get hands-on experience with portfolio manage-ment. By playing the game, you can find out investment terms, gain confi-dence in your decision-making, become familiar with financial markets, see how others are faring, and have lots of fun. Your success is measured by how many hypothetical dollars you make each month.

Online investment simulation games are easy to play, and many of the simula-tion game Web sites provide helpful investor lessons and insights. You don't need any prior experience to enter the game. Complete the free registration and in many cases win prizes for your savvy investment strategies.

Here's an overview of how these games work: After you register, decide how much of your fantasy cash you want to invest. To purchase stock, just click a tab that is named something like Buy Order. To sell, click Sell Order. Enter the quantity and the ticker symbol (the abbreviated name of a publicly owned company that is used when trading on an exchange) of your choice. The pro-gram does the rest. When you click Update, the program assigns your portfo-lio a rank. If your profits pile up faster and higher than other game players' profits do, you get a better ranking. For a handy list of links to stock market games and simulations, see Stocks2Games at www.stocks2games.com.

Playing the stock market for fun in a no-money, no-risk game can help you get started with understanding the financial market and trading online. Here are some examples of online stock simulation games:

- **Final Bell Play the Market Game** (www.sandbox.net/finalbell/ pub-doc/home.html) shows you how to take control of your financial future today. You can explore new investing strategies while you master online trading in this risk-free stock market simulation.

- **MarketPlayer.com** (www.marketplayer.com), shown in Figure 2-7, enables participants to build their hypothetical $1-million hedge fund stock portfolio and compete with other contestants in a month-long test of their financial skills. Trading is continuous, and performance is updated daily. The monthly grand prize is $200 in real cash.

✔ **Money.com Stock Tournament** (`www.stocktournament.money.com`) provides an investment simulation game that puts your stock-picking skills to the test. If you want a few ideas, check out what the game's leaders hypothetically own.

✔ **Virtual Stock Exchange** (`www.virtualstockexchange.com`) is a stock simulation game that enables you to trade shares like a real brokerage account. You can test your latest profit-making strategy with stocks you are thinking about purchasing. This Web site also provides research reports, market news, and charting.

Figure 2-7: MarketPlayer's Stock Competitions help investors measure their ability to make money investing a portfolio of stocks.

Chapter 3

Making Your Money Work Harder

In This Chapter

▶ Using the Internet to simplify your financial planning

▶ Moving from saver to investor

▶ Setting your financial objectives and reaching them

▶ Bulletproofing your investing

*Y*ou may not have a formal investment plan, but you probably do some financial planning, even if it's only noting the bills that need to be paid on the back of your paycheck envelope. However, if you want to be a successful online investor, you need to do a little more homework to get your financial ducks in a row.

In this chapter, I show you how to make your money work as hard as you do. I explain what you need to do before you begin investing, as well as how the Internet can help you get started. I spell out how you can move from saver to investor. I illustrate how you can use an online worksheet to determine your starting point and use an online calculator to compute your personal net worth. I show you how to determine your investment objectives and figure out how much you need to earn to meet those goals. I provide guidelines for setting a ten-year goal and setting aside emergency funds. I also show you where to go online for financial planning resources, how to determine your risk-tolerance level, and how to start maximizing your personal wealth now.

Using the Internet to Simplify Financial Planning

Many people find it difficult to shake off the notion that if they're not wealthy, they don't need to do any financial planning. Stock market volatility, inflation, changing interest rates, unemployment, illness, and hard times are part of life.

To do no financial planning or to let others (your spouse, employer, broker, or financial advisor) do all your planning is to flirt with disaster. Remember that no one cares more about your financial well-being than you do.

The Internet makes financial planning easier than ever before. The Web has hundreds of online worksheets, calculators, and other tools that can easily put you on the right track. This chapter shows how you can start maximizing your personal wealth by

- ✔ **Analyzing your current financial position.** After all, you can't get to your financial finish line if you don't know your starting point. The Internet provides many online net-worth worksheets and calculators to make this task easier.

- ✔ **Finding out where your cash is going each month.** Your financial well-being doesn't depend on how much you make; it depends on how much you spend. If you don't know how much you're spending, the Internet can help you gain an understanding of your spending habits and assist you in creating a budget you can live with.

- ✔ **Deciding your financial objectives.** Do you want to purchase a house in five years or retire early? The Internet can help you achieve your goal by helping you develop a workable plan.

- ✔ **Building your financial base so that you can start accumulating real wealth.** This approach to investing offers a diversified system that provides financial growth and protection. Discover how you can build a financial base to maximize your personal wealth.

The joys of compound interest

The most powerful investment returns are stable, compounded returns. Regardless of what's happening in the economy or stock market, you can always count on the magic of compounding. Over time, a modest but steady rate of compound interest can build into a sizable nest egg.

Table 3-1 provides examples of how much you need to save each month to reach a specific financial goal. For example, assume that you need $10,000 for your investment nest egg (retirement fund, house down-payment fund, college expenses fund, or some other large financial goal). If you save $147.05 per month for five years at a 5 percent rate of return, you'll have the money you need. The second part of Table 3-1 shows that if you put away only $139.68 a month for five years at a 7 percent rate of return, you'll have $10,000. That's the magic of compounding.

Table 3-1 Monthly Savings Needed to Reach Your Financial Goal

Dollars Needed	Years to Achieve Goal at a 5% Rate of Return		
	5 Years	**10 Years**	**20 Years**
$5,000	$73.52	$32.20	$12.16
$10,000	$147.05	$64.40	$24.33
$20,000	$294.09	$128.80	$48.66
$50,000	$735.23	$321.99	$121.64
$300,000	$4,411.37	$1,931.97	$729.87

Dollars Needed	Years to Achieve Goal at a 7% Rate of Return		
	5 Years	**10 Years**	**20 Years**
$5,000	$69.84	$28.89	$9.60
$10,000	$139.68	$57.78	$19.20
$20,000	$279.36	$115.56	$38.40
$50,000	$698.40	$288.90	$96.00
$300,000	$4,190.40	$1,733.40	$576.00

Want to be a millionaire? Go to FinanCenter at www.financenter.com. Click the Savings icon and then click the calculator titled "What will it take to become a millionaire?" Enter the required data and then click Calculate. The results show how much you need to invest today to be a millionaire in the future.

The Internet provides many online calculators to assist you with calculating compound interest. To use these calculators, all you need to know is the amount you want to save, the average rate of interest you expect to receive, frequency of compounding (monthly, weekly, and so on), and how long you plan to save. The following Web sites can help you get started:

- ✔ **AARP Webplace** (www.aarp.org/confacts/money/compinterest. html), shown in Figure 3-1, provides information on types of interest and links to a variety of online interest calculators.

- ✔ **Dinkytown.net Compound Interest Calculator** (www.dinkytown.net/ java/CompoundInterest.html) can show you how the different ways interest is calculated can affect your savings.

- ✔ **Federal Reserve Bank of Chicago** (www.frbchi.org/calculators/ calc_launch.html) provides online calculators that compound interest yearly or daily.

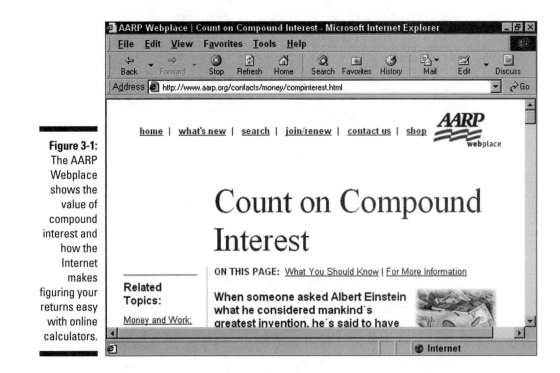

Figure 3-1:
The AARP Webplace shows the value of compound interest and how the Internet makes figuring your returns easy with online calculators.

Investing versus playing the lottery

Investing in what's hot without doing the research is like buying a lottery ticket. The chances of your investment being a success have the same odds (about a million to one). Investing isn't like buying a lottery ticket. To invest wisely, you need to understand an investment's liquidity (how fast can you get your money?), safety (will you get all your money back?), and rate of return (how much will your money earn?). Often, investors expect too much too soon from their investments.

One way to remove much of the risk and emotional turmoil of investing is to invest fixed amounts of money on a regular basis. This type of investing is called *dollar-cost averaging.* For more information on dollar-cost averaging, check out these helpful sites:

- **Institute of Systematic Investing Research** (`www.isir.com/finance/`) provides education and related links to help investors understand the benefits of dollar-cost averaging. Check out the dollar-cost averaging site of the week.

- **iVillage** (`www.ivillagemoneylife.com/money/articles/ 0,4029,12401~335,00.html`) offers an informative article about the advantages of dollar-cost averaging.

- **Montgomery Funds** (`www.montgomeryfunds.com/Fundamentals/ index.html`) includes dollar-cost averaging in the site's basics of investing. Discover how to determine your goals, how to manage different types of investment risk, and how to get ahead with dollar-cost averaging.

- **The Mutual Fund Reporter** (`www.mutualfundreporter.com/ investor_education/dollar_cost_avg.htm`) provides a quick overview of the advantages of dollar-cost averaging.

Moving Some of Your Savings to Investments

The beginning of personal wealth is the accumulation of capital that you can use for investing. This capital often begins with savings and expands into other types of more profitable investments. Savings are the beginning of your capital accumulation. Families need a regular savings program that's between 5 and 10 percent of take-home pay per month. Some people even manage to put away 15 percent. Getting into a regular rhythm with saving is important.

Additionally, individuals and families need emergency funds. Folks with fluctuating income, few job benefits, and little job security may need to have a larger emergency fund. Families with two wage earners may need a smaller emergency fund.

A general rule is to have three to six months of take-home pay in a savings account (or a near-cash account similar to a market fund with check writing privileges) for emergencies. If you don't have an emergency fund, you need to increase your savings. Payroll deduction plans into a savings account or money market fund are often the most painless way to achieve the best results. On the other hand, if you've been saving a surplus, you may want to consider using these funds for investing.

Every successful investor starts with a financial plan. The plan includes clearly stating your financial objectives, saving a certain amount of money each month, developing investment asset allocation strategies, and so on. Here are a few examples of Internet sites that can assist you in building your financial plan:

- **BankSite.com** (`www.banksite.com/online/blc/testyourself/ resultfinplan.htm`) has an online Financial Planning Test that you can take as the first step toward developing your own personal financial plan. Discover if you should be investing a portion of your money in addition to saving it.

✔ **Charles Schwab** (www.schwab.com) can help your financial planning with online calculators, tools, and advice. Go to the home page and click Getting Started. The next screen shows financial tools that include a step-by-step guide to retirement. Other online planning tools include an investor profile, general goal planner, retirement planner, IRA analyzer, and college planner. Quick Links provides easy access to the Customer Center Demo and FAQs (answers to frequently asked questions).

✔ **Fidelity Investments** (www100.fidelity.com) provides a personal resource center, information about workplace savings plans, and details about how financial advisors can help you put it all together. The asset allocation planner demonstrates how you can develop an investment strategy to meet your financial goals.

✔ **Vanguard Online Planner** (majestic.vanguard.com/GUIDE/DA) can assist you in creating a personal financial plan based on the information you enter. Free of charge, Vanguard offers three ways to map out your financial strategies.

Calculating Your Current Assets Using the Internet

The first step in getting to where you want to go is figuring out where you are now. I know that calculating your net worth doesn't sound exciting, but consider this exercise the creation of a starting line for your online investment program. Later, you can compare your increased net worth to this starting line.

One of the things that can make calculating net worth difficult is organizing all your personal finance data and sorting it into the right asset classes. Finding the data you need for entries can be time-consuming. You can use the following suggestions to help you organize your data for the categories used to calculate your net worth:

✔ **Liquid assets:** To find the value of your investments, refer to your most recent bank and brokerage statements.

✔ **Property assets:** For real-estate assets, use your most recent property appraisal or check with a realtor who knows your neighborhood.

✔ **Vehicles:** Remember to deduct depreciation from the original cost.

✔ **Jewelry, art, and collectibles:** Use your insurer's appraised value or your best estimate.

✔ **Other assets:** Use your best estimate of each asset's resale value.

Many professional financial planners tell you that most people don't know their net worth and that when potential customers make a ballpark guess, they usually aren't even close. The Internet provides many online calculators that can assist you in determining your exact net worth. These calculators do much of the work for you. For a sampling of the Internet's many online net worth calculators, visit the following sites:

- ✔ **American Express** (home3.americanexpress.com/advisors/tools) provides a wide range of online financial planning tools. Click Net Worth to get started on calculating what you own.

- ✔ **Money.com** (www.money.com/money/depts/investing/tools/ networth/introduction.html) offers a seven-step plan to see how much you are worth and how it compares to other Americans.

- ✔ **SmartMoney** (www.smartmoney.com/ac/estate/index.cfm?story= networth) has easy-to-use, no-fuss, and no-muss online calculators to assist you in determining how well you are doing.

Financial planners suggest that as you go through life, one of the primary financial goals is to increase your net worth. Online calculators are designed to help you determine your current net worth and enable you to track changes in your net worth over time.

Accumulating Something to Invest

Saving and investing are different, although savings are often the source of funds for investing. *Savings* are a set level of funds that you put aside regularly, usually at a low interest rate. You can easily access savings, and often they are insured by a financial institution.

Investment funds are the funds that you don't have earmarked for the rent, groceries, taxes, and so on. You place these funds in securities that can increase or decrease in value. They may earn interest or dividends, but you have no guarantee of increased value or future income. (Investment funds should be free of any obligations. Good examples of investment fund sources are inheritances, gifts, and disposable income.)

If you want to start investing but are having trouble making ends meet, you may be due for a financial health checkup. You can test your financial fitness by visiting the Quicken site at www.quicken.com/saving/checkup. Answer a series of questions covering key areas, such as investments, debt management, and retirement planning. After you complete the questionnaire, you get a summary based on your financial objectives along with a set of suggestions and remedies.

Setting — and Reaching — Your Goals

Determining how much you need to earn requires having a clear understanding of where you are and where you expect to be in the coming years. Here's an example to show the factors you need to consider when setting a ten-year goal:

Suppose that you're married, both you and your spouse have relatively well-paying jobs, you own a home (with a hefty 30-year mortgage), you have $5,000 in an IRA, and you're vested in your employer's pension. You have two children; one is 6 years old, and the other is 7. You expect that both children will want to go to college.

Your financial objectives for the next ten years are pretty clear: You need to raise the cash to send your children to college and still cover your other obligations. What about the ten years after that? Do you want to retire early? How much cash will you need for a comfortable retirement? Will your investment strategies get you to your financial objectives? How much of your income should you invest?

Setting your financial objectives

Financial planning involves setting objectives. Achieving these objectives is the finish line, and to reach it, you need to set strategic and tactical goals. *Strategic* goals are long-term and tend to be general. These goals can be wishes like "I want to be a millionaire by the time I'm 50." Financial planning *tactical* goals are short-term and specific, like "I want to save $5,000 this year." Your financial plan needs to include both strategic and tactical goals. Write them down and file them. Once a year, open the file and check on your progress. If your life situation changes, update your goals.

How you achieve your financial objectives is where your investment program enters the picture. But stop and evaluate your financial situation before you start investing. You want to be certain that you're financially ready to be an investor. You don't want to pay penalties due to early withdrawals, suffer excess brokerage fees, or lose income from your Treasury securities because you needed the cash and had to sell your investments earlier than planned. Before investing, be sure that you have the following:

   ✔ **An emergency fund:** For most people, the first thing on their list should be an emergency fund, which exists to protect them from unexpected situations. Unexpected expenses can include uninsured medical costs, property losses, and unemployment. (A recent survey indicated that only 17 percent of 1,000 respondents had a sufficient emergency fund, and one out of every five respondents didn't even have an emergency fund.)

✔ **Adequate insurance:** You need insurance to cover disability, health, life, automobiles, and property.

✔ **The ability to pay the monthly bills without stretching:** For many people, the goal is to pay the monthly bills without relying on future cash sources (that year-end bonus you were promised) or credit cards. For other people, the goal is to pay their children's college tuition, take care of their parents, or help their children with the down payment for their first car or home. Some goals include taking an ocean cruise, purchasing a vacation home, making home improvements, or purchasing a new home. Whatever your goals, make certain that they don't prevent you from covering your monthly bills.

Where do you stand?

If you use a credit card to pay for everyday expenses but you don't pay off the card balance at the end of the month, you aren't ready to be an investor. You need to change your spending habits and pay off those credit cards before you begin investing.

Interest rates on credit-card debt are often between 16 and 21 percent. Over the last 50 years, the average annual return on stocks is 13 percent. Even if your investments beat the market, you'll still have a difficult time covering your credit-card interest expenses.

The pitfalls of paycheck-to-paycheck accounting

Your income level doesn't determine whether you'll be financially successful. Financial success means not having to stretch to pay the monthly bills, living a comfortable lifestyle, and having the resources necessary for your family and retirement.

Why you should start now

The best argument for why you should start investing is to do the math and compare the results. For example, if a 25-year-old invests about $100 a month (at a 12 percent return) until age 65, the investment will be worth $1 million. For someone older to make that much money it's much harder. To have a $1-million nest egg at 65, a 40-year-old needs to invest $600 a month at a 12-percent return for 25 years. (Assuming that all returns are reinvested and the investments escape taxes.)

How much you earn today leads you to ask the following questions that impact your investing decisions:

✔ Do you need more income now?

✔ How much time (in number of years) do you have to meet your financial goals?

✔ Do you require a stable rate of capital appreciation or are you willing to speculate?

Can you pass a Debt Repayment Test? Many lenders use a 36-percent rule. That is, if your monthly debt is greater than 36 percent of your income, lenders may not approve your loan application. For example, if your gross monthly income is $6,000, your combined expenses can't exceed $2,160 ($6,000 x 0.36 = $2,160). Individuals with higher debt-to-income ratios have a hard time qualifying for a loan and aren't likely to have any funds available for investing.

Deciding How Much Risk You Can Take

Your investment decisions need to take into consideration your attitudes about risk. The amount of risk you can tolerate often depends on your knowledge of investments, your experience, and your personality. Each person has his or her own style and needs. Knowing exactly what your risk-tolerance level is can help you select investments that offer the highest return for the investment's level of risk.

The Internet provides many personal investment profiles — for example:

✔ **Bank of America Investment Services** (www.bankofamerica.com/ investments/index.cfm?template=inv_tools_profile.cfm&from= eba) offers a survey of 11 questions. Enter your answers, and the online calculator suggests an investment allocation strategy that suits your current needs and situation.

✔ **Bank of Hawaii** (www.boh.com/invest/paccen/invest/calculator/ index.asp) offers a seven-question worksheet to assist you in identifying your investor profile and risk tolerance. (Remember, there are no right or wrong answers.)

✔ **PrudentialSecurities.com** (www.prudentialsecurities.com/ financial_concerns/quiz.htm) provides a helpful investment personality quiz. For each statement, choose the response that most accurately reflects your feelings or behavior.

- ✔ **Safeco Mutual Funds** (`www.safecofunds.com/safecofunds/investor`) has a questionnaire that can help you determine your personal comfort zone with regard to risk. At the Safeco Investor Services page, click Risk Tolerance.

- ✔ **UMB Bank** (`www.umb.com/invest/retirement/investor.html`) helps you determine your investor type with ten questions. Results indicate whether you are a conservative, balanced, or aggressive investor, and which investment offered by your retirement plan suits your needs.

Establishing Your Investment Plan

Many people want to jump into investing before they know where they are and where they're going. Investing is always a risk, and you need to understand how this risk relates to your financial base.

Figure 3-2 shows a diagram of your financial base that uses information from the North Dakota State University (NDSU) Extension Service (`www.ext.nodak.edu/extpubs/yf/fammgmt/he258w.htm`). The first (bottom) level is your budget, setting up a savings plan for an emergency fund, acquiring insurance, and developing a home ownership plan. The second level is developing a savings plan that meets your short-, intermediate-, and long-term financial goals. The third level is having six months of take-home pay ready for emergencies. The fourth level is keeping your contributions to your individual retirement plan on track.

Figure 3-2 shows how successful investors use a "financial pyramid." Regardless of your financial history, your current net worth, or how large your paycheck is, the pyramid crumbles if any of the foundation is missing.

Figure 3-2:
Diagram of an investor's financial base.

Stocks, Bonds, Real Estate, Collectibles, and Other Investments			
Mutual Funds			
Qualified Retirement Plan			
Half-a-Year's Income in Low Risk Investments			
Systematic Savings Plan to meet short term goals, intermediate, and long-range goals			
Budget	Emergency fund	Insurance	Home mortgage

SOURCE: North Dakota State University, NDSU Extension Service (www.ext.nodak.edu/extpubs/yf/fammgmt/he258w.htm)

Don't let this happen to you. For some individuals, establishing a sturdy foundation takes years. For others, it means simply reallocating assets. After your financial foundation is set in place, you'll be ready to invest in mutual funds and then in stocks, bonds, real estate, and collectibles.

Determining How Much You Can Invest

Deciding how much you can invest isn't based on guesswork. It requires some analysis and setting up a budget. A budget is a blueprint that guides you through the process of paying bills, purchasing needed items, putting money into savings, and knowing how much you can invest. Where you can often run into problems is not budgeting for predictable but occasional expenses. Occasional expenses can include car repairs, annual life insurance premiums, and tuition.

Gaining a good understanding of how much money you can expect to earn and understanding where your cash goes are the first steps to determining how much you can invest. Make a budget using pen and paper, Internet tools, or personal financial software like Money 2000 (microsoft.com/money) or Quicken 2000 (www.quicken2000.com) to track your finances. Because the pen-and-paper method is too time-consuming, and personal software programs can be costly and difficult to learn, I recommend using Internet tools. The Internet offers many online budgeting resources that are free, easy-to-use, and quick.

Using the Internet to control your finances

Whatever your personal situation dictates, you can find investments that are tailor-made for your requirements. Determining how much money to invest (or whether you have any money to invest) is a big step in the right direction.

The hundreds of existing online calculators can make setting up a budget almost painless. Using the following online calculators can help you determine your *net cash flow,* which is the amount of money that comes into your household each year and the amount of money you spend:

✔ **Dinkytown.net** (www.dinkytown.net) offers an online calculator called the Home Budget Analyzer. At the home page, find the Personal Finance category and then click Home Budget Analyzer. Enter your income and expenditures and discover how much you can invest. Additionally, you can compare your budget breakdown to predetermined targets to help you pinpoint areas that need improvement.

✔ **FinanCenter** (www.financenter.com) offers a "How Much Am I Spending?" calculator that you can access by clicking the Budget icon. This calculator shows your income, how much you're spending, and the amount available for investment. The online calculator even derives the future value of your investments if invested for ten years. With this feature, you know exactly what the benefits are of changing your spending habits.

✔ **MoneyMinded** (www.moneyminded.com) provides an interactive monthly budget worksheet to assist you in creating your personalized cash flow analysis. *Note:* The folks at MoneyMinded suggest that you calculate your monthly savings as an expense.

✔ **Understanding and Controlling Your Finances** (www.bygpub.com/finance/CashFlowCalc.htm) provides an online calculator that shows your income and expenses and determines whether you're living within your means.

The shortfall problem

A *surplus* means that you have excess funds — that is, money that may be available for investment. A *shortfall* means that you're living beyond your means and may need some assistance with debt management. If you spend more than you make, you may need to make some lifestyle changes. Here are two examples of Internet sources that can help you with the shortfall problem:

✔ **Nolo.com** (www.nolo.com/encyclopedia/dc_ency.html#Subtopic156) offers expert advice on how to avoid overspending, strategies for repaying debts, ten tips on how to steer clear of financial trouble, and suggestions of ways to avoid bankruptcy.

✔ **Ohio State University Extension** (www.ag.ohio-state.edu/%7eohioline/home/money) offers a tutorial for managing your money. The tutorial includes six lessons: Where do I begin?; Where does your money go?; Stop spending leaks; Developing a spending plan; How much credit can you afford?; and Keeping records in order.

Investing in Securities That Meet Your Goals

Investors often receive hot tips from neighbors, e-mail messages, and message boards or chat rooms. However, studies indicate that chasing these investments, even if the investments are top performers, rarely produces the returns investors expect. Keep in mind that each security purchase is part of your investment plan, which is tied to your long-term goals. Specifically, how you choose to invest your capital (in mutual funds, stocks, bonds, Treasury securities, money market funds, and other types of investments) depends on the following considerations:

- ✔ Your required rate of return
- ✔ How much risk you can tolerate
- ✔ How long you can invest your capital
- ✔ Your personal tax liability
- ✔ Your need for quick access to your cash

Checking Out What the Experts Are Doing

After factoring all the elements of this chapter into your investment plan, you may want to find out which stocks are creating the biggest buzz on the Internet and find out what the experts are doing. Keep in mind that you can follow investment candidates for years cost-free. Here are some of the better Internet investment starting points:

- ✔ **Investorguide** (www.investorguide.com) offers links to thousands of investor-related sites. This well-organized guide includes site reviews, summaries, and an extensive section on initial public offerings (IPOs).

- ✔ **Morningstar** (www.morningstar.com) specializes in mutual funds. This Chicago-based independent rating company site includes information about stocks and mutual funds, easy-to-use screening tools, and research sources.

- ✔ **The Syndicate** (www.moneypages.com/syndicate) offers informative articles on investor topics, more than 2,000 links to related investor sites, and information on brokers, bonds, and more.

- ✔ **Wall Street Research Net** (www.wsrn.com) focuses on stock market research. The site offers more than 65,000 links to company information, the economy, market news, investor reports, quotes, mutual fund indexes, and more.

- ✔ **Zacks Investment Research** (www.zacks.com) specializes in free and fee-based investment research. Get company reports, broker recommendations, analysts' forecasts, earnings announcements, and more.

Tracking and Measuring Your Success

After selecting, analyzing, and purchasing securities, your work still isn't done. Managing your investment portfolio can help you squeeze every bit of profit from your investments and realize your financial goals. You need to find information on changing market conditions, study analytical techniques, and update your financial plan regularly. The Internet provides many portfolio-management tools that include all these features. (See Chapter 16 for more details about online portfolio tracking.)

If you want to calculate your returns or expected returns with pencil and paper, it's relatively easy, assuming that no additional purchases or redemptions were made during the period you're calculating (other than the reinvestment of dividends, interest payments, or capital gains distributions). To calculate your return, start with the ending balance and subtract the beginning balance. Divide this number by the beginning balance and then multiply by 100 to determine a percentage. This percentage is your return. Here's the formula:

Total Return = [(Ending Balance – Beginning Balance) / Beginning Balance] x 100

For example, suppose that you invest $10,000 in stocks on January 1, 2000, and on December 31, 2000, your account has a value of $12,174:

1. **Start with the ending balance and deduct the beginning balance:**

   $12,174 – $10,000 = $2,174

2. **Divided the result by the beginning balance:**

   $2,174 / $10,000 = 0.21740

3. **Multiply the result by 100:**

   0.2174 x 100 = 21.74%

   Your return is 21.74 percent.

A return of 21.74 percent in one year (by anyone's standard) is pretty good. This rate means that for each dollar invested, you earned $0.22. To determine whether this rate of return "beat the market," you need to compare it to the appropriate benchmark. See Chapter 8 for more information on where to find benchmarks and indices online.

Setting realistic expectations

When you start your investment program, don't expect to become a millionaire overnight. History has shown that the market has many ups and downs. However, when looking at the long term (five years or more), investors have been rewarded for their patience. Additionally, riskier investments held over the long term provide higher rewards than low-risk investments. As you can see from the following statistics, less risk equals less return. For example, the 73-year average annual return (1926 to 1998) for U.S. Treasury bills was 5.7 percent, the return for long-term corporate bonds was 5.7 percent, and the return on the S&P 500 Index was 11.2 percent.

Bulletproof Investing

This chapter details the beginnings of the investment process, and if you glanced through, you can see that selecting securities isn't the first thing investors do. Choosing investments is just one of many elements in the process. To bulletproof your investing, you need to complete the many tasks detailed in this chapter. The following checklist outlines how you can bulletproof your investment plan:

- ✔ **Determine where you stand.** Gain a good understanding of what your financial commitments are for now and the future. Make certain you have an emergency fund and a savings plan.

- ✔ **Clearly state your financial goals.** How much do you need? When do you need it? How much risk can you tolerate? If you lost the principal of an investment, could you mentally recover and invest again?

- ✔ **Determine the appropriate allocation of your personal assets for your age (young adult, middle aged, retiree, and so on).** Develop a regular investing program and stick to it regardless of market volatility.

- ✔ **Select the investments that meet your financial goals and risk-tolerance level.** How much time do you have (in years) to invest? Should you be an active trader and invest often during the day or a passive investor with a buy-and-hold policy? (See Chapter 4 for details on answering such questions.)

- ✔ **Analyze your investment candidates.** Before you call your online broker, make certain that you can tell a child in two minutes or less why you want to own a particular investment. Determine how long you plan to hold the security, and decide at what price you will sell (and take your profits or cut your losses).

✔ **Select an online broker that suits your needs.** Avoid mutual fund *loads* and high fees. Use automatic investment plans, dividend reinvestment programs, investment clubs, and other programs to reduce brokerage commissions. (See Chapter 6 for more information.)

✔ **Monitor your portfolio and reevaluate your goals on a regular basis.** Rank the performance of your investments and make the appropriate changes. You can expect that changes in general market conditions, new products that are introduced, and new technology will change how established businesses operate. Use this information to gain an understanding of when to hold and when to fold.

For more information about the investment process and bulletproofing your portfolio, check out Investor Home at www.investorhome.com/toc.htm.

Chapter 4

Selecting an Online Broker and Trading Online

• •

In This Chapter

▶ Checking out online brokerages

▶ Paying the lowest commissions available

▶ Opening your electronic brokerage account

▶ Increasing your profits by choosing the right trading techniques

▶ Getting a grip on electronic communications networks (ECNs), after-hours trading, and wireless trading

• •

*I*n this chapter, I show you how to save money on trades, gain control over your investments, and enter trades from your computer 24 hours a day, 7 days a week. You just need to get the hang of a few online trading basics and the risks that any investor faces.

This chapter describes three types of online brokerages: full-service, discount, and deep-discount. Each type of broker offers a different range of services. Of the three types, full-service brokerages typically charge the highest online commission, but they also offer extensive online services and customer service, lots of online research, and initial public offerings. Discount brokerages offer lower commissions, limited online services and features, minimal research features, and usually do not offer initial public offerings. Deep-discount brokerages charge the lowest commissions. These bare-bones operations offer no-frills online trading, with no research features and no initial public offerings. Within these three categories, you'll find a wide range of relationship service levels, reliability, and ease of use.

Occasionally, an inexpensive broker costs you more money. For example, if you require real-time stock quotes and subscribe to an online service, the cost is about $30 per month. If you select a broker who has a commission rate that's higher than some others but includes free online securities quotes, you may save money. This chapter also describes some of the additional features of brokerages, such as extended trading hours. This information can help you decide which brokerage is right for you.

All trading accounts require you to complete an application form and to open and maintain a minimum cash account balance. While your electronic brokerage is processing your account (which takes two to three weeks), you can turn to this chapter to find out where you can practice trading online and how to increase your profits by using the right trading strategies. This chapter also explains the impact of electronic communications networks (ECNs) on both traditional and online investors and how wireless trading is taking online investing to a new level of convenience.

Selecting the Right Online Brokerage

Today, you can divide online brokerages into three categories:

- ✔ **Full-service brokerages:** These brokerages often offer extensive services, investment advice, and branch locations. Full-service brokerages tend to attract bigger accounts and are frequently early industry leaders. Good examples of this type of online brokerage include Fidelity (www300.fidelity.com), Charles Schwab, shown in Figure 4-1 (www.schwab.com), and Waterhouse (www.waterhouse.com).

- ✔ **Discount brokerages:** These firms offer some site content and fewer services than full-service brokerages. Examples of discount online brokerages include Accutrade (www.accutrade.com), DLJ Direct (www.dljdirect.com), Discover (www.discover.com), E*Trade (www.etrade.com), and Quick and Reilly (www.quick-reilly.com).

- ✔ **Deep-discount brokerages:** These brokerages are used primarily by active traders interested in low prices. These traders want bare-bones features and fast service. Examples of deep-discount brokerages include Ameritrade (www.ameritrade.com), Datek (www.datek.com), and Suretrade (www.suretrade.com).

In the future, however, the border between these categories will likely be harder to identify as online brokerages add features and start charging "fees for services rendered." For example, if you wanted to have a face-to-face meeting with your broker to complete a complex transaction, you would pay a full-service brokerage fee. Later, if you placed an online trade with the same brokerage, you would pay a discounted brokerage fee.

You can easily locate a broker via the World Wide Web. For a good alphabetical list of licensed brokers, see the Invest-FAQ at invest-faq.com/links/trading.html.

Figure 4-1:
New online investors often begin with full-service brokerages like Charles Schwab.

Checking Out Prospective Brokers

The Securities Investor Protection Corporation (SIPC) provides account protection for brokerage accounts in a way that's similar to how the Federal Deposit Insurance Corporation (FDIC) insures bank accounts. Each customer's account is protected to $500,000, and some brokerages have additional insurance. If your brokerage firm goes belly-up, you're covered. However, if you make poor investment selections, you can lose all your money.

As an investor, you're wise to look into the background of a brokerage firm before investing. The Central Registration Depository (CRD) — a registration and licensing database used by regulators throughout the securities industry to collect data about securities firms and their brokers — is available at your state securities agency or the National Association of Securities Dealers (www.nasdr.com/2000.htm). Additionally, each month the New York Stock Exchange releases a disciplinary action list at www.nyse.com.

You can check several sources to find out whether the broker you are considering is registered. The National Association of Securities Dealers Regulation Web site (www.nadr.com) has investor services that enable you to request background information about your broker through NASD Regulation's Public Disclosure Program. Your state securities regulator can tell you whether the broker you're considering is registered, and some state securities commissions provide cautionary lists at their Web sites — for example, the Oklahoma Securities Commission site at www.securities.state.ok.us.

Getting Online Trading Services for Less

As I mention at the beginning of this chapter, no two brokerages are alike. Furthermore, individual brokerages may change their services and fees to keep pace with their competitors. To find the online broker that best meets your needs, you must investigate the prices, services, and features that various brokers offer.

Make certain that your brokerage doesn't charge you for services that are free elsewhere. For example, say that an online brokerage charges a flat fee of $15 for your trade. If the brokerage adds a postage and handling fee of $4 for your transaction, your transaction actually costs $19. That's 27 percent higher than you expected. Other hidden fees may include

- ✔ Higher fees for accepting *odd-lot orders* (orders of less than one hundred shares)

- ✔ Higher fees for certain types of orders (see "Increasing Profits with Simple Order Specification Techniques," later in this chapter)

- ✔ Fees for sending out certificates (some firms charge $50 per certificate)

- ✔ Fees to close your account

- ✔ Fees to withdraw funds from your trading account

Trading online for $15 or less

The rapid growth of the Internet, technological advances, and more brokerage evolution have led to low commissions for online trading. Generally, all Internet brokers can handle any type of basic transaction with a minimum of human contact. This lowers the cost of doing business and permits low commissions. Many reputable online brokerages can complete your trade for $15 or less. Table 4-1 lists several brokerages that offer low-cost online trading.

Table 4-1	You Can Trade Online for $15 or Less	
Brokerage Center	*Web Address*	*Commission Structure (Less Than or Equal to 1,000 Shares)*
American Express Brokerage	`www.americanexpress.com/trade`	$14.95 (free with certain accounts)
Ameritrade	`www.ameritrade.com`	$8 market order; $13 limit order
CompuTEL	`www.computel.com`	$14 market; $19 limit; plus $2.50 service fee
E*Trade	`www.etrade.com`	$14.95 listed market; $19.95 NASDAQ/limit/stop; $6.95 market
Fidelity Investments	`personal100.fidelity.com`	Active Traders: $14.95; Regular Traders: $25
NDB Online	`www.ndb.com`	$14.75 market; $19.95 limit
Quick & Reilly's Quickway Net	`www.quick-reilly.com`	$14.95 market; $19.95 limit
Scottrade	`www.scottrade.com`	$7 market; $12 limit
SiebertNet.com	`www.siebertnet.com`	$14.95
SureTrade	`www.suretrade.com`	$7.95 market; $9.95 limit
TD Waterhouse Securities	`www.waterhouse.com`	$12 (for up to 5,000 shares)
Web Street Securities	`www.webstreetsecurities.com`	$14.95

Note: *Market orders* are instructions for the broker to immediately buy or sell a security for the best available price. *Limit orders* are trading orders that specify a certain price at which the broker is to execute the order. For more information, see "Increasing Profits with Simple Order Specification Techniques," later in this chapter.

Finding online brokers with no or low initial account minimums

One of the things that many investors may find prohibitive about online trading is the initial minimum deposit required for opening a cash account. This requirement means that the broker already has your money when you request a trade. However, this requirement is changing, just like everything else on the Internet. Table 4-2 lists several online brokerages that offer cash accounts with no minimum deposit or a low minimum deposit.

Table 4-2	Minimum Amounts to Open Trading Accounts with Some Online Brokers	
Brokerage Center	**Web Address**	**Minimum to Open Cash Account**
American Express Brokerage	www.americanexpress.com/trade	$0
BCL Online	www.bclnet.com	$0
DLJDirect	www.dljdirect.com	$0
FirstTrade.com	www.firsttrade.com	$0
Freeman Welwood Online	www.freemanwelwood.com	$0
My Discount Broker	www.mydiscountbroker.com	$0
NDB Online	www.ndb.com	$0
Quick & Reilly's Quickway Net	www.quick-reilly.com	$0
SiebertNet.com	www.siebertnet.com	$0
SureTrade	www.suretrade.com	$0
Trading Direct	www.tradingdirect.com	$0
Wall Street Electronica	www.wallstreete.com	$0
Web Street Securities	www.webstreetsecurities.com	$0
Dreyfus Brokerage	www.tradepbs.com	$1,000
E*Trade	www.etrade.com	$1,000
EmpireNow.com	www.empirenow.com	$1,000
TD Waterhouse Securities	www.waterhouse.com	$1,000
TradeOptions	www.tradeoptions.com/cgi-bin/tohome.cgi	$1,000

Brokerage Center	Web Address	Minimum to Open Cash Account
WellsTrade	www.wellsfargo.com/ wellstrade	$1,000
Ameritrade	www.ameritrade.com	$2,000
Datek Online	www.datek.com	$2,000
InvesTrade	www.investrade.com	$2,000
J.B. Oxford & Co.	www.jboxford.com/ 0_0_brokerage_services.htm	$2,000
Morgan Stanley Dean Witter	www.online.msdw.com	$2,000
Mr. Stock	www.mrstock.com	$2,000
Regal Discount Securities	www.eregal.com	$2,000
Scottrade	www.scottrade.com	$2,000
Sloan Securities	www.sloansecurities.com	$2,000
TradeStar Investments	www.savoystocks.com	$2,000
USRICA.com	www.usrica.com	$2,000

Commission structures change radically from firm to firm. One reason for this wide range is that some Internet brokers include special or additional features. When deciding which broker is best for you, factoring in some or all of the features that I list in this section is probably wise. First, consider whether each broker offers the following features in your cash account:

- ✔ Low minimum amount required to open an account
- ✔ Low monthly fees with minimum equity balance
- ✔ No additional charges for postage and handling
- ✔ A summary of cash balances
- ✔ A summary of order status
- ✔ A summary of your portfolio's value
- ✔ A historical review of your trading activities
- ✔ No charges for retirement account maintenance

When comparing brokers, consider whether each broker offers the following account features:

- ✔ Unlimited check-writing privileges
- ✔ Dividend collection and reinvestment
- ✔ Debit cards for ATM access
- ✔ Interest earned on cash balances
- ✔ Wire transfers accepted
- ✔ No IRA inactivity fees

You should ascertain which of the following types of investments the broker enables you to trade:

- ✔ Stocks (foreign or domestic)
- ✔ Options
- ✔ Bonds (corporate or agency)
- ✔ Treasury securities
- ✔ Zero-coupon bonds
- ✔ Certificates of deposit
- ✔ Precious metals
- ✔ Mutual funds
- ✔ Unit investment trusts

Finally, you need to determine whether the brokerage offers the following analytical and research features:

- ✔ Real-time online quotes
- ✔ Reports on insider trading
- ✔ Economic forecasts
- ✔ Company profiles and breaking news
- ✔ Earnings forecasts
- ✔ End-of-the-day prices automatically sent to you

Adding new features to Web sites is a routine occurrence in the online brokerage world, as are changes in the online brokerage's internal database for better and more personalized reporting. Therefore, even though an online brokerage doesn't have all the features you desire, that brokerage might offer the missing items in the near future. For example, you probably won't need to contact customer service very often, but when you do, you want excellent service. Frequently, this means being able to talk immediately with a sales representative. In response to this need, many online brokerages now offer a "chat button." Click the button and a chat window opens in which you can talk directly with a sales representative. Online brokerages that offer this feature include National Discount Brokers (`www.ndb.com`), AB Watley (`www.abwatley.com`), and Datek (`www.datek.com`).

One feature that's of interest to frequent traders is real-time quotes. Some brokerage firms offer real-time quotes for free, other firms offer a limited number for free when you open an account or make a trade, and several firms charge $30 a month for nonprofessional, real-time quotes.

With nearly 100 online brokerages to choose from, finding the one brokerage that meets all your needs can seem like an impossible dream. Money.com (`www.money.com/broker`) has made selecting an online brokerage easier than ever before. Money.com provides an easy-to-use, interactive questionnaire that can assist you in quickly finding the online brokerage that is geared for your type of investing and has the features you need.

Rating Online Brokers

Online brokerage rankings are often based on the trade execution process, ease of use, customer confidence, on-site resources, relationship services, commissions and overall costs. The following Web sites offer ratings that can help you determine which online brokerage meets your needs:

- ✔ **American Association of Individual Investors** (`www.aaii.org/survey`) requires you to complete a short survey to gain access to its ratings of online brokerages. Completing the questionnaire is worth your time and effort to gain access to the in-depth results. See the top ten vote getters, find out how discount brokers rate, and see how your online brokerage compares.

- ✔ **Forrester Research** (`powerrankings.forrester.com/ER/ PowerRankings/Industry/0,2142,3,FF.html`) serves up its Power Ratings based on interactive consumer surveys and unbiased expert analysis. The goal of Forrester's brokerage ratings is to provide consumers with objective research to assist them in selecting an online brokerage.

✔ **Gomez Advisors** (`www.gomezadvisors.com`) is a Boston-based independent rating agency that specializes in online investing. This firm has developed a quarterly Internet Broker Scorecard to help investors select the online broker that's right for them.

✔ **Money.com** (`www.money.com/money/broker/index.html`) ranks the top 15 online brokerages based on their ease of use, customer service, system responsiveness, products and tools, and total cost. Discover if your investor profile matches your online brokerage.

Don't assume that you always get what you pay for. The Keynote Web Broker Trading Index (`www.keynote.com`), shown in Figure 4-2, illustrates the average response time in seconds and the success rate for creating a standard stock-order transaction on selected brokerage Web sites. At the home page, click Performance Indexes ☞ Broker Trading Index. Using Keynote's Web Broker Trading Index, you can easily see that some high-priced online brokerages aren't as fast or as reliable as their lower-priced competitors.

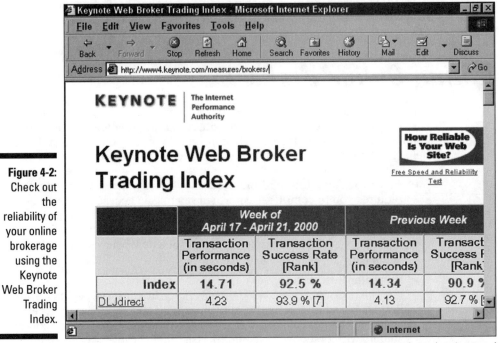

Figure 4-2: Check out the reliability of your online brokerage using the Keynote Web Broker Trading Index.

	Week of April 17 - April 21, 2000		Previous Week	
	Transaction Performance (in seconds)	Transaction Success Rate [Rank]	Transaction Performance (in seconds)	Transact Success F [Rank]
Index	14.71	92.5 %	14.34	90.9 %
DLJdirect	4.23	93.9 % [7]	4.13	92.7 % [

Opening Your Online Brokerage Account

Internet brokerage firms are basically cash-and-carry enterprises. They all require investors to open an account before trading — a process that takes from two to three weeks to complete. Account minimums vary from $0 to $10,000.

All Internet brokers require that you complete an application form that includes your name, address, Social Security number, work history, and a personal check, certified check, or money order for the minimum amount needed to open an account. Some brokers accept wire transfers or securities of equal value. All brokerages are required by law to have your signature on file. Figure 4-3 shows the online application form for CompuTEL Securities (www.computel.com).

To speed up the application process, you can complete application forms online or fax them to the Internet broker. You must then follow up by sending the completed, written, and signed forms via U.S. mail within 15 days, or the account is canceled. The Internet broker then verifies all the information on the form and opens your account. Investors receive a personal identification number (PIN) by mail. After you receive your PIN, you're ready to begin trading.

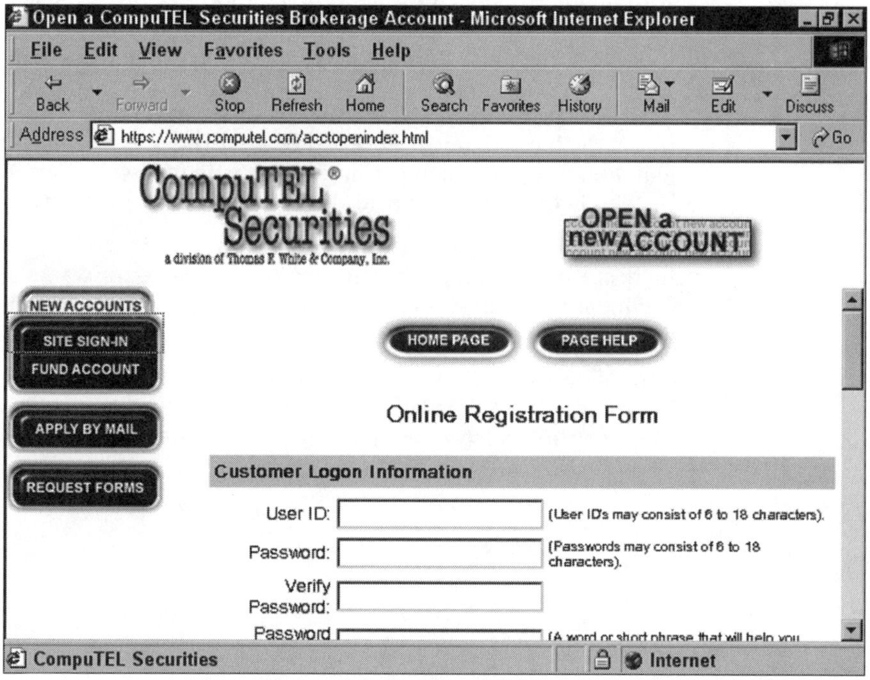

Figure 4-3:
The online application form for CompuTEL Securities.

Increasing Profits with Simple Order Specification Techniques

Traditional brokers recommend the order specifications for your stock transactions and confirm that your transaction was completed. Specifying security execution orders is one of the expert services that brokers use to justify their fees. Order specifications define how your request is completed. One type of order specification is called a *day order*. Day orders are good only on the day you place the order.

Another type of order is the Good Till Canceled (GTC) order. The GTC order is open until it is executed or canceled. For example, an investor wants to buy a certain company's shares, but not until the shares are a few dollars cheaper. The investor specifies a GTC order and determines when the order will expire. If the company's shares reach the predetermined limit (today, tomorrow, next year, or next decade), the order is filled.

Trading online means that you are now in charge of specifying your stock order. Knowing how to designate the terms of your order can increase your chances of execution at the price you want. As you look over your online order form, you'll notice different ways of specifying how the order should be executed. In the past, your traditional broker decided which approach was best. With online trading, you select the method you feel is best.

Here are four of the more popular ways to specify your stock order:

- **Limit orders:** Orders in which buyers or sellers specify the top price they are willing to pay or accept. For sell orders, the *limit* specified is the minimum price at which the investor is willing to sell. For buy orders, the limit is the maximum price that the investor is willing to pay.

- **Market orders:** Any order (buy or sell) to be executed immediately at the best price available. In other words, the investor wants to buy or sell a stated number of shares at the best price at the time the order is placed.

- **Stop:** After a security reaches the price set by the investor, the order becomes active. When the order is activated, the order will be executed. However, the investor isn't guaranteed the execution price.

✔ **Stop-limit orders:** After a security reaches the investor's predetermined price, the order is activated. The order can only be executed at the set price or better, so the order might not be completed.

You may want to use a *limit order* when purchasing or selling *odd lots* (less than 100 shares of any one stock). This type of order can increase your chances of getting filled at your price. Odd lots rarely get the best price because they must be bundled with other orders.

Many online brokerages have handy online trading demos that can assist you in practicing trading online. For example, DLJ Direct (www.dljdirect.com) and Ameritrade (www.ameritrade.com), shown in Figure 4-4, have handy online trading demos that can assist you in practicing trading online.

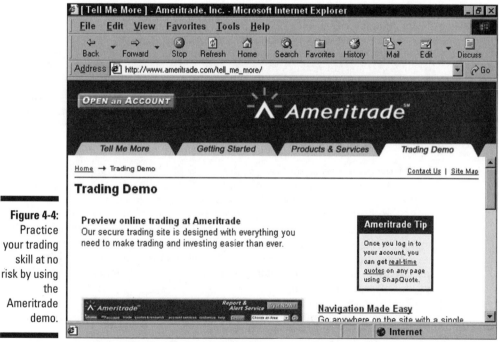

Figure 4-4:
Practice
your trading
skill at no
risk by using
the
Ameritrade
demo.

It's Not Your Grandfather's Market Anymore

Recent changes in SEC regulations and technology have transformed how investors interact with the stock market. I explain these changes in the following sections, and I show you how these changes enable online investors to make more money on their investments. In the following sections, you gain an understanding of what happens after you click your mouse button to execute an online trade. You also discover how you can avoid hidden transaction costs by using an electronic communications network (ECN) and how you benefit from ECNs even if you never use one.

How ECNs work

In 1988, the Securities and Exchange Commission (SEC) made it mandatory for NASDAQ market makers to accept buy and sell orders of up to 1,000 shares via an automated small-order execution system (SOES). This opened the door for the so-called "SOES bandits," who later became known as day traders. This also led to the development of the first electronic communications networks (ECNs), and in January 1997, the SEC approved the first four ECNs. Today, there are nine ECNs.

Stocks are traded by *specialists* on the NYSE and by *market makers* in the NASDAQ market. For example, the NASDAQ requires at least two market markers for each listed stock. This creates a market in which the stock is bought and sold. On ECNs, computers replace specialists and market makers. Anyone can purchase NASDAQ-traded equities through a brokerage that uses an ECN. Investors buy stock through an online broker, and if the broker's computer finds a seller in an ECN, the investor's order is executed with no human intervention. (And because computers never sleep, ECNs open the way for after-hours trading.)

To gain some insight into how ECNs work, compare how investors purchase equities on the NYSE, NASDAQ, and ECNs.

Buying stock on the NYSE involves the following steps:

1. **The broker sends a buy order to a specialist on the exchange floor.**

2. **The specialist looks for sellers on the trading floor or in an electronic order book.**

3. **If the specialist finds enough sellers to match the offer price, the specialist completes the transaction.**

Here are the steps for buying stock on the NASDAQ:

1. **The broker consults a trading screen that lists how many shares various market makers are offering to sell and at what price.**

2. **The broker picks the best price and sends an electronic message to the market maker, who must sell the shares.**

In contrast, buying stock on an ECN involves these steps:

1. **The broker sends a buy order to an ECN.**

2. **The computer looks for matching sell orders on the ECN.**

3. **If the computer finds enough sellers to complete the trade, the transaction is executed. Otherwise, the order isn't executed.**

Understanding inside spreads

One of the first steps in understanding trading is to define the players. What day traders really focus on are the activities of market makers. A *market maker* represents an institution (such as Lehman Brothers, Merrill Lynch & Co., Prudential Securities, and so on) that wants to *make a market* in a particular NASDAQ stock. The market maker is a specialist on an exchange or a dealer in the over-the-counter market who buys and sells stocks, creating an inventory for temporary holding. The market maker provides liquidity by buying and selling at any time. However, the market maker isn't under any obligation to buy or sell at a price other than the published bid and ask prices.

The downside of being a market maker is that you are obligated to purchase stocks when no one wants them. The upside of being a market maker is that you get to pocket the profits of a spread. A *spread* is the difference between a bid and ask price. For example, a stock with a bid and ask price of 15 x 15¼ has a spread of ¼. The bid price is $15 and the sell price is $15.25. By selling 1,000 shares at $15.25, the market maker profits by $250.

Spreads are often just a few cents for each stock. However, these pennies quickly become dollars due to high trading volume. Last year, NASDAQ market makers earned $2 billion from spreads. Day traders have sliced into some of these profits. Recent reports indicate that market maker spreads are down by 30 percent.

The existence of several kinds of spreads has caused some confusion. The following list defines some of these spreads:

- ✔ **Dealer spread:** The quote of the individual market maker. A market maker never earns the entire spread. The market maker needs to be competitive on either the bid or offer side of the market. The dealer is unlikely to be at the best price (the highest price if selling and the lowest price if buying) on both sides of the market at the same time.

- ✔ **Inside spread:** The highest bid and lowest offer being quoted among all the market makers competing in a stock. Because the quote is a combined quote, it's narrower than an individual dealer quote.

- ✔ **Actual spreads paid:** The narrowest measure of a spread, because it's based on actual trade prices. The actual spread paid is calculated by measuring actual trade prices against the inside quotes at the time of the trade.

Datek (www.datek.com), shown in Figure 4-5, offers the Datek Streamer to nonprofessional users, giving access to free, dynamically updating real-time quotes for up to 20 securities in one window. Now you can watch the market move in real-time without purchasing additional hardware or software.

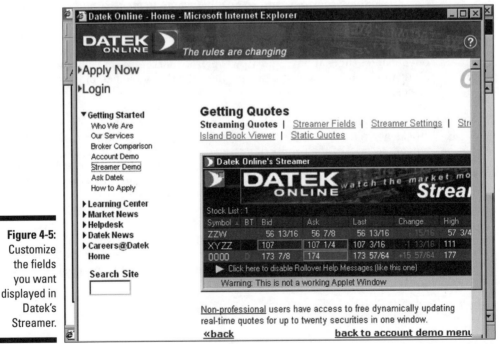

Figure 4-5:
Customize the fields you want displayed in Datek's Streamer.

Finding Online Brokerages with Night Trading

Until recently, only professional traders and institutions could trade outside the official market hours of 9:30 a.m. to 4:00 p.m. EST. Many online brokerages use ECNs to offer individual investors access to both morning and evening extended-hours trading sessions. For many online brokerages, the morning session begins at 8:00 a.m. EST and ends when traditional trading begins at 9:30 a.m. The evening session begins after the traditional markets close at 4:00 p.m. and continues until 8:00 p.m. EST.

All trades placed during these sessions are represented exclusively on ECNs. For example, Datek (www.datek.com) accounts must be enabled for participation in extended-hours trading sessions.

NASDAQ and NYSE equities are available for trading during extended hours. Usually, only limit orders are accepted for after-hours sessions. Sometimes, the commissions and fees for trading limit orders during extended hours differ from the limit order fees for traditional trading sessions. Orders are in round lots (100 shares). Orders traded during extended-hours trading sessions have the same trade date as orders executed during that day's traditional trading session.

Join the after-hours club

After-hours trading is one way an online brokerage can increase revenue. As of this writing, six brokerages command 80 percent of all online trading accounts. Each of these online brokerages has an "after-hours" club:

- Charles Schwab (www.schwab.com): REDIBook
- E*Trade (www.etrade.com): Instinet
- Waterhouse (www.waterhouse.com): Island
- Datek (www.datek.com): Island
- Fidelity (www300.fidelity.com): REDI Book
- Ameritrade (www.ameritrade.com): A combination of Island, Market XT, Knight/Trimart, and the Chicago Stock Exchange

Different brokerages offer different extended trading hours, trade different securities (just NASDAQ or certain securities), and have different rules about joining the club. Table 4-3 shows the after-hours club rules for several major online brokerages.

Table 4-3	Examples of After-Hours Trading	
Online Brokerage (URL)	*Limit Order Online Trading Costs for 1,000 Shares or Less*	*Hours for Trading on the NYSE and NASDAQ*
A.B. Watley (www.abwatley.com)	$9.95 per trade for standard accounts	8:30 a.m. to 8:00 p.m. EST
Ameritrade (www.ameritrade.com)	$13 per trade	4:15 p.m. to 6:30 p.m. EST
Datek (www.datek.com)	$9.99 per trade	8:00 a.m. to 9:30 a.m. and 4:00 p.m. to 8:00 p.m. EST; NASDAQ only
DLJdirect (www.dljdirect.com)	$20 per trade	8:00 a.m. to 9:15 a.m. and 4:15 p.m. to 7:00 p.m. EST; NASDAQ and some listed stocks
Dreyfus (www.dreyfus.com)	$15 per trade	4:00 p.m. to 8:00 p.m. EST
E*Trade (www.etrade.com)	$14.95 for listed market orders. $19.95 for limit and unlisted orders.	4:05 p.m. to 6:30 p.m. EST
Fidelity Online (www300.fidelity.com)	$30 per trade	4:30 p.m. to 8:00 p.m. EST; NASDAQ and some listed stocks
JB Oxford (www.jboxford.com)	$19.50 per trade	8:45 a.m. to 4:45 p.m. EST
Morgan Stanley Dean Witter Online (www.online.msdw.com)	$29.95 per trade	4:30 p.m. to 8:00 p.m. EST
Mydiscountbroker (www.mydiscount broker.com)	$12 per trade	4:00 p.m. to 8:00 p.m. EST
Muriel Siebert (www.msiebert.com)	$37.50 per trade	7:30 a.m. to 9:00 a.m. and 4:00 p.m. to 6:00 p.m. EST; phone orders only for after-hours trading
Schwab (www.schwab.com)	$29.95 per trade	4:30 p.m. to 7:00 p.m. EST

Night trading limitations

ECNs are not isolated trading "islands;" rather, they are just like any partici-
pant in the NASDAQ market. Most, if not all, NASDAQ market participants,
including ECNs and market makers, are linked to a system called Select Net.
As long as ECNs and the overall NASDAQ market are linked to Select Net,
ECNs are not likely to fragment or reduce liquidity in the market. However,
extended-hours trading does have some limitations:

- ✔ News stories may have a greater impact on stock prices.

- ✔ Some stocks will be very liquid during after-hours trading, and some will
  not be liquid at all.

- ✔ Investors may encounter wider spreads between bids and offers than
  during traditional market hours. Stock prices may be more volatile.

- ✔ Investors may be competing against professional traders with more
  information and analysis.

Sources for extended-hours stock information

With unprecedented access to information about securities and trading,
investors now enjoy narrower spreads, lower execution costs, and faster execution speeds. For example, the average investor can access the following
premarket information:

- ✔ **MarketXT** (www.marketxt.com) provides investors with access to in-
  depth financial information. Through the affiliate Web sites of subscribing brokerage-firms and the MarketXT Web site, investors can receive
  breaking news, closing results, market data, and charts.

- ✔ **Zacks** (www.zacks.com), **Reuters Before the Bell** (www.reuters.com),
  and **CBS MarketWatch** (www.cbsmarketwatch.com) offer summaries of
  premarket trading. CBS MarketWatch also provides Instinet quotes for
  actively traded stocks and companies that have released important
  news.

And here are a few examples of after-hours trading information now available
to the average investor:

- ✔ **Stockwinners** (www.stockwinners.com) provides premarket and after-
  hours market prices.

- ✔ **Quote.com** (www.quote.com/quote.com) provides after-hours market
  updates.

> ✔ **Reuters After the Bell by Yahoo!** (`search.news.yahoo.com/search/news?p=after+the+bell&n=10`) and **Reuters After the Bell by DLJ Direct** (`www.dljdirect./dljd/qnnewsab.htm`) offer highlights of significant after-hours trading activity.
>
> ✔ **Nite Traders Online** (`www.nitetradersonline.com`) provides after-hours news from CBS MarketWatch, WorldlyInvestor.com, Bridge News, Business Wire: Financial, Internet Wire: Financial News, and more.

Some online brokerages provide extended-hours quotes. For example, account holders at Charles Schwab (`www.schwab.com`) can go to the real-time quote box on the stock trading Web page. When you enter the ticker symbol of the equity you are interested in, include the letter 'e.' (For example, type **IBMe** for the extended-hours trading price of IBM.) The price quoted will be the extended-hours price.

Going from Hardwired to Wireless Trading

Imagine that you are on your way to work, when the radio broadcasts news that a company you are interested in has just dropped to $35 a share. You're on your way to the mandatory weekly meeting but want to catch this opportunity. You take out your personal digital assistant (PDA) and log on to your brokerage. You get a real-time quote and set up a limit order: If the stock falls to $33, you'll purchase 100 shares. You execute your order and receive a confirmation. Total transaction time: less than a minute.

The Internet revolutionized investing in the '90s by enabling investors to connect with the markets online. By the year 2000, everyone was getting wired. Now, however, everyone is getting unwired! The next revolution for investors is the proliferation of wireless, mobile appliances that give you instant Internet connections from the palm of your hand, anywhere and anytime.

Today, the fastest growing categories of consumer electronics are lightweight PC laptops, cell phones and PDAs — all unwired devices that provide easy Internet and e-mail access. Not only can you send and receive messages and trade stocks while you sit in traffic or on the beach, you can also zap data between devices without a wire. What makes this unwired world possible is highly complex digital and analog technologies on a single chip developed by such companies as Integration, Inc., a semiconductor design and manufacturing firm in Silicon Valley.

The implications for investors are huge now that wireless devices are available from the major brokerage firms. You don't have to be wired in order to be connected to the stock market anymore! Here are a few examples of online brokerages that are offering wireless trading:

- ✔ **Ameritrade** (www.Ameritrade.com) supports Sprint Web telephones and Palm V and Palm VII organizers.
- ✔ **Charles Schwab** (www.schwab.com) has developed PocketBroker(tm), a wireless investing product.
- ✔ **DLJ Direct** (www.dljdirect.com) supports Web phones, Palm VII, Palm III with modem, Windows CE handheld PCs, Web phones, and pagers.
- ✔ **Dreyfus** (www.tradepbs.com) supports Palm III with modem, smart phones, and RIM pagers.
- ✔ **Fidelity** (www.fidelity.com) supports Palm VII, Sprint phones, and RIM pagers.
- ✔ **Morgan Stanley Dean Witter** (www.msdw.com) supports Palm III with modem.
- ✔ **SiebertNet** (www.siebertnet.com) supports SiebertBroker.
- ✔ **Suretrade** (www.Suretrade.com) supports all PDAs like Palm and Web phones, Windows CE-based handheld devices, and two-way interactive pagers.

Be sure to ask how security works for your brokerage's wireless service. For example, WAP (Wireless Access Protocol), an emerging standard for cell phone browsers, has recently received criticism for a transaction problem. At one point during a WAP transaction, the data must decrypt itself, leaving you with no security. Someone could intercept your transmission and know exactly what you are doing. Industry professionals are currently working on the problem and hope to find a solution soon.

Part II
Finding the Right Investments

In this part . . .

The Internet offers plenty of resources that can help you turn your hunches into investment strategies, and the chapters in this part of the book highlight the best Internet sources for tools and information related to mutual funds, stocks, and bonds. This part of the book shows you how to locate mutual funds online, how to analyze a prospectus, and how you can buy a no-load mutual fund through an online brokerage. You find out how to use Internet screens to locate stock candidates. You also discover how to use online tools to analyze stocks, as well as how to find earnings forecasts and online sources that can assist you in deciphering company annual reports. You explore one of the easier ways to value bonds, and you find out how you can purchase bonds online and directly from the Federal government without a broker.

Chapter 5

What's So Great about Mutual Funds?

In This Chapter

▶ Understanding why mutual funds are so wonderful

▶ Finding mutual fund resources on the Internet

▶ Buying mutual funds online

▶ Selling a mutual fund

▶ Starting a mutual fund account with as little as $50

---

*W*ant to participate in spectacular stock market profits but you're scared of the risks? Want to start investing but you don't have $1,000 to $2,500 for an initial minimum balance? Don't want to pay high brokerage commissions and fees? Well, you may want to consider a *mutual fund* (a managed investment company that is ready to purchase shares and constantly offers new shares to the public). When you buy shares in a mutual fund, you are really buying shares of an investment company. The investment company's assets are stocks, bonds, certificates of deposit, and so on.

Mutual fund mania is rampant. Everyone is talking about mutual funds. Mutual funds are rapidly becoming the most popular way for Americans to invest — which is remarkable, considering that before the 1920s mutual funds didn't even exist. In the 1940s, only 68 funds existed, with $400 million in assets. Today, more than 9,000 mutual funds are available.

In this chapter, I explain how you use the Internet to select mutual funds, and I list the latest Internet tools and resources to help you select, buy, and sell mutual funds. I also provide step-by-step instructions for opening a mutual fund account online, and I show you how to use the Internet to start a mutual fund account for as little as $50.

Mutual Fund Mania

Mutual funds offer a good solution for individuals who don't have the time and the technical knowledge to track individual stocks. Mutual funds are a convenient way of investing in stocks, bonds, cash, gold, and so on. In a mutual fund, professional managers pool the money of small investors. The goal of the investment company is to make more money for the small investors. In return for handling the investments, a fee is paid to the investment manager of a mutual fund for supervising the investment portfolio and administering the fund. Management fees are normally calculated as a percentage of the total assets of the fund.

Often, the portfolio manager and technical analysts invest in a collection of about 35 securities. However, any one fund can include anywhere from 20 to 200 securities. The portfolio manager expects these investments to earn interest from bonds, dividends from stocks, capital gains from buying and selling stocks at opportune times, and any other spin-off profits that can increase the value of the mutual fund. The mutual fund doesn't pay any taxes because all the profits are distributed as dividends and capital gains to the small investors (the shareholders).

The shareholder pays the management fees, registration fees, expenses for annual meetings, custodial bank and transfer agent fees, interest and taxes, brokerage commissions, marketing costs, and sometimes expenses related to the distribution of fund materials (prospectus, annual statement, and so on). These fees and expenses are usually deducted from the dividends paid to shareholders.

Visit Brill's Mutual Funds Interactive at `www.fundsinteractive.com/newbie.html` for more information about mutual funds. This Web site offers tutorials for beginners interested in mutual fund investing. For example, Figure 5-1 shows "Funds 101 — The Essential Resource for the New Mutual Fund Investor." Also, check out *Investing For Dummies,* 2nd Edition, by Eric Tyson, MBA (published by IDG Books Worldwide, Inc.).

Mutual funds are a good investment choice because funds offer individual investors several benefits that they don't ordinarily receive:

> ✔ **Diversification:** Mutual funds add securities to a portfolio so that the portfolio's unique risk is lowered. In other words, mutual funds enable you to spread your risk by purchasing several types of investments in one fund. For 75 percent of the fund, no single security can be greater than 5 percent of the fund's total assets. However, 25 percent of the fund's total assets can be in any one issue.

Before you purchase a fund, read the prospectus and see how the assets are allocated. Well-diversified funds provide lots of investor protection. If one stock loses half its value in one day, the effect on the entire fund is small. On the other hand, if one stock skyrockets, you won't be able to buy that yacht you want.

✔ **No broker required:** If you're confident about your investment choices, you're likely to purchase no-load mutual funds directly from the mutual fund company, instead of paying a *load* (a broker's commission). For more information about no-load funds, see Chapter 6.

✔ **No investor homework:** The mutual fund does the tracking and record keeping for you.

✔ **Professional management:** The professional managers, employed by the fund, search for fast-growing investments on your behalf. To have these professionals working for you full-time provides you with competitive advantages over other investors.

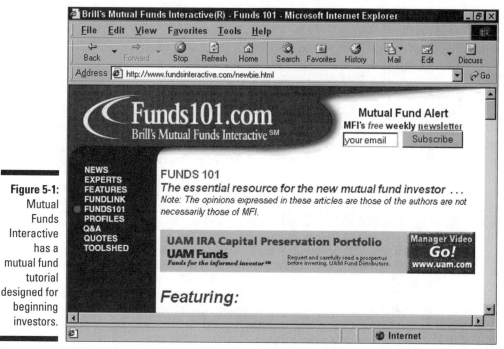

Figure 5-1:
Mutual
Funds
Interactive
has a
mutual fund
tutorial
designed for
beginning
investors.

Mutual Funds Interactive ® is a registered trademark of Brill Editorial Services.

Finding Mutual Fund Information on the Internet

The Internet provides many mutual fund supersites that are timely, interesting, and best of all, useful. Here are a few examples of these all-purpose sites:

- **Charles Schwab & Co., Inc.** (www.schwab.com) provides the Mutual Funds Marketplace, with a comprehensive list of mutual funds with Morningstar Ratings.

- **CBS MarketWatch — Super Star Funds** (cbs.marketwatch.com/news/ newsroom.htx) provides articles, news, market data, fund research, links to fund sites, mutual fund tutorials for new investors, market data, portfolios, and a stock chat room.

- **Fund Focus** (www.fundfocus.com) provides free quotes, performance reports, and investment kits for more than 10,000 U.S. mutual funds. Discover the top 15 funds, use the glossary to define mutual fund investing terms, and get free e-mail alerts about updated performance reports.

- **Mutual Fund Magazine** (www.mfmag.com) requires your free registration, but the site is worth registering for. This online magazine has a wide variety of features, departments, screens, reports, online calculators, and tools to assist you in making your mutual fund selections.

- **Mutual Funds INVESTOR'S CENTER** (www.mfea.com) provides a news center, information about the new tax rules, links to mutual funds, and a research center that enables you to track from a list of more than 1,000 funds.

Buying Mutual Funds

Mutual funds can give you a much better return than savings accounts, money market deposit accounts, or certificates of deposit. However, the Federal Deposit Insurance Corporation (FDIC) doesn't insure mutual funds. The FDIC doesn't even insure the mutual funds sold by your bank. Even mutual fund portfolios consisting only of guaranteed U.S. government bonds contain some element of risk. On the other hand, returns from stock mutual funds average about 12 percent a year, whereas savings accounts may earn only 4 percent. Although your savings account pays 4 percent year after year, your mutual fund may be up 35 percent this year and down 10 percent the next.

Over the years, the stock market has outperformed any other investment. Unlike a mutual fund, however, individual investors frequently can't purchase a large number of different securities to diversify their investment risk. Buying shares in a mutual fund solves this problem. When you invest in a mutual fund, the diversity of the portfolio reduces the risk of losing your total investment. Selecting the right fund may be difficult, but you can find plenty of online help.

Assume that you have $1,000 to invest in a mutual fund. With your investment, you're purchasing a share of the total assets in the fund. If the share price of the fund is $10 per share, you can purchase 100 shares. The price of each share is the Net Asset Value (NAV). The fund manager calculates the NAV of the mutual fund by adding up the value of the securities in the fund and dividing by the number of outstanding shares.

The NAV increases and decreases as the market fluctuates. The Securities and Exchange Commission (SEC) requires that the NAV of each mutual fund be calculated and published for investors at the end of each business day. Here are a few examples of online quote servers that provide mutual fund NAV information:

- ✔ **CNNfn** (www.cnnfn.com) is affiliated with Cable News Network (CNN) and provides links to financial sites, investment articles, market information, and online research sources. Market information shows the current level, amount of change, and time of the last update for the Dow Jones Industrial Averages, NASDAQ composite, S&P 500, Russell 2000, NYSE Composite, Dow Transports, Dow Utilities, Amex Composite, and S&P Futures. For mutual fund data, click Stock Quotes and then enter the ticker symbol for your mutual fund or stock. CNNfn provides charts and company snapshots of selected firms. For mutual funds, CNNfn provides the latest performance data from Lipper Analytical.

- ✔ **PC Quote** (www.pcquote.com) offers five levels of service that range from $75 per month to $300 per month or $750 per year to $3,000 per year for real-time quotes, charts, and more. (See the Web site for details.) Free services include ticker symbol lookup, current mutual fund and stock prices, fundamental data, Market Guide company snapshots, Zacks Investment Research broker recommendations, annual earnings and earning estimates, current company news, charts of a company's stock price history and volume, and market indexes. Overall, you can search for stocks, bonds, futures, options, mutual funds, and indexes by entering the mutual fund ticker symbol in the Quote Tools box. You can also maintain as many as five portfolios with 20 ticker symbols in each portfolio.

- ✔ **Quote.com Mutual Funds** (www.quote.com/quotecom/funds) provides free tools and quotes for mutual funds. Get a market overview, charts, and Lipper and Morningstar performance reports for mutual funds that interest you. Quote.com Mutual Funds also provides a very informative mutual fund tutorial. Quote.com has several packages of services. The investor package is $7 per month for premium fundamental information, premium news, and real-time streaming charts. (You pay exchange fees for real-time streaming information for the three major U.S. exchanges: NYSE, NASDAQ, and Amex.) At $9.95 per month, the Trader package is for active investors who are less concerned with premium fundamental information (but still want basics like company reports, SEC filings, news, and more) and want streaming, real-time information.

A better way to buy mutual funds

If you purchase a load fund, it costs the same amount whether you purchase it through a broker or directly from the mutual fund company. However, you really don't need to pay a "load" to get a great mutual fund. One of the advantages of no-load mutual funds is that you can purchase them directly from the mutual fund company and skip paying a sales commission. In the past, if you purchased a no-load fund through a broker, you were charged a brokerage fee. Now, many discount brokerages and large mutual fund companies offer no-load funds (and even some load funds) with no transaction fees. (Brokers receive a portion of the fund's annual expenses instead.)

The primary advantage of purchasing a mutual fund through your online broker is the convenience. You can purchase several mutual funds in the same fund family and thus save time and effort because you don't have to call several mutual fund companies to open accounts and make your purchases. If you are unhappy with one of the mutual funds, you can swap it with another mutual fund in the same family at no cost, subject to certain restrictions. At the end of the month, you receive only one statement that covers all your funds. Your online brokerage provides you with one statement for your taxes, which simplifies the process of calculating the tax you owe on your profits.

Purchasing several mutual funds from one firm can help you with your investment tracking. Many online brokerages allow you to download your brokerage statement to personal finance programs such as Money 2000 and Quicken 2000. (For more information on downloading your brokerage statement and managing your portfolio, see Chapter 16.) For more information about one-stop shopping for your mutual funds, check out Table 5-1.

Table 5-1	Commission-Free Mutual Funds	
Broker (URL)	*Number of Funds Available*	*Fees and Restrictions*
American Express (www.americanexpress.com/direct)	2,000	No transaction fee if held for 180 days. Transaction fee: $39.95. Investment minimums: $2,000 for new accounts; $1,000 for retirement accounts; $500 for additional deposit

Broker (URL)	Number of Funds Available	Fees and Restrictions
Charles Schwab (www.schwab.com)	more than 1,000 no-load funds	Investment minimum/ subsequent: Brokerage: $2,500/$500; IRA: $1,000/ $500; Custodial: $1,000/ $100. Mutual Fund OneSource Service: $0 fees for no-load mutual funds. Transaction fees may apply to no-load or low-load funds not part of OneSource Service.
Datek Online (www.datek.com)	more than 5,000	$9.99 no-load transaction fee; load sales charge
Dreyfus Brokerage Services (www.edreyfus.com)	59 no-load fund families	$35 fee if not held 180 days
E*Trade (www.etrade.com)	more than 5,000	$25.95 for transaction-fee funds and for selling no-transaction-fee funds within 90 days
M. Siebert (www.msiebert.com)	more than 8,395 (includes 2,410 no-load, 1,045 with no transaction fee)	$35 per transaction for funds with transaction fee; minimum investment $5,000 ($2,000 for IRA)
National Discount Brokers (www.ndb.com)	more than 9,800	$20 transaction fee for 1,964 no-loads; minimum holding period
Waterhouse Securities (www.waterhouse.com)	more than 9,000; more than 1,400 no-load with no transaction fee	$24 transaction fee
Web Street Securities (www.webstreet securities.com)	more than 4,000	$14.95 fee for transactions under $500; minimum three-day holding period

Note: *Transaction fees apply to open-end mutual funds only. Some funds may also charge sales and redemption fees. Please read the prospectus and check the brokerage Web site for details as the terms and conditions of these transactions are subject to change.*

If you have to pay a sales charge for purchasing your mutual fund, deduct this amount from your return for the year. For example, if you pay a 5-percent sales charge for your $1,000 investment in mutual funds, the amount invested in the funds is $950. If the fund increases by 10 percent in one year, you have a $1,045 investment. Your true yield is $95, or 9.5 percent ($95 ÷ $1,000) — not the full 10 percent.

On the other hand, if you purchase a no-load mutual fund, your yield is 10 percent because you don't pay the sales fee. Your original $1,000 investment in mutual funds is now worth $1,100, which is $55 more than the fund with the sales fee.

Here are a few examples of firms that can sell you a mutual fund without a sales charge (or load):

✔ **Invesco** (`www.invesco.com`) provides plenty of information about its no-load funds. If you're a beginning investor, you'll appreciate the useful advice at this site. The site includes online prospectuses, charts to compare rates of return, and a list of the firm's financial services.

✔ **Janus** (`www.janus.com`) has a family of no-load funds. The site provides account access, brief overviews of fund performance, application forms, investor chats, and articles. If you want a prospectus, just ask for one at this Web site; Janus mails one to you.

✔ **Vanguard** (`www.vanguard.com`), one of the larger mutual fund families, has around 90 funds that don't charge sales fees. The Vanguard Web site includes brief fund descriptions, downloadable prospectuses, and an education center. This site offers an online library, online calculators, a portfolio planner, a listing of Vanguard's upcoming events (such as end-of-the-year returns), and investment articles.

Opening a mutual fund account

Before you invest in a mutual fund, read the fund's prospectus so that you understand exactly what you're investing in. Next, fill out the online account application form for the mutual fund company. SEC regulations require your signature to open an account. Figure 5-2 shows the application form for Lipper Funds, Inc., at `www.lipper.com/howto.htm`. This site indicates all the necessary steps for opening an account.

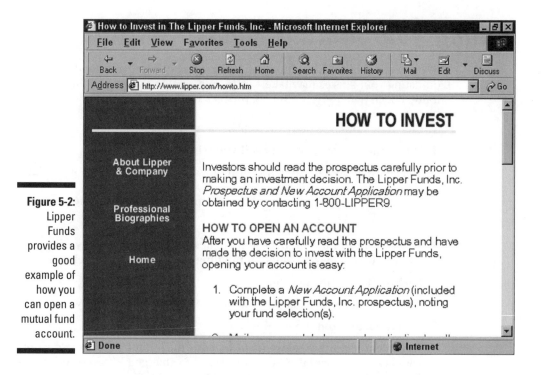

Figure 5-2:
Lipper
Funds
provides a
good
example of
how you
can open a
mutual fund
account.

For specific details about opening an account, contact the fund company or broker. In general, you need to complete the following steps:

1. **Indicate your fund selections.**

2. **Mark what type of account you want: individual, joint, or trust.**

3. **Include your Social Security number.**

4. **Mark whether you want check-writing privileges.**

5. **Indicate whether you want direct or automatic deposits (when you sell or if you receive a dividend) from a checking account or a paper check.**

6. **Mail your completed account application form and your check, made payable to the mutual fund.**

Selling Your Mutual Funds

The prospectus of a mutual fund details how you can sell your funds. Liquidating your shares may take a little time, so don't wait until the last minute to sell. Generally, the selling process works like this:

1. **Call your fund company or your broker.**

2. **Direct the representative to sell your shares.**

   You get that day's closing price, provided that you call before 4 p.m. EST.

If you are holding the certificate shares of a mutual fund, the selling process involves additional steps:

1. **Write a letter to the fund's agent requesting redemption of your fund shares at their market value at the time your request is received.**

2. **Enclose the certificates you hold.**

   If a custodial bank holds your shares, this step isn't necessary.

3. **Sign the letter and the certificates.**

4. **Have your signature guaranteed by your local bank or broker-dealer who is a member of the New York Stock Exchange (NYSE) or the National Association of Securities Dealers (NASD).**

5. **Insure the mailing for the full market value of the securities on the date they're sent.**

   Federal law requires redemption within seven days of when the fund's agent receives your request.

Starting Your Mutual Fund Account with as Little as $50

You don't need a great deal of money to buy a mutual fund. Before you start reading prospectuses, find out which mutual funds have automatic investment plans (AIPs). A mutual fund with an automatic investment plan often allows you to invest as little as $50 per month, after you meet the minimum investment.

The Internet provides information about which mutual funds offer AIPs. Table 5-2 shows a few examples of online mutual funds with automatic investment plans.

Table 5-2	Avoiding Minimum Deposit Requirements			
Fund Name (URL)	*Number of Funds*	*Minimum Initial Investment*	*Minimum Subsequent Investment*	
AARP (www.scudder.com)	3	$50	$50	
Alleghany (www.alleghanyfunds.chicago-trust.com)	11	$50	$50	
Ariel (www.arielmutualfund.com)	2	$50	$50	
Bramwell (www.bramwell.com)	2	$50	$50	
Dreyfus Founders (www.founders.com)	10	$50	$0	
Fidelity (www400.fidelity.com)	1	$0	N/A	
Fremont (www.fremontfunds.com)	10	$50	$50	
Gabelli (www.gabelli.com)	2	$0	$100	
INVESCO (www.invesco.com)	30	$50	$50	
Reynolds (www.reynoldsfunds.com)	2	$50	$50	
Strong (www.strong-funds.com)	51	$50	$0–$50	
T. Rowe Price (www.troweprice.com)	71	$50	$50	
TIAA-CREF (www.tiaa-cref.org)	6	$25	$25	
Transamerica (www.transamerica.com)	2	$50	$50	
USAA (www.usaa.com)	19	$0	$50	
Vanguard (www.vanguard.com)	1	$50	$50	
Westcore (www.westcore.com)	11	$0	$50	

Source: Mutual Fund Education Alliance (www.mfea.com/funddata/fund50.htm)

After you select several mutual funds with AIPs, ask for the funds' prospectuses and application forms. You can request the forms online, by telephone, or by mail. Fill out the section marked automatic investments and complete the form. You are authorizing the mutual fund company to make regular electronic withdrawals from your checking account. Many funds let you decide how much you want to invest. For example, you may decide to invest $50 per month or $25 every payday. If you reinvest your fund's cash distribution, you'll enjoy the benefits of compounding, and your capital gains can add up quickly.

As a starting point, you can visit some of the Web site listed in Table 5-2 to see what these firms offer. For example, Strong's Web site (`www.strong-funds.com`) includes the Strong Learning Center, shown in Figure 5-3. At the home page, click Learning Center for an online tutorial about mutual fund investing basics, information about how mutual funds are divided into different asset classes, and investments topics such as dollar-cost averaging. (See Chapter 3 for details about dollar-cost averaging.)

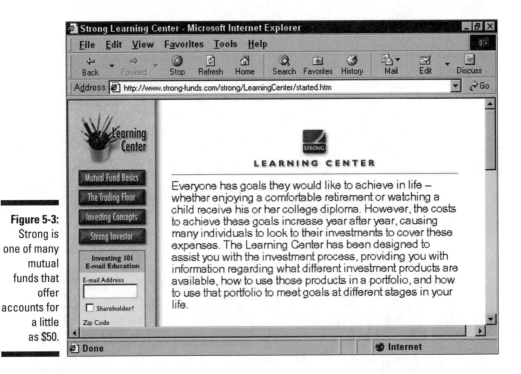

Figure 5-3: Strong is one of many mutual funds that offer accounts for a little as $50.

Chapter 6

The Keys to Successful Internet Mutual Fund Investing

T his chapter provides you with all the basic online tools for identifying mutual fund candidates. I present some general information about mutual fund investment, including types of funds, fees, and potential risks. I offer suggestions about where to find mutual fund facts and figures online. I also describe several online screening tools that can help you choose the mutual fund that best meets your needs. These mutual fund screens vary from simple to more advanced. By the way, the best online mutual fund screen is the one that includes the investment criteria you feel are important.

Mutual Fund Basics

With more than 9,000 funds to choose from, selecting a mutual fund has become a complex process — meaning that online screening tools are more important than ever before. When you select your investment criteria, you need to consider several factors:

✔ How long do you plan to own the mutual fund?

✔ How much risk to your principal can you tolerate?

✔ Which mutual fund category meets your personal financial objectives?

Which funds you select depends on the answers to these questions. If you need your money in a year and can't afford much risk because, for example, you plan to use the money to purchase a house, you want to consider a safe, short-term bond fund. On the other hand, if this money is your retirement fund that you don't plan to tap for ten years and you can stomach some ups and downs, you should consider a growth stock fund.

Before you start screening mutual fund candidates, you need to understand some general information: the types of funds you can choose, the fees that mutual fund companies charge, the types of risks associated with mutual funds, and how to read a prospectus.

Discovering the differences between open-end and closed-end mutual funds

An *open-end mutual fund* has an unlimited number of shares. You can buy these shares either through the mutual fund company or your broker. The Securities and Exchange Commission requires that each mutual fund company calculate the NAV of each fund every day at the close of business.

A *closed-end mutual fund* is a hybrid: part mutual fund and part stock. A closed-end mutual fund is a publicly traded investment company with a limited number of shares. It doesn't stand ready to redeem its own shares from shareholders, and rarely issues new shares beyond its initial offering. That's why it's a "closed fund." You can only buy or sell these shares through a broker on the major stock exchanges. The value of these shares isn't calculated by using the NAV methodology. Instead, shares are valued by using a method similar to bonds and are traded at either a discount or a premium. Market prices of publicly traded closed-end mutual fund shares are published daily.

Closed fund types include closed-end stock funds (investments in common and preferred stocks), closed-end bond funds (investments in a range of bonds), closed-end convertible bond funds (have portfolios of bonds that can be converted to common stocks), closed-end single country funds (that specialize in stocks from one country or geographical region), and so on.

Minimizing fees

Loads are the fees with which mutual fund companies compensate the broker who sold you the fund. About half of all stock and bond funds have loads; money market funds normally don't have loads. Loads and other fees are important because they are deducted from your investment returns.

Loading it on

A *front-end load* is the most common type of fee that mutual fund companies charge. Investors pay this fee when they purchase shares in the mutual fund. No additional fees are charged for redeeming or selling your mutual fund shares. By law, front-end loads can't be greater than 8.5 percent. Loads average 5 percent for stock funds and 4 percent for bond funds.

The less common *back-end load* fee is charged when you sell or redeem the shares. Back-end fees are usually based on time, starting at 5 percent during the first year and declining a percentage point a year — by year five, no fees are charged. However, back-end load funds often have Rule 12b-1 fees, which are usually the amounts charged to investors for promoting the mutual fund. Fees range from 0.25 percent to 0.30 percent but can be as high as 1.25 percent. Rule 12b-1 fees are included in the fund's expense ratio.

Rule 12b-1 marketing fees increase manager fees and aren't related to maximizing shareholder wealth. As an investor, you need to be on the lookout for these expenses when you read the prospectus.

Generally, funds with back-end fees are more expensive than funds with front-end fees due to the high Rule 12b-1 fees. However, if you are willing to hold your investment for five years or more (which really, you ought to, if you're investing in stocks), you pay no load (back-end loads usually disappear after five years).

Excluding the maximum fee for front-end loads of 8.5 percent, mutual funds can't charge more than 7.25 percent for the life of the investment. Overall, load fees vary from 4.0 percent to 8.5 percent of the NAV for the shares purchased.

What does all this fee information mean? If you purchase 300 shares at $10 per share with an 8-percent front-end fee, you're purchasing only $2,760 worth of shares. The other $240 goes to compensate the broker who sold you the fund. In other words, your investment needs to increase by $240 just to break even.

Taking it off

Some funds have no loads, which means that they have no front-end or back-end fees. These no-load funds generally don't have a sales force, so you have to contact the investment company to make a purchase. Nevertheless, no-load funds do charge service fees, proving that there's no such thing as a free lunch. Mutual fund companies charge annual fees for their management services, deducting these amounts before calculating the NAV.

Annual fees for the fund managers are about 0.50 percent of the fund's net assets. Other service fees include legal and auditing fees, the cost of preparing and distributing annual reports and proxy statements, director's fees, and transaction expenses. When added to the management fee, a fund's total yearly expenses can range from 0.75 to 1.25 percent of fund assets.

Experienced mutual fund investors typically avoid funds with expense ratios greater than 1.25 percent.

Some mutual fund companies may have low up-front fees but charge high rates for managing fund operations. The prospectus details whether the mutual fund charges these fees.

Understanding Mutual Fund Risks

Mutual funds provide statements about their objectives and risk posture (which is briefly explained in qualitative terms in the prospectus). Rather than provide precise information to help you evaluate the riskiness of a mutual fund, however, these statements typically offer vague, general explanations of a fund's approach to risk. For more precise, statistical evaluations of a fund's risks, you can turn to independent mutual fund rating services such as Morningstar (`www.morningstar.com`).

Morningstar and other independent rating services calculate such statistics as the standard deviation of a fund's return. I don't want to turn this chapter into an introductory statistics course, but I can tell you that standard deviation helps you judge how volatile, or risky, a fund is. This statistic shows you how much a fund has deviated from its average return over a period of time. Figure 6-1 shows Morningstar's rating for a mutual fund, which you can find at `quicktake.morningstar.com/Funds/Ratings/_RPMGX.html`.

Standard deviation offers a clear indicator of a fund's consistency over time. A fund's standard deviation is a simple measure of the fund's highest and lowest returns over a specific time period. Just remember this point: The higher the standard deviation, the higher the fund's risk.

For example, if the 3-year return on a fund is 33 percent, that statistic may mean that the fund earned 11 percent in the first year, 11 percent in the second year, and 11 percent in the third year. On the other hand, the fund may have earned 28 percent in the first year, 5 percent in the second year, and 0 percent in the third year. If your financial plan requires an 11-percent annual return, this fund is not for you!

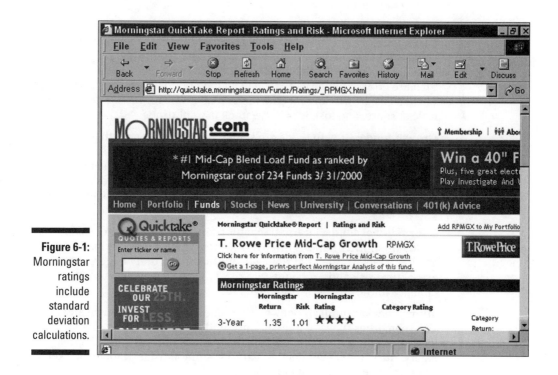

Figure 6-1:
Morningstar
ratings
include
standard
deviation
calculations.

A Fund for You, a Fund for Me

You can choose from a wide variety of mutual fund categories. As a matter of fact, so many types of funds are available that you're almost guaranteed to find a fund that is an excellent fit for your personal financial objectives. You can summarize the funds into nine groups:

✔ **Aggressive growth funds:** Aggressive growth funds tend to be investments in small, young companies and may involve the use of options and futures to reap greater profits. Aggressive growth funds primarily seek increases in capital gains. If the stock market is hot, these funds often provide the biggest returns of all mutual funds, mostly due to the capital gains of the stocks in the funds. They typically drop the most, though, when the market is cold. Their volatility makes them a poor choice for the short-term investor.

✔ **Bond funds:** Investment grade bond funds usually have less risk than funds with stocks, but they are not risk free. These types of bond funds are usually good investment choices for short-, medium-, and long-term investors who desire low risk. Investment grade bond funds focus on current income. For more information on bonds, see Chapter 12.

✔ **Growth and income funds:** Funds in the growth and income category target a steady return with capital growth potential. They often invest in companies that are growing, as well as in companies that are paying high or increasing dividends. Growth and income funds are more diverse than are growth funds; — they may include bonds — and are less risky. This means growth and income funds reap fewer rewards if the stock market soars, and lose less if the stock market drops.

✔ **Growth funds:** Growth funds are similar to aggressive growth funds but have less risk. They may invest in larger, well-established firms with a long track record of earnings that may continue to grow faster than average. These funds also seek stocks with capital gain potential. In addition to stocks, these funds generally include bonds and cash equivalents. Growth funds are best for investors with medium- to long-term objectives.

✔ **International funds:** International funds include a mix of stocks and bonds from other nations or governments. These funds are subject to several types of risks that domestic mutual funds don't experience, such as political risk and exchange rate risk (losing money because of changes in the currency exchange rate).

✔ **Money market funds:** Money market funds provide less return and less risk than other types of mutual funds and are good investments for short-term investors. The principal advantage of these funds is their safety. Also, if you ever need to get to your money fast, money market funds may be the type of fund for you.

✔ **Balanced funds:** Balanced funds are a mix of stocks, bonds, and Treasury bills, and possibly some foreign assets. Each fund has a different strategy for determining its asset allocation mix.

✔ **Dividend funds:** Dividend funds are investments in common and preferred stocks offered by corporations that generate a high, steady stream of dividend income. In Canada, the dividends are usually eligible for the dividend tax credit, thereby increasing the after-tax yield to the unit holder. This makes dividend funds attractive to Canadian investors who prefer to pay the lower tax rates on dividend income than the higher tax rates on interest income.

✔ **Equity funds:** Equity funds have a higher risk than money market or bond funds, but they also can offer the highest returns. A stock fund's NAV can rise and fall quickly over the short term, but historically stocks have performed better over the long term than other types of investments. Not all equity (stock) funds are the same. For example, some equity funds specialize in growth or technology stocks.

Table 6-1 provides a brief overview of the time period and risk-tolerance level of the major mutual fund categories. Please note the difference in risk level between money market funds (that are not insured by the Federal Deposit Insurance Corporation) and money market deposit accounts (MMDAs) that are insured.

Table 6-1	Choosing the Right Type of Mutual Fund	
Investment Time Period	*Risk-Tolerance Level*	*Category of Mutual Fund*
Less than 2 years	Minimum risk to principal	Money market fund (not an MMDA)
	Some risk to principal	Bond fund (short to intermediate bond fund)
Between 2 and 4 years	Minimum risk to principal	Money market fund (not an MMDA)
	Some risk to principal	Bond fund (short to intermediate term)
	Moderate risk to principal	Bond fund (intermediate to long-term)
Between 4 and 6 years	Minimum risk to principal	Money market fund (not an MMDA)
	Some risk to principal	Bond fund (short to intermediate)
	Moderate risk to principal	Growth and income funds
	Excessive risk to principal	Growth funds and international funds

Set realistic expectations for your investment choices. The Internet provides many information sources about the average rates of return for different categories of mutual funds. You can find out how the fund category you select stacks up against other categories of funds at the Wall Street Journal Interactive Web site (www.wsj.com). Starting at the home page, click Money & Investing ☞ Mutual Funds Center. Under Leaders and Laggards (Monthly Tallies), click Mutual Fund Yardsticks.

Finding Facts and Figures Online

This list of online information services can assist you in finding the right mutual fund:

✔ **Find a Fund** (www.findafund.com) features quotes, top mutual fund performers, and lists of mutual funds by name, category, and ticker symbol. Investigate the similarity between two mutual funds by examining recent trends and prices. Brush up on mutual fund basics and create a portfolio and have e-mail sent to you each month to update you on your portfolio's performance.

- **Mutual Funds Interactive (The Mutual Funds Homepage)** (www.brill.com) offers tutorials for beginning mutual fund investors, interviews, descriptions of fund strategies with top mutual fund managers, analyses of the mutual funds market, and links to mutual fund home pages.

- **Standard & Poor's Micropal** (www.micropal.com) provides fund information and monitoring for more than 38,000 funds across the globe on a daily, weekly, and monthly basis. Additionally, Micropal supplies summaries on the funds it monitors.

- **The Street.com** (www.thestreet.com), shown in Figure 6-2, provides fund profiles and scorecards at quote.thestreet.com/cgi-bin/texis/FundSB. You can search Lipper Analytical's top performers for the week. Additionally, you can search funds by asset size, category, fund symbol, or fund name.

- **The Wall Street Journal** (interactive.wsj.com) provides information on mutual funds as part of its Money & Investing section. This free information includes news and features, statistics on the top performers in various fund categories, mutual fund profiles, scorecards, and closed-end fund prices.

Figure 6-2: The Street.com provides the capability to search for mutual fund reports and statistics.

Locating and Reading the Prospectus

Fast EDGAR Mutual Funds Reporting is located at www.sec.gov/edaux/mutual.htm. This Web site, shown in Figure 6-3, provides prospectuses for more than 7,000 mutual funds. If you know the name of the fund you're interested in, you can investigate the fund's activities at this site. Target your search by determining the range of dates you want, which filing forms (quarterly, annually, and so on) you want to read, and the name of the specific fund.

If you don't know the exact name of the fund you want, refer to Morningstar at www.morningstar.com. Morningstar provides a mutual fund search engine. Just enter what you know of the mutual fund's name. The search engine's results provide you with several mutual funds that have similar names. It is likely that the mutual fund you are seeking is one of the funds listed.

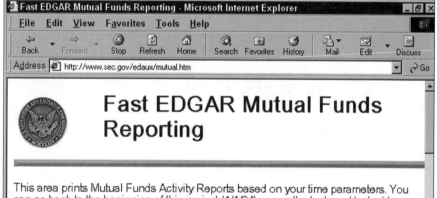

Figure 6-3:
Get the prospectus for the mutual fund you are investigating online from Fast EDGAR.

After you find the prospectus you want, download it to your computer so that you can read it at your leisure. Here's how you download a prospectus that you have accessed via the Fast EDGAR Mutual Funds Reporting Web site:

1. **With the prospectus displayed in your Web browser, choose File⇨Save.**

   Your browser displays the Save As dialog box.

2. **Enter a filename for the prospectus and select the directory in which you want to save the file.**

3. **Click Save.**

   Your browser saves the prospectus on your computer. If you have a dial-up connection to the Internet, you can disconnect from your ISP.

4. **Minimize your Internet browser.**

5. **Open your word-processing program.**

6. **Open the prospectus file.**

   You can now read the prospectus at your leisure offline.

Checking the facts

When you read the prospectus you have downloaded, look for the following information:

- ✔ **Investment objectives:** The first paragraph of the prospectus describes the fund's investment objectives and lists the types of securities the fund invests in. If the fund doesn't meet your investment objectives, you can stop reading and start evaluating another fund.

- ✔ **Fees:** The SEC requires all mutual funds to list all fees, costs, and expenses in a table at the front of the prospectus.

- ✔ **Additional expenses:** Additional expenses may be for extra services, such as printed shareholder materials, toll-free telephone numbers with 24-hour service, accumulation plans that reinvest your distributions (shareholder profits), and related support and guidance.

- ✔ **Performance:** Year-to-year data for the last ten years (or less if the fund isn't that old) in condensed financial statements indicates the fund's performance. Statistics track the fund's NAV, shareholder distributions, and expenses. For funds that include stocks, the prospectus may also include dividends and price information. Many funds provide graphs that show how a $1,000 investment in the fund increased or decreased over a ten-year period.

> ✔ **Statement of additional information:** This section of the prospectus covers fund details and complex items such as the biographies of the fund's directors, the fund's objectives, and contracts for professional services. These reports are free to the fund's shareholders that request them.

The SEC requires the prospectus to indicate what fees the fund charges for a $1,000 investment with a 5-percent return redeemed at the end of one year, three years, five years, and ten years. Keep in mind that both load and no-load funds have management fees and operating expenses that are charged to the fund.

Getting it right

Reading a mutual fund prospectus is not the most exciting thing you could be doing on a Saturday night, but you'll discover many useful facts and disclosures required by the Federal law. The mutual fund's prospectus may stimulate many questions, but here are a few that you should get answers to before you invest:

> ✔ **Is the fund's performance steady?** Over the last ten years (or life of the fund if it is younger) are one or two good years responsible for the fund's overall performance?
>
> ✔ **How does this mutual fund compare to similar funds in terms of performance and expenses?** Keep in mind that higher expenses result in lower investor returns.
>
> ✔ **What's the standard deviation or risk level of the fund?** How does this compare to similar funds? (Remember, if the fund has a higher level of risk, it should have a higher level of return. This is your just reward for taking additional risk.)
>
> ✔ **What's the fund "turnover ratio" like?** The turnover ratio indicates how actively the fund's managers are trading securities. The higher the fund turnover rate, the higher the brokerage's charges. High transaction costs can take a bite out of investor returns.
>
> ✔ **In the "how to purchase shares" and "how to redeem shares" sections of the prospectus, are there any initial sales charges?** Is there a required minimum investment amount or a minimum amount for subsequent investments? Will you be charged a fee for switching from one fund to another fund in the same fund family? Will you be charged a redemption fee when you sell your shares?

It is unlikely that the prospectus will have an up-to-the-minute listing of the securities currently held by the mutual fund. Check out the fund's current holdings at Morningstar (www.morningstar.com), Smart Money (www.smartmoney.com), or a similar mutual fund supersite.

How to Screen Mutual Funds Online

The Internet provides a variety of mutual fund screening tools that sort thousands of mutual funds by criteria that you select. For example, you may want one type of fund for your children's education — something long-term because you don't need the money for 10 to 20 years — and a different fund for your retirement to help you reduce your current tax liabilities. With these online screening tools, you can evaluate several funds that meet your financial needs.

Most of the stock-screening sites on the Internet are free. These database searches are an inexpensive way to isolate mutual funds that meet your special criteria. Some databases list funds incorrectly or have outdated information. However, they are useful for pruning a large list of candidates to a manageable short list.

Some mutual fund screening programs — for example, Quicken's Mutual Fund Finder (www.quicken.com/investments/mutualfunds/finder/) and MSN's Money Central (moneycentral.msn.com) — are for beginners to use. Others, such as Thomson Investors Network (www.thomsoninvest.net), require some practice.

Each screening site uses different criteria to sort mutual funds. You have to decide which criteria you care about and then use the site that offers the criteria you want. Any way you look at it, the selection of the right mutual fund is still up to you.

Here's an overview of the features of three mutual fund screens that are better for beginning online investors:

✔ **MSN MoneyCentral** (moneycentral.msn.com/investor/finder/ mffinder.asp) has a mutual fund screen that you access by clicking Finder. The Easy Fund Finder is designed to let you search a database of over 8,000 mutual funds for the one fund that meets your needs and investment objectives. MoneyCentral also offers 11 prebuilt mutual fund screens. Just click Predefined Searches for screens that include the criteria that you feel are the most important when selecting a mutual fund. Examples of the prebuilt screens include: Safety first funds; Do-it-yourself funds (this screen lets you experiment with your own pain threshold); Foreign stock funds; High-yield bond funds; Hot, no-load funds; Large blend funds; NAIC equity screen; NAIC fixed-income screen; Small cap growth funds; Specialty technology funds; and Top-rated funds. You can also design your own mutual fund screens.

✔ **Morningstar** (www.morningstar.com) offers a free, independent service that evaluates more than 18,000 mutual funds. From Morningstar's home page, click Funds ☞ Fund Selector. The free screen lets you set the criteria for fund type, cost and purchase options, ratings and risk, returns, and portfolio. The advanced search function is comprehensive; expect great performance and historical data. However, you have to be a premium member — $9.95 per month or $99 per year (after 30-day free trial.)

✔ **Quicken.com** (www.quicken.com) provides its mutual fund screen free of charge. At the Quicken.com home page, click Search for More Mutual Funds to access the prebuilt mutual fund screens. Popular Searches uses preset criteria that match popular investing strategies. Easy Step Search has additional variables and is geared for more experienced investors. Full Search has 20 basic variables, includes Value Line and Morningstar ratings, and provides side-by-side comparisons of up to eight funds. You can move freely between different searches to sample each screen.

The following three mutual funds screens are great for more experienced investors:

✔ **Forbes Mutual Fund Tool** (www.forbes.com/tool/toolbox/lipper/screen.asp) lets you screen the Lipper database of more than 6,000 mutual funds. You select the criteria that match your investment objectives by choosing screening fields you like by using pull-down menus and clicking the box next to the category. Just click the categories you are interested in and then click the Screen button to access the database and see which funds score best.

✔ **Smart Money Interactive** (www.smartmoney.com) has a do-it-yourself mutual fund finder that searches a database of over 6,000 mutual funds. You can screen for dozens of factors. For additional help, the screen provides current averages for criteria such as standard deviation and beta. To analyze your selections, click Analyze First 15 Funds. This function sorts your best candidates so that you can compare and print your results.

✔ **Thomson Investors Network** (www.thomsoninvest.net), shown in Figure 6-4, offers a free, newly enhanced mutual fund screener. At the home page, click Funds ☞ Fund Screening. The fund selection wizard presents a wide variety of selection criteria. The criteria selections are divided into categories such as objectives, performance, expenses, holdings, and risk. Enter the criteria that are important to you. When you have completed your selections, click Show Results.

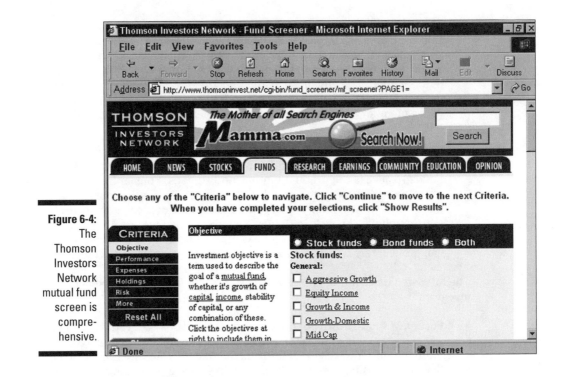

Figure 6-4:
The
Thomson
Investors
Network
mutual fund
screen is
compre-
hensive.

Buying mutual funds your way

You have your choice of three ways to purchase mutual funds. First, you can send an application directly to the mutual fund company. (You can do this online, by fax, or via U.S. mail.) Second, you can purchase mutual funds through your full-service or online broker and pay a brokerage fee (even if you are purchasing a no-load fund). Finally, you can purchase a no-load mutual fund via the Internet *free of any*

transaction charges through an online mutual fund supermarket, such as Schwab's One Source program (www.schwab.com) or DLJ Direct's FundCenter (www.dljdirect.com). (Don't forget to read the purchase instructions. At some online mutual fund supermarkets, you may find a few restrictions, such as minimum purchase amounts.)

Chapter 7

Online Analysis, Buying, and Selling of Mutual Funds

*W*hen selecting a mutual fund, investors often look for relative performance over the last ten years, five years, and three years to see how the fund reacts to different economic conditions and stock market environments. Other factors in selecting a mutual fund include evaluating the fund manager's experience and record, the fund's level of consistency, and the fund's major investment holdings.

In this chapter, I show how you can match your financial objectives and risk-tolerance level to the right mutual funds. As a result, you can decide how much you should invest in a particular type of fund. This chapter includes instructions about how to read an online mutual fund listing. I also describe how to use online mutual fund ratings to assist in selecting the very best mutual funds for your personal portfolio. I compare mutual fund rating systems and provide a short list of online mutual funds that you can purchase without a broker. I also provide step-by-step directions on how to purchase mutual funds with a broker and how to tell when it's time to sell.

Going Online with Mutual Funds

Mutual funds are great for investors who lack capital, technical knowledge, and the time to establish and maintain a diversified stock or bond portfolio. The advantages of mutual funds are easy access to your assets, the ability to sell the funds if you need to, and professional management.

A wide difference exists in the kinds of mutual funds available. Many large mutual fund companies manage *families* of funds. A mutual fund family is a group of mutual funds all under the same management. Today, you can select from more than 9,000 different mutual funds from over 700 fund families. Most likely, one of these funds meets your personal objectives and risk-tolerance level. If you aren't satisfied with the fund you select, you can always switch from one fund to another in the same fund family (often without any additional costs).

You can find information about a fund's goals, strategies for reaching those objectives, performance, management, and fee structures in the fund's prospectus. Prospectuses are often located at the fund's Web site (for example, T. Rowe Price's site at `www.troweprice.com`), and they're also filed at the Securities and Exchange Commission's Web site at `www.sec.gov`.

Mutual funds fall into two main categories: *open-end funds* (which can continuously acquire new funds for investment through the sale of additional shares) and *closed-end funds* (which initially raise capital by selling a fixed number of shares, and then those shares are bought and sold on a stock exchange).

Different funds have different fees. Some funds have *front-end loads* (a sales commission when you buy the fund) or *back-end loads* (a sales commission when you sell the fund), and some funds have *no loads* (no sales commissions).

For a list of a few no-load mutual funds, visit `www.noload.com` and click Mutual Funds Research Reports.

All funds have fees and expenses, but the amounts vary. In addition to sales and redemption fees, the mutual fund's prospectus indicates the fund's management and administration expenses. The fund's investment advisor generally receives 0.5 to 1.0 percent of the fund's average daily net assets. Administrative expenses include legal, auditing, and accounting costs, along with the fees for directors and the costs of preparing the annual report and proxy statements. These administrative expenses are added to the investment advisory fee. The total costs often average between 0.75 percent and 1.25 percent of fund assets. Savvy mutual fund investors are wary of funds that charge more than 1.25 percent.

In 1980, the SEC passed Rule 12b-1, which allows mutual fund companies to charge advertising and marketing expenses. These costs typically range from 0.25 percent to 0.30 percent and can be as high as 1.25 percent. Some mutual funds charge these fees and others don't, so read the prospectus carefully.

Figure 7-1 shows the Web site of the Mutual Fund Education Alliance (`www.mfea.com`), a not-for-profit trade association of the no-load mutual fund industry. The Web site's Mutual Fund Investor's Center is designed to serve investors who want to use mutual funds to reach their financial goals. The site provides links to profiles on performance data for no-load mutual funds, lists of funds with the lowest initial minimum deposit, lists of funds with the lowest expenses, comparative indexes, and other relevant mutual fund information.

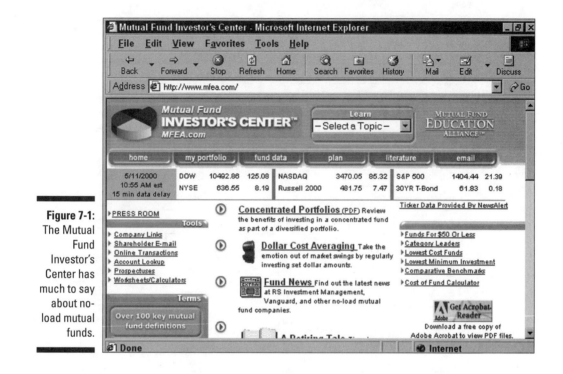

Figure 7-1: The Mutual Fund Investor's Center has much to say about no-load mutual funds.

Finding the Right Mix of Investments

Asset allocation is the specific amount of money that you spend for each type of investment. In Wall Street-speak, the term describes how you diversify your financial assets (stocks, bonds, and cash) by amounts that you determine. Asset allocation also means trying to squeeze every bit of return out of each asset type, given the level of risk. Overall, the right asset allocation approach is the one that works best for you. It should take into consideration your age, the amount of time you can invest your money, your financial goals, your risk-tolerance level, and the impact of taxes on your investment decisions.

Table 7-1 shows all the ingredients for finding the combination of assets that may be just right for you. The source of this guideline is Value Line (www.valueline.com). The table shows Value Line's definitions of nine investor types. The types are categorized as conservative, moderate, and aggressive. The investment time frame fills out the picture. The investment period can be short-term, medium-term, or long-term.

Table 7-1	Mutual Fund Asset Allocations Based on Investor Risk-Tolerance Levels		
Risk	**Time Frame**		
	Short-term (0 to 2 years)	**Medium-term (3 to 5 years)**	**Long-term (6 years and greater)**
Conservative Investors	#1	#2	#3
Stocks	0%	30%	50%
Bonds	0%	25%	50%
Cash	100%	45%	0%
Moderate Investors	#4	#5	#6
Stocks	10%	55%	65%
Bonds	30%	35%	35%
Cash	60%	10%	0%
Aggressive Investors	#7	#8	#9
Stocks	30%	70%	100%
Bonds	30%	30%	0%
Cash	40%	0%	0%

Source: *Value Line Mutual Fund Survey,* **How to Invest in Mutual Funds** *(1995), Value Line Publishing, Inc., New York, NY.*

Many mutual funds match the asset allocation table shown in Table 7-1. You can start with one mutual fund or you can purchase a mutual fund for each allocation. If you purchase several mutual funds, you can diversify your risk even more. For example, to complete your portfolio, you may want to buy a money market fund, a stock mutual fund, and a fixed-asset (bond) mutual fund. It's your money and your choice.

Matching Mutual Funds to Your Financial Objectives

Table 7-2 shows how you can match mutual fund categories to your financial objectives and risk-tolerance level. After you read Table 7-1, decide which of the nine investor types most closely matches your personal financial plan and risk-tolerance profile. For example, Investor Type #1 is a conservative investor who is investing for the short-term. Investor Type #9 is an aggressive investor who is investing for the long-term. For more detail about the investor types, visit the Value Line site at www.valueline.com. Table 7-2 shows what categories of mutual funds are right for your investor type. The percentages listed in Table 7-2 match the recommended allocations shown in Table 7-1. (For details about fund types, see Chapter 6.)

Table 7-2	Suggested Mutual Funds for Nine Types of Investors		
Investor Type	*Cash*	*Stocks*	*Bonds*
1	(100%) Money market fund		
2	(45%) Money market fund	(30%) General equity	(25%) Intermediate fixed-income partial equity funds (asset allocation); Tax-free fixed income funds (municipal bonds)
3	(0%)	(50%) General equity funds (income, growth)	(50%) Taxable fixed-income funds (government agency, and income); Fixed-mortgage income, partial equity funds (asset allocation)
4	(10%) Money market fund	(30%) General equity funds (income)	(60%) Short-term fixed-income funds (diversified); Fixed-income partial equity funds (asset allocation and balanced)
5	(10%) Money market fund	(55%) General equity funds (growth, income)	(35%) Intermediate fixed-income funds (diversified); Intermediate fixed-income partial equity funds (balanced); Tax-free fixed-income funds (municipal bonds)
6	(0%)	(65%) General equity funds (growth, growth and equity)	(35%) Fixed-income bonds (diversified, corporate); Fixed-income partial equity funds (balanced); Tax-free fixed-income funds (municipal bonds
7	(40%) Money market fund	(30%) General equity funds (aggressive growth, small cap)	(30%) Short-term fixed-income funds (corporate high-yield); Short-term fixed-income partial equity funds (convertible)

(continued)

Table 7-2 *(continued)*

Investor Type	Cash	Stocks	Bonds
8	(0%)	(70%) General equity funds(aggressive growth, small cap), Specialty equity (technology,other)	(30%) Intermediate fixed-income (corporate high yield); Intermediate fixed-income partial equity funds (flexible); Tax-free fixed-income funds (municipal bonds)
9	(0%)	(100%) General equity funds (aggressive growth, growth, and growth and income); Small cap equity funds; Specialty equity (technology, other); International equity (European, foreign, global, or Pacific stock)	(0%)

Interested in finding specific mutual funds in the categories that match your individual personal finance profile? Stock Smart (www.stocksmart.com) can assist in finding the mutual fund that is right for you. When you reach Stock Smart, click Test Drive Free! for a seven-day trial. Enter the information requested and then wait for Stock Smart to send you an e-mail message with your trial subscription user name and password. Use this information to log on. After you log on, you can quickly change the user name and password to what you'd usually use.

Now, for the fun part, click Mutual Funds ☞ Tools ☞ Mutual Funds Screening. The Mutual Funds Screening Web page asks three questions: What is your investment goal? What is the term of your investment? How much are you going to invest? Answer these three questions and then click Submit. (The terms used in the questionnaire are explained further down the Web page.)

The results page shows the outcome of all your clicking and answering. The screening program suggests how much money you should invest, and in what type of mutual funds, based on your investor profile. Below this suggestion are about 50 funds that meet your investing criteria. Funds have year-to-date (YTD) ratings, fund names, assets, 13-week returns, YTD returns, and standard deviations. Click a hyperlinked description, such as YTD return, and the program sorts the 50 investment candidates so the highest YTD return is listed first. A monthly subscription to Stock Smart is $19.95, and an annual subscription, with a 10-percent discount, is $215.46.

Using the Internet to Help You Choose the Best Funds in Each Class

Past performance doesn't guarantee future performance. However, investors often use annualized returns to compare funds. The Internet offers tables of fund comparisons for each month and for periods ranging from one month to ten years or more. For example, *Business Week* (www.businessweek.com) has a Mutual Funds Corner that provides listings of the returns for the best funds, the bond fund leaders, and the worst funds.

Comparing a fund to similar funds is a good way to examine a fund's performance. Organizations such as Morningstar (www.morningstar.com) have mutual fund tables that make comparisons easy by grouping fund classes (see Chapter 6 for details about fund classes) and including the averages for each category. A fund's capability to consistently outperform similar funds is one sign of good quality. In contrast, you should avoid funds that have consistently underperformed for three years or more.

Make certain that the funds you're comparing are similar. A big difference exists between an aggressive growth fund and a growth fund. To verify your analyses, check the prospectus of each fund. The fund's investment objectives are listed in the first paragraph. You may discover that the fund that looked so attractive at first is too risky for you.

Following a mutual fund checklist

As you select your first mutual fund, consider several factors described in the following checklist:

- ✔ **The fund manager:** Often a fund is only as good as its management. If the fund manager has shown great performance in the past, future performance is likely to be above average. If the fund manager has been replaced, past performance becomes less meaningful and may even be worthless. A poor-performing fund that gets a new fund manager may turn around and become a top performer.

- ✔ **The stability of the fund's philosophy:** If the fund seems unclear about its financial goals and is switching investment methods, it may be in trouble.

- ✔ **The size of the fund:** Good fund candidates have at least $50 million under management and should be large enough to keep up with institutional investors. At the opposite end of the spectrum, funds with more than $20 billion tend to have problems with being too large.

- ✓ **The objectives of the fund:** Some funds focus on specialty or sector funds (gold funds, biotech funds) and often offer great returns. However, they aren't good funds for the online investor who wants to own just one mutual fund. If you own just one specialty fund, you lose the advantage of diversification.

- ✓ **Fees:** A debate has raged during the last ten years about which is better: no-load or load mutual funds. All the studies indicate that paying a sales commission doesn't ensure a greater return. However, investing in a fund with high fees and high returns is better than investing in a fund with low fees and poor performance.

- ✓ **Purchase constraints:** Although some funds require a minimum initial investment of $5,000, many good funds don't have this requirement. If you enroll in a fund's automatic investment program, the minimum initial investment amount is usually waived. Additionally, many fund minimums are waived or substantially reduced for IRA investments.

For additional information about selecting mutual funds, see Morningstar (www.morningstar.com). Morningstar has a learning section (just click Learn) and helpful articles. One such article is titled "Select Your First Fund."

Reading an online mutual fund listing

As a general rule, mutual fund listings are slightly easier to read than stock listings. (See Chapter 8 to find out about stock listings.) Some online sources and newspapers list mutual funds differently. Table 7-3 shows how the Wall Street Journal Interactive Edition (www.wsj.com) shows the performance of a mutual fund profile. The name and ticker symbol of the mutual fund are listed first.

You can use a company lookup to find the ticker symbol of the mutual fund you're researching. Many online sources, such as the *Wall Street Journal* (www.wsj.com), have company lookups. These handy tools are often listed next to the quote server tools so that you don't have to change to another Web site. Enter the full or partial name of the fund you are interested in. The company lookup tool provides a hyperlinked list of potential matches. Click the ticker symbol that you think matches the fund you are researching. If the symbol doesn't represent the correct fund, click the Back button and try another candidate.

The Net Asset Value (NAV) of the fund and the changes in the fund's value for that day appear under the ticker symbol information (refer to Table 7-3). The NAV is the sales price of one share of the fund. (The NAV is calculated by dividing the value of the fund by the number of shares.) The change in price for the day appears below that, and is the *bottom line* for investors. Table 7-3 indicates that the example fund increased by $0.12. The fund's NAV 52-week high and low are in the next column.

Table 7-3 How to Read an Online Mutual Fund Listing			
Title of Fund:		Dreyfus Growth Opportunity Fund, Inc.	
Symbol:		DREQX	
Net Asset Value:	9.97	52-Week High	10.94
Change:	+0.12	52-Week Low	8.51
Performance			
	Total Return		Percentile within Objective
Year-to-date	3.9%	D	34
1-Year	4.5%	D	26
3-Year (annualized)	16.0%	D	27
5-Year (annualized)	11.5%	E	15
Fund Information			
Investment Objective:		Growth Funds	
Fund Manger (Tenure):		Timothy M. Ghriskey (since 1995)	
Minimum Initial Investment		$2,500	
Maximum Sales Charge:		0%	
Maximum Redemption Charge:		0%	
Total Expense Ratio:		1.06%	
Total Net Assets:		$406,200,000	
Phone:		800-383-9387	

Source: Wall Street Journal Interactive (www.wsj.com)

The *Performance* section of Table 7-3 indicates the total performance of the fund for the time periods of year-to-date, one year, three years (annualized), and five years (annualized). A total return assumes that all dividends have been reinvested at the share price on the day of payout. The annualized returns are the compounded annual rate of investment return expressed as a percentage. These amounts are also important to investors. They indicate how much the fund has gained or lost in a specific time period. (These figures are calculated before subtracting for sales fees.)

The *Wall Street Journal* has its own rating system. The Percentile Within Objective is a comparison of the fund to other like funds (aggressive funds to aggressive funds, growth funds to growth funds). The fund is ranked in two ways. The letter score shows the ranking of the fund. A score of "A" indicates that the fund is in the top 20 percent, B is the next 20 percent, C is the middle 20 percent, and D is the next 20 percent. A score of "E" indicates that the fund was in the bottom 20 percent of the objective in that time period. The fund illustrated in Table 7-3 has a year-to-date rank of D, indicating that, at this time, the fund is below the middle rating and in the bottom 40 percent of the objective.

Percentile scores are the actual ranking within the objective. Table 7-3 shows that the year-to-date performance of the fund has a score of 34, which indicates that the fund did better than 34 percent of the funds in its category in the same time period. This information means that 66 percent of the funds performed better than our example did.

The *Fund Information* section of Table 7-3 shows basic fund information. Investment objective data indicates how the fund is categorized by its investment objectives. (The *Wall Street Journal* uses 28 categories.) Click the Investment Objective link to see the definition of this category and a listing of the top winners and losers in this investment objective. Other fund information includes the fund manager's name and length of tenure, minimum initial investment amount, maximum sales and redemption charges, expense ratio (which is the percentage of average net assets devoted to expenses and distribution (12b-1 fees) as reported in the annual report), and total asset size of the fund.

Assessing mutual fund performance

No hard-and-fast rules exist about how to assess a mutual fund. However, the following list provides easy-to-use guidelines to assess the performance of your mutual fund investment candidates. After your assessment, each fund will require additional analysis. Only funds that meet all the following criteria should be selected for further research. They are likely to reduce your chances of losing money without lowering your mutual fund returns.

- ✔ **Tax liabilities and returns:** All mutual fund performance is shown on a pre-tax basis. This is reasonable because different investors are in different tax brackets. If you are investing through taxable accounts (which are different from nontaxable accounts that might include your IRA or other tax-exempt investments), you should only compare the after-tax returns of the funds you are analyzing. This comparison enables you to compare apples to apples instead of apples to oranges.

- ✔ **The impact of short-term performance:** Ignore short-term performance. Short-term returns are heavily influenced by fluctuations in the market and are valueless.

✔ **Inconsistent returns:** Avoid funds that have inconsistent returns when compared to unmanaged indexes. In other words, when you compare your fund to the appropriate benchmark, take into consideration the consistency of the two funds. If your fund is more volatile than the benchmark, it may have more risk than you expected. For a quick list of mutual fund benchmarks, see Lipper, Inc., with its affiliated companies (www.lipperweb.com), which currently tracks the performance of approximately 32,000 funds worldwide with assets in excess of $6 trillion U.S. dollars.

✔ **Fund ranking when compared to like funds:** The fund's performance is ranked within the top 20 percent to 50 percent or better of its type. Make certain that your analysis compares growth funds to growth funds and value funds to value funds.

✔ **Fund ranking when compared to unmanaged indexes:** The fund's performance and risk level is better than an unmanaged index for 1-, 3-, and 5-year time periods. Compare the fund's performance (before mutual fund costs). A broad-based U.S. stock fund should be compared to the S&P 500 (www.stockinfo.standardpoor.com) or the Wilshire 5000 Index. Small company funds should be compared to the Russell 2000 Index.

✔ **The fund's price/earnings (P/E) ratios are 15 to 25:** P/E ratios above 30 tend to be high-risk.

✔ **The fund's standard deviation:** The higher the standard deviation, the higher the risk. The fund's Morningstar standard deviation for 3 years is 17 or lower. If you are using the Value Line-calculated standard deviation (which is different), the standard deviation for 3 years is 12 or lower.

✔ **The fund's risk value:** Value Line rankings range from 1 (low risk) to 5 (high risk). If the Value Line risk rating is 1, it is in the top 10 percent of the safest funds. With the Morningstar rating system, a 5-star rating indicates that the fund is within the top 10 percent of the safest funds.

The evaluation criteria in the preceding list are a good starting point for your analysis. As you become a more sophisticated investor, you're likely to modify, delete, and add criteria. This customization ensures that your mutual fund selections meet your individual risk-tolerance level and financial objectives.

The Ratings War

Mutual fund companies don't show you the standard deviation or the betas (a measurement of the volatility of a security with the market in general) of their mutual funds. However, you don't have to make your investment decision without these bits of vital information. Many Web sites offer information on the ranking of mutual funds. Rankings are useful because they help you digest important performance and risk statistics into one measure. Here are a few examples of Web sites that offer information on the ranking of mutual funds:

- ✔ **Barron's** (www.barrons.com)
- ✔ **Business Week** (www.businessweek.com)
- ✔ **Forbes** (www.forbes.com)
- ✔ **S&P Mutual Fund Profiles and Stock Guides** (www.stockinfo.standard poor.com)
- ✔ **Wall Street Journal** (www.wsj.com)

Two of the more popular online rating services are Morningstar and Value Line. Morningstar (www.morningstar.com) is a free service. Value Line (www.valueline.com) is a fee-based service.

The Morningstar rating system

Morningstar is an independent, Chicago-based firm that has been evaluating mutual funds and annuities since 1984. The organization currently evaluates more than 7,500 mutual funds.

Morningstar uses historical data to develop its ratings. The unique feature of the rating system is that it penalizes mutual funds for excess risk that doesn't result in excess returns. Morningstar rates funds for consistently giving the highest returns and adjusts for risk as compared to funds in the same category.

Morningstar's five-star system is as follows:

- ✔ **Five Stars:** In the top 10 percent of performance; produces substantially above-average returns
- ✔ **Four Stars:** In the next 22.5 percent of performance; produces above-average returns
- ✔ **Three Stars:** In the middle 35 percent of performance; produces average returns
- ✔ **Two Stars:** In the lower 22.5 percent of performance; produces below-average returns
- ✔ **One Star:** In the bottom 10 percent of performance; produces substantially below-average returns

The Value Line rating system

Value Line uses a dual rating system that includes overall rank and measures various performance criteria, including risk. Funds are ranked from 1 to 5, with 1 having the highest rank (the best risk-adjusted performance) and the best risk ranking (the least risky).

Value Line uses historical data to develop its ratings. The five-number system is as follows:

- ✔ **1:** In the top 10 percent; highest overall performance and lowest risk

- ✔ **2:** In the next 20 percent; above-average performance and lower risk

- ✔ **3:** In the middle 40 percent; average performance and average risk

- ✔ **4:** In the lower 20 percent; below-average performance and higher risk

- ✔ **5:** In the lowest 10 percent; lowest average performance and highest risk

Value Line's Mutual Survey for Windows (www.ec-server.valueline.com) is a data/software service that includes extensive capabilities for viewing, sorting, screening, graphing, and preparing reports on more than 9,500 mutual funds. The service has a two-month trial subscription for $50 and an annual subscription for $345 with monthly updates. Users can also access weekly updates online by clicking Data Updates. The software is available on CD-ROM for Windows-based computers. The CD-ROM provides access to reports on mutual funds exactly as published in the Value Line Mutual Fund Survey.

When using mutual funds ratings, you must keep two things in mind. First, past performance does not predict future performance. Second, comparing the ranks of two different mutual fund categories is meaningless. For example, you can't compare the ranks of a municipal-bond fund against an aggressive-growth fund.

Using Scoreboards and Ratings

In this chapter, I present three different rating systems: the *Wall Street Journal,* Morningstar, and Value Line. The *Wall Street Journal* (www.wsj.com) ranks mutual funds from A to E, with A the top scorer. Morningstar (www.morningstar.com) rates mutual funds from five to one star, with five stars the top performers. And Value Line (www.valueline.com) categorizes mutual funds from 1 to 5, with 1 taking top billing.

In the best of times, the same fund can be ranked a five-star Morningstar winner and a number-one mutual fund by Value Line. Sometimes, a mutual fund's score can indicate a top performer by one mutual fund rating service and a loser by another mutual fund rating service. Why the difference?

Some mutual funds scores are *risk adjusted* and some are *absolute*. Risk-adjusted scores punish mutual funds for inconsistent returns and reward others for stability. For example, the risk-adjusted mutual funds rating can

✔ Penalize a fund for radically changing from its previous performance. Additionally, a fund can be penalized for *exceeding* its previous performance. In other words, the fund can receive a lower rating because of unexpected increases in returns. This rating penalty can be just as bad as the penalty for an unexpected decrease in returns.

✔ Reward mediocre fund performers. They can receive a higher rating because of their stability.

Conservative investors prefer to use risk-adjusted scores. Other investors prefer to use the absolute numbers. The best approach is to have a clear understanding of the differences in the ranking systems.

The analysis of mutual funds includes more research than selecting a fund by its rating. Remember that the more informed you are, the better your decision-making will be.

Buying Mutual Funds Online: No Broker Needed

You can purchase a mutual fund without a broker. All you have to do is contact the company directly. Table 7-4 lists a few online mutual fund companies. The table shows the name of the mutual fund company, its Internet address, the minimum investment required, the number of funds the mutual fund company has (as of this printing), and whether the company has an automatic investment plan (AIP). Usually, if you enroll for the automatic investment plan, you don't have to deposit the required initial minimum investment amount.

Table 7-4	Examples of Online Mutual Fund Sources			
Company	*Internet Address*	*Minimum Investment (Non-IRA Accts.)*	*No. of Funds*	*AIP?*
AIM Funds	www.aimfunds.com	$500	50+	Yes
Alliance Funds	www.alliance-capital.com	$250	118	Yes
Columbia Funds	www.columbia funds.com	$1,000	13	Yes

Company	Internet Address	Minimum Investment (Non-IRA Accts.)	No. of Funds	AIP?
Dreyfus Funds	www.dreyfus.com	$2,000	150+	Yes
Evergreen Funds	www.evergreen-funds.com	$1,000	70+	Yes
Fidelity Funds	www.fidelity.com	$2,500	253	Yes
INVESCO Funds	www.invesco.com	$1,000	48	Yes
Janus Funds	www.janus.com	$2,500	19	Yes
John Hancock Funds	www.jhancock.com	$1,000	71	Yes
Kemper Funds	www.kemper.com	$1,000	50+	Yes
Merrill Lynch Funds	www.plan.ml.com/products_services	Varies	100+	Yes
Nations Funds	www.bankofamerica.com/nationsfunds	1,000	44	Yes
Oppenheimer Funds	www.oppenheimerfunds.com	$1,000	65+	Yes
Paine Webber Funds	www.painewebber.com	$1,000	86	No
Prudential Funds	www.prudential.com	Varies	50+	Yes
Putnam Funds	www.putnaminv.com	$500	116+	Yes
Schwab Funds	www.schwab.com	$1,000	29	Yes
Scudder Funds	funds.scudder.com	$2,500	47	Yes
Smith Barney Funds	www.smithbarney.com	$1,000	60+	Yes
Stein Roe Funds	www.steinroe.com	$2,500	21	Yes
Strong Funds	www.strongfunds.com	Varies	30	Yes
Vanguard Group	www.vanguard.com	Varies	90	Yes

Buying Mutual Funds Online: Using an Online Broker

You have many choices in how you purchase mutual funds. In addition to purchasing directly from the mutual fund company, you can purchase mutual funds through registered representatives of banks, trust companies, stockbrokers, discount brokers, and financial planners. To purchase mutual funds via the Internet, go to an online broker's Web site. (I list a few examples later in this section.)

Register by completing the online application form. You have to provide information about your income, net worth, Social Security number, and the type of account you desire. Sometimes, you can open an account based on the quality (credit-worthiness) of your information.

The Internet is constantly changing, so check out the online brokerage's latest rates, new special mutual fund purchase programs, and brokerage statement download capabilities before sending in your application for a trading account.

To have a fully functioning account, brokerages are required to have your signature on file. After they have your signature on file, you can buy or sell as much as you want.

After you open your account, you can log on to the Internet, go to your brokerage Web site, and enter orders by completing the online form. You can access your account at any time, check your investments, and monitor your investments by using online news or quote services.

Here are a few examples of online brokers that sell load and no-load mutual funds:

- **Ameritrade** (www.ameritrade.com) is a New York-based firm that charges a flat rate of $18 per mutual fund trade. This firm trades stocks, funds, and options. An initial investment of $2,000 is required to open an account.

- **E*Trade** (www.etrade.com) is a Palo Alto, California-based firm that charges a flat rate of $24.95 per mutual fund trade. The minimum deposit to open an account is $1,000. E*Trade is available on America Online and CompuServe.

- **National Discount Brokers** (www.ndb.com) is a Chicago-based firm that requires an initial investment of $2,000 to open an account, and charges $20 per mutual fund trade.

The Right Time to Sell Your Mutual Funds

If your fund becomes one of the worst performers, consider selling. However, you need to look at more than just the fund's rating. Here are a few guidelines for determining when to sell a fund:

- You may want to sell if you have "overlapping" stocks in your portfolio. Let's say you own two growth mutual funds. You use Morningstar's portfolio X-ray feature (`portfolio.morningstar.com`) and discover that you own a double dose of stock in the same company. To keep diversified, you may want to sell.

- Look at the performance of comparable mutual funds. If a similar fund's overall performance is down 10 percent, your fund is down 16 percent, and your fund's performance consistently trails its peers, your fund may be a loser.

- If your fund has *drifted* from its original investment objectives, it's not meeting your asset allocation goals. You'll lose all the benefits of diversification if you have two mutual funds investing in the same asset class.

- Keep track of changes in your fund's management. If the fund hires a new money manager, that person may have a different investment strategy.

- You may want to sell if your mutual fund's expenses have been creeping up, you inherited the fund, or your broker sold you a fund with a high 12b-1 fee. High fund fees reduce your returns and make the fund less profitable than similar funds with lower expenses.

- In a volatile market, you may discover that you are a more conservative investor than you imagined. If you can't sleep at night, sell your fund.

- You are going to pay taxes on your capital gains. One of your mutual funds is posting negative returns. You may want to consider selling the losing fund to offset your tax liabilities.

- If the fund increases by three or four times its original size in a short time period, and its performance starts to decline, you may want to sell. As the fund keeps growing and growing, the professional money manager can't invest in the securities he or she knows and loves best, so the fund may start to acquire poor or average performing assets.

- Consider your needs. If you purchased the fund for a specific purpose and your life circumstances change, you should sell the fund and purchase one that meets your needs — even if the fund is doing well.

Figure 7-2 shows FundAlarm (`www.fundalarm.com`), a free, noncommercial Web site. FundAlarm provides objective information to help individual investors decide whether to sell a mutual fund. For details about how you can be automatically notified about when it's time to sell your mutual funds, see the Web site.

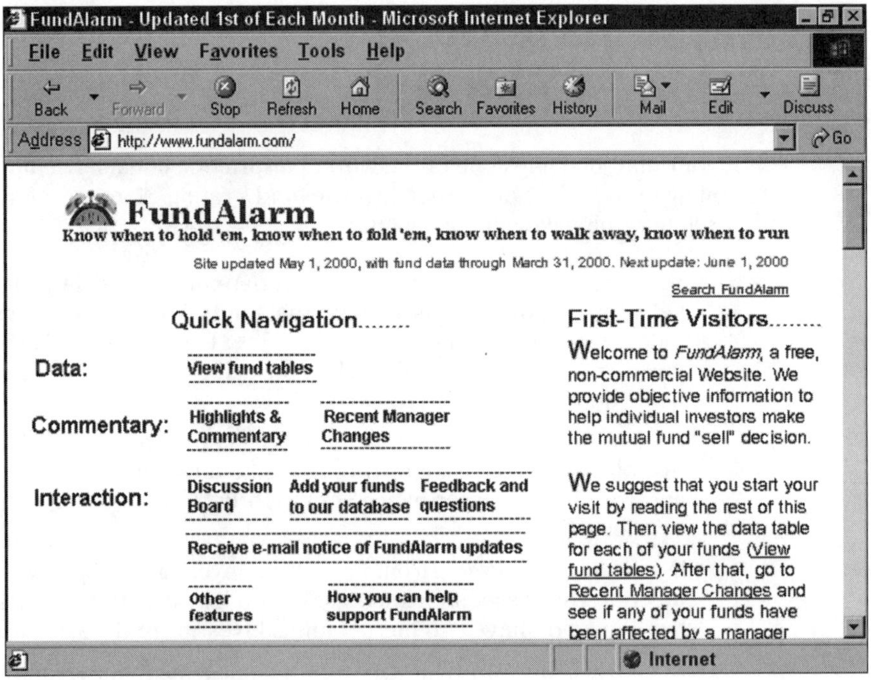

Figure 7-2:
FundAlarm automatically notifies you about changes in your mutual fund.

Funds that underperform in the short term can still be sound investments. For example, in 1999, Sequoia Fund ended up in the red, with a loss of 16.5 percent. For the last three years, however, its average annual return is a healthy 20.7 percent. Additionally, Sequoia Fund outperformed the S&P 500 Index in two of the last three years.

Chapter 8

The Basics of Stocks and Rates of Return

In This Chapter

▶ Getting your financial house in order to begin wealth-building

▶ Matching your investment objectives to the right investments

▶ Finding and reading online stock quotes

▶ Using models to value stocks

*T*he focus of this chapter is stock selection. The savvy online investor prospects all possible stock candidates, looking for companies that are exceptional in some way and positioned to perform well in the future.

In this chapter, I discuss using the Internet to decide which types of securities are right for you. I also show you how to keep current with online news services, read a stock table, and find the ticker symbols of securities online, so that you can make wise investment decisions.

Taking Stock of You

Most people spend the bulk of their income on no-frills necessities such as housing, food, transportation, and education. People who don't invest often believe that they can't afford to do so. Investing today usually means giving up some immediate pleasure, such as a European vacation, taking the family to see a play, or going to that great new restaurant. However, even a small amount of money invested each month can make a big impact on long-term financial security. For example, you can start a mutual fund automatic investment program with as little as $50 (see Chapter 5 for details).

Investing can help you stay ahead of inflation and assist you in accumulating real personal wealth with the power of compounding. Successful investing has several key factors, some of which must be in place before you invest your first dollar:

✔ **Know yourself.** How much risk to your savings can you tolerate and still sleep at night? How much experience, technical knowledge, and time do you have for making investment decisions?

✔ **Know your goals and the time you have to accomplish those goals.** Understand exactly what's needed to achieve your financial objectives.

✔ **Decide how you want to allocate your assets into the three main classes: stocks, bonds, and cash.** You decide how much you want to invest in each class based on how much risk you can tolerate, your required rate of return, and the investment time period.

✔ **Select specific investment candidates in the three asset classes.** Bear in mind the importance of compounding and the impact of taxes and fees on your returns.

✔ **Determine investment criteria for selecting the right investments.** How much risk can you take? How long can you invest your cash? What is your required rate of return? (For more help in determining your personal investment criteria, see Chapter 3.)

✔ **Keep current with changes in the economy and other factors that affect your investments.** Strive to make proactive rather than reactive investment decisions. You can keep current by using the online news services listed in this chapter and in this book's Investing Online Directory. I offer additional how-to information in Chapter 11.

✔ **Decide how you plan to define success for your investment selections.** Monitor your investments and keep good financial records.

You can find many asset allocation worksheets on the Internet. Check out the Accutrade Asset Allocation Worksheet (www.accutrade.com/fhtml/assetallocation.fhtml). This free, easy-to-use worksheet can immediately assist you in matching your risk-tolerance levels to your financial goals. Make certain you make time to answer several time-horizon and risk-aversion questions.

Understanding Stocks

When you buy shares of a company, you purchase part ownership in that company. As a shareholder, you also expect to receive *capital appreciation* on your investment — the difference between your purchase price and the market price of your shares. If the company prospers, your shares of stock increase in value. If company performance declines, the market value of your shares also decreases.

As a shareholder, you're entitled to periodic cash dividends. (The board of directors decides whether dividends are paid.) The amount of cash dividends paid per year can vary, but they're generally predictable.

Some successful firms like Berkshire Hathaway and Microsoft do not pay dividends. These companies usually plow dividend payout funds back into the company to finance expansion. This increases the value of the company and the price of shares stockholders own. In other words, if all goes as planned, the stockholders get capital appreciation instead of a dividend check. Some investors in high tax brackets prefer this approach. They don't have to pay taxes on capital appreciation until they sell the stock. With dividends, investors have to pay the taxes right away.

The *annual return* is the percentage difference of the stock price at the beginning of the year from the stock price at the end of the year plus any dividends paid. The price at which you can buy or sell a share of common stock can change radically. As a matter of fact, stock prices are so volatile that accurately predicting annual returns is impossible. (If we had this gift, we would all be rich!)

Common stock returns can vary — for example, from a depressing −43.34 percent in 1931 to a thrilling 53.99 percent in 1933. However, over 73 years, investments in the stock market have consistently outperformed any other type of investment. For example, the return on $1 invested in the S&P Index from the year-end of 1925 through 1998 is worth $2,350.89. A dollar invested for the same 73 years in Treasury bonds is worth $43.93.

For answers to questions like "What is stock?," "Why does a company issue stock?," "Why do investors pay good money for little pieces of paper called stock certificates?," "What do investors look for?," and "What about ratings and what about dividends?," see Investor FAQs (Frequently Asked Questions) at invest-faq.com/articles/stock-a-basics.html.

Types of Stock

Just like other investments, several types of stocks are available to try. Each stock type has characteristics, benefits, and drawbacks that you should be aware of before you invest. The following sections offer a quick summary to help you gain an understanding of these financial instruments.

Common stocks

When people think about investing, they tend to think primarily of common stocks. After all, it's difficult not to be bombarded daily with stock market news and commentary. Additionally, American history is filled with stories about how the Vanderbilts, Rockefellers, Carnegies, and other turn-of-the-century entrepreneurs made their fortunes on Wall Street with common stocks.

Both new and old companies sell common stock to raise capital to fund operations and expand their businesses. Common stocks represent shares of ownership in a corporation. Shareholders have a right to dividends and can vote on mergers, acquisitions, and other major issues affecting the corporation. Additionally, shareholders have a voice in the election of the board of directors. Dividends are paid at the discretion of the board of directors. The liabilities of being a shareholder are limited. Shareholders can't lose any more than the amount of their investments.

Preferred stocks

Preferred stocks are also equity stocks in a corporation. However, preferred stockholders cannot cast their votes on issues regarding company management. For this trade-off, the stockholder gets another benefit: a fixed dividend. Preferred stock is sold at par value (face value). The par value of preferred stocks is usually $25, $35, or $100. The company assigns a fixed dividend. Preferred stocks (sometimes called hybrids, because they include the features of both stocks and bonds) compete with bonds and other interest-bearing financial instruments, which means that the amount of the dividend is affected by the current interest rate at the time that the preferred stock is issued. Higher dividends tend to be issued when interest rates are high. Lower dividends are issued when interest rates are low. Preferred stockholders are paid their dividends regularly, and the stock has no maturity date.

Stock rights and warrants

Stock rights are derivative financial instruments that are similar to stock options. Stock rights allow current shareholders to purchase stock ahead of the public and directly from the company with no commissions or fees, and usually at a discount of 5 to 10 percent. The life of a stock right is generally only 30 days. During this time, the investors can exercise their rights, purchase shares at a discount, and sell them for a quick profit. If investors don't want to purchase the shares outright, they can sell the stock rights for a profit. After the expiration date, stock rights have no value, so stock right investors need to be quick.

Warrants are a way to gain control of a large amount of stock without having to purchase it outright. Warrants are options to purchase a pre-set amount of stock at a pre-set price, during a specified time period (5 years, 10 years, 20 years, or perpetually). At the time the warrant is issued, the price is fixed above the market price. Warrants have no voting rights or claims on corporate assets. When the warrant expires, it has no trading value. Warrants only have value if the stock is trading at a price that is above the amount stated on the warrant. Often, warrants are sold with bonds, as part of an initial public offering, or as part of a merger or acquisition.

DowJones.com World of Stocks (www.dowjones.com) can assist you in gaining an understanding of the different types of stocks you can purchase. After all, there are thousands of investment candidates available from around the world. To narrow the field, see DowJones.com's special section on Common versus Preferred stock.

Picking the Right Stock for the Right Goal

Selecting your own stocks can be hard work. The exciting thing is that the Internet has much of the information you need, and most of this information is free. With the power of your computer, you can utilize Internet data to gain real insight. As you start to determine which stocks you're interested in, you should be aware of the different types of stocks. Stocks have distinct characteristics, and as general economic conditions change, they behave in special ways.

Write a short list of your financial goals and then investigate how different types of stock relate to those objectives. Different stocks have different rates of return — some are better for young, aggressive investors; others are better for retirees or for people in high tax brackets. Here are a few examples of the different types of stocks:

- **Blue-chip stocks:** Usually the most prestigious stocks on Wall Street. They're high-quality stocks that have a long history of earnings and dividend payments. These stocks are often good long-term investments.

- **Cyclical stocks:** Stocks of companies whose fortunes rise when business conditions are good. When business conditions deteriorate, their earnings and stock prices decline. These companies are likely to be manufacturers of automobiles, steel, cement, and machine tools.

- **Seasonal stocks:** Similar to cyclical stocks, their fortunes change with the seasons. Good examples of seasonal companies are retail corporations whose sales and profits increase at Christmastime.

- **Defensive stocks:** Tend to be stable and relatively safe in declining markets. Defensive stocks are from companies that provide necessary services, such as electricity and gas, which everyone needs regardless of the economic climate. Companies in this category also provide essentials such as drugs and food, so their sales remain stable when the economy is depressed. (**Note:** Defensive stocks are *not* related to the military.)

- ✔ **Growth stocks:** Growth companies are positioned for future growth and capital appreciation. However, their market price can change rapidly. Rather than pay dividends, growth companies typically spend their profits on research and development to fuel future growth. These stocks are good for aggressive, long-term investors who are willing to bet on the future. If you're in a high tax bracket, these stocks may be for you; low dividends mean fewer taxes. But if expected earnings don't match analyst predictions, expect a big decline in stock price.

- ✔ **Income stocks:** Purchased for their regular, high dividends, income stocks usually pay bigger dividends than their peers do. Income stocks are attractive to retirees who may depend on their dividends for monthly expenses. Income stocks are often utilities companies and similar firms that pay higher dividends than comparable companies. These companies are often slow to expand because they spend most of their cash on dividend payouts. During times of declining interest rates, bonds are better investments.

- ✔ **International stocks:** Investors in these stocks often believe that U.S. domestic stocks are overpriced. These investors are seeking bargains overseas. However, international stocks include some risks that U.S. stocks don't have, such as trading in another currency, operating in a different economy, being subject to a different government, and using accounting standards that do not follow U.S. generally accepted accounting principles. Public information may have to be translated, which causes delays and sometimes miscommunication. All these elements add cost and risk to foreign stocks.

- ✔ **Speculative stocks and initial public offerings:** Speculative stocks are easy to identify because they have price/earnings (P/E) ratios that are frequently twice as high as other stocks. For example, the S&P 500 Index has a median P/E ratio of 30, and the NASDAQ Index has a median P/E ratio of 51. A second type of speculative stock is an initial public offering (IPO). This type of stock often has no track record. A good example of speculative stock is Netscape; its stock price is high, and revenues are small.

- ✔ **Value stocks:** Some Wall Street analysts consider these stocks to be bargains. These stocks have sound financial statements and earning increases, but are priced less than stocks of similar companies in the same industry.

Analyzing Stock Sectors

All good analysts evaluate their decisions by looking at several factors. One is selecting the type of stock that meets your financial goals. Two different types of stocks can be in the same stock sector. Using sector analysis, investors try to anticipate the economy to capitalize on market trends. One approach to this type of analysis is to analyze market sectors such as basic industries, consumer staples, consumer services, energy, financials, industrials, technology, transports, and utilities.

As you track these market sectors, you look at trends and analyze market peaks (high points) and troughs (low points). To take advantage of these market trends, investors sell at or just before the market sector's peak and buy just before the market's economic trough.

Here are a few examples of online sources for more information about analyzing in stock sectors.

- **Briefing.com** (`www.briefing.com/intro/i_ratings.htm`), shown in Figure 8-1, provides sector ratings. Each sector rating indicates whether the sector outperformed, slightly outperformed, was average, slightly underperformed, or underperformed. Additional information includes a descriptive narrative and date of the review. The free services page provides the most recent sector analysis. For all sectors, investors can consider the free trial of Briefing.com's full stock analysis service, which is $9.95 per month or $100 per year. The professional version is $25 per month, or $250 per year.

- **On the Money** (`www.onmoney.com`) has a terrific article about understanding stocks. At the home page, click Investing. Then, click the Investing Center icon to get to the section called Six Kinds of Stocks.

- **Smart Money** (`www.smartmoney.com`) provides breaking news that is divided by sectors. From the home page, click Tools ☞ Sector Tracker. Sector Tracker enables you to follow 120 industry groups in ten market categories and thus see which industry sectors are peaking. You can click any of the sectors to see the companies that make up that sector.

- **Stock Chart** (`www.stockchart.com`) has a wide variety of charts, including charts of market sectors that let you see the performance of important market relationships. Additionally, these charts can assist you in comparing the performance of related indexes. Stock Chart also includes tools, commentary, and educational resources.

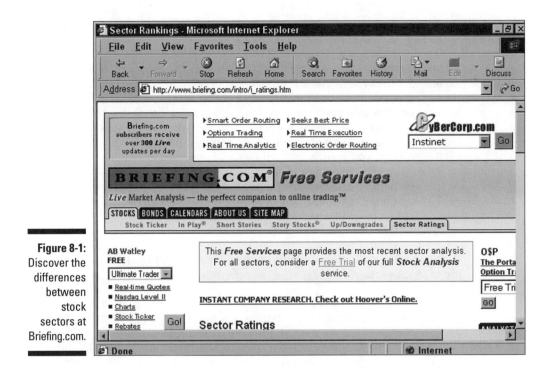

Figure 8-1:
Discover the
differences
between
stock
sectors at
Briefing.com.

How to Read a Stock Chart or Table

Most newspapers and many Internet sites, such as The Wall Street Journal Interactive Edition (www.wsj.com) and Barron's (www.barrons.com), have a listing of the day's stock activities. Table 8-1 shows the information you find in a typical listing from the Wall Street Journal Interactive Edition. (The values in the table are hypothetical.) The stock detailed is Compaq (CPQ). Compaq designs, develops, manufactures, and markets a wide range of computing products, including desktop and portable computers.

Table 8-1	Reading the Stock Pages at the Wall Street Journal Interactive Edition
Entry	*Value*
Date	November 16, 2000
Last	66 $\frac{7}{16}$
Change	+3 $\frac{1}{8}$
Volume	14,122,200

Entry	Value
Time	4:21 p.m. EST
Exchange	NYSE
Day Open	64⅞
Day High	67³⁄₁₆
Day Low	64⅛
Close	62⁹⁄₁₆
Change	+ ⁵⁄₁₆ (Previous day)
Volume	9,323,900 (Previous day)
52-Week High	79⁹⁄₁₆
52-Week Low	28¹³⁄₃₂

Here's how to interpret all this information about Compaq's stock:

- **Last: 66⁷⁄₁₆.** The dollar amount of the last price for the Compaq stock. (All stock prices are customarily shown in fractions instead of decimals.)

- **Change: +3⅞.** The change in the current price to the day's last price. This change compares the current price to the previous day's closing price. It is the amount of today's gain or loss.

- **Volume: 14,122,220.** The volume or number of shares traded that day.

- **Time: 4:21 p.m. EST.** The time of the price quote. Some Internet quote services provide real-time quotes; others may be delayed as much as 20 minutes.

- **Exchange: NYSE.** The exchange that the stock is traded on. Compaq is traded on the New York Stock Exchange (NYSE).

- **Day Open: 64⅞.** The price of the stock at the beginning of the day.

- **Day High: 67³⁄₁₆.** The highest stock price of the day.

- **Day Low: 64⅛.** The lowest stock price of the day.

- **Close: 62⁹⁄₁₆.** The closing price from the previous day.

- **Change: + ⁵⁄₁₆.** The change from the closing price of the previous day. This change compares yesterday's price at this time to yesterday's closing price.

- **Volume: 9,323,900.** The number of shares traded as of this time, on the previous day.

- **52-Week High: 79⁹⁄₁₆.** The highest stock price in the last year.

- **52-Week Low: 28¹³⁄₃₂.** The lowest stock price in the last year.

The Wall Street Journal Interactive Edition is continually updated. For more about how this financial newspaper is structured, see `interactive.wsj.com/edition/resources/documents/help.htm`. (This page is for subscribers, but you can see samples of the information this site offers.)

Finding Ticker Symbols and Stock Prices Online

A ticker symbol is the letter code representing the company's name in the listing for a publicly traded security. For example, if you want to find the current price for a share of Compaq's stock (as I do in the preceding section of this chapter), look for the company's ticker symbol — CPQ. Ticker symbols for companies traded on the NYSE have one to three letters; stocks traded on NASDAQ have four or five letters.

Many commercial organizations provide ticker symbols and quotes on the Internet. Figure 8-2 shows one such company, called PCQuote.com (`www.pcquote.com`). This excellent quote service has a link to a symbol lookup page and other features that make it a good place to start researching stock prices. You can type in the partial name of a company, and the PC Quote program automatically finds the ticker symbol.

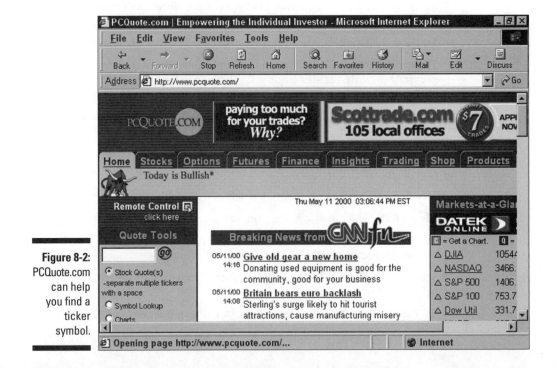

Figure 8-2: PCQuote.com can help you find a ticker symbol.

PCQuote.com offers five levels of service that range from $75 per month to $300 per month — or $750 per year to $3,000 per year — for real-time quotes, charts, and information. Free services include ticker symbol lookup, current stock prices and fundamental data, Market Guide company snapshot, Zacks Investment Research broker recommendations, annual earnings and earning estimates, current company news, charts of the company's stock price history and volume, and market indexes. You can search for stocks, bonds, futures, options, mutual funds, and indexes. You can also maintain as many as five portfolios of 20 ticker symbols each.

If the PC Quote program can't find the company's ticker symbol based on the partial name you enter, it suggests several candidates, including the ticker symbol, company name, and stock exchange. You can scroll through the companies until you find the one you want. Click the company's name, and the program fetches the latest stock prices. (The free service is delayed 20 minutes. Quotes are real-time for subscribers.)

PC Quote can look up five ticker symbols at a time; just leave a space between each company's name or ticker symbol as you enter them. Many other quote services can accommodate only one ticker symbol or company name at a time.

PCQuote.com provides links to charts, news, earnings information, fundamental analysis data, and Securities and Exchange Commission (SEC) filings that detail the company's financial position. Stock price data includes the amount of the last sale, time of the last sale, net change, percent change, highest sale of the day, name of the exchange, previous closing price, opening price, and volume. PCQuote.com also shows the following information:

- **52-week high:** The highest stock price in the last year.

- **52-week low:** The lowest stock price in the last year.

- **Annual dividend:** The total of cash payments made to stockholders by the corporation.

- **Dividend yield:** The current annualized dividend paid on a share of common stock, expressed as a percentage of the current market price of the company's common stock.

- **Earnings per share (EPS):** The company's earnings for the last 12 months divided by the number of common shares outstanding.

- **Beta:** The relationship between the investment's returns and the market's average returns, expressed as a number with one decimal place.

- **Price/earnings ratio:** The price the market places on the firm's earnings. For example, if a firm has an earnings per share of $2 and a stock price of $50, its price/earnings ratio is 25 ($50 ÷ $2).

- **Amount of shares outstanding:** The total number of shares the firm has issued to common stockholders.

Free real-time stock quotes

In the past, the average investor had to wait for newspapers to discover stock prices. Today, real-time and 20-minute-delayed stock quotes are available on the Internet. In fact, during the last few years, the number of Web sites offering free real-time and delayed stock quotes has proliferated. Here are a few examples of online quote servers:

- ✔ **FreeRealTime.com** (www.freerealtime.com) requires registration for your free access to real-time stock quotes, financial news, and corporate profiles. There is no limit on the number of quotes you can get per day.

- ✔ **InfoSpace** (www.infospace.com/info/rtq/index.htm?) offers free real-time stock quotes. To use the service, you must register online. Each user is allowed 50 free quotes per day.

- ✔ **Thomson Real Time Quotes** (www.thomsoninvest.net.) offers investors up to 50 free real-time stock quotes with your free registration. At the home page, click Real-Time Quotes for registration information.

Free wireless stock quotes

With wireless Internet connections, you can have stock quotes delivered to wireless devices such as alphanumeric pagers, digital telephones, and PDAs (Personal Data Assistants). Here are two services that support wireless connections:

- ✔ **MSN Mobile** (mobile.msn.com) has a free service that provides alerts on stock quotes based on dozens of preset options from MSN Money Central.

- ✔ **Yahoo! Mobile** (mobile.yahoo.com) provides stock alerts via your mobile device. The service is free for registered Yahoo! members.

Check this book's companion CD-ROM for stock tickers you can easily add to your desktop PC. This way, you can easily check your investments or see how that new stock is performing.

Fee-based stock quotes

If you are a frequent or active investor, you probably want to track the stocks you are trading in real-time. In the past, individual investors did not have access to this type of information at any cost. Today, you can access real-time quotes from your wireless handheld device or at your home or office computer. Here are a few examples of what's available on the Internet:

- ✔ **Briefing.com** (www.briefing.com) has two levels of premium service. The first level, called Stock Analysis, is $6.95 per month (with a free trial) and includes stocks on the move, technical stock analysis, earnings calendar, splits calendar, stock ratings, upgrade/downgrade reports, and company reports. The highest level of service, called Professional, is $25 per month (with a free trial) and includes many advanced investor services. Briefing.com also provides a free introductory service that includes market comments, quotes, charts, portfolio tracking, sector ratings, and an economic calendar.

- ✔ **Data Broadcasting Corporation** (www.dbc.com), shown in Figure 8-3, retrieves as many as seven ticker symbols at one time. Quotes include last price, change, currency, percent change, opening price, day low, day high, previous day's closing price, and volume. The ticker symbol lookup requires you to click where the stock is traded (for example, North America) and then click the first letter in the company's name. Next, you have to scroll through a list of all stocks beginning with that letter. DBC offers real-time quotes in three different packages. Access to wireless real-time quotes is $49 per month. Signal Online offers a real-time quotes service for active trading in stocks, futures, and options for $150 per month. StockEdge Online provides real-time continuous equity quotes, via the Internet, for $79 per month.

- ✔ **Interquote** (www.interquote.com) offers real-time, continuously updated quotes for $69.95 per month or $629.55 per year. The InterQuote software comes with an easy-to-use spreadsheet format, time and sales, and charting with analytics and options tables. There is a one-time start-up fee of $75. For delayed quotes, the price is $240 per year with a one-time set-up fee of $25. For a limited package of real-time quotes, the cost is $450 per year with a one-time set-up charge of $50. Each package has a free seven-day trial.

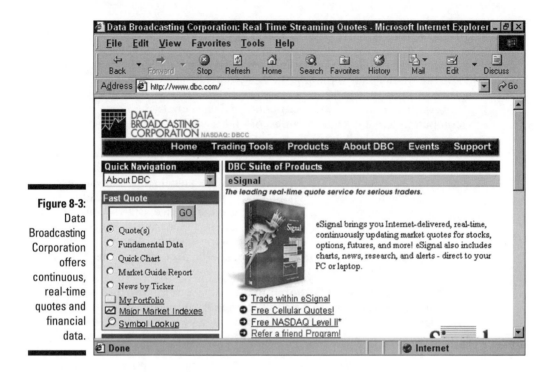

Figure 8-3:
Data
Broadcasting
Corporation
offers
continuous,
real-time
quotes and
financial
data.

What Does the S&P 500 Have to Do with Anything?

You can measure how good or bad an investment is by comparing it to a market index. For example, the Standard & Poor's (S&P) 500 tracks a broad group of large capitalization stocks that are traded on the New York Stock Exchange and NASDAQ/AMEX. (I define the term *large capitalization stocks,* or *large cap stocks,* later in this section.) You can see the S&P Web site at www.stockinfo.standardpoor.com.

Each stock in the S&P 500 Index is weighted by the relative market value of its outstanding shares. Overall, the index represents the performance obtained in the stock market for large capitalization stocks. This index provides performance information so that you can compare the stocks in your portfolio to the market. If your returns are better than the market, you're doing well. If your returns are lower than the market, you need to re-evaluate your stock selections.

When you compare the performance of your stock to a market index, you can determine whether the stock outperformed the market, maintained the market rate, or underperformed. As Table 8-2 shows, however, not all market indexes are alike. The Dow Jones Industrial Average is the most well-known index, but it includes only 30 large, mature, consumer-oriented companies. The Wilshire 5000 is the most comprehensive index of common stock prices regularly published in the United States, and may be the best indicator of overall market performance. As you can see in Table 8-2, the S&P 500 tracks the performance of large capitalization stocks. In other words, the S&P 500 isn't the appropriate index for evaluating the performance of your small capitalization stock.

Table 8-2	Comparing Apples to Apples with the Right Index
Index	*Type of Security*
Dow Jones Industrial Average	Large capitalization stocks
Financial Times World	World stocks
Lehman Bros. Corporate Bonds	Corporate bonds
Lehman Bros. Government Bonds	U.S. Treasury bonds
Morgan Stanley EAFE	International stocks
Russell 2000	Small capitalization stocks
S&P 500	Large capitalization stocks
Wilshire 5000	Entire market

Source: Jim Jubak, The Worth Guide to Electronic Investing (1996, Harper Business, New York, NY).

Table 8-3 helps to explain why the S&P 500 may not be the appropriate index to compare to your small capitalization stock. *Capitalization* (or *cap*) is the total number of shares outstanding multiplied by the current stock price of those shares. For example, a firm with 1 million common shares outstanding at $55 per share has capitalization of $55 million, which makes the company a small cap firm. Table 8-3 shows a quick estimate of how the capitalization of different companies sorts out.

Table 8-3	Defining the Capitalization of Companies
Category	*Capitalization*
Micro cap	Less than $50 million
Small cap	$50 million to $500 million
Mid cap	$500 million to $5 billion
Large cap	More than $5 billion

According to Standard & Poor's, small capitalization stocks have outper-formed large capitalization stocks over time. Over certain short-term periods, however, this may not hold true. From 1983 to 1990, small capitalization stocks, as a group, underperformed larger capitalization firms. From 1991 to 1993, both small and mid capitalization firms have outperformed large capitalization companies. During times of market volatility, small capitalization stocks tend to fall faster and harder than their bigger siblings. For example, between June 12 and August 23, 1996, NASDAQ was down 7.48 percent. During the same time period, the MicroCap 50 was down 24.52 percent.

Financenter (`www.financenter.com`) can answer many of your investing questions by automatically calculating your investment gains or losses. Go to the home page and click Investing ☞ Calculate Answers. You'll discover a page of hyperlinks that are divided into categories such as Investing. In the Investing section, check the questions for Stock Calculators. Financenter provides free online calculators to answer such questions as:

✔ What is my return if I sell now?

✔ Should I sell before or after one year?

✔ What selling price provides my desired return?

Valuing Stocks

Stocks are more difficult to value than bonds. Bonds have a limited life and a stated payment rate. Common stocks don't have a limited life or an upper dollar limit on cash payments. This uncertainty makes stocks harder to value than bonds. Many ways exist to value common stock. Overall, the value of a stock is the present value of all its future dividends. However, common stock-holders aren't promised a certain dividend each year. The dividend is based on the profitability of the company and the board of directors' decision to pay dividends to stockholders.

The second source of return for a stock is the increased market price of the stock. If the company decides not to pay dividends, and reinvests profits in the firm, the company's future profits and dividends should grow. This additional value should be reflected in a stock price increase in the future.

Fundamental analysis seeks to determine the intrinsic value of securities based on underlying economic factors. It is the most widely accepted method for determining a stock's true value, which you can then compare to current prices to estimate current levels of mispricing. Fundamental analysts usually forecast future sales growth, expenses, and earnings.

Quick valuations with online fundamental analysis

Tradtrek.com (www.tradetrek.com/fund-analysis) offers fundamental analysis of your stock selection. Results indicate a six-month price target for the stock you are investigating. At the home page, click Top Feature ☞ Fundamental Analysis. Then, enter the ticker symbol of the stock you want to analyze and click Go to retrieve the default parameters.

Review the default parameters to make any changes you think are necessary. Click Recalculate to generate results. (Don't be surprised if stocks with sky-rocketing P/E ratios are rated as overpriced. You may have to use another investment model to determine the right fair value.)

Using the Net to calculate fair value

If you are averse to math, the Value Point Analysis Financial Forum at www.eduvest.com can help. The Value Point Analysis Financial Forum, shown in Figure 8-4, includes a community of investors who share information about their stock picks and their analyses using the Web site's valuation model. To use the model, at the home page click Value Point Analysis Model. Just enter the factors used by the model. For additional insight, you can post your results and get feedback from others. All this at a price you can't beat — it's free.

Figure 8-4: Value Point Analysis calculates the fair value of a stock so that you don't have to do the math.

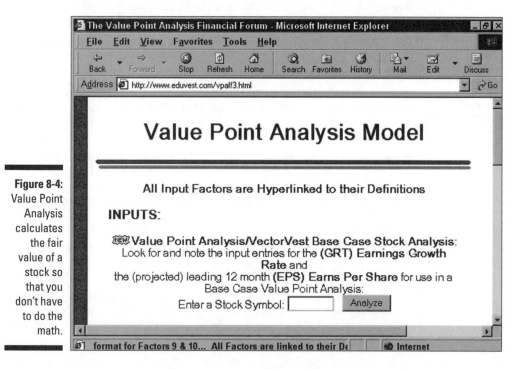

To determine the intrinsic value (and what some people feel is the real value) of a stock, the Value Point Analysis Model uses 12 factors. (I define and discuss these factors in Chapter 9.) Overall, the Value Point Analysis Model, which was designed in 1979, is used to evaluate a stock's worth in terms of its fundamental economic underpinnings and the general money market. The model uses the following factors:

1. **Corporate name, ticker symbol, and exchange of a stock.** This information is used to identify the specific stock you are analyzing.

2. **Number of the corporation's shares outstanding (in millions).** This number represents how many other common shareholders will be paid dividends.

3. **Long-term debt (in millions).** Long-term debt is the amount of any loans or outstanding bonds that mature in five years or more. Debts with terms of one to four years are considered short- or mid-term liabilities.

4. **Current dividend payout ($ per share).** This number is the annualized amount of this year's dividend. For example, imagine that we are in the middle of the second quarter. The first quarter dividend is $0.25. The company pays dividends each quarter. The annualized current dividend is $1.00. (In other words, 4 x $0.25 = $1.00).

5. **Book value or net worth ($ per share).** Many company reports have calculated this number for you. This value is often listed at the bottom of the balance sheet. The formula to calculate net worth is total assets less total liabilities. For example, total assets of $100 million less total liabilities of $75 million equals a net worth of $25 million. Net worth divided by the number of outstanding shares equals the book value per share.

6. **Projected earnings ($ per share).** Many company reports include expert forecasts of expected earnings. For example, if earnings for one year are $1.00, and next year the earnings are $1.10, the growth rate is 10 percent.

You can use experts' earnings forecasts or the amount you believe is correct for your analyses. Remember that each quarter you may see "earnings surprises," and individual investors have often outsmarted the so-called experts.

7. **Projected average growth in earnings (percent).** Without revenue (sales), you have no profits (earnings), and corporate earnings are what make stocks valuable. At the beginning of each company's annual report is a letter from the CEO. In this letter, the CEO usually states what he or she expects sales to be for the next year. You may or may not agree with this statement. Enter the percentage amount that, in your judgment and based on your research, is correct.

8. **Current earnings ($ per share).** Current earnings are often called Earnings Per Share, and are calculated for you at the bottom of the income statement. In case you have to do your own math, take the net after-tax income and divide it by the number of outstanding shares of common stock. For example, $1.5 million net after-tax income divided by 1 million shares is $1.50 per share.

9. **Current sales price ($ per share).** Check with an online quote server for the current sales price of a share of stock.

10. **Number of years the earning growth rate is expected to be sustained (1, 1.5, 2.0 years, and so on).** Some companies have variable growth rates, and others have a steady increase that can go on for ten years or more. You need to decide whether the company will sustain its growth rate and for how long. This decision is a judgment call that investors have to make.

11. **Current yield of AAA Bonds (percent).** Luckily, the Value Point Model fills this number in for you.

12. **Projected change of AAA Bonds (percent, 100 basis points = 1%).** The Value Point Analysis Model enters a default amount here. If you agree with the amount, don't change it.

Valuation model input and results

No investor wants to pay more for a stock than it is worth. The following mini-table illustrates the input data and results for an online stock valuation using the Value Point Analysis Model, which can help you determine a stock's fair value. An example of user input and results looks like this:

Description	*Model Input*
1. Stock Name, Ticker Symbol, and Exchange	Example Corporation, EXCC, NYSE
2. The number of shares in millions, greater than 0	1,010.00
3. The long term debt in millions of dollars	28,200.00
4. Current dividend in $/sh (xx.xx), annual	8.00
5. Book value or net worth in dollars/sh	20.12
6. Projected earnings in $/sh, annual	8.80
7. Projected average growth in earnings (%)	5.00
8. Projected average growth in sales (%)	5.00
9. Current yield of AAA bonds, greater than 0	6.55
10. Projected change of AAA bonds(%)	0.00
11. Current earnings in $/sh, annual amount	8.17
12. Current price in $/sh, greater than 0	138.00
13. Number of years the earnings growth rate is expected to be sustained (for example, 1, 1.5, 2, and so on)	1.00

Description	*Stock Evaluation Results*
NAME SYM EXCH	Example name, Example symbol, NYSE
VALUE POINT ($/sh)	133.55
PROJECTED EARNINGS ($/sh)	8.80
PROJECTED P/E	15.18
VALUE POINT /CURRENT PRICE	0.97
CURRENT P/E	16.89
CURRENT YIELD (%)	5.80
CURRENT PRICE. ($/sh)	138.00
RELATIVE RISK FACTOR	0.90

This table indicates that the Value Point-determined fair value for the stock is $133.55. The model forecasts earnings of $8.80 and a projected P/E ratio of 15.18. The Value Point price is 0.97 of the stock's current price. The stock's current P/E ratio is 16.89. The current yield is 5.80 percent, and the current price is $138. The model assigns a relative risk factor of 0.90 to its estimate of the stock's fair value.

In summary, this chart indicates that the stock's intrinsic value is $133.55. The stock is currently selling for $138.00. This amount is greater than $133.55, which indicates that the stock is overpriced. If I were you, I wouldn't even think about buying this expensive stock. However, if you already own the stock, it might be a good time to sell.

You can visit the following Web sites for more about fundamental analysis and valuing stocks:

- **Dow Jones University** (www.dju.com) offers an online course about the fundamental analysis of common stocks. The advanced course focuses on the math used to assess a stock's worth to quantitatively assess the fair market value of a stock. The course includes examples and exercises. At the home page, click Course Catalog ☞ Fundamental Analysis of Common Stocks. On the resulting page, you can test yourself using the Fundamental Analysis of Common Stocks Quiz. You can also view sample lesson pages and review the course summary ($49 per course).

- **J & E Research, Inc.** (www.jeresearch.com) is a group of PhDs and MBAs who specialize in financial modeling, research, and analysis. Try their Stock Analysis program. It uses an Excel spreadsheet that can assist you in completing the fundamental analysis of any stock.

- **Simtel** (ftp.urz.uni-heidelberg.de/ftp/pub/simtel_win95/finance/) offers many downloadable financial management programs that can help value stocks and other securities.

Chapter 9

Internet Stock Screening

●●●

In This Chapter

▶ Getting familiar with online stock screens

▶ Building your first stock screen

▶ Locating online and PC-based stock screens

▶ Using prebuilt stock screens

▶ Getting online stock recommendations from the experts

●●●

S tock screening boils down to finding the answer to one fundamental question: Which stock (among all stocks) should I buy right now? Of course, finding the answer to this question requires asking many more specific questions about stocks — questions that are difficult to answer without the help of computerized databases.

This chapter shows how you can use the Internet and PC-based stock screening tools to whittle down the universe of stocks to a manageable few candidates. You can then analyze your short list of stocks for gems that may bring you above-average returns. This chapter also tells you where to find daily or weekly results of prebuilt stock screens.

Finding the Best Stock Electronically

Screening is a process that permits investors to discover and distill information within a larger set of information. The Internet provides many screening tools that help you prospect stock issues. The goal of stock screens is to point out which stocks are worth your research and analysis time.

Some people believe that using a stock screen is like panning for gold. You use your computer to screen ("pan") for investment "nuggets" from a long list of possibilities. The online investor sets the objectives of any single screen. Different people get different results because no two people have exactly the same selection criteria or investment philosophy.

Overall, the benefit of stock screens is that they let you generate your own ideas — ideas that generate profits based on your investor savvy. Stock-screening programs enable you to go beyond finding good stock investments and assist you in finding the very best stocks.

To identify investment candidates, the stock screen uses your preset criteria, such as *growth* (stocks that are expanding faster than the market or their peers), *value* (stocks that have strong financial statements but are selling at prices below their peers), or *income* (stocks that provide higher than average dividends).

Depending upon the criteria you select, you may have to run several iterations of the stock screen. For example, your first screen may result in several hundred possibilities. Because you can't investigate and analyze so many candidates, you have to run a second screen of these results. This fine-tuning should lead to a manageable list of investment candidates that you can research and analyze — perhaps between 10 and 20 candidates. It is likely that you can quickly pare this number down by using common sense and your investor savvy.

Choosing the criteria for your first stock screen

Typically, you build a stock screen by accessing an online stock-screening tool and filling out an online form. I offer examples of the variables used in these forms later in this chapter, in the section "Important ratios for screening stocks." The first stock screen that you develop may include quantifiable variables that you believe are the most important — for example:

- **Earnings growth:** The percentage of change between current earnings and earnings for the last quarter or last year.

- **Recent earnings surprises:** The difference between predicted and actual earnings.

- **Price/earnings (P/E) ratio:** The current price of the stock divided by the earnings per share — that is, net income divided by the total number of common shares outstanding. For example, value stocks have P/E ratios below 10 or 12, and growth stocks have P/Es above 20.

- **Dividends:** The annual cash dividend paid by the company.

- **Market capitalization:** The number of outstanding shares multiplied by the current stock price of those shares. Market capitalization is sometimes abbreviated to *cap*. This value is a measurement of the company's size. Firms with high market capitalization are called "large cap" and companies with a low market capitalization are called "small cap."

Fine-tuning your stock screen

After you select your initial screening criteria, you click Submit, Sort, or a similar command. A list of stock candidates appears. Often, this list includes several hundred stocks. This number is still too large to research, so you should narrow this list by selecting more variables.

You may have some special knowledge about the industry you work in. You may have used certain products over the years and can use your knowledge to your advantage. However, keep in mind that a good product doesn't necessarily mean a good company. You may want to filter out companies that you just don't understand. You may also want to filter out companies about which you lack information. Without at least some basic information, you can't perform a complete analysis.

Using your stock screen results

After you complete your second stock screen and sort the data, you should have a list of about 10 to 20 companies. Start a file for each firm and begin to gather data for your analysis. At this point, you may discover that some companies aren't worth additional research — a finding that further reduces your short list. For example, the company may have filed for bankruptcy, or it may be targeted for Federal investigation. Maybe the company recently paid a large fine for shady dealings, or the executive management was recently indicted for fraud, misconduct, or some other crime.

Check out the stock screen at Daily Stocks (www.dailystocks.net). After you reach the Daily Stocks home page, click either Advance Stock Screen or Basic Stock Screen. The basic stock screens are prebuilt. With the advanced stock screens, you enter the industry and criteria that you feel are important. You can then query the database for fundamental and historical stock information by using your own investment criteria.

Important ratios for screening stocks

Every industry has its own language, and the financial industry is no exception. In the following sections, I define the key terms that the finance industry uses for stock-screening variables.

Figure 9-1 shows Hoover's StockScreener. Using the StockScreener, you can choose the original stock screen, which uses up to 22 variables and sorts the results alphabetically. You can also use any of Hoover's three prebuilt stock screens to analyze growth, value, and high-yield stocks. To access Hoover's StockScreener, go to the home page(www.hoovers.com) and click Money ☞

Stock ☞ Screener. Hoover's StockScreener lets you sift and sort information to generate customized results that are as broad or narrow as you need. Each stock screen's results are hyperlinked to a Hoover's *company capsule* (a snapshot of the company), as well as the company's home page, stock quotes and charts, SEC filings, and investment news.

Beta

Beta is the measurement of market risk. The beta is the relationship between investment returns and market returns. Risk-free Treasury securities have a beta of 0.0. If the beta is negative, the company is inversely correlated to the market — that is, if the market goes up, the company's stock tends to go down. If a stock's volatility is equal to the market, the beta is 1.0. In this case, if the stock market increases 10 percent, the stock price increases 10 percent. Betas greater than 1.0 indicate that the company is more volatile than the market. For example, if the stock is 50 percent more volatile than the market, the beta is 1.5.

Book value

Book value is the original cost, less depreciation of the company's assets and outstanding liabilities. (*Depreciation* is the means by which an asset's value is expensed over its useful life for Federal income tax purposes.)

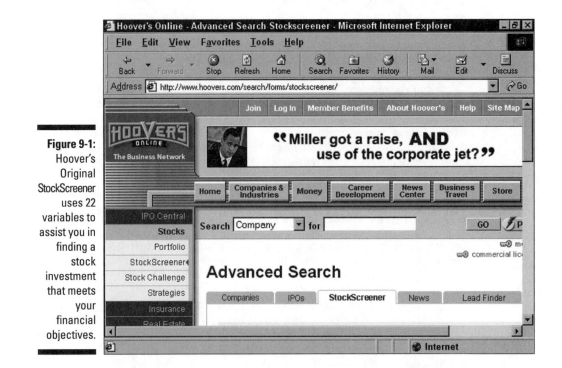

Figure 9-1: Hoover's Original StockScreener uses 22 variables to assist you in finding a stock investment that meets your financial objectives.

Cash flow to share price

The ratio of *cash flow to share price* is the company's net income plus depreciation (expenses not paid in cash) divided by the number of shares outstanding. For companies that are building their infrastructure (such as cable companies or new cellular companies) and, therefore, don't yet have earnings, this ratio may be a better measure of their value than earnings per share (EPS).

Current ratio

Current ratio is current assets divided by current liabilities. A current ratio of 1.00 or greater means that the company can pay all current obligations without using future earnings.

Debt to equity ratio

To determine the *debt to equity ratio,* divide the company's total amount of long-term debt by the total amount of equity. (*Equity* is defined as the residual claim by stockholders of company assets, after creditors and preferred stockholders have been paid.) This ratio measures the percentage of debt the company is carrying. Many firms average a debt level of 50 percent. Debt to equity ratios greater than 50 percent may indicate trouble. That is, if sales decline, the firm may not be able to pay the interest payments due on its debt.

Dividends

Dividends are paid quarterly out of retained earnings. However, some high-growth companies reinvest earnings and don't pay dividends.

Dividend yield

Dividend yield is the amount of the dividend divided by the most current stock price. You can use dividends as a valuation indicator by comparing them to the company's own historical dividend yield. If a stock is selling at a historically low yield, it may be overvalued. Companies that don't pay a dividend have a dividend yield of zero.

Earnings per share (EPS)

Earnings are one of the stock's more important features. After all, the price you pay for a stock is based on the future earnings of the company. The consistency and growth of a company's past earnings indicate the likelihood of stock price appreciation and future dividends. An *earnings per share* is often referred to as EPS.

Market capitalization

Market capitalization is the total value of the firm. It is calculated by multiplying the number of outstanding shares times the current stock price of those shares. Market capitalization is sometimes called *market value.*

P/E ratio

You calculate the *price/earnings ratio* by dividing the price of the stock by the current earnings per share. A low P/E ratio indicates that the company may be undervalued. A high P/E ratio indicates that the company may be overvalued.

Price-to-book value ratio

Price-to-book value ratio is tangible assets less liabilities, and the price-to-book value is the current price of the stock divided by the book value. If the company has old assets, this ratio may be high. If the company is a new start-up with fixed assets that have not been depreciated, this ratio could be very low. Therefore, you need to compare this ratio to industry standards and other information about the company.

Return on equity (ROE)

Return on equity (ROE) is usually equity earnings as a proportion of net worth. You divide the most recent year's net income by shareholders' equity (*shareholders' equity* is assets minus liabilities) to calculate ROE.

Shares outstanding

The term *shares outstanding* refers to the total number of shares for a company's stock. To determine the firm's outstanding shares, you need the most recent data. The shares outstanding can be calculated by taking issued shares on the balance sheet and subtracting treasury stock. *Treasury stock* is stock issued but not outstanding by virtue of being held (after it is repurchased) by the firm.

Watching Out for Investment Risks

No one invests in securities to lose money. However, each security has its own fine print. The Securities and Exchange Commission (www.sec.gov) has put together a list of some things to watch for:

- ✓ The higher the return, the greater the risk. You may lose some or all of your investment.

- ✓ Some investments can't be easily sold or converted to cash. For example, you may have a hard time selling a municipal bond before it matures.

✔ If you want to sell an investment quickly, you may have to pay some penalties or transaction charges.

✔ Investments in new companies or companies that don't have a long history may involve greater risk.

✔ Securities, like mutual funds, are not Federal Deposit Insurance Corporation (FDIC)-insured.

✔ The securities you own may change due to corporate reorganizations, mergers, or third-party actions. You may be asked to sell your current shares, or you may be offered new shares due to this activity. Make certain that you understand the complexities of this investment decision before you act.

✔ Past performance of a security is no guarantee of future performance.

Using Online Stock Screens

Web-based stock screens can require between 2 and 80 variables. Their computerized stock databases can include anywhere from 1,000 stocks to more than 13,000 stocks. Additionally, some computerized stock databases are updated daily, weekly, or monthly. The best stock screen is the one that includes your personal investment criteria. Here are a few examples:

✔ **Financial Web** (www.financialweb.com) has Super Screener, an online stock-screening tool. Select from the criteria listed and then click Go at the bottom of the page. You may find the industry comparisons of interest. All criteria are optional.

✔ **Market Guide's NetScreen** (www.marketguide.com) is a powerful online stock-screening tool that is designed to meet the needs of the experienced investor. Using 20 variables, you can screen more than 13,000 publicly traded companies. The stock screen makes use of 80 variables so you can create customized screens for your different financial objectives.

✔ **NASDAQ-Amex Stock Screening** (www.amex.com/sitemap/tour_screening.stm) offers an interactive stock screening tour with instructions on how to use the NASDAQ-Amex Stock Screening tool. In one search, you can find as many as 100 NASDAQ, Amex, and NYSE stocks that meet your criteria. Check out the sample screening criteria to improve your results.

✔ **Stock Selector** (`www.stockselector.com`) has basic and advanced stock screens. With the basic stock screen, just click the criterion that meets your objective. With the advanced stock screen, enter a value for each item you want to search. You can also indicate that you want to find investment candidates above or below the industry average. For criteria you do not want to include, leave the items blank.

✔ **Wall Street Research Net** (`www.wsrn.com`) includes the stock screen shown in Figure 9-2. This stock screen is designed for beginning and advanced investors who want an easy-to-use, quick search tool that focuses on price and yield, growth, and size. At the home page, click Screening. Enter the required information for the QuickSearch and click Submit Query.

✔ **Zacks** (`www.zacks.com`) provides several types of stock screening tools. At the home page, click Screening. You'll find an overview of the screening tools, a custom screening tool, and predefined screens. If you need assistance, just click Screening Help.

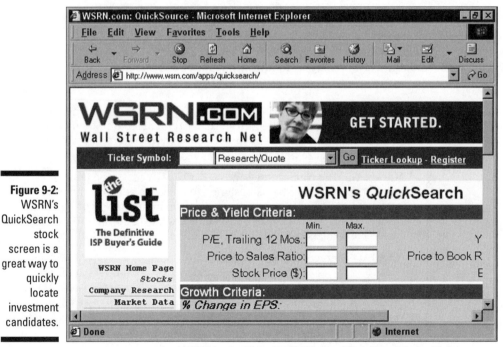

Figure 9-2:
WSRN's
QuickSearch
stock
screen is a
great way to
quickly
locate
investment
candidates.

Using Stock Screening Software

PC-based stock screens use their own stock screening software and databases. The advantage of these programs over Web-based stock screens is that they use hundreds of variables to screen stocks. I describe a few examples in this section.

STB Prospector II (www.better-investing.org/computer/stbpro.html) examines all the companies and helps beginning and experienced investors find the best stocks in any category they choose. The program displays each company easily and quickly, and graphs up to 20 different financial items to help visualize historical information. Prospector II is a Windows-based, menu-driven program with a Screening Wizard to search for investor preferences (Growth, Quality, Safety, and so on). The program also provides fully customizable criteria setup and reports.

Prospector II offers unique company ranking reports and graphs, at a cost of $95 for NAIC members and $84 for Computer Group (CG) members. The STB Prospector requires the NAIC S&P data files, which are sold separately. This service automatically updates price information through your modem. A one-time purchase is $52 for NAIC or CG members, and $104 for nonmembers (which includes NAIC membership for one year). Monthly subscriptions are $169 for CG members, $179 for NAIC members, and $221 for nonmembers; this includes NAIC membership for one year. For a test drive, you can download a free demo at www.better-investing.org/computer/demoinst.html.

Equis International MetaStock(Professional 7.0 (www.equis.com), shown in Figure 9-3, is designed for beginning and experienced investors. MetaStock analyzes stocks, bonds, commodities, futures, indices, mutual funds, and options to assist investors in making better-informed decisions. You can generate your own buy and sell signals and test your investment strategies to see how much you would have made before using real money.

The Explorer(tm) function is an analysis tool that performs in-depth "explorations" of up to 12,000 securities at one time. It can compare, rank, sort, and filter securities; list multiple indicator values for multiple securities; show securities with current buy and sell signals; and search for any technical criteria that you select. Results can be saved to lists for future reference. The price of MetaStock 7.0 for Windows is $1,495.

MetaStock Pro 7.0 also enables investors to analyze investment data in real time. The new data management model in this version of MetaStock Pro enables traders to access current and historical price data from Data Broadcasting Corporation's (www.dbc.com) eSignal(r) Internet data service directly online, without storing it on a local drive. With eSignal, you get all equities, futures, and option financial data for $150 per month when you prepay your annual subscription, or $175 monthly. For more information on rates, see eSignal at www.esignal.com/pricing.

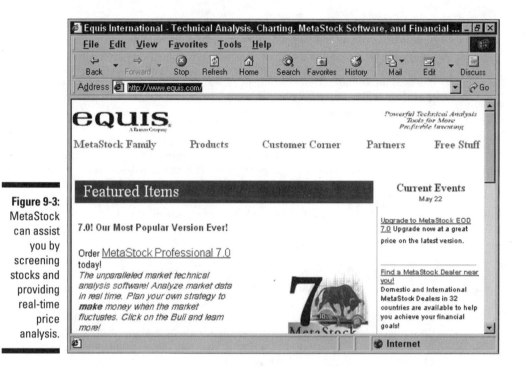

Figure 9-3:
MetaStock
can assist
you by
screening
stocks and
providing
real-time
price
analysis.

American Association of Individual Investors (www.aaii.org) offers Stock Investor, a quarterly version of the American Association of Individual Investors (AAII) software program and database. Stock Investor features a new graphical user interface. In addition to company fundamentals of over 8,000 stocks, it has a screening and navigation tool to narrow your choices to the handful matching your investment criteria. Stock Investor Pro provides deeper data and more frequent updates. With the enhanced Stock Investor Pro version, data is combined with over 1,500 data fields per company to help you keep abreast of the market. The increased frequency of monthly updates can assist you in being better prepared to take advantage of changes in the market. Stock Investor is $99 for members and $148 for nonmembers. Stock Investor Pro is $198 for members and $247 for nonmembers.

Telescan's Investor's Platform (TIP) (www.telescan.com) is Windows-based investment software that assists investors in spotting profitable investments. The program includes the ProSearch 5.0 screening module and Analyzer, Telescan's charting and research program. The program requires access to the Telescan database, which offers statistical and textual information on more than 120,000 stocks, mutual funds, bonds, options, futures, commodities, industry groups, and market indexes. The database contains historical price and volume information dating back to 1973, and the latest online quotes on securities listed on the New York, American, NASDAQ, and Canadian exchanges, as well as the Futures and Options markets. The TIP software is $349, plus unlimited access via your Internet provider to company charts, technical analysis, news, and quotes, any time of day for $34.95 per month. Pro Search, the screening tool, is available separately for $249, plus $18 per month for unlimited access via your Internet provider.

Using Those Terrific Prebuilt Stock Screens

The Internet provides many prebuilt stock screens that use pre-selected criteria. Some of these screens may make your work easier because they already include the investment criteria that you feel are most important. In the following paragraphs, I describe a few examples.

MSN MoneyCentral (moneycentral.msn.com/investor/finder/welcome.asp) offers the Investment Finder, which identifies stocks and mutual funds that best match your investing strategy. The 17 prebuilt stock screens are based on criteria favored by MoneyCentral Investor editors and well-known professionals. Each stock screen enables you to quickly search a database of more than 17,000 securities.

Quicken.com — Popular Stock Searches (www.quicken.excite.com/investments/stocks/search/) uses a large database that's owned by Disclosure, an independent financial information company. Figure 9-4 shows the Quicken.com prebuilt stock screen for Popular Searches (at the Search entry page, just click Popular Searches).

Quicken's Stock Evaluator compares your search results and explains the benefits and limitations of using each variable as a stock selection criterion. The prebuilt stock screens are divided into three categories:

- ✓ **Popular Searches:** Uses preset criteria that match the most popular investing strategies.

- ✓ **EasyStep Search:** Walks you through six steps that use important variables one step at a time. Each step provides definitions about the variable and shows why the variable is important in your stock search.

- ✓ **Full Search:** Uses 33 variables on one page and many advanced search options.

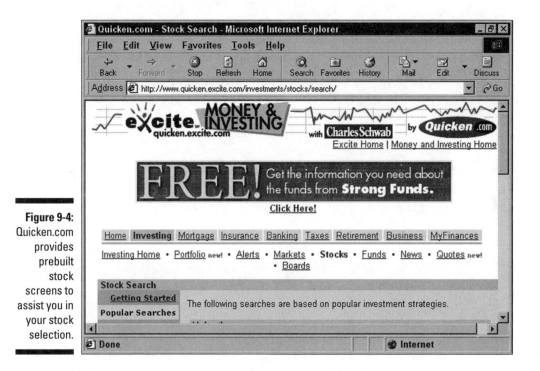

Figure 9-4:
Quicken.com
provides
prebuilt
stock
screens to
assist you in
your stock
selection.

MarketPlayer (www.marketplayer.com) requires your free registration. After you register, click Screening. MarketPlayer provides instructions, sample screens, and an advanced stock-screening engine. Instructions for using the engine are easy to understand, but you should allow some time for getting used to the program.

MarketPlayer, shown in Figure 9-5, features simple industry stock screens that you may find useful. With over 100 screening ratios, MarketPlayer offers a unique screening environment for the serious investor. (If you're an experienced online investor, the prebuilt sample screens may provide some ideas about how you can improve your own screens.)

Many online brokerages offer stock screens. Using a stock screen provided by your online brokerage can save you time and effort. A few examples of online brokerages that provide stock screens are Accutrade (www.accutrade.com), Ameritrade (www.ameritrade.com), and DLJ Direct (www.dljdirect.com).

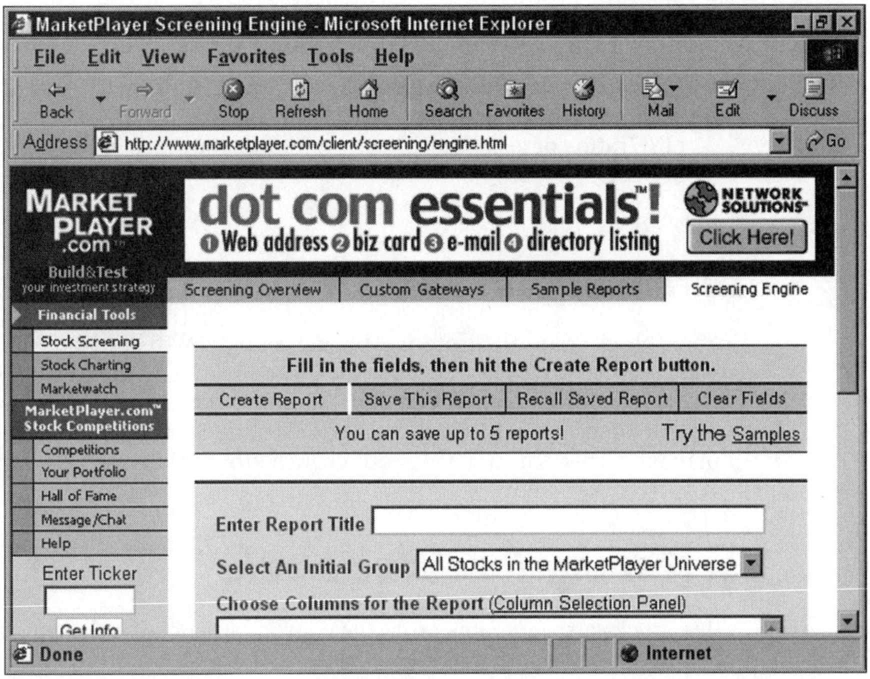

MarketPlayer.com is a trademark of Paradigm Investment Services, Inc. All rights reserved.

Figure 9-5: MarketPlayer provides more advanced stock screens for serious investors.

Determining Your Own Investment Criteria for Stock Screens

This section outlines several ways to set up stock screens that may be beneficial for your information mining. I offer a few examples of ways you can build stock screens to discover specific categories of stocks. I use the categories of growth stocks, income stocks, and value stocks for these examples.

Screening for growth stocks

Growth stocks are expanding at rates faster than their counterparts. They have different degrees of risk and are a way of betting on the future. Your stock screen for growth stocks may consider the following criteria:

✔ **Basic growth:** Any stock that has an earnings growth of 15 percent or more in one year.

✔ **Long-term growth:** Any stocks that grew 15 percent or more in one year over the past five years. (Companies must have historical EPS records of over five years.)

✔ **Earnings for growth:** Stocks that have a price-to-earnings ratio that is equal to or less than the growth rate of the stock plus its dividend yield.

✔ **Aggressive growth companies with low P/E ratios:** Stocks with annual earnings growth of more than 24 percent and P/E ratios of less than 15. (P/E ratios of less than 15 are preferable, but rare in the current market.)

Screening for income stocks

Income stocks tend to be stodgy, boring, slow-growth companies that are steady income producers. You may want to include dividend yield in your stock screen for income stocks. For example, you may screen for any stocks with a dividend yield that's at least equal to the S&P 500 and never falls below 4 percent. (This criterion rules out growth stocks that don't pay dividends.)

Screening for value stocks

Value stocks are companies that have strong financial statements and good earnings, but are traded at stock prices that are less than their industry peers. Here are some criteria that you may want to include in your stock screen for value stocks:

✔ **Book value:** Stocks for which the book value of the company is less than 80 percent of the average S&P 500 stock.

✔ **Debt/equity ratio:** Stocks for companies with a debt/equity ratio of 50 percent or less.

✔ **P/E ratio:** Stocks for which the average of the company's five-year earnings is not less than 70 percent of the average P/E ratio of the S&P 500. Don't include stocks with a P/E ratio greater than 12. (A low P/E ratio may indicate that the stock is selling at a bargain price.)

✔ **Underpriced stocks:** Three criteria exist for this section of the value stock screen:

- Small cap stocks with *quick ratios* (current assets less inventory divided by current liabilities) greater than 1.0 and return on assets (ROA) greater than 0.0

- A price to earnings ratio (P/E ratio) that is half of that industry's average

- A price-to-book value ratio of 80 percent or less, and a price-to-sales ratio of 33 percent or less

Screening for Investment Bargains

Investors are always searching for a *competitive edge* that will enable them to *beat the market*. (Beating the market is usually defined as selecting stocks that *outperform* — that is, provide greater returns than — the S&P 500 Index.) The following sections describe several stock screen variables that you may want to factor in to your stock selection strategy. However, keep your risk-tolerance level. After all, you do want to sleep at night.

Stocks selling at below book value

Some stock screens enable you to sort for stocks that have a current selling price below book value. *Book value* is defined as the depreciated value of a company's assets (original cost less accumulated depreciation) less the outstanding liabilities.

Purchasing stocks selling at below book value may be a bargain hunter's dream, but will require additional research on your part. A company's total assets are often the accounting values of assets purchased over time; in other words, the historical price of an asset less depreciation. For example, the firm may have fully depreciated a 20-year-old building. The sales value of the building may be in the millions, but the listed value listed on the balance sheet may be zero. (This difference causes the book value to be understated.) Or the building may have environmental problems (due to improper disposal of industrial wastes, for example) that will cost the owners millions to clean up. In this case, the book value is overstated.

Before purchasing the stock, the prudent investor determines why a company is selling at below book value. Check out these good online sources for this type of data: Companies Online (www.companiesonline.com) and the company's annual, quarterly, and other miscellaneous reports filed with the Securities and Exchange Commission (www.sec.gov).

Try different approaches to your research. For example, you may be able to discover some interesting facts about the company if it was a failed merger or acquisition candidate. If a large corporation or an investment bank didn't want to buy the company, you may want to follow suit.

Securities selling below liquidation value

Your bargain hunting may guide you to screening for stocks that are selling below their liquidation value. *Liquidation value* of a company is defined as the dollar sum that could be realized if an asset were sold independently of the going concern. (Assets are listed in company annual reports. Good Internet sources for these reports include Disclosure at www.disclosure.com and Dunn & Bradstreet at www.dnb.com.) For example, say that no market demand exists for the company's barrel staves and buggy-whips, and the company discontinues those product lines. The machinery used to manufacture those products still bears value. The appraised value of the manufacturing equipment is determined as a separate collection. The values of the firm's ongoing or discontinued operations are not factored into this price.

Stocks selling at below liquidation value may be valuable, but you should consider the priority of claims if the company is forced into bankruptcy. Claims against company assets are paid in the following order: (1) secured creditors; (2) expenses incurred for administration and bankruptcy costs; (3) expenses incurred after filing bankruptcy; (4) salaries and commissions (not to exceed a set amount) that were earned within three months of filing bankruptcy; (5) Federal, state, and local taxes; (6) unsecured creditors; (7) preferred stock; and (8) finally you, the common stockholder.

Stocks with low P/E ratios

The price/earnings (P/E) ratio is the current price of a stock divided by the earning for one share of stock, and is the value that the investment community places on $1 of the company's earnings. For example, if the current price of the stock is $60 and the earning per share (for the last 12 months) is $3, then the P/E ratio is 20 ($60/$3).

Note: In Wall Street-speak, the earnings per share (EPS) for the last 12 months when used in the preceding formula is often called the *trailing P/E ratio*. You are likely to see the trailing P/E ratio listed as a variable in the online stock screens.

P/E ratios vary by industry, so unless you find out the industry average, you can't determine whether a stock has a low P/E ratio. Luckily, Hoover's (www.hoovers.com) Company Capsules and Zacks Company Reports (my.zacks.com/index.php3) provide this information for free. When analyzing a P/E ratio, you want to look at the trend of the company's P/E ratio over the last five to seven years. Companies that the investment community expects to grow will have higher P/E ratios than others in the same industry.

Bargain hunters may want to set the variables in their stock screens for low P/E ratios because a company with a P/E ratio of 20 is a more expensive stock than one with a P/E ratio of 10. However, companies with low P/E ratios may be *cheap* for good reason. For example, one way to analyze the P/E ratio is to compare it to the company's growth rate. The company's P/E ratio and growth rate should be equal. The stock price is the present value of all the future earnings. Therefore, if the P/E ratio is low, the company may be plagued by slow growth.

What a low P/E ratio is or what it indicates may be difficult to determine. For example, the company may have a low P/E ratio because investors are bailing out, which can drive the stock price down and make the stock appear inexpensive. Say that a $60 stock drops to $30 per share. The P/E ratio will be reduced to 10 ($30/$3). The stock is now half-priced, but it may not be a good purchase if the company is headed toward bankruptcy or has a major problem.

Companies reporting deficits

You may want to set up your stock screen to determine which companies in a certain cyclical industry are reporting deficits (losses). Cyclical stocks are dependent on external environmental factors, such as the national economy, housing sales, and consumer confidence. You can check out these good online sources of industry information: Lexis-Nexis (www.lexis-nexis.com) and US STAT-USA (www.stat-usa.gov). Cyclical stocks have peaks (high points) and valleys (low points) in their revenues, profits, and stock prices. These peaks and valleys can mean that some cyclical companies with strong foundations may be experiencing flat earnings or deficits due to their business cycles.

Be certain that you understand the company's business operations. High fliers can crash and burn. For example, you may want to avoid companies that have no earnings or stock prices based on planned new products, corporate restructuring, or strategic partnering.

The trick with cyclical stocks is to purchase the stock when it's in a valley in the cycle and sell when it's near the peak. A good indicator that the upward part of the cycle may be about to begin is when the P/E ratio is high and the EPS (earnings per share) is low. Other external environmental factors may indicate that the stock is approaching its peak. For example, a sudden drop in housing starts might indicate that your shares in a furniture company are near their peak and it's time to sell.

Prospective turnaround candidates

Using stock screen variables to locate companies that are laggards in sales, earnings, and profits is one way to locate turnaround candidates. The value of investing in turnarounds is that the stock may increase two or three times as the company becomes successful. (A rare few companies will increase ten times. The 40 times increase for Chrysler may be the biggest increase on record.)

Early-stage companies often have ups and downs, but mature companies that have problems frequently don't get a second chance to improve their fundamentals. These fallen angels often have problems with inconsistent product quality, respond slowly to changing market conditions, have high operating costs, low employee involvement, poor customer service, and inadequate methods of allocating resources. Often, management is negative, risk-averse, and bureaucratic. All these factors prevent the company from becoming competitive. The result is that analysts and investors are waiting for a turnaround that never appears.

The preceding situation highlights how timing is everything when investing in troubled companies. The company has to survive long enough to get well. For troubled companies, a larger, more mature company that owns real estate and has cash on hand is superior to a small company with limited resources and rented office space. After all, the company needs to be solvent in order to make a comeback.

Don't be fooled by quick profits when the company starts slashing budgets and implementing a recovery plan. These short-term gains will likely disappear as customers become wary of doing business with the troubled company. The comeback road is bumpy. Many companies get off to false starts and then stumble. Some pick themselves up again.

Chapter 10

Researching Individual Stocks

*I*n the past, only large financial institutions had access to high-quality financial data. Clients didn't have anywhere else to go for stock advice, which meant that bankers and stockbrokers charged customers hefty commissions for their research and recommendations. Much of this data is now available on the Internet. Some of the databases are free, and some are fee-based. Databases that charge fees require subscription fees — payment by the month, by database, or by document.

Even with free or low-cost information, researching stocks is still hard work. Doing so requires good judgment, the ability to fit all the bits and pieces of information together, and excellent decision-making skills. If you're thinking about investing in stocks, you need to research the following information:

- ✔ **Companies:** Profiles, management, financial health, insider trading, potential mergers, and acquisitions.

- ✔ **Industries:** Industrial markets, industrial standards, and trends.

- ✔ **Economic indicators:** The national, regional, and local economics.

- ✔ **Other factors:** New legislation, technological breakthroughs, and new stock offerings.

Often, the best starting point for researching the stock of a certain company is the annual report. The best place to find annual reports is on the Internet. This chapter shows you how to locate annual reports by using a search engine, special company locator sites, investor supersites, and EDGAR — the Securities and Exchange Commission's online database.

Publicly traded companies are required to file quarterly reports with the Securities and Exchange Commission (www.sec.gov). These reports provide updates of the company's activities since it filed its annual report. If the company is going through a momentous change (such as a merger or acquisition), it's required to file more often.

You can find important information about a company in the annual report, but annual reports require careful reading. This chapter shows you how to download an annual report and analyze any publicly traded company. After all, reading a company's annual report is a little like kicking the tires of a used car. You want to make certain that you get what you think you're buying.

Finding Financial Statements Online

If you're a stockholder, you automatically receive the company's annual report. Annual reports are also free for the asking to anyone else. All you have to do is call the firm's investor relations department and request a copy.

For online investors, getting annual reports is even easier. The Internet provides four sources for annual reports:

- ✔ **Annual report Web sites:** These Web sites are designed for investors, shareholders, and money managers who want instant access to company annual reports. Many sites include additional company quarterlies, fact books, and press releases.

- ✔ **Company Web sites:** Many companies have sites on the Internet that include their annual reports. You can use special corporate linking sites and commercial search engines to find these company sites.

- ✔ **Investor compilation sites:** These Internet investor supersites often include annual reports, company news, earnings forecasts, and other useful information.

- ✔ **Securities and Exchange Commission (SEC) filings:** The SEC does a good job of making electronically filed company reports available online to the public.

In the following sections, I show you how to find annual reports using these sources.

For annual reports, and just about anything else you want to know about a company, Just Quotes (www.justquotes.com) is a valuable tool for all online investors. Enter the name or the ticker symbol of the company you want to research in the search form. Just Quotes will build a customized page with hundreds of direct links for corporate news, information, and charts.

Accessing Web sites that specialize in annual reports

The Internet features Web sites that focus on the individual investor's need for company information. These sites deliver annual reports in a variety of ways. For example, you can order hard copies of the original reports, immediately access online annual reports, or view annual reports in their original formats using free Internet plug-ins. Here are a few examples of these investor information services:

- ✔ **The Annual Reports Library** (www.zpub.com/sf/arl/index.html), founded in 1983, includes more than 1.5 million original annual reports from corporations, foundations, banks, mutual funds, and public institutions located throughout the world.

- ✔ **Disclosure** (www.disclosure-investor.com), shown in Figure 10-1, provides SEC filings, financial information on more than 12,000 U.S. public companies, financial data on over 13,000 global companies, and company press releases. The SEC information, corporate snapshots, and company PRNewsire press releases are free. Profile and Company tear sheets and profiles investment tear sheets are $3 and $500 each, respectively. (*Tear sheets* are one-page reports that consolidate company financial information.)

- ✔ **Investor's Relations Information Network** (www.irin.com) offers over 32,500 free company annual reports in their original formats. Annual reports may include photographs, graphs, and text. You use the Adobe Acrobat Reader program to read the information, which comes to you in the form of PDF (Portable Document Format) files. (With Acrobat Reader, you can read PDF files on Windows, Macintosh, DOS, and UNIX operating systems. You can download a free copy of Acrobat Reader from Adobe's Web site at www.adobe.com or by clicking a link on the IRIN Web site.) To find an annual report, just enter the first few letters of the ticker symbol or company name.

- ✔ **Public Register's Annual Report Service** (www.prars.com) is free and provides both online and hard-copy annual reports from more than 3,000 companies. Some annual reports are in PDF files, which you can read with Adobe Acrobat Reader. (You can download a free copy of the Adobe Acrobat Reader from this Web site.) Search criteria for finding an annual report include any or all of the following items: industry, ticker symbol, state of business, exchange, or all companies beginning with a certain letter.

- ✔ **Report Gallery** (www.reportgallery.com) offers 2,200 annual reports that cover the majority of Fortune 500 companies. Report Gallery also offers international annual reports, financial links, and a link to Finance Wise, a financial search engine.

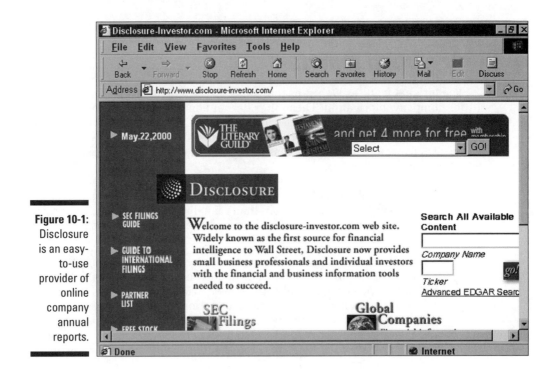

Figure 10-1:
Disclosure
is an easy-
to-use
provider of
online
company
annual
reports.

Using a search engine to find an annual report

Many publicly traded companies have Web sites on the Internet. These sites often include the company's annual report as part of the firm's public relations and investor services.

To find these annual reports, you can start with a commercial search engine, such as AltaVista (`www.altavista.com`), Infoseek (`www.go.com`), or Excite (`www.excite.com`). After you access one of these *search engines* (Web-based tools that enable you to hunt for Web sites on topics that you specify), you simply enter words or phrases that describe the information you want to find, and then you click the Search button. To find a company report, you enter the company name, a plus sign (+), and the words *annual report* in quotation marks, as in the following example:

```
Microsoft + "annual report"
```

Using Web sites that link to company home pages

Many Web sites provide links to the home pages of large businesses. Here are two examples of these sites:

- **Global Securities Information, Inc.** (www.gsionline.com/websites. htm) provides links to the home pages of large corporations. This index provides Internet users with easy access to information provided by public companies. Information provided by public companies includes SEC annual reports, SEC quarterly reports, proxy statements, and press releases.

- **Web100** (metamoney.com/w100), shown in Figure 10-2, provides links to the 100 largest U.S. and international businesses on the Internet. You can sort the database by company name or industry.

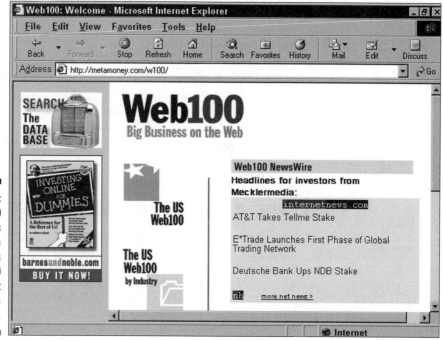

Figure 10-2: Web100 provides links to the home pages of the 100 largest businesses on the Net.

Finding online annual reports: Investor supersites

If using a commercial search engine or a special business Web site locator doesn't lead you to the annual report you desire, try an investor supersite. You can find many such investor directories on the Internet. Here are a few examples:

- ✔ **Financials.com** (www.financials.com) offers investor content that is useful, current, and available at a single location at no cost. Among other things, the Web site provides quotes, company data, charts, portfolio tracking, educational resources, research, and annual reports on more than 3,000 companies.

- ✔ **Financial Web's SmallCap Investor** (www.financialweb.com/editorial/smallcap) is a compilation site of information that is geared for individuals interested in investing in small companies. The research center includes small company stock research reports and company profiles, stock quotes and graphs, company news, and links to SEC filings.

- ✔ **Hoover's Online Company Profiles** (www.hoovers.com) includes company profiles and annual report information on more than 25,000 publicly traded, private, and international firms. You can get capsule information for free; you pay a fee for access to the entire database.

- ✔ **Zacks Investment Research** (my.zacks.com), shown in Figure10-3, has a database of more than 7,000 U.S. and Canadian companies. The site also tracks 200 industry groups. Just enter the company's ticker symbol for estimates, company quotes, charts, news, snapshots, and company reports (in PDF files).

Researching a company's SEC filing

In the United States, publicly traded companies are required to file business and financial information with the Securities and Exchange Commission (SEC). These reports are entered into a government-sponsored database called EDGAR (www.sec.gov). The SEC's EDGAR service provides downloadable data that can be accessed by individual investors. You also can save SEC reports on a disk and read them at a later time. One disadvantage of this free service is that financial data can't be downloaded to your spreadsheet program.

Annual reports may include more than 50 pages and often exceed 100 pages. For example, the 10-K annual reports include descriptions of the business, business properties, legal proceedings, stockholder voting matters, selected financial data, management's discussion of the firm's financial condition and results of operations, financial statements and supplementary data, changes in accounting procedures and financial disclosures, insider transactions, executive compensation, and leasing agreements.

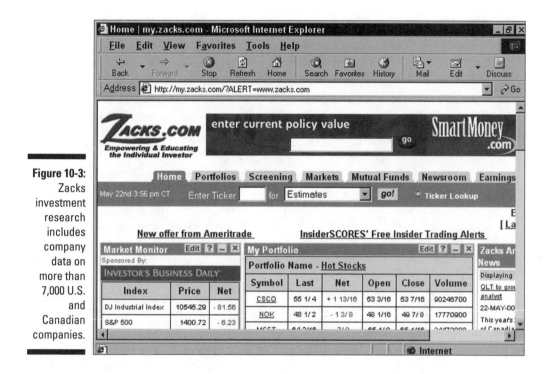

Figure 10-3:
Zacks
investment
research
includes
company
data on
more than
7,000 U.S.
and
Canadian
companies.

When you search the EDGAR database, you're asked for the report number of the document you want. The reports are numbered in the following manner:

- **10-K reports:** Annual reports that include shareholder information covering the firm's fiscal year.

- **10-Q reports:** Quarterly reports that include shareholder information for the firm's last quarter.

- **8-K reports:** Interim reports covering an odd period due to a merger, acquisition, or other event.

- **S-1 registration:** Forms required for businesses that want to offer stock to the public; often used for initial public offerings.

- **S-3 registration:** Registration of a secondary offering; necessary form to offer stock to the public after an initial public offering.

- **14-A form:** Information about voting matters and candidates seeking election to the board of directors; this form is also called a proxy.

Trivia from the Annual Reports Library

Can you name . . .

1. The oldest still operating library in the world?

2. The first people who used handwriting?

3. Who founded the first "members only" library? And when?

4. Where and when was the first tax-supported library?

5. Who said, "Never judge an annual report by its movie"?

6. The oldest printed annual report?

7. The world's longest printed annual report?

8. The first annual report with CD-ROM and diskette copies?

9. The annual report with sunflower seeds?

10. The annual report that included a saliva drug screening kit?

11. The smallest/shortest annual report?

12. The annual report that had a penny glued to the cover?

13. The annual report that smelled of spices?

14. The annual report that came wrapped in a reusable canvas sack?

15. The annual report that included water?

16. The first annual report that included coupons for all the company's products?

17. Who said, "The real purpose of a library is to trap the mind into doing its own thinking"?

18. The annual report cut into the shape of a deck of playing cards?

19. The annual report that's covered with a laced-up sleeve that you have to unlace before you can read the report?

20. The annual report that reads like and follows along like a game of monopoly?

21. The annual report that put a warning on its front cover stating, "WARNING: This Report is NOT interactive NOR entertaining"?

22. The annual report that came inside a bank coin bag which, when unzipped, revealed a simulated checkbook and $100 bills all wrapped together and, when opened, revealed the annual report?

Give up?

For the answers, see The Annual Reports Library at www.zpub.com/sf/arl. At the ARL home page, click Trivia from the Annual Reports Library.

Downloading SEC filings in just three clicks

When you find the annual report you want, save it to a floppy disk or your computer's hard disk. After you download the report and save it on your computer, you can read the file at your leisure. You can also use your word processor's snappy text-search features to find the important information you need.

After you find the report you want, you can save the data in just three clicks:

1. **Click the File menu at the top-left corner of your Internet browser screen.**

2. **Click Save.**

   Your browser displays a dialog box asking you which drive you want to save the data on and which name you want to file it under.

3. **Enter a name for the file and specify where you want to save the file.**

   Use the company's name, initials, or ticker symbol for the filename and a file extension of .TXT or .DOC.

4. **Click Save.**

   You're finished downloading a 50-page document from the Internet.

To read the file, just start your word-processing program and open the file.

If the columns are out of alignment, you may need to adjust the font size for the entire document.

Dissecting the Annual Report

Despite their glossiness, annual reports often present many unglamorous but truthful statements about a company. Corporate challenges are often treated with amazing frankness.

The National Association of Investors Corporation (NAIC) (www. better-investing.org) is a nonprofit educational organization that supports individual investors and investment clubs. The association offers downloadable demos of its investment analysis, stock screening, and portfolio management software programs. The programs are designed for computer novices. If you are math averse, using these demos may be a good way to approach the ratio analysis tasks described in this section.

In general, annual reports consist of nine sections:

- ✔ Letter to the shareholders
- ✔ Company overview
- ✔ Ten-year summary of financial figures
- ✔ Management discussion and analysis of operations
- ✔ Independent auditor's report
- ✔ Financial statements

✔ Subsidiaries, brands, and addresses

✔ List of directors and officers

✔ Stock price history

As you start analyzing annual reports, you're likely to notice that each company has its own style and approach. Additionally, writing the annual report is often an ongoing company project and not something that happens just at the end of the fiscal year. As you read the annual report, you may notice that some sections are clear and straightforward. Other sections may be almost indecipherable and require your close attention. Several sections may be lengthy and others provide just a brief overview. These inconsistencies are normal because different company departments and individuals write different sections of the annual report.

The following guidelines can help you find your way through the various sections in an annual report:

✔ **Reading the letter to the shareholders:** Although you usually find the letter to the shareholders within the first couple of pages of the annual report, save reading this letter for last and then compare it to the facts you uncover about the company. Is the CEO being truthful with the shareholders? What is the CEO's view of the company's operations? What does this letter tell you about the character of the CEO?

✔ **Viewing the company overview:** After the letter to the shareholders, the annual report usually presents an overview of the company, which includes a description of the company's products and its channels of distribution.

✔ **Figuring out the ten-year summary of financial figures:** Companies often provide selected financial data. The ten-year summary of financial figures should indicate the steady growth of the company, if there was steady growth.

✔ **Analyzing the management discussion and analysis of operations:** The management discussion, which is one of the more significant sections of the annual report, usually focuses on corporate operations. This section addresses such issues as how technology has impacted the company, how the company copes with competition, and what management expects to accomplish in the next year.

✔ **Scrutinizing the independent auditor's report:** Toward the back of the annual report, you generally find an opinion letter with a title like *Report of Independent Auditor* or *The CPA Opinion Letter*. Keep in mind that the company pays the auditor — a fact that may sometimes lead to a biased annual report. (During the savings-and-loan crisis, for example, the annual reports of many thrifts didn't reveal their shaky financial situations.)

The first part of the auditor's opinion is standard. The key words you're looking for are "in our opinion, the financial position stated in the annual report has been fairly stated in all material aspects and in conformity with generally accepted accounting principles," or something to this effect. If this statement isn't used, a problem may exist.

✔ **Examining financial statements:** Many companies belong to conglomerates that operate in numerous industries and countries. In such cases, it isn't possible to compare company performance to any industry average. The only way you can judge whether the company's performance is improving or declining is by comparing current financial ratios to the firm's previous ratios.

Often, the notes to the financial statements are the most revealing part of a financial statement. Notes define accounting policies and disclose any pending litigation and environmental issues.

✔ **Finding out about subsidiaries, brands, and addresses:** Knowing what the company owns and where the company operates is important. This can help investors evaluate the political risk of their investments. For example, during the time of South Africa's apartheid, many individuals boycotted Eastman-Kodak. They protested how Kodak products were used in South Africa. In this age of social conscience investing, you may not want to own stock in a company that supports initiatives and products that you disagree with or believe are unsuitable.

✔ **Perusing the list of directors and officers:** The board of directors listing usually appears on the last page of the annual report. Few reports provide details about the experience and professional backgrounds of these individuals. (Director biographies are usually included on the company's proxies to assist you in voting for new or incumbent candidates for the board of directors.) If you feel that this information is intentionally deleted, you can call the company's investor relations department and ask for a background biography of each director.

✔ **Investigating the stock price history:** Evaluating the company's stock price history may provide you with some useful insights. For example, is the current stock price the highest in the history of the company?

The Internet provides many resources about reading and understanding company annual reports. Here are a few examples:

✔ **ABC News** (`abcnews.go.com/sections/business`) offers an article titled "Secrets of the Annual Report: Finding Key Facts in a Sea of Numbers and Words." At the Business page, click Your Money. Scroll down to Investing Archive and click Secrets of the Annual Report.

✔ **IBM Financial Guide** (`www.ibm.com/investor/financialguide`) provides information about how to analyze financial statements. According to IBM, financial statements and their accompanying notes attempt to explain a company's financial performance and recent financial history. Financial statements are used to evaluate a company's overall performance, identify strengths and weaknesses, anticipate future successes or problems, and ultimately help decide whether the company is a good investment opportunity.

✔ **University of South Florida** (`www.coba.usf.edu/departments/ management/facualty/rouse/finstate.htm`) **provides a lengthy article written by Maryann Rouse. This piece covers the basics of accounting, an overview, and suggestions for analysis of the balance sheet and income statement. The article concludes with an explanation of the relationship between the balance sheet and income statement and an overview of the cash flow statement.**

TIP

Entrepreneurial Edge Online (`edge.lowe.org/resource/bizbuild`) **is an** online resource that can assist you in analyzing a balance sheet. This Internet source provides an introduction to accounting terminology and examines the concepts of assets, liabilities, and net worth in a way that helps you relate them to your investments. It explains the step-by-step process of creating a balance sheet and shows you how to use a balance sheet to analyze a company's liquidity and leverage.

When analyzing the financial statements and developing ratios, you should note the following information:

✔ **Growth in sales:** Are sales increasing or decreasing?

✔ **Growth in profits:** Are profits growing as fast as sales? Are high interest payments eating away at profits?

✔ **Profits:** Have earnings per share increased every year? (If not, why not? There may be a logical answer. For example, an aluminum company's profits may not rise every year because the commodity price of aluminum fluctuates.)

✔ **Research and development spending:** Does the company spend the same amount on research and development as similar firms?

✔ **Inventory:** Are inventories going up or down due to a change in accounting procedures?

✔ **Debt:** Are debts increasing?

✔ **Assets:** Are most of the company's assets leased?

✔ **Litigations:** Are there any pending litigations (lawsuits)?

✔ **Pension plan:** Is the pension plan in bad shape?

✔ **Changes in procedures:** Is the company using accounting changes that may inflate earnings?

Analyzing a Financial Statement

Companies often use their annual reports to attract new investors; you can guess that these reports contain some marketing fluff and exaggerations. Most of this embellishment is self-evident. Analyzing a company with a calculator, paper, and pencil will take you about an hour, and the results of this examination can help online investors make investment decisions.

Buying stock in a company without reading the annual report is like buying a used car without seeing it. Here's a checklist of the information you need to consider while you review a company's annual report:

- **Profitability:** How much money did the company make last year?

- **Survivability:** How is the company coping with competition?

- **Growth:** Is the company expanding? How fast is this expansion?

- **Stability:** Is the company subject to radical changes from year to year?

- **Dividends (if any):** Is dividend growth constant? How does it compare to the industry averages?

- **Problems:** Does the company have any pending lawsuits? Any other problems?

- **Risks:** Is the company subject to any environmental, political, or exchange rate risks?

- **Other factors:** Is the management team experienced? Does the company need more executive talent?

EDGAR Online (www.edgar-online.com) is a value-added SEC database provider. Free services include, among other things, access to the SEC database back to 1994, exclusive of today's filings. The EDGAR Online search engine allows you to search by date, company, ticker symbol, people, type of filing, industry, and location. You can import reports to word-processing programs and financial data to Lotus or Excel spreadsheet programs. The premium service is $9.95 per month, which includes all the free services, plus a Watchlist that notifies you when companies that you select file SEC documents. In addition, EDGAR provides features that enable you to discover executive salaries, stock options, corporate board memberships, and individual insider trading. (You may want to know whether the company CEO gave himself a big salary increase as sales revenues dropped and profits dwindled.)

You Don't Have to Be a Math Whiz to Calculate Ratios

You may want to calculate several ratios that you can then compare to the company's previous ratios and to industry averages. Industry averages provide a benchmark for your analysis. Here are some of the ratios that provide investor insights:

- ✔ Last closing stock price (price per share)
- ✔ P/E ratio (current price per share divided by annualized earnings per share)
- ✔ Dividend yield (annual dividend divided by price)
- ✔ Return on equity ratio (net income available to common stockholders divided by common equity)
- ✔ Debt to equity ratio (total debt divided by common equity)
- ✔ Percentage change in EPS (earnings per share) from the last quarter (current EPS divided by last quarter's EPS less 1.00)
- ✔ Earnings growth rate (net income from this year divided by last year's net income less 1.00)

Company solvency ratios include:

- ✔ Current ratio (current assets divided by current liabilities)
- ✔ Debt ratio (total debt divided by total assets)

Several software programs can assist you in using the financial data in annual reports to calculate financial ratios — for example:

- ✔ **Edgar Online** (www.edgar-online.com) requires registration for guests and subscribers. Guests have limited access to SEC filings, alerts, and news. Visitors have full access to historical filings since 1994. SEC filings can be downloaded to Excel, Lotus, or other types of spreadsheet programs for customized analysis. Subscribers have full access to the Web site. There are four levels of subscribers. Level One subscribers get 25 SEC filings for $9.95 per month and can purchase insider-trading filings for $2 each. Level Two subscribers get 125 SEC filings per month and 25 insider-trading filings for $49.95 per month. Level Three subscribers get 250 SEC filings per month and 50 insider-trading filings for $99.95 per month. Journalists and student subscribers get 25 SEC filings per month and can purchase insider-trading filings for $14.25 per month.

✔ **Spreadware** (www.spreadware.com) provides Business Financial Analysis for Windows and Macintosh. This easy-to-use software performs financial statement analysis, cash-flow forecasting and analysis, and ratio analysis. The financial statement analysis includes cash-flow analysis, easy-to-use standard data entry, and the popular Z-Score model, which helps predict the likelihood of a business going bankrupt. The software costs $89.

✔ **SPREDGAR 2000** (www.spredgar.com), shown in Figure 10-4, is a Microsoft Excel add-in that can convert the text of SEC database reports to your Excel spreadsheet. An avid investor who wanted to find a way to manage awkward or cumbersome public data developed the program. SPREDGAR calculates and graphs 30 standard financial ratios of over 9,000 companies from SEC 10-K and 10-Q filings. There is a one-day free trial. You can download a full-featured evaluation copy of SPREDGAR 2000 and generate spreadsheets with financial ratios and cash flow for 10-K and 10-Q SEC Edgar filings. Student/educator purchase price is $150; all other purchases are $250. It costs $49.95 to upgrade a Version 1 license.

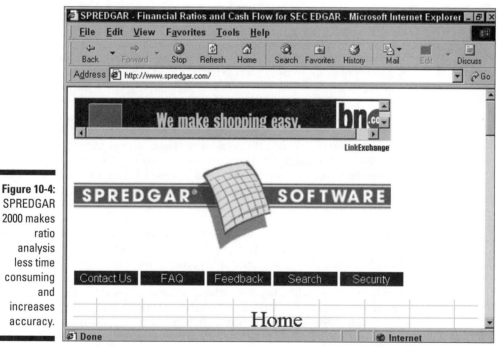

Figure 10-4:
SPREDGAR 2000 makes ratio analysis less time consuming and increases accuracy.

SPREDGAR is a registered trademark of Spredgar Software.

Utilizing Prepared Online Ratio Analysis

Many organizations provide online annual reports that include ratio analyses, performance statistics, accounting notes, and other relevant information. You can download, print, and save all these reports. Much of the downloaded data is ready for your spreadsheet program and your analytic skills; however, you may need to reformat some data, and some data you can't change into a spreadsheet.

Here are two online sources of prepared online ratio analysis and company information:

 ✔ **Thomson Investor Net** (www.thomsoninvest.net/stocks/ report_example.sht) enables members to create and maintain 25 portfolios of up to 25 securities each, receive 25 in-depth company reports per month on more than 7,000 companies, receive 25 in-depth mutual fund reports per month, access company financials and stock research, receive commentary and special announcements via e-mail, and use LiveTicker to monitor their portfolios from their desktop. Company reports include a comparison of the firm's ratios to industry averages. Subscriptions are $34.95 per year. Guest members can purchase company reports for $2.50 each. There is a free 30-day trial.

 ✔ **Market Guide** (www.marketguide.com), shown in Figure 10-5, has a database of more than 12,000 publicly traded companies, and is constantly being updated with new companies and new corporate information. At the home page, enter the company name or ticker symbol of the company you want to analyze. Click Annual Balance Sheet or Annual Income Statement. Next, click in the left margin under Analysis and then click Comparison. The Ratio Comparison page shows the ratios for the accounts on the financial statement you selected. These ratios are then compared to the industry, sector, and S&P 500. If you are unsure of how to use the Comparison Report, click the hyperlinks to an easy-to-understand explanation.

Financial statement analysis involves examining the company's annual report and ratio analysis. However, looking beyond the firm's numbers and evaluating changes in accounting procedures that may hide serious problems is also important. For example, how the firm accounts for depreciation and the valuing of inventory can radically vary between similar firms in the same industry. These accounting procedures can result in earnings per share (EPS) that aren't truly representative of the firm's performance, especially when they're compared to the company's previous EPS and the industry standard. An inaccurate EPS number can lead to big surprises toward the end of the year when the company doesn't perform as expected.

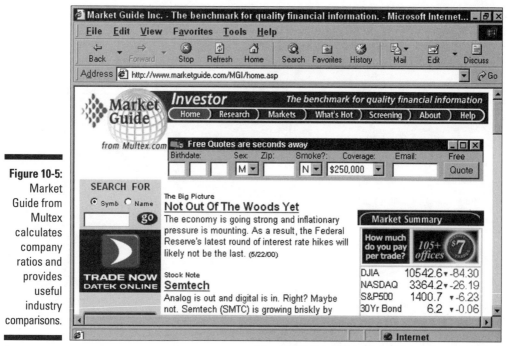

© Copyright 2000, Market Guide Inc. Market Guide is a Multex.com Inc. Company

Figure 10-5:
Market
Guide from
Multex
calculates
company
ratios and
provides
useful
industry
comparisons.

Chapter 11

Digging Deeper: Researching Investment Candidates

In This Chapter

▶ Turning your hunches into investment strategies

▶ Comparing stock returns to other investments

▶ Getting hard data on the economy

▶ Researching stocks online with hard facts

▶ Paying the right price for stocks

*Y*ou may use an online stock screen (see Chapter 9) to whittle down the number of common stock investment candidates you're considering. Or you may select a few companies because you know something about the products they sell. Maybe you work in the industry or have used the company's products or services over a long period of time.

After you find a few investment candidates, you can use online sources to download the annual reports of the companies that you find interesting (see Chapter 10). You read the financial statements, and you calculate the ratios that are important to investors. You may think that you're done, but you need to do a little more research before you contact your online broker.

The next step involves digging deeper to understand the economic environment in which your investment candidate operates. In this chapter, I help you locate the online sources that you can use to determine where the company stands in its industry and what type of marketing techniques it's using to maintain and increase revenues. I show you where to find out what the experts are saying about your stock pick and where to go online to find analysts' earning estimates. I also point out where you can get historical stock price information. After you have all these hard facts, you can make your investment decision.

Many investors do not have the confidence to select their own stocks. This chapter shows how you can conduct your own online research to find winning investments. Many of the sources I list in this chapter are the same sources that full-service brokers use in their stock analyses.

Turning Your Hunches into Investment Strategies

Every online investor has his or her own research system for investigating investment candidates. What makes any system work is that it's repeatable, and it ensures that you don't make investment decisions based on emotional factors. The following guidelines can assist you in turning your hunches into investment strategies. You begin by gathering all the facts:

1. **Find the candidates that you want to research.**

   Match your hunches about stocks that are positioned to be top performers to your investor profile, and use a stock screen or some other method to identify investment candidates. (For more information about researching individual stocks, see Chapter 10. For in-depth coverage of Internet stock screens, refer to Chapter 9.)

2. **Trim your list of candidates.**

   Locate the online annual reports for your short list of stock candidates using the techniques I outline in Chapter 10. Conduct your analysis to reduce the list to several companies

3. **Find out more about each company.**

   Use this background information to put each company into a broader context using the sources I detail in this chapter. For example, is the company a market leader?

   The good news is that the Internet has tons of this type of information, and most of it is free. Here are some examples of sources for this information (I list Internet resources for the following categories of information later in this chapter):

   • **News:** Read the company's press releases and keep current with breaking news. Try to connect isolated news articles to spot trends.

   • **Industry:** Read news articles and industry trade journals to spot patterns that may indicate technological breakthroughs or new products. Does the industry have problems with oversupply, and if so, how does this situation affect the profits of the company you're researching?

   • **Economics:** Note how changes in the national, regional, and local economies affect your investment candidates. Will a rising dollar lower corporate returns? What are the Wall Street economists saying?

   • **Market:** What's happening in the stock market? Are prices and trading volume increasing? Are insiders purchasing stock?

- **Analysts' evaluations:** Most publicly traded companies have Wall Street analysts who often provide opinions about the firm. Study what the analysts are saying about the company. What they say may provide you with leads for additional research.

- **Earnings estimates:** Keep current with the earnings estimates of professionals. Are the estimates going up or down?

- **Historical prices:** Sometimes you can tell where a company is going by seeing where it has been. Evaluating a company's past stock prices may provide you with new insights.

4. **Decide whether the company is a low-priced, high-quality stock or a loser.**

   When you put all the facts together, you gain a good understanding of what causes the company's stock price to rise or fall. Additionally, you know what's normal for the company.

5. **Ask yourself "What if?"**

   For example, what if sales drop by 10 percent, like they did five years ago? What if the material the company uses to manufacture its product becomes scarce — would this scarcity cause the cost of goods to increase? Would such a change reduce profits so much that the company couldn't pay its interest expense? Would the company be forced into bankruptcy?

6. **To complete your investment strategy, determine how risky the stock is.**

   Could you lose your entire investment? If so, you need to add a *risk premium* to your required rate of return. This risk premium compensates you for the additional risk of your investment. Should the return be ten times your investment or maybe even 50 times your initial investment? Making this decision can be difficult, because everyone defines risk differently, and everyone has a different risk-tolerance level. So what's normal anyway?

Conquering Uncertainty with Online Research

You can use the Internet to get background company information by accessing one of the many free and fee-based databases, where you can dig up all kinds of facts and opinions about a company. Some of this information can provide you with new insights, ideas, and leads about additional research. Overall, this information can provide you with an understanding of how a company works within the economy, how it copes with the competition, and how it ranks within its industry. This information is often critical to your investment decision.

With millions of Web pages on the Internet, finding exactly what you're looking for can be a challenge. However, uncovering one small fact can make the difference between purchasing a mediocre stock and buying a stock that can bring you exceptional returns. As you surf the Internet, you may encounter sites that discuss stocks, markets, and online trading. In the following sections, I help you locate the right online sources to assist you in finding the background information you need to complete your company research.

Gaining new investor insights with breaking news

Daily news and press releases can assist you in keeping current with your investments or investment candidates. These sources often provide the first glimpse of why a stock price is rapidly increasing or falling like a stone. One of the advantages to these online sources is that they have *archives,* where you can check past company events that made news.

Here are a few Internet resources for finding press releases and breaking news:

- **AJR NewsLink** (`ajr.newslink.org`) provides over 18,000 links to newspapers and magazines. Select from more than 3,400 U.S. online newspapers and 2,000 non-U.S. papers. Discover many of the links to 23 of the 50 largest U.S. magazines that are online.

- **Bloomberg.com** (`www.bloomberg.com`), shown in Figure 11-1, includes newswire articles, edited columns, audio clips about current market performance, and other information about stocks, bonds, markets, and industry. The site is well organized and provides access to current market statistics, business and financial news, major newspaper stories, Bloomberg columns, and financial analysis tools. (Bloomberg charges a fee for subscribing to its magazine, but you can search its Web site for free.)

- **Industry Watch** (`generic.yellowbrix.com/pages/generic/Headlines.nsp?`) provides top news stories for specific industries. The search engine invites you to select a category. Scroll through the list and select the industry you want to research. You may find the news Executive Summaries of special interest.

- **National Public Radio** (`www.npr.org`) offers news and analysis of breaking stories in such categories as the U.S., World, High Tech, Business, Health & Science, and Arts.

- **Newsday.com** (`www.newsday.com/ap/national`) provides an Associated Press news feed online. Breaking news is divided into categories, such as Top News, International, National, Washington, Business, and Wall Street.

✔ **Venture Wire** (www.venturewire.com) requires your registration for a free daily e-mail newsletter that provides private company business news. This is a great source for information about the day's events in venture-backed information technology companies.

✔ **The Wall Street Journal Interactive Edition** (www.wsj.com) contains recent news, business, and market columns from *The Wall Street Journal*. Articles have links to charts, graphs, and tables. Daily news is continually updated. The site includes closing stock prices and a summary of each day's activities.

Don't forget The Wall Street Journal Interactive Briefing Books. These handy summaries include a company's background, financial overview, stock performance, company news, press releases, and corporate snapshot.

The firm offers a two-week free trial. Subscribers to the print version of *The Wall Street Journal* pay $29 per year for the Internet version of *The Journal*. Other subscribers pay $59 per year. For an additional fee, you can gain access to a much larger database of business research.

✔ **WSRN** (www.wsrn.com) provides a good starting place for your search for company information. WSRN has more than 500,000 links to Internet financial sources to help professional and individual investors. The site is divided into eight sections: company information, economic research, market news, news, research publications, mutual funds, broker services, and what's new.

Start at the Research a Company page and use the links to get SEC filings, quotes, graphs or charts, news, earnings estimates, research reports, and summaries.

✔ **Yahoo! Broadcast** (www.broadcast.com) provides breaking news divided into Business & Finance, Computer & Technology, and News & Politics. In the Business & Finance category, you'll find earnings calls and a search engine so you can locate information on specific companies.

Locating company profiles and related data

In much the same way as the literary world includes biographies of famous people, the world of finance has *company profiles*. Company profiles include all the events that make a company what it is today. You can keep all of a company's pertinent facts handy by obtaining a company profile. Company profiles are often designed for investors and highlight investor-related information.

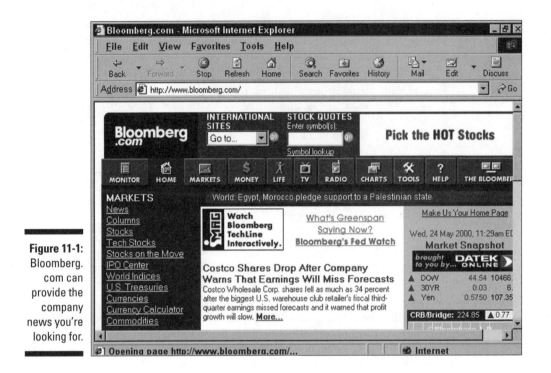

Figure 11-1:
Bloomberg.
com can
provide the
company
news you're
looking for.

Here are a few online sources for obtaining company profiles:

- **Company Sleuth** (www.company.sleuth.com) features a free service that provides daily e-mail updates on your stocks, investments, competitors, and clients. Follow the activities of your investments to know the next move to make. This information includes patents, trademarks, URLs, insider-trading information, analysts' reports, Yahoo! and Motley Fool message board discussions, Usenet discussion forums, SEC filings, stock quotes, and breaking corporate news.

- **Corporate Information** (www.corporateinformation.com) includes 15,000 research reports, 20,000 corporate profiles, 1,700 profiles in French, 600 profiles in Spanish, and other resources. Just enter the company name and search.

- **Corptech** (www.corptech.com) offers Web-based business and financial information to professionals who need quick access to reliable corporate, industry, and market intelligence. Individuals can find sales, marketing, finance, and management information such as news, trade press, executive biographies, and analyst reports, in addition to numeric information such as company financial results, stock quotes, and industry statistics. The database includes over a million global public and private companies from more than 25 information providers drawing upon over 2,500 sources of content. Some information is free with registration. Prices vary.

✓ **Hoover's Online** (www.hoovers.com), shown in Figure 11-2, includes free information on over 9,000 publicly traded companies. You can find ticker symbols, company locations, and sales figures at this Web site. A company profile includes the firm's address, phone numbers, executive names, recent sales figures, and company status. This site has links to stock quotes and SEC financial data. Basic service is free. The price of a membership is $14.95 per month, or $109.95 per year.

✓ **Individual.com** (finance.individual.com/ticker_lookup.asp) offers easy access to the latest stock quotes: Just click the first letter of the name of the company you are researching and then click the name of the company. On the stock quote page, click the Profile link for a snapshot of the company. Other information includes charts, news, earnings, financials, and SEC filings.

✓ **SiliconValley.com** (www.sv.com) provides a database of 150 of the largest publicly traded companies in California's Silicon Valley. You can search by company name, stock symbol, industry type, location, product, and company size. Company profiles include information on benefits, corporate culture, and financial history for the three most recent years.

✓ **Transium Corporation** (databex.transium.com) unifies 300,000 company profiles, mainstream and specialty articles into useable categories and subcategories. Just enter the name or the ticker symbol of the company you are researching. Abstracts are available for free. Fees for full-text articles vary but are affordable.

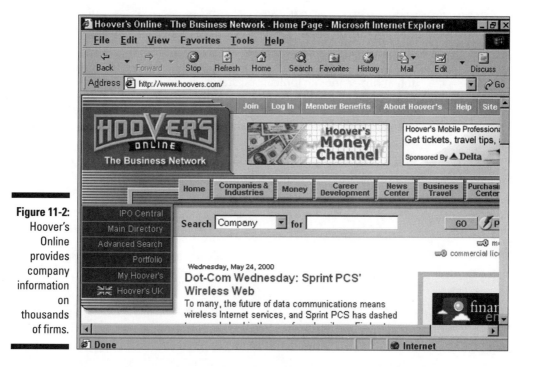

Figure 11-2:
Hoover's
Online
provides
company
information
on
thousands
of firms.

Finding industry and statistical information

Annual reports often provide good insights into the forces that drive certain industries. However, this information may not be enough to answer your questions.

Independent research about how a company is doing in its industry is often available from trade associations and periodicals. Market research sites are helpful for determining how the company of your choice stacks up. Here are some online sources for industry and statistical information:

- ✔ **Fedstats** (www.fedstats.gov) enables you to search 14 Federal agencies for a specific statistic at the same time. You can also search press releases, regional statistics, and policies.

- ✔ **Fuld & Company** (www.fuld.com/i3/index.html) provides a free listing of industry-specific Internet resources. The firm divides industries into 27 categories.

- ✔ **Hoover's Online** (www.hoovers.com) has lists of companies that are part of a certain industry or sector. At the home page, click Companies & Industries ☞ Industries. Hoover's has researched and written over 45 in-depth overviews of various industry groups. You'll find them archived at www.hoovers.com/industry/archive/0,2048,169,00.html.

- ✔ **Michigan Electronic Library** (mel.lib.mi.us/business/BU-IPmenu.html) lists 30 basic industries and provides links to industry publications.

- ✔ **STAT-USA** (www.stat-usa.gov), shown in Figure 11-3, is sponsored by the U.S. Department of Commerce. This site provides financial information about economic indicators, statistics, and news. The site also includes data about state and local government bond rates, foreign exchange rates, and daily economic news about trade and business issues. Statistics include interest rates, employment, income, price, productivity, new construction, and home sales.

- ✔ **Yahoo! Industry News** (biz.yahoo.com/industry) categorizes the business world into 10 major industries, each of which has subcategories. Click the appropriate subcategory for industry press releases and current news.

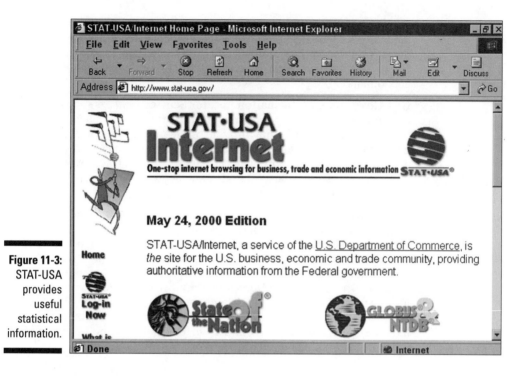

Figure 11-3:
STAT-USA
provides
useful
statistical
information.

Gathering economic and related data

Many individuals try to predict economic trends, but few (if any) are successful. However, having a good understanding of current economic conditions and where they're headed is vital to your comprehension of a company in its broader context. After all, many companies are sensitive to changes in the economy.

The Internet has many sources for economic information. Here are a few examples:

✔ **U.S. Census Bureau** (www.census.gov): Shown in Figure 11-4, this site provides information about industry, statistics, and general business. *Current Industrial Reports* provides production, shipment, and inventory statistics. *Census of Manufacturers Industry Series* includes industry statistics (some of this information may be outdated). *The Census of Wholesale Trade* contains data about organizations that sell merchandise to retailers, institutions, and other types of wholesalers. The *Survey* provides updates about current and past statistics of monthly sales, inventories, and stock/sales ratios. *Today's Economic Indicator Report* provides information about government and related entities releasing economic reports on industrial production, and consumer sentiment.

✔ **The Dismal Scientist** (www.dismal.com): This site provides metropolitan, state, and local economic data and analysis, in addition to forecasts, demographic data, and statistics. Don't let the name throw you; this Web site is designed for people who want to use economic data but aren't economists.

✔ **GSA Government Information Locator Service** (www.gsa.gov): Government agencies are now required to provide and maintain a database of the information they provide to the public. Most agencies are using the Internet to meet this requirement. This site includes many U.S. government agency reports in either full-text or abstract forms. Most information resources are cataloged and searchable. Searches can include more than one agency.

✔ **Internet Federal Reserve sites** (www.bog.frb.fed.us/otherfrb.htm): This site provides links to all the Fed home pages. Publications by this organization include high-quality statistics, analyses, and forecasts of regional, national, and international economic and financial conditions. Publications include *Economic Trends* (from Cleveland), a monthly report on the GDP (Gross Domestic Product), consumer income, housing starts, producer price index, and consumer price index. *U.S. Financial Data,* published weekly in St. Louis, includes statistics on money supply, interest rates, and securities yields. Regional economic indicators are published in the *Fed Flash.*

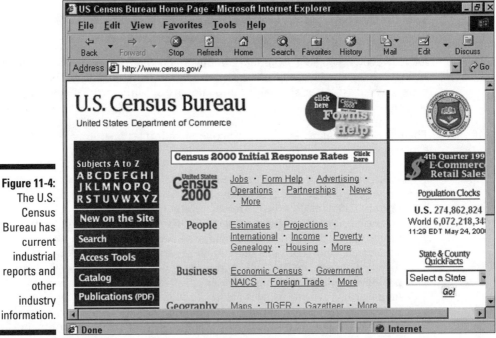

Figure 11-4:
The U.S. Census Bureau has current industrial reports and other industry information.

The Economic Statistics Briefing Room (www.whitehouse.gov/fsbr/esbr. html) is designed to provide easy access to current Federal economic indicators. Links are to Federal agencies that maintain and update information. The estimates for economic indicators presented in the Briefing Room are based on the most currently available values.

Collecting market information

Understanding the current market environment can help you select a stock that can provide you with your required return. This information can give you a better understanding of what drives the company's stock price.

Here are some online sources for market information:

- **Clearstation** (www.clearstation.com) is free with your registration. You can personalize the market data you want, and you can track your portfolio. Get information about the major indexes, analyst's upgrades and downgrades, and earnings surprises, as well as market updates and stock investment ideas.

- **FreeRealTime.com** (www.freerealtime.com) provides market data for free with your registration. You can get news, real-time streaming quotes, analysis, earnings reports, information on what's hot and what's not, and start a watchlist. In real-time, find out which stocks are the most active, and which are the biggest gainers or losers on the NASDAQ, NYSE, AMEX,, and Over the Count Bulletin Board (OTC BB).

- **Holt Stock Report** (metro.turnpike.net/holt) provides indexes; averages; information about foreign markets; issues trades; new highs and lows; currency; gold; interest rates; most active issues on the NYSE, NASDAQ, and AMEX; stocks whose trading volume was up by more than 50 percent that day; and stocks that reached new highs or lows.

- **Prophet** (www.prophet.com) provides market information and charts for stocks, funds, futures, options, and indices; market data such as end-of-day updates and historical data on CD-ROM; online portfolio tracking; and investment discussions.

- **Quote.com** (www.quote.com/quotecom), shown in Figure 11-5, provides free, unlimited, delayed security quotes from U.S. and Canadian exchanges; limited balance-sheet data; some company profile information; an unlimited number of updates for a portfolio of up to seven securities; daily, weekly, and monthly stock price charts; daily market index charts; daily information for major industry groups; and foreign exchange rates.

Basic service is $9.95 a month. Subscribers get all the free services, updates of two portfolios of up to 50 securities each, *Newsbytes News Network* news, any ten historical data files, any ten customized charts that you may want, and annual reports ordering service (for printed copies sent by U.S. mail). Extra service is $24.95 per month, which includes all the basic services plus more historical data, charts, and reports. Premium service and other types of services escalate from there.

✔ **Wall Street City** (www.wallstreetcity.com) provides free market data about U.S. stocks, the Dow Jones averages, U.S. futures, bonds, Canada, Latin America, Europe, Asia, Australia, and Africa. At the home page, just click Market.

Checking out analyst evaluations

Often, stock prices move because analysts recommend or criticize a company. Although these opinions are "informed," they're still opinions and shouldn't overshadow your own good judgment. For example, assume that an analyst suggests buying a stock and forecasts the price to increase to a record high. Over the year, the stock reaches the mark, and then the analyst places a hold on the stock. (A "hold" is a suggestion to investors that they neither sell nor buy the stock.) This hold may look like an unfavorable mark against the stock, but the stock performed just as expected and is currently a good investment.

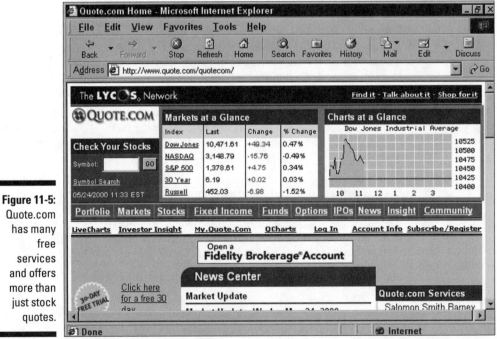

Figure 11-5:
Quote.com has many free services and offers more than just stock quotes.

The Internet now has many analyst reports by individual Wall Street analysts and groups of Wall Street analysts who study a particular stock. However, many of these firms participated in the financing of the companies they're analyzing. Consequently, you rarely see a "sell" recommendation. Additionally, you may see that analysts' opinions vary. Feel free to disagree with their conclusions, but know what the professionals are saying about a company that interests you.

Here are several examples of sites where you can check out analysts' evaluations:

- ✔ **Financial Web** (www.financialweb.com) offers one of the Internet's better Web sites for discovering what brokerages are recommending. At the home page, click Research. Next, in the box titled Brokerage Search, enter the ticker symbol of the stock you are researching. Click Go. You may discover a large number of brokerage evaluations and a wide range of opinions.

- ✔ **S&P Personal Wealth** (www.personalwealth.com) provides its subscribers with Word on the Street — coverage of analysts' recommendations for different stocks. The service offers a 30-day free trial, and subscriptions are $9.95 per month.

- ✔ **W3OTC.com Research Reports** (www.w3otc.com/discover/research.htm) offers reports on selected small cap issues with analyst ratings and initiations coverage.

- ✔ **Zacks Investment Research** (my.zacks.com) provides estimated earnings reports based on analyst opinions. The site includes a listing of current earnings surprises, recommendations, and the company's annual balance sheet and income statement.

Tracking down earnings estimates

The price you pay for a stock is based on its future income stream. If earnings estimates indicate that the earnings per share is dropping, the stock price you pay today may be too high for the true value of the stock.

Here are two Internet sources for earnings estimates:

- ✔ **CBS MarketWatch: Analyst Rating Revisions** (cbs.marketwatch.com/news/current/ratings.htx?source=htx/http2_mx) is updated throughout the trading day. The revised analyst reports show the name of the company, the broker, the new and old ratings, and comments.

✔ **Thomson Investors Network** (www.thomsoninvest.net/FirstCall/intro.sht), shown in Figure 11-6, provides a listing from First Call (www.firstcall.com). Free First Call Snapshot reports offer earnings data, including current quarter and current fiscal year estimates, recommendations, and price to earnings ratios. Estimate revision reports are also available. These reports show revisions to the fiscal year estimates, as determined by broker coverage. The listing includes positive and negative revisions from the last 30 days for heavily followed companies (those that are covered by four or more brokers) and underfollowed companies (those covered by less than four brokers). To access the First Call Center, at the home page, click Earnings.

Researching historical prices

Seeing where a company has been is always important in order to get a feeling about where it's going. Here are a few Internet sources for historical prices:

✔ **BigCharts** (www.bigcharts.com/historical), shown in Figure 11-7, provides graphs of historical stock prices. At the home page, click Historical Quotes. The BigCharts tool enables you to look up a security's exact closing price. Type in the ticker symbol and a historical date. The closing price is listed, and a mini-graph charts the closing price and the daily closing prices for one full month before and after the date you are researching.

✔ **Quote.com** (www.quote.com) provides historical data files as an additional service ($1.95) for current subscribers. Four types of historical data are available:

- U.S. stocks — daily history from October 1988 to the present.

- U.S. commodity futures — daily history from April 1994 to the present.

- Indexes and indicators — daily history from October 1988 to the present.

- Foreign stocks and commodities — daily history from April 1994 to the present.

✔ **Stockmaster** (www.stockmaster.com) charts historical stock prices for one month, two months, three months, six months, and year-to-date, in addition to one year, two years, three years, five years, and ten years. Just enter the ticker symbol of the stock you are researching in the text box labeled Quote & Chart.

✔ **Yahoo! Finance** (chart.yahoo.com) offers historical quotes at no charge. Just enter the starting date (month, day, and year) and the end date (month, day, and year) of the time period you are researching. Indicate whether you want daily, weekly, or monthly prices (or dividends), enter the ticker symbol, and then click Get Historical Data.

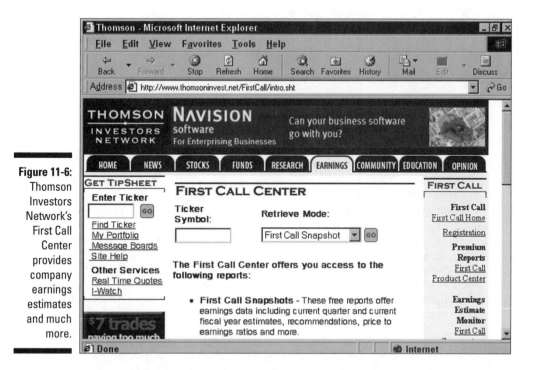

Figure 11-6: Thomson Investors Network's First Call Center provides company earnings estimates and much more.

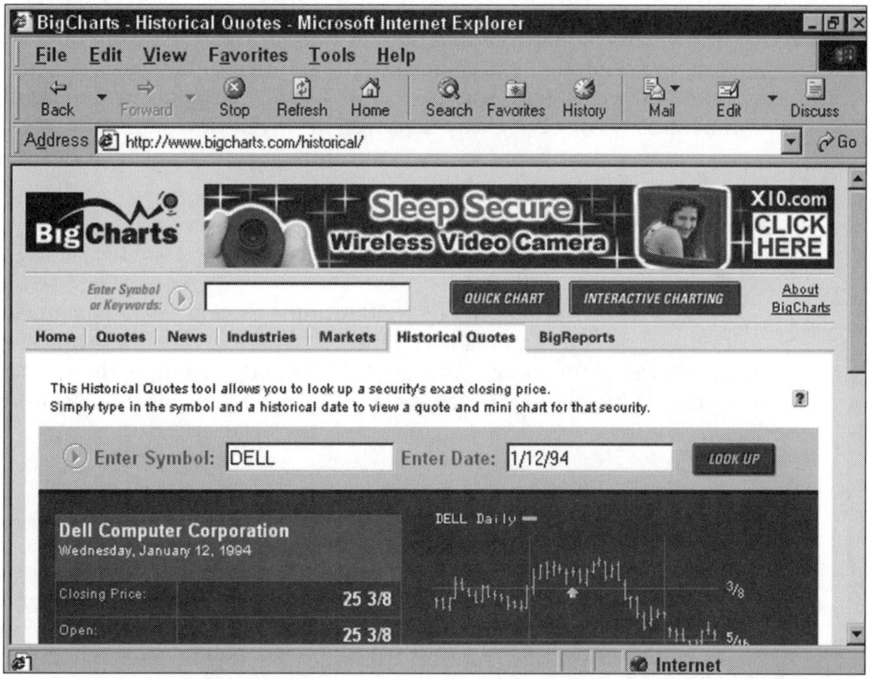

Figure 11-7: You can easily get historical stock quotes at BigCharts.

Source:www.bigcharts.com

SLS Reference Service assists local libraries in gathering information and educating staff. The organization supports three key functions: reference, consultation, and continuing education. With these goals in mind, SLS provides a great online article titled, "Stock Answers: Finding Historical Stock Prices" at www.sls.lib.il.us/reference/por/features/99/stock.html.

Forecasting earnings and the stock market level

An investor who could accurately forecast a company's earnings, general market conditions, national economic activity, or interest rates, would make extraordinary returns. Over the years, intrepid investors have studied these factors and determined that the most important factors in separating the winners from the losers are profitability and the general stock market level. However, when academics have studied past earnings, they've discovered that historical earning trends were not predictors of future earnings. This information only confirms what investors already know: Past performance does not guarantee future returns.

You can forecast the general stock market level using several methods, but not one of them is consistently reliable. For example, the short-term interest ratio theory (the short interest rate for the month divided by the mean daily volume for the same period) theorizes that a very high short-term interest ratio of 2.00 indicates a bull market (up), and a short-term interest ratio of .80 indicates a mildly bearish market (down). When first introduced, this approach was a good way to predict the direction of the market. But over time, this theory hasn't worked well for investors.

Paying the Right Price

You can use several methods to determine the *fair value* of a stock (for a definition and discussion of fair value, see Chapter 8). The following sections illustrate three of the more popular methods of determining the right price for a stock: (1) fundamental analysis, (2) technical analysis, and (3) market timing.

Getting down to fundamentals

Fundamental analysis focuses on the underlying economics of the company being researched. Analysts try to forecast sales, earnings, and expenses, which in turn are used to forecast the company's stock price or returns. All U.S. business schools support this methodology because fundamental analysis seeks to paint the whole economic picture of the company being analyzed.

Fundamental analysis relies on forecasts of the economy, the industry, and the company's commercial prospects. Analysts use fundamental analysis to determine the intrinsic value or fair value of a stock (see Chapter 8 for details). The fair value is compared to market values to determine whether the stock is underpriced or overpriced. In other words, the objective of fundamental analysis is to locate mispriced stocks or undervalued stocks. Fundamental analysis is the most frequently used approach for common stock valuations.

If the stock has higher risk than usual (due to past volatility, political turmoil, or other factors), the investors include a *risk premium* in the required rate of return. This risk premium serves to compensate the investor for the higher than normal risk.

Money.com (`www.money.com`) offers "Calculate the Value of Your Return," a fundamental online analysis calculator that can assist you in determining the fair value of a stock. To determine the right price to pay for you next stock, go to the Money.com home page and then click Calculate Your Return. Just enter the company name or ticker symbol and follow the instructions in the worksheet. The Fair Value Worksheet automatically evaluates your investment candidate. Results indicate the fully adjusted price/earnings ratio and this year's estimated per-share earnings. The Web site also includes information about how the system works and how to find investment bargains.

Proceeding with caution

After crunching all the numbers, it's time for a reality check. The fundamental analysis methodology is limited because it often assumes that the investor holds the stock until termination of the company. If you hold the stock for a short time, you may not get all the expected returns. Additionally, investors and analysts can make errors in dividend projections or may ignore relevant external factors that can result in not valuing the stock correctly. Before you log on to your broker, you need to review your analysis and the data you collected. This is your money and your investment decision. What do you think is going to happen to this company in the future?

Analysis for value shopping

If you're a bargain shopper, you understand how difficult it is to separate the treasure from the trash. This search for value extends to investors who are seeking securities that seem underpriced relative to the fair value or financial prospects. Experts have a variety of opinions about how to decide whether a stock is undervalued (and unloved) or just a loser.

The Leuthold Group at T. Rowe Price (`www.troweprice.com`) has developed one approach. At the T. Rowe Price home page, enter **Value Investing** in the Search Function box and click Go. At the search results screen, click Value Investing.

Table 11-1 shows a snapshot of this methodology. This is one way of separating the winners from the losers. The Leuthold Group suggests that investment candidates meet at least six of the following factors (see Chapter 9 for more information on ratios).

Table 11-1	Value Investing (Spotting the True Bargains)
Factor	**Analysis**
Price/book value (1)	Never over 2.0X
Price/earnings ratio (2)	Using five-year average earnings never over 12X
Ratio of cash per share to price per share (3)	At least 10%
Dividend yield (The annual dividend divided by the market price)	Never below 3%
Price to cash flow	80% or less of the S&P 500 cash flow ratio
Ratio of long-term debt (plus unfunded pension liabilities) to total capital	The debt-equity ratio should be under 50% (include unfunded pension liabilities in the debt)
Financial strength	Creditworthiness should be at least equal to the industry average. The S&P rating should be at least B-

The following are explanations of the terms used in Table 11-1:

- **Price/book value (P/BV) (1):** Expresses the current selling price divided by book value. If the current selling price of the stock is below this amount, the stock is underpriced. Then again, the company may be on the verge of bankruptcy, and that may be why the stock price is depressed.

- **Price/earnings ratio (P/E ratio) (2):** Reflects how many years of current earnings must be earned to purchase one share of stock. For example, if annual earnings are $2 and the stock is selling at $30, the price/earnings ratio is 15 ($30⁄2). Many investors believe that the higher the P/E ratio, the better. If investors expect earnings to decrease, the P/E ratio will decrease to below the industry average.

- **Cash flow per share (3):** Expresses the firm's net income plus depreciation and amortization expenses, divided by the number of outstanding shares.

Note: For more information on many of these terms, see Chapter 9.

Getting technical: Technical analysis

Technical analysis focuses on stock data analysis and stock market statistics. Analysts search for early indicators of pattern changes. As soon as analysts identify the beginnings of a change in a pattern, they use it to predict the future. However, this methodology fails to recognize that stock prices change when the consensus of the investment community's opinion concerning the value of the stock changes. Additionally, market timing is a popular valuation methodology and is similar to technical analysis. This approach uses stock market cycles to gauge when investors should enter or exit the market.

Technical analysis values a stock by tracking price trends of stocks, bonds, commodities, and the market. Technical analysis makes three assumptions:

- ✔ The past action of the stock market is the best indicator of future performance.

- ✔ 80 percent of the stock's performance is outside of the company's control, and 20 percent of the stock price is due to the stock's unique factors.

- ✔ The stock market is based on 85 percent psychology and 15 percent economics.

Although technical analysis consists of many approaches, the most popular approach is the Dow Theory. The Dow Theory is based on _The Wall Street Journal_ founder Charles H. Dow's methodology for identifying signals of bull and bear markets. The theory suggests that as soon as the market heads in one direction, it stays that course until canceled (stopped) by both the Dow Jones Industrial Average (DJIA) and the Dow Jones Transportation Averages (DJTA). (It takes both averages to indicate that the market has changed its course.)

Technical analysis uses the Dow Theory to analyze individual stocks. However, Dow developed this methodology to predict changes in the general market. He did not expect his theory to be applied to individual stocks. For more on the Dow Theory, see E-Analytics at www.e-analytics.com/f13.htm.

The Dow Theory maintains that there are three major market movements. The first is the daily fluctuations that represent normal activity. The second is intermediate or secondary movements that last about two weeks to a month and point out the long-term trends of the market. The third is long primary trends that indicate either a bull or a bear market.

Stocktrader (www.stocktrader.com) is a discount brokerage with a Web site that provides links to online technical analysis tools, software programs, and other data.

For a more detailed explanation of technical analysis techniques, check out Decision Point at `decisionpoint.com/TAcourse/TAcourseMenu.html`.

Technical analysis requires large amounts of information (usually historical price and volume data) that can be manipulated with technical analysis software programs. Some programs are designed for different types of securities and for specific indicators and markets. Additionally, some programs are designed for beginners, while others are for professionals. Here is a short list of available programs:

- ✔ **Equis International** (`www.equis.com`): Analysts sometimes refer to Equis International's MetaStock Professional as the Granddaddy of technical analysis software. MetaStock Professional costs $350. The Web site includes back issues of the Equis newsletter, files of tips, system tests, and custom formulas for use with the software. A downloadable demo is available.

- ✔ **Insiders TA** (`www.stockblocks.com`): This program uses box charting to highlight each trading period's volume and high and low prices. Insider's TA costs $70 and offers a downloadable demo at the Web site.

- ✔ **Stable Technical Graphs** (`www.winterra.com`): You use this Windows-based program for analyzing stocks, bonds, commodities, mutual funds, indexes, and options. Stable Technical Graphs costs $50 and offers a downloadable evaluation version of the software.

- ✔ **Vector Vest** (`www.vectorvest.com`): This program uses fundamental valuation and technical analysis to rank over 6,000 stocks each day. Stocks are ranked for value, safety, and timing. Go to the Web site to sample the program. Just enter the ticker symbol of the company you're analyzing.

Stocks and Commodities (`www.traders.com/documentation/survey/98softwr.html`) offers reviews of technical analysis software. You can view a survey of a program's features by clicking the name of the software product.

Market timing

The underlying theory of market timing is that you purchase stocks when prices are low and sell when prices are high. The market timing strategy is based on reams of historical data that are used to discover patterns and relationships that affect investment returns. Market timing software uses this data to detect or anticipate changes in market patterns. Market timers note that the market can underperform for long periods of time. This low performance can reduce returns for buy-and-hold investors who decide to go ahead and sell before the next upswing. Market timers point out that their buy-and-hold approach prevents these emotional *sell* reactions by investors.

Statistics indicate that a buy-and-hold strategy can outperform the market timing strategy. See the Syndicate (www.moneypages.com/syndicate/buy holdhtml) article on "A Case for Buy and Hold." The table at this site shows the results of a University of Michigan study in which the S&P annualized return for 1982 to 1987 was 26.3 percent for the full 1,276 trading days. If the investor is out of the market on ten of the biggest gain days, returns are reduced to 18.3 percent. If the investor is out of the market for 40 of the biggest gain days, returns drop to 4.3 percent.

These percentages point out the biggest problem with market timing: the need to predict when to get into the market and when to get out of the market (in addition to ensuring that the timing strategy will make enough increased returns to offset trading costs). A buy-and-hold strategy makes certain that the investor is in the market for the days with the biggest gains. For more information about market timing, check out First Capital Corporation (www.firstcap.com). This site provides two free newsletters. *Market Timing* presents a short-term technical approach for the stock and bond markets. *Global Viewpoint* provides a weekly technical analysis of world markets that includes interest rates, foreign exchange, spot stock indices, and commodities. You can search back issues online. Both newsletters include recommendations, tips, illustrations, and charts.

Chapter 12

Going with Fixed-Income Securities: Which Type Is Best for You?

*B*onds are similar to stocks because you make money in two ways. The first way is *capital appreciation;* the bond increases in value if interest rates decline, which means that you can sell the bond at a *premium*. That is, you can sell the bond for more money than you paid for it. (The profit you make is called *capital gains*.) The second way to make money is the periodic interest payment that you receive during the bond term.

Bonds are often called *fixed-income investments*. They represent debts or IOUs from the issuer. The amount of the loan is the *principal;* the compensation given to the investor is called *interest payments*. In this chapter, I show you how the Internet provides information about Treasury, Federal agency, municipal, and corporate bond auctions and offerings, historical and current yield rates, education, and tax information.

Bonds can be virtually risk-free and guaranteed by the U.S. government, or they can be speculative, high-flyers that can crash and go into default. You may decide that these investments aren't for you, but if you own a mutual fund, you may already be invested in the bond market.

Generic Features of Bonds

Bonds are simply defined as long-term promissory notes from an issuer. Issuers tend to be large organizations, like the Federal government and its agencies, and state and local governments. Bonds are contracts that state the interest payment (coupon rate) to be paid to the investor, the *par value* (principal or face value of the bond), and when the par value will be repaid to the investor. Overall, bonds provide the investor with security and a fixed income under a legal contract.

Bondholders want to minimize the business, market, and political risks of investing. From the date of issue, the bond's rate of interest payments (the coupon rate) and maturity date don't change. The price of the bond (the par or face value of the bond when it's issued) can vary during the bond term depending on changes in interest rates. Generally, if interest rates increase, the bond's value falls. On the other hand, if interest rates decline, the value of the bond increases.

A different type of bond contract is a *variable-rate note* or *floating-rate note*. A few corporate bonds have floating rates. The coupon rate is fixed for a short period of time and then varies with a specific short-term rate (such as a Treasury bill). With floating-rate notes, the investor's interest payments go up and down rather than the price of the bond.

Corporate and municipal bonds are usually purchased through a broker. Treasury securities (bills, notes, and bonds) can be purchased directly from the government, without a broker.

The most popular bonds are often long-term debt that matures in ten or more years. A bond is a commitment by a public or private entity to pay the bond-holder certain interest payments at specific times and the *principal* (the original investment) at the end of a specified time period.

Bonds have clearly stated terms and maturity dates. These terms can be as short as 13 weeks or as long as 30 years. Sometimes you can't recover your investment until the bond matures. If you have to sell the bond before it matures, you may have a difficult time finding a buyer. The broker's commission takes some of your return, and you lose the sizable return you were going to receive on your original investment.

Bonds have their own terminology that you need to understand:

- ✔ **Par value:** Refers to the face value of the bond and the amount returned to the bondholder at maturity. Most corporate bonds have a par value of $1,000; many Federal, state, and local bonds have par values of $5,000 or $10,000.

- ✔ **Coupon interest rate:** Indicates what percentage of the par value of the bond is paid out annually in the form of interest.

- ✔ **Maturity:** Indicates the length of time until the bond issuer returns the face value to the bondholder and terminates the bond.

- ✔ **Current yield:** Refers to the ratio of the annual interest payment to the bond's current selling price. For example, assume that the bond has an 11 percent coupon rate, a par value of $1,000, and a market value of $700. It has a current yield of 15.71 percent ([0.11 x $1,000] ÷ $700).

> ✓ **Yield to maturity:** Indicates how much you would pay today for the future benefits of the bond. Yield to maturity is the investor's required rate of return used as the discount rate to arrive at the current value of a bond. (The current value of a bond is determined by the present value of future interest payments and the repayment of the principal at maturity.)

Special benefits and exposures

As evidence that there are no guarantees with bonds, the 1994 bond market experienced worldwide losses of around $1.5 trillion. (Among other things, this was attributed to the Peso Crisis in Mexico.) Since that time, the market has radically changed. It's no longer the sleepy market it was before derivatives and similar financial instruments were introduced (see Chapter 17 for more information). However, if you know what you are doing, bonds can provide a fixed cash flow over time. A fixed cash flow from bonds is important if you are planning a comfortable retirement.

The benefit of a fixed cash flow isn't cost free. Bond returns are usually lower than other investments because of the risk and return trade-off. (High risk brings high returns, and low risk brings low returns.) Bonds are contracts for a certain amount of interest payments along with repayments of the principal at the end of a specified period. The investor can make financial plans based on these contracts. Stocks have no guarantees (or limits) on dividend payments and the sales price. A stock's dividends and value can skyrocket or plummet.

Table 12-1 shows the historical risk and return trade-offs of different types of bonds compared to different types of stocks over the last 50, 20, 10, and 5 years. For instance, a comparison of the annualized returns of stocks to corporate bonds for the last five years indicates that investing in stocks would have delivered more than twice the returns of bonds (a return of 24.1 percent versus a return of 8.7 percent). And stock investments provided three times the return of Treasury securities (a return of 24.1 percent versus a return of 6.2 percent).

Table 12-1	Historical Returns for Different Types of Investments			
	Annualized returns for periods ended 12/31/98			
	50 Years (%)	20 Years (%)	10 Years (%)	5 Years (%)
Small company stocks	14.8	16.0	13.2	13.2
Large company stocks	13.6	17.8	19.2	24.1
Corporate bonds	6.2	10.9	10.9	8.7
35-year Treasury bonds	6.2	9.9	8.7	6.2
30-day Treasury bills	5.1	7.2	5.3	5.0
U.S. inflation	3.9	4.5	3.1	2.4

Source: T. Rowe Price (www.troweprice.com/retirement/historical.html)

For more information about investing in bonds, see the following Internet sites:

- **Bank of America Investment Services, Inc.** (www.bankofamerica.com/investments) can assist you in determining which types of bonds are right for you. At the Investment page, click Education ☞ Bonds.

- **DowJones.com** (dowjones.wsj.com/d/perfin-guide-bonds-future.html) provides an overview of the different types of bonds, who issues bonds, how to make money with bonds, and how bonds are sold.

- **Investing In Bonds.com** (www.investinginbonds.com/investing-2col.shtml) can help you get educated about investing in bonds. This site even has a yield calculator so you can compare your returns to other types of investments.

- **The Investment FAQ** (invest-faq.com/articles/bonds-a-basics.html) provides investors with a good idea of what bonds are all about. If you want to start your bond education with something that doesn't have lots of finance jargon, this is a good place to begin.

Using the Internet to find new bond offerings

New bond issues generally provide a slightly better yield than comparable issues of existing bonds offered on the secondary market. That's because bond issuers are anxious to get the new bonds sold.

Here are several useful online sources for information about new bond offerings:

- **A. G. Edwards** (www.agedwards.com/bondpub/curr_mbi.shtml) provides a sampling of the bonds it offers. Additionally, you can access a sample of several upcoming new issues that A. G. Edwards expects to underwrite.

- **The Bond Buyer** (www.bondbuyer.com) covers the municipal bond market in minute detail. The online publication provides daily municipal bond news, analysis, and commentary. Five bureaus and 30 reporters cover the bond market geographically and topically. This online edition of *The Bond Buyer* covers new municipal bond offerings, city and state officials involved in issuing debt, underwriters and underwriting, brokerages, and bond lawyers. The subscription-based service has a free 30-day trial, and the subscription rate is $1,550 per year. (A printed version of *The Bond Buyer* is also available.)

✔ **Fidelity Brokerage Service** (`personal300.fidelity.com/news/ calendars`) provides a list of new fixed-income offerings. You'll find everything from CDs to municipal bonds. You can even check out current offerings.

✔ **Salomon Smith Barney Municipal New Issue Calendar** (`www.smith barney.com/prod_svc/bonds/munical.html`), shown in Figure 12-1, provides a free listing of new municipal free issues and bond issues that Smith Barney is involved in, intends to bid on its own, or is part of a syndicate. (A syndicate is a group of investment bankers that jointly share in the underwriting, distribution, selling, and management of a new issue.) The bonds listed at the Web site are updated weekly but are subject to prior sale (and may not be available).

Finding bond indexes and historical data online

Bond indexes are designed to represent either the average yield to maturity or the average price on a portfolio of bonds that have certain similar characteristics. Historical data can also provide bond performance insights. The Internet offers several sources for these averages and historical data. Here are a few examples:

✔ **Bondsonline** (`www.bondsonline.com/bcgraphs.htm`) provides charts and historical data that compare various bond market sectors and stock market indexes — for example, a comparison of the 30-year Treasury bonds, 10-year Treasury notes, and the Dow Jones Industrial Average. This site also offers a comparison of tax-free municipal yields as a percentage of U.S. Treasury yields.

✔ **Federal Reserve Bank of St. Louis** (`www.stls.frb.org`) lists the monthly interest rate for each type of Treasury security. Files for specific Treasuries (for example, the one-year Treasury bill rate — auction average) and a downloadable zipped file that contains all the Interest Rate Series (historical archives of interest rate data) that are available.

✔ **Moody's Investor Services** (`www.moodys.com`) provides long-term corporate bond yield averages based on bonds with maturities of 20 years and more. Corporate bond averages are sorted into average corporate, average industrial, and average public utility groups, and by bond ratings.

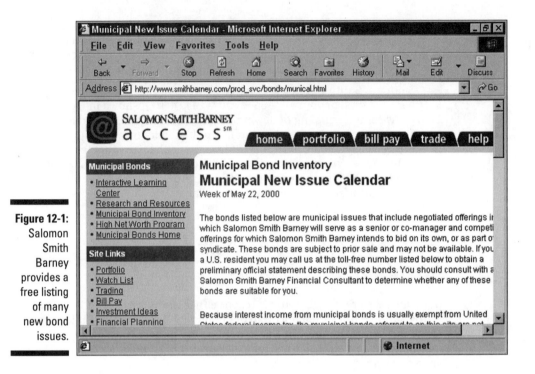

Figure 12-1:
Salomon
Smith
Barney
provides a
free listing
of many
new bond
issues.

Risks and stability

Moody's Investor Services (www.moodys.com), Standard & Poor's Corporation (www.standardpoor.com), Fitch Investor Services, L.P. (www.fitchibca.com), and Duff & Phelps Credit Rating Company (DCR) (www.dcrco.com) are the best-known and most prominent credit-rating agencies. These companies assess the risk of bonds by studying all the bond's information and then assign the bond a rank that reflects the issuer's ability to meet the promised principal and interest payments. This rating may change during the life of the bond, and a change in the rating can dramatically change the value of the bond.

All the credit rating companies rate bonds in descending alphabetical order from A to C, but each company uses a somewhat different letter scheme. For a comparison of the leading bond rating agencies' alphanumeric grading systems, see Equity Analytics at www.e-analytics.com/bonds/bond19.htm.

Ratings are not absolute measures of quality. Each rating takes into consideration such factors as the issuer's past earnings record and future earnings expectations, the financial condition of the issuer, the nature of the issuer's business, the backing for a particular issue, and the rating agency's appraisals of the issuer's management.

The rating agencies warn investors that a bond's rating isn't a "buy" recommendation. However, due to the risk-reward ratio, bonds with higher ratings offer lower yields; bonds with lower ratings, which represent a riskier investment, offer higher yields.

How Small Investors Can Make Money with Fixed-Income Investments and Bonds

Banks and savings and loan associations have developed new ways of keeping customer assets in their financial institutions. They often offer a variety of investment plans that provide higher returns than traditional fixed-rate savings accounts. For example, many savings and loan associations allow their customers to invest in commercial paper (uninsured promissory notes to large business entities) instead of certificates of deposit (an insured type of time deposit).

Small investors seeking greater returns may want to consider the following types of fixed-income and bond investments:

- ✔ **Fixed-rate certificates:** In the past, Federal regulations required a minimum deposit amount of $1,000 with maturities of at least four years for fixed-rate certificates of deposit (CDs). Financial institutions now set their own minimum amounts (which often range between $100 and $500) for time periods including three months, six months, one year, two years, and five years.

  Banks impose hefty penalties for early withdrawals. These fees can wipe out any gains you may have made.

- ✔ **Small-saver certificates:** Deposits do not require any minimum amount according to Federal banking laws, but many banks have established a minimum requirement of deposits of $100 to $500. Maturities are generally 30 months, and the interest paid is slightly below the 30-month Treasury yield. Expect high penalties for early withdrawals.

- ✔ **Six-month money market certificates:** These certificates are for investors with more cash (there is a $10,000 minimum) than time. Yields are higher than those for short-term money market certificates. The interest rate paid is generally slightly higher than the six-month Treasury bill rate. Like the saver certificate, the interest rate ceiling of a six-month money market certificate is a floating interest rate until you purchase the certificate. After you purchase the certificate, the rate is locked until the certificate matures. When the certificate matures, you are free to reinvest (rollover) your investment. If the current Treasury security rate is higher, you'll make more money.

✔ **Short-term bond funds:** By purchasing short-term, no-load bond funds, investors can earn higher-than-passbook returns and still have lots of liquidity. Some bond funds even have limited check-writing privileges. (Writing a check is certainly more convenient and inexpensive than placing a sell order.)

With short-term bond funds, small investors tend to pay more for bonds than professional bond fund managers (who keenly watch every movement of the bond market). Bond funds come in two flavors: tax-free and taxable. If you are in a high-income bracket, tax-free bonds may be to your advantage. However, all these benefits aren't cost-free. Investors will incur an annual fund management fee that averages 0.2 percent. (That is, $200 for every $100,000 invested in the fund.)

Investors can enjoy the type of liquidity that bond funds offer but not pay management fees by purchasing Treasury securities directly from the government. (For details, see "The Four Basic Types of Bonds," later in this chapter.) If you want to buy directly from the government but want to avoid doing the paperwork yourself, brokerages like Schwab can complete your transaction for about $50.

The Internet provides more information about fixed investments for small investors. You can discover online what the benchmark rates are and which financial institutions have the best deals. Here are a few examples:

✔ **Federally Insured Savings Network** (www.fisn.com) specializes in insured certificates of deposit (CDs). The firm researches across the nation for the safest and highest CD rates. Discover definitions of fixed-rate jumbo CDs, fixed-rate callable CDs, fixed-rate fixed-term CDs, and stock market CDs.

✔ **IBC's Money Fund Selector** (www.ibcdata.com/basics.htm) provides information about what a money fund is, the difference between taxable and tax-free money funds, a discussion about how safe money funds are, and how to read a money fund prospectus.

✔ **Money-rates.com** (www.money-rates.com), shown in Figure 12-2, has market updates; information about the economy; consumer interest rates; and investment rates for money market funds, certificates of deposit, Treasury securities, and special bank offerings.

✔ **Rate.Net** (www.rate.net) provides information on the best 30-, 60-, 180-day, and one-year jumbo CDs in the United States. All rates are current within the last seven days but are subject to change at any time. (***Note:*** A jumbo CD is $100,000.)

Checking out the best online banking deals on the Internet

My favorite place for locating banks that offer online banking and evaluating the best online banking deals is Bank Rate Monitor (www.bankrate.com). At the home page, click Online Finance for information about special online offerings. Click Internet Banking Deals to find an extensive listing of instituions that offer special deals via the Internet. Some instituions even offer more than one deal. Find out whether the bank offers a free trial period for online banking services, the monthly online banking fee, and the availability of any free bill-paying sessions per month. This Web page also shows how you can access the bank via the Internet, an online service such as AOL, or a dial-up network with Microsoft Money, Quicken, or a proprietary program.

You can also search for the best savings rates nationwide, search for the best local annual percentage rate, and check out today's averages. Today's averages shows the best rates for today, last week, and six months ago for MMAs, interest-bearing checking accounts, 3-month CDs, 6-month CDs, 1-year CDs, 2-year CDs, 2.5-year CDs, 3-year CDs, and 5-year CDs.

Bank Rate Monitor has several thousand Web pages of timely bank fees and rates. It's a free nationwide consumer source for rates and news on auto loans, checking account fees, ATM fees, credit card rates, home equity loan rates, IRA rates, money market account rates, personal loan rates, and online banking fees.

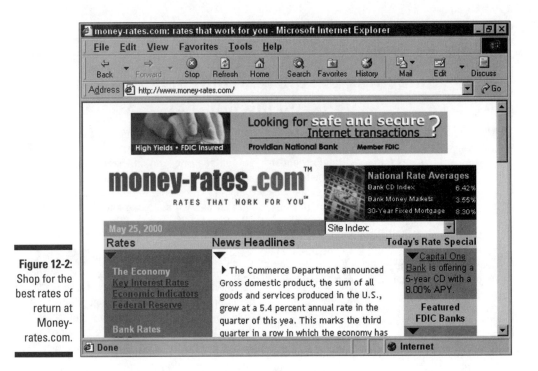

Figure 12-2: Shop for the best rates of return at Money-rates.com.

When to Choose a Money Market Deposit Account (MMDA)

Your online banking program can provide you with information about your money market deposit account (MMDA). An MMDA is a good place to keep your emergency fund and to park funds temporarily. *(Emergency funds,* as I explain in Chapter 3, are generally three to six months of take-home pay that you put in a savings account — or a near-cash account similar to a market fund with check-writing privileges — for emergencies. If you don't have an emergency fund, you need to increase your savings.) An MMDA is a savings account with several unique features. You can withdraw the money whenever you like, and you can write up to three checks per month.

Most banks have a minimum balance for this type of account. As long as you maintain the minimum balance, you earn the money market rate of interest (currently, about 4.5 percent). If the balance falls below the required minimum balance, you earn the current NOW account interest rate, and you may incur a service charge (usually about $5). All in all, an MMDA is the perfect place for your emergency fund.

Choosing between money funds and money market accounts

Your bank may have money market deposit accounts and money fund accounts. The two types of accounts are easily confused, but big differences exist between them.

Money market deposit accounts (MMDAs) are Federal Deposit Insurance Corporation (FDIC)-insured up to $100,000. *Money funds* are mutual funds offered by an investment trust company in short-term (no more than 90 days), safe investment opportunities such as bonds. These funds are *not* FDIC-insured.

Three types of money funds are available:

- ✔ General-purpose funds invest in short-term debt instruments such as certificates of deposit, Treasury securities, and short-term corporate IOUs.
- ✔ Government funds usually invest in U.S. Treasury securities.
- ✔ Tax-exempt funds invest in short-term municipal bonds (which are federally tax-exempt and sometimes state tax-exempt).

BanxQuote (`www.quote.com`) is a good online source for the best rates for money market deposit accounts. BanxQuote shows rates and allows searches by location or terms. Data include the financial institution's name and contact information and the money market account's rate of return.

Opening a high-yielding deposit account

After you find a great MMDA or CD account rate, how do you open an account? Don't worry — it's easy. Just follow these simple instructions:

1. **Call the bank's toll-free number to open an account.**

2. **Ask for the person who supervises personal accounts.** (Some banks have a "national desk" for out-of-town customers like you.)

3. **Tell the contact person how much you have to invest and the type of account you're interested in.**

4. **Ask for the latest interest rate and annual percentage yield (your return).**

5. **Find out when you will begin earning interest and when you can first withdraw funds.**

6. **Ask for an application to open an account.**

7. **Complete the application forms and signature cards; make copies for your records.**

8. **Send the completed bank forms and your check by U.S. mail.**

    The bank confirms your deposit by return mail.

The Four Basic Types of Bonds

Many organizations issue bonds, but the following types of organizations issue most bonds:

- The Federal government (Treasury securities)
- Federal government agencies (agency bonds)
- State and local government agencies (municipal bonds)
- Corporations (corporate bonds)

Uncle Sam's bonds: Treasury securities

Treasury securities are U.S. government securities called Treasury bills, notes, and bonds. These securities are a major source of government funds and a key investment for many consumers. The U.S. government is highly unlikely to default on its Treasury securities, but if it does, your dollar is also probably worthless, so your investment is, essentially, risk-free.

The disadvantage of the risk-free rate of Treasury securities is that it's generally considered the bottom of the yield pile — the lowest yield you can get. As the level of risk gets greater, the reward also increases. You can expect a better yield (but more risk) from corporate bonds with similar maturities.

You can purchase Treasury securities without a broker, directly from the government, in a program called Treasury Direct. Check out www.publicdebt.treas.gov/sec/sectrdir.htm for more information about Treasury Direct and instructions on how to open an account.

The Treasury Direct program enables investors to participate in regularly scheduled auctions. The minimum investments are $10,000 for bills, $5,000 for notes maturing in less than five years, and $1,000 for securities that mature in five or more years. Your interest payments are paid into your Treasury Direct account, as is a security's par value at maturity.

See the Bureau of Public Debt's Web page at www.publicdebt.treas.gov/servlet/OFAnnce for more information about Treasury auction dates.

Treasury bills are sold for less than their face value. The discount represents the interest the investor earns. Interest income on Treasuries is usually exempt from state and local taxes but is subject to Federal taxes.

Internet information on Treasury securities

For more information on U.S. Treasury securities, see the following Web sites:

- ✔ **The Investment FAQ** (www.invest-faq.com/articles/bonds-treas.html) has a useful article about the difference between Treasury bills, notes and bonds. The article also includes a discussion of zero-coupon bonds.

  The Investment FAQ (www.invest-faq.com/articles/bonds-treas-direct.html) also provides useful information about how to open a Treasury Direct account so you can purchase Treasuries directly from the Federal government.

- ✔ **The Syndicate** (www.moneypages.com/syndiate/bnds/tauction.html) provides an overview of how to purchase treasury securities. At the Federal government's Public Debt Web site located at www.treas.gov/domfin/auction.htm, you can find the U.S. Treasury Auction schedule.

If you are uncertain about the fixed-income market and how much you should pay for a bond, the Financial Forecast Center (www.neatideas.com), shown in Figure 12-3, can assist you. Forecasts are based on data from the last ten years and a forecasting methodology. You may find this information useful for spotting market trends.

Savings bonds: The easiest way to save

Series EE savings bonds are easy to buy. You can purchase them at any bank. In addition, some employers have savings bonds automatic investment programs. The employee has a certain amount of money deducted from his or her paycheck, and that money is used to purchase savings bonds. For some people, this kind of investment program is the easiest and only way they can save money.

The full faith and credit of the United States back U.S. savings bonds. The Series EE savings bonds that you buy today earn market-based rates for 30 years. However, you can cash in the bonds at any time after six months from the purchase date.

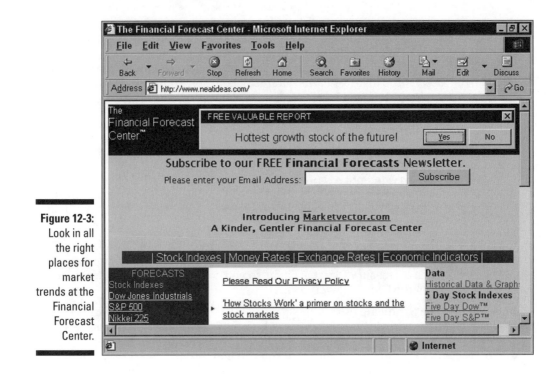

Figure 12-3:
Look in all
the right
places for
market
trends at the
Financial
Forecast
Center.

Income from U.S. savings bonds is exempt from state and local income tax. You can also defer paying Federal income tax on the interest until you cash in the bond or until it stops earning interest in 30 years. If you use savings bonds for educational purposes, they may provide you with additional tax savings.

Figure 12-4 shows the Web site for the Bureau of the Public Debt at `www.publicdebt.treas.gov/sav/sav.htm`. This site provides information about the different types of savings bonds and notes that are available.

Federal government agency bonds

Agency bonds are similar to Treasury bonds but have marginally higher risk and higher returns. They can be sold at $1,000 to $25,000 and sometimes more. Federal agencies issue bonds to support housing (either with direct loans or the purchase of existing mortgages); export and import activities with loans, credit guarantees, and insurance; the postal service; and the activities of the Tennessee Valley Authority.

Figure 12-4:
Bureau of
the Public
Debt
provides a
vast amount
of
information
on savings
bonds.

Not all government agency bonds are equal. The full faith and credit of the U.S. government guarantee many issues. Although government agency bonds aren't a direct obligation of the U.S. government, they offer little, if any, credit risk. However, some bonds (for example, those of the Tennessee Valley Authority) do not have this guarantee.

The Internet provides additional information on specific types of government agency bonds. The following are two examples:

✔ **Fannie Mae** (www.fanniemae.com/financilinfo.index.html) provides investors with background information about the bonds it issues. In the Search In box, select Investor. In the Search For box, type **Bonds** and then click Search. A list of hyperlinked topics appears. Check out bond topics that interest you.

✔ **Ginnie Mae** (www.ginniemae.com) is a government agency that specializes in non-conforming home loans. Consequently, this agency is always issuing to fund its activities. For investor information, click Guides.

The beauty of tax-free municipal bonds

Towns, cities, and regional and local agencies issue municipal bonds. Municipal bonds usually have lower interest rates than comparably rated corporate bonds and Treasury securities. The minimum amount required for investment in municipal bonds is $5,000, and municipal bonds are sometimes issued at a discount. This discount compensates investors for the additional risk that these bonds may have due to the financial difficulties of some local governments.

The most important feature of municipal bonds is their tax-exempt feature. In subsequent judgments based on the 1819 *McCullough v. Maryland* ruling, the Federal, state, and local governments don't possess the power to tax each other. Consequently, municipal bonds can't be subject to Federal tax. Additionally, income from state and local municipal bonds can't be taxed if purchased within the geographic area. For example, Virginia residents don't pay state taxes on Virginia bonds. However, residents of California are subject to state income taxes on their Virginia bonds. This tax-exempt feature makes municipal bonds very attractive to investors in high tax brackets. You treat capital gains on such bonds as normal income.

Three primary types of municipal bonds exist. Each bond type has special features:

- **General obligation bonds** are backed by the full faith and credit of the issuing agency. For municipal bonds, *full faith and credit* also means the taxing power of the issuing municipality.

- **Revenue bonds** are backed by the funds from a designated tax or the revenues from a specific project, authority, or agency. These bonds are not backed by the full faith and credit (or the taxing power) of the issuing agency. In other words, revenue bonds are only as good (and as creditworthy) as the ventures they support.

- **Industrial development bonds (IDBs)** are used to finance the purchase or construction of industrial facilities that are to be leased to businesses. Leasing fees of the facilities are used to meet construction expenses and the repayment requirements of the bonds. Often, these bonds provide inexpensive financing to firms choosing to locate in the geographical area of the issuer. Examples of IDBs are bonds for the construction of piers and wharves.

Municipalities can also issue short-term securities called tax-exempt commercial paper and variable-rate demand obligations.

The Bond Market Association / Bloomberg National Municipal Bonds Yields (www.Bloomberg.com/markts/psa/muni.html) provides investors with an overview of the national municipal bonds yields for triple A-rated, tax-exempt, insured revenue bonds. This information is designed to be used as a benchmark for particular categories of municipal bonds. Benchmarks are useful when you are determining whether a municipal bond is priced above or below the average market rate.

The following brokerages provide a variety of bond information such as frequently updated offerings for individual investors, informative articles, and starter kits. The offerings shown at these Web sites are used for information purposes only. The securities listed by these firms are subject to changes in price and availability.

- ✔ **First Miami Securities** (www.firstmiami.com/yields.html) is a financial institution that provides tables and charts of investment-grade municipal bond yields, among other things.

- ✔ **J. C. Bradford Municipal Bonds** (www.jcbradford.com/personal/bonds.htm) provides a state by state listing of its current municipal bond inventory and selected Municipal Research reports that can be viewed either as a standard file or in PDF files.

- ✔ **Lebenthal & Company** (www.lebenthal.com), shown in Figure 12-5, will send you a "Bond Kit" that is designed for first-time municipal bond purchasers. The Bond Kit covers general obligation and revenue bonds, bond insurance, coupons, taxes, and how to sell your bonds.

- ✔ **Stone & Youngberg** (www.styo.com) offers weekly listings of mortgage-backed securities, corporate bonds, and municipal bonds. At the home page, click Weekly Market Update for the listing of the municipal bond type you are researching.

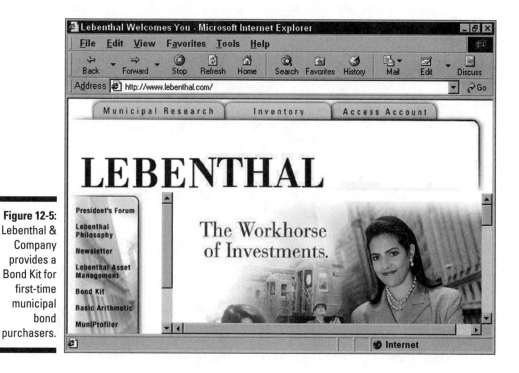

Figure 12-5: Lebenthal & Company provides a Bond Kit for first-time municipal bond purchasers.

Floating with corporate bonds

Corporate bonds are a major source of corporate borrowing. When corporations make corporate bonds, they "float a bond issue." Such bond issues take the form of either *debentures* (which are unsecured corporate bonds backed by the general credit of the corporation) or *asset-backed bonds* (which are backed by specific corporate assets like property or equipment). Income from these bonds is taxable. However, top-rated corporate bonds are often almost risk-free and have a higher return than Treasury securities. Corporate bonds are generally considered safer than stocks because of two factors:

- ✔ **The bonds state exactly how much the corporation will pay the bondholder.** Shareholders are entitled to cash dividends, but payment and the amount of the dividend is at the discretion of the corporation.

- ✔ **Bondholders are creditors.** They receive payment before the corporation can distribute any cash dividends to shareholders, which means that bondholders have greater protection in getting at least some return on their investment. (In bankruptcy, bondholders are paid from corporate assets before common stockholders.)

Some risk of default always exists. In the 1980s, many companies used junk bonds to finance highly leveraged takeovers of rival companies. Their bonds were rated noninvestment grade and speculative by the bond-rating agencies. Due to the additional risk, these bonds paid above-average interest rates. For some bondholders, these bonds were a windfall. For bondholders who invested in the corporate bonds of companies that failed, their bonds went into default and became worthless junk.

Some professional money managers are required by law to purchase investment-grade securities so that they can't purchase junk bonds. These organizations generally limit their corporate bond purchases to issues rated B or higher by Moody's Investors.

Using the Internet to select bonds

The Internet provides many online tools to help you make bond selections. Some Web sites include search engines that sort through thousands of bond offerings while looking for bonds that meet your criteria. These services are free but often accompanied by a sales pitch. The Internet provides many tools and resources for analyzing bonds. Here are some popular bond sites:

- ✔ **Bond Agent** (www.bondagent.com) is an online bond brokerage firm that requires your free registration in return for use of its powerful search capabilities. Investors are free to search for corporate and municipal new issues and breaking bond news.

- ✔ **Bond Resources** (`www.bondresources.com`) includes news, analysis, charts, rates, and education for Treasuries and municipal, agency, and corporate bonds. At the home page, just click Corporate.

- ✔ **CBS Bellwether Bonds Report** (`www.cbsmarketwatch.com`) provides constantly updated bond market news and data about corporate bonds. From the home page, click Market Data ☞ Bonds ☞ Corporates.

- ✔ **MCM Watch** (`www.mcmwatch.com`) offers real-time direct Internet access to MCM's global fixed-income, equity, and foreign exchange analyses. Discover the trading volume of different kinds of corporate bonds for the last week, year-to-date, and prior year with CorporateWatch. The service offers a free 30-day trial and costs $450 per month.

- ✔ **The Standard & Poor's Blue List** (`www.bluelist.com/bltsdemo.dem`) shows current municipal and corporate bond offerings. This Web site has a static demo scan of its "Blue List Offerings" available to individual investors. The demo scans a maximum of 14 items and is designed to demonstrate the company's software. You can search the database for state issuers, maturity dates, lot size of the issue, coupon, and CUSIP.

CUSIP is a numbering system endorsed by major segments of the financial community. See the CUSIP service bureau operated by Standard & Poor's for the American Bankers Association at `www.cusip.com` for more information about CUSIP numbering.

Two Alternate Types of Bonds

Two relatively new types of bonds may be of interest to online investors: zero-coupon bonds and Eurobonds. I describe these newer bond types in the following sections.

Zero-coupon bonds

Zero-coupon bonds offer no interest payments but are put on the market at prices substantially below their face values. The return to the investor is the difference between the investor's cost and the face value received at the end of the life of the bond.

If you don't rely on interest payment income, zero-coupon bonds may be the way to go for your nontaxable retirement plan (such as an individual retirement account, Keogh plan, or other nontaxable pension fund). The Internal Revenue Service taxes zero-coupon bonds as if investors received regular interest payments. This tax is based on amortizing the built-in gain over the life of the bond. In other words, for taxable accounts, investors have to pay taxes on income they haven't received, but for nontaxable accounts, they're a great investment choice.

Some brokerages offer *Treasury strips*. Large companies purchase 30-year Treasury securities and clip the interest-bearing coupons. The brokers then sell these Treasury coupons like zero-coupon bonds. You purchase the Treasury strip at a discount (say $4,300) and redeem the coupon at face value ($5,000). Treasury strips are like zero-coupon bonds because no interest is paid during the maturity term.

If you are looking for more information about zero-coupon bonds, the Internet provides many educational articles — for example:

- **Federal Reserve Bank of New York** (www.ny.frb.org/pihome/fedpoint/fed42.html) has an overview of zero-coupon bonds and strips, as well as a short history of Treasury zero-coupon bonds and strips.

- **Deloitte & Touche** (www.dtonline.com/pfa/zeros.htm) provide useful examples of how zero-coupon bonds can increase returns and eliminate reinvestment risk.

- **Financenter** (www.financenter.com) can help you decide whether a Treasury security, municipal or corporate bond is better for you than a zero-coupon bond. At the FinanCenter home page, click Investing ☞ Calculate Answers. Search for "Should I buy a zero coupon bond?" and enter the appropriate data in the online calculator.

Eurobonds

Investments in foreign securities typically involve many government restrictions. Eurobonds are bonds offered outside the country of the borrower and usually outside the country in whose currency the securities are denominated. For example, a Eurobond may be issued by an American corporation, denominated in German deutsche marks, and sold in Japan and Switzerland.

For additional information about Eurobonds, see the following sites:

- **Bradynet CyberExchange** (www.bradynet.com) provides bond prices, analysis, research, ratings, news, information about new issues, and forums. Enter **Eurobonds** in the Search engine on the home page and select Search Bradynet. You get a page that includes a demonstration program that searches for specific Eurobond issues.

- **Barclays Capital** (www.barclayscapital.com/euroidx/data/Summary.shtml) offers a summary, by country, of the Euro Government Bond Indices. The various charts show all maturities index, index weights, capitalization profile, and yield versus duration in graph and table form.

- **Petercam Eurobonds** (www.petercam.be) provides valuation techniques for Eurobonds, benchmarks, and information about Eurobond primary and secondary markets. At the home page, click Eurobond Desk.

J.P. Morgan & Company, Inc. (www.jpmorgan.com) provides a government bond index that is a widely used benchmark for assessing and quantifying risk across international fixed-income bond markets. If you're looking for benchmarks, go to the J.P. Morgan home page and click Index.

The indexes measure the total, principal, and interest returns in each market and can be reported in 19 currencies. You can compare Eurobonds to the index in order to provide a realistic measure of market performance.

Chapter 13

Valuing, Buying, and Selling Bonds Online

*I*n this chapter, I show you how to analyze, buy, and sell a variety of fixed-income investments. I explore the benefits of savings bonds, detail new regulations, and explain the limitations of this type of investment. I also show you where to find the Savings Bond Wizard, which you can use to determine the exact value of your savings bonds.

This chapter also explains how to purchase Treasury securities without a broker. You can now purchase Treasury securities online or over the phone with *Buy Direct!,* a U.S. Treasury Department-sponsored program. In addition, you can access your account online to see your online statement. Other online services include helpful information — for example, dates of government auctions, Treasury yields, auction results, and instructions about how to open your investor's account at Treasury Direct (the master record of the securities you own that is maintained by the Federal government).

For online investors interested in paying the right price for a bond, this chapter shows how to value all types of bonds and determine bond yields (returns). Doing so may sound complicated, but with a little practice, you'll be calculating your returns in no time. This chapter also explains where to buy bonds online, and offers a hot strategy that can protect you from interest rate risk.

Nice and Simple: Savings Bonds

For many people, the only way they can save money is by purchasing savings bonds. The United States Treasury Department offers three main types of savings bonds:

- ✔ **Series EE:** You pay half the face value of a Series EE bond at the time of purchase, and you receive the face value when the bond matures. The interest rate isn't fixed, so the maturity term is variable. However, most bonds mature in 18 years and don't accrue any more income after 30 years. The minimum denomination is $50, and the maximum denomination is $10,000.

- ✔ **Series HH:** A Series HH bond pays interest directly to your account at a financial institution every six months. These bonds have fixed interest rates for ten years and earn interest up to 20 years. Series HH bonds are available in denominations of $500, $1,000, $5,000, and $10,000.

- ✔ **Series I:** A Series I bond has a fixed interest rate combined with semiannual inflation adjustments to help protect purchasing power. Series I bond earnings are added every month, and interest is compounded semiannually. They are sold at face value in denominations of $50, $75, $100, $200, $500, $1,000, $5,000, and $10,000 and earn interest for as long as 30 years.

Check for old bonds in your safe-deposit box or among the papers of elderly relatives. More than $2.3 billion in savings bonds have never been redeemed.

Hanging on to your old bonds may seem like a good idea, but after specified periods they no longer pay interest.

Where to buy bonds

About 55 million people own savings bonds, and around $15 billion worth of savings bonds are sold per year. Different sources exist for purchasing savings bonds:

- ✔ **Banks, credit unions, and other financial institutions:** Many financial institutions are qualified as savings bond agents. These agents accept the payments and purchase orders for the EE bonds and then forward the orders to a Federal Reserve Bank, where the bonds are inscribed and mailed. Allow 15 days for delivery.

- ✔ **Bond-a-Month programs:** Many financial institutions offer savings bonds through a "Bond-a-Month" savings plan. With this plan, you can automatically buy bonds on a regular schedule (not necessarily a bond a month). Contact your financial institution for more information.

✔ **Easy Saver:** You can purchase bonds automatically for yourself or anyone you choose with a regularly scheduled deduction from your bank account. You select the amount, the recipient, and when you want the bond issued. For details, see the Easy Saver section of the Bureau of the Public Debt (`www.publicdebt.treas.gov/mar/maressav.htm`), shown in Figure 13-1.

✔ **Employer sponsored payroll savings plans:** More than 45,000 employers participate in employer-sponsored payroll savings plans.

✔ **Federal Reserve banks:** If you write to your local Federal Reserve Bank for an application, you can purchase savings bonds by mail. The Federal Reserve Bank of New York (`www.ny.frb.org/pihome/svg_bnds`) provides the addresses of the 12 regional Federal Reserve banks.

Now you can buy savings bonds online 24 hours a day, 7 days a week. As of this writing, you can purchase up to $1,000 face value ($500 purchase price) in a single online transaction at the Federal government's Savings Bond Connection Web site located at `www.publicdebt.treas.gov/ols/olshome.htm`.

Figure 13-1:
Easy Saver is an automatic investment plan for buying U.S. savings bonds.

You can get additional information about savings bonds from the following Internet sources:

- **The Bureau of the Public Debt** (`www.publicdebt.Treas.gov/sav/savbene.htm`) provides information on the benefits of savings bonds, and covers interest rates and maturity periods.

- **The Federal Reserve Bank of New York** (`app.ny.frb.org/sbr`) has an online savings bond redemption calculator. Fill in the blanks and click Compute Values. A maximum of five years of data is displayed for each computation.

- **Savings Bond.com** (`www.savingsbond.com`), sponsored by Lexington Software, provides useful information on just about any savings bond topic you can imagine.

- **The Savings Bond Informer** (`www.bondinformer.com`) provides information about how well your savings bonds are performing, suggestions about which bonds to cash if you need the money, and the tax consequences of your savings bond investments.

The good and the bad about savings bonds

The returns on savings bonds are so low that they'll never make you rich. In fact, returns are so low that large pension funds and other big investors don't purchase savings bonds. However, for many individuals, savings bonds are the best approach for saving money. Savings bonds offer the following advantages:

- **You can save automatically:** Employers who sponsor savings bond programs can automatically deduct an amount that you designate from your paychecks. For many people, this program is a painless way to save money.

- **You can diversify your risk:** If you already have investments in stocks and bonds, you may want to invest in savings bonds and thus add a no-risk element to your portfolio.

- **Your investment is safe:** In exchange for a low return, savings bonds offer absolute safety of principal — they're no-risk investments.

- **You don't pay any sales commissions:** Savings bonds don't require the services of a broker to help you purchase them, thus you pay no sales commissions.

- **Your minimum investment is low:** The minimum investment in savings bonds is $25, and employer-sponsored plans can make the per week minimum even lower.

- **You pay no or low taxes:** The difference between the purchase price and the redemption value of EE bonds, and the payments made on HH bonds, comes in the form of interest. This interest income is subject to Federal income tax, but not state or local income taxes. You can defer paying Federal income tax on the interest until you cash in the bonds.

✔ **You gain education tax benefits:** For EE bonds purchased after 1989 and cashed to pay tuition and post-secondary education fees, the interest earned is not subject to Federal income taxes.

Downloading the Savings Bond Wizard

Savings bonds have always been easy to purchase and are popular gifts for new parents and grandchildren. But as easy as these financial instruments are to buy, they are equally difficult to value. This difficulty can be especially troublesome if you need to cash in a bond before it matures. Additionally, bondholders may have problems keeping an accurate inventory of the savings bonds they have on hand.

Recognizing this problem, the Federal government developed a nifty program that does all the work for you. The accompanying figure shows a page from the Web site of the Bureau of the Public Debt at `www.publicdebt.treas. gov/sav/savwizar.htm`. This site contains the Savings Bond Wizard, a free savings bond software program. To download the program, just click the appropriate link.

The Savings Bond Wizard's features enable you to print a copy of your bond inventory. (After a flood or fire, this inventory is an invaluable record of the bondholder's investment.)

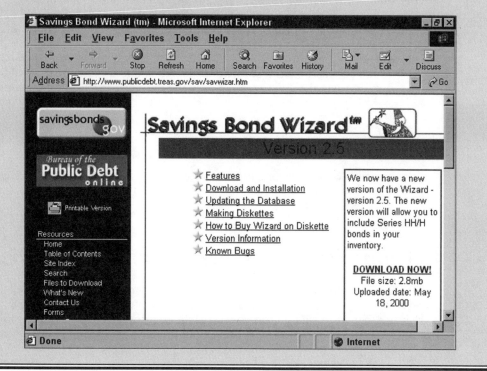

EE bonds don't pay accrued interest in periodic cash payments, as HH bonds do. An alternative investment exists for people who are about to retire and want an investment that pays interest in cash: Sell the savings bonds, pay the tax, and use the proceeds to purchase 20-year Treasury securities. The Treasury securities pay interest in cash so that retirees can use it for living expenses. *Note:* If selling your E and EE bonds puts you in a higher tax bracket, sell them over a two-year period.

Just Uncle Sam, Treasury Securities, and You

The Federal government sells Treasury securities to the public to pay off maturing debt and to raise the cash needed to operate the Federal government. These securities are sold at 150 auctions throughout the year. There are three types of Treasury securities. All Treasury securities have a minimum purchase of $1,000, and additional purchase increments of $1,000. The chief difference between Treasury securities is the life of the obligation:

- **Treasury bills (T-bills)** mature in three months, six months, or one year. Treasury bills are purchased at a discount, so interest is actually paid. You write a check for $10,000, and the government refunds the discount (which equals the interest rate determined at auction). In other words, your return is the difference between the purchase price and the maturity value.

- **Treasury notes** are considered intermediate-term securities and mature in two to ten years. They provide state and local tax-exempt interest payments to noteholders.

- **Treasury bonds** are long-term securities that have maturities that range from 10 years to 30 years. Interest paid to bondholders is exempt from state and local taxes.

Buying Treasury securities via the Internet

Treasury securities may not look very lucrative if you're used to double-digit returns, but they're excellent investments for investors who can't tolerate risk. In other words, if you're a conservative investor, U.S. Treasury securities may be your type of investment. You can now purchase Treasury securities over the Internet or by telephone.

The Internet purchase program is called, *Buy Direct!,* and you can submit a noncompetitive bid (which I explain later in this section) via the Internet (or by calling 800-943-6864). The price of the security is debited from the account you previously designated to receive Treasury Direct payments. (This is called a Treasury Direct account. I show you how to open your own account later in this section.) Tender forms and payments may also be submitted electronically through your financial institution or government securities broker or dealer.

Opening your account

Treasury Direct is a book-entry system that is managed by the Federal government. After you open a Treasury Direct account, you can purchase bonds from the government without a broker. Treasury Direct provides a statement of account whenever you make a change to your account (for example, when you buy more Treasury securities, sell your securities, or reinvest earnings).

If you purchase Treasury securities directly from the Federal government, they are issued in a book-entry form that is held in the Bureau of the Public Debt's Treasury Direct system (www.publicdebt.treas.gov/sec/sectrdir.htm). The securities are issued to your individual account. In contrast, if you purchase Treasury securities using a broker, they are issued in a commercial book-entry form, which means that the securities are held in the name of your broker or dealer. The broker then maintains records of each individual investor's Treasury securities.

You can see your account balance online at www.publicdebt.treas.gov/sec/sectdes.htm. Just go to Virtual Lobby, type in your Treasury Direct account number, and click Enter the Lobby.

Maintenance charges are $25 per year for each $100,000 in your account. Treasury Direct provides information about how to open and maintain a Treasury Direct Investor Account at www.publicdebt.treas.gov/sec/secacct.htm.

 You can request that an account be set up before you purchase your first Treasury security by submitting a New Account Request form. Just print the form located at www.publicdebt.treas.gov/sec/secform1. Fill in all the required information and mail the form to your local Federal Reserve Bank. Don't send any cash; it's free. For the address, go to www.publicdebt.treas.gov/sec/secfrb.htm, type in your zip code and press the Locate button. In the next screen, you'll see the local address of your nearest Federal Reserve Bank.

Now you can download the application form, print it, fill in the blanks, and then mail the completed form to your local Federal Reserve Bank. (You need Adobe Acrobat Reader 4.0 to display and print the form. You can download the free Acrobat Reader program from www.adobe.com.)

How to buy

Figure 13-2 shows a calendar of upcoming auction dates at the Bureau of the Public Debt (www.publicdebt.treas.gov/of/ofaucrt.htm). The Bureau of the Public Debt provides a constantly updated three-month calendar of tentative auction dates (www.treas.gov/domfin/auction.htm) so that you can plan ahead. Official auction dates are announced about seven days before the securities are offered.

Treasury bills, notes, and bonds are sold through competitive and noncompetitive bidding:

- **Noncompetitive bid:** You agree to accept a rate determined by the auction, and in return you're guaranteed that your bid successfully results in purchasing the security you desire. Most individual investors submit noncompetitive bids. Noncompetitive bids from individual investors can't exceed $5 million for the same offering of Treasury notes or bonds.

- **Competitive bid:** For a bill auction, the investor submits an offer — or *tender* — specifying a discount rate to two decimal places (for example 5.12 percent). For a note or bond auction, the investor submits a tender specifying a yield to three decimal places (for example, 5.123 percent). Common fractions may not be used. If the bid falls within the range accepted at the auction, the investor is awarded the security. If the bid is at the high rate or yield, the investor may not be awarded the full amount bid. Most financial institutions (banks, insurance companies, brokerages, and so on) submit competitive bids.

You can obtain all the order forms, instructions, auction dates, auction results, and other related information you'll need to purchase Treasury securities, at the Bureau of the Public Debt Web site (www.publicdebt.treas.gov). You can download and print forms, send e-mail requests for forms, or have forms mailed to you. This site also provides details about how to purchase Treasury securities without a broker (a great money-saving feature for investors).

Don't let the jargon of Treasury securities make purchasing seem more complex than it really is. A noncompetitive bid is similar to a market order (you definitely get the security, but you don't know what price you receive), whereas a competitive bid is similar to a limit order (you know what price you get, but you don't know whether you definitely get the security).

You may want to consider accumulating cash in a money market account (for any purpose other than education). The interest rate paid is often as good as or better than an investment in Treasuries, and you have much more liquidity (you don't have to wait three months to five years to get your money back).

U.S. Treasury Borrowing - Auction Calendars - Microsoft Internet Explorer

File   Edit   View   Favorites   Tools   Help

Back   Forward   Stop   Refresh   Home   Search   Favorites   History   Mail   Edit   Discuss

Address | http://www.treas.gov/domfin/auction.htm | Go

Auction Calendars

TENTATIVE SCHEDULE OF ISSUES TO BE ANNOUNCED AND AUCTIONED IN MAY 2000 [1]

Monday	Tuesday	Wednesday	Thursday	Friday
1	2	3	4	5
8	9 Auction 5 year note [2]	10 Auction 10 year note [2]	11	12
15	16	17 Announce 2 year note	18	19
22	23	24 Auction 2 year note [3]	25 Announce 52 week	26

Done   Internet

Figure 13-2:
To find out about upcoming auctions, visit the Bureau of the Public Debt.

Tendering your offer

Select the issue you want to bid on and then complete the correct *Treasury Direct Tender Information* form at www.publicdebt.treas.gov/sec/secform.htm. Finish the form by making either a competitive or noncompetitive bid, which is called a *tender*. State how many securities you want to buy, the maturity term, and include full payment payable to your local Federal Reserve Bank. You can make payments by direct deposit, certified check, matured Treasury obligation, personal check for notes and bonds, and U.S. currency if presented in person.

When completing the Treasury Direct Tender Information form, you must decide whether you want to send in a competitive or a noncompetitive bid. (Institutional investors always submit competitive bids.) A noncompetitive tender specifies the discount rate with two decimal places that you're willing to pay (for example, 6.12 percent). If your bid is too high and the issue is purchased at a lower rate, you may not get the securities you want.

Detailed directions about how to complete the Treasury Direct Tender Information form and acceptable ways to pay for the Treasuries are available at the Bureau of the Public Debt (www.publicdebt.treas.gov/sec/secform1.htm#buying).

Cashing in or rolling over your Treasury securities

Treasury bills mature in 13, 26, or 52 weeks. When your Treasury bill matures, you have two choices. First, you can roll over your investment and reinvest in the face value of another T-bill (with the same or a different maturity). For information about reinvesting, see the appropriate form at `www.publicdebt.treas.gov/sec/secform1.htm#reinvest`. Second, you can cash in and have the proceeds deposited to your Treasury Direct account. For example, say that your $15,000 Treasury bill with a maturity term of 13 weeks matures. You can elect to reinvest in another $15,000 Treasury bill for 13, 26, or 52 weeks (with a noncompetitive bid). If you do not elect to reinvest your $15,000 at maturity, your Treasury Direct Account is credited with $15,000, or a check for $15,000 is sent to your home.

Selling your Treasury securities

The good news is that you can sell your Treasury securities before they mature, with or without a broker. The first approach is to sell your Treasury securities through a broker. The second approach is to let the federal government sell your Treasury securities. The bad news is that both approaches cost you extra money.

If you need to sell your Treasury security, the Federal government will help you. You can sell directly through Treasury Direct — you don't need a broker. The government will get quotes from different dealers, and you get the best price offered. The fee is $34 for each security sold. You can even have the proceeds from the sale of the Treasury security deposited directly to your checking account, less the transaction fee. For additional information, see `www.publicdebt.treas.gov/sec/secform1.htm#selling`.

In a secondary market for Treasury securities, investors can sell Treasury securities before they mature through a brokerage. For instance, assume that you purchased a six-month Treasury bill. Three months later, you decide to sell. Other investors will purchase the Treasury bill at a slightly higher price than what you paid because it is closer to maturity. Brokerage fees vary for these services, so shop around for the best price.

You can also purchase Treasury securities in the secondary market — that is, through your full-service or online brokerage — if you want to have securities (money) come due on a specific date to meet a financial objective.

Online sources for more information

Information provided by the government is written in a way that makes purchasing Treasuries seem more difficult and complex than it really is, but don't get discouraged. For more information about understanding and purchasing Treasury securities, refer to the following online resources:

✔ **Bondtrac** (www.bondtrac.com) is for professionals, but provides some information for individual investors. Investors can view a descriptive list (no ratings, issuer or yield information) of around 8,000 government agency, municipal, and corporate bonds that can be purchased from a brokerage.

✔ **GovPX** (www.govpx.com) provides some quotations of U.S. government securities in the Daily Treasury Report. Additionally, the report includes statistics on trading volume and is updated several times a day. Subscribers get in-depth information such as access to active lists of Treasury bonds, notes, and bills with each financial instrument's account (CUSIP — Computerized Uniform Securities Identification Program) number, coupon rate, and maturity date. Lists include buyers' bid prices, sellers' asking prices, changes from the prior trading day, and yields. End-of-the day quotes are delivered by e-mail ($200 per month).

✔ **PC Trader** (www.pctrader.com) offers a GovPX full feed package that includes U.S. Treasury and Government markets. Subscribers have full access to GovPX quotes ($165 per month) that are used by many professional traders.

✔ **Quote.com Street Pricing** (www.quote.com) provides quotes for Treasury securities and government agency securities. Specific information includes interest rates and spreads, quotes on active Treasuries, and quotes on government agency securities. Cost is $9.95 per month for the basic service.

✔ **Smart Money** (www.smartmoney.com), shown in Figure 13-3, provides useful information about bonds. At the home page click the Bonds tab for key interest rates, bond market updates, a bond calculator, and a glossary. Educational articles include bond strategies, short-term bond investing, bond allocation, and a bond primer.

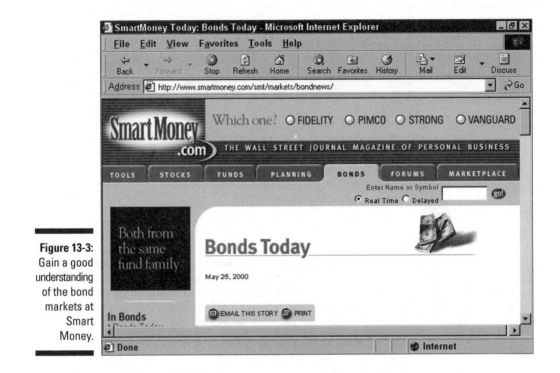

Figure 13-3:
Gain a good understanding of the bond markets at Smart Money.

Fraud alert! Some fraudsters employ scams that involve the renting or leasing of U.S. Treasury securities. Usually, the securities offered don't exist (the offer is for bearer securities in an amount that exceeds the amount that remains outstanding on the bearer form for a particular security) or are not owned by the party making the offer (the securities do not exist or are owned by someone else who is not aware of this transaction). If you are approached by one of these offers, ask the individual to produce the securities or otherwise prove ownership. He or she will be unable to do so, and will offer excuses such as "they are frozen at my bank," "a wealthy philanthropist has assigned them to us to assign to others for infrastructure or humanitarian purposes in third world countries and wishes to remain anonymous," or "bank secrecy laws of this country (often Great Britain, Greece, or South Africa) prevent such a verification." Additionally, the scam artist, in an effort to fool you, will misuse Public Debt forms as evidence of ownership, misuse CUSIP numbers as evidence of ownership, and claim that the scam has been certified by a well-known or official organization.

The Math of Bonds

The bond market is dominated by institutional investors (insurance companies, pension funds, mutual funds) that account for 80 to 85 percent of all trading. Individual investors tend to purchase municipal and corporate bonds because of their lower denominations (around $1,000) and tax-exempt features. However, the impact of individual investors can also be felt through the purchases of mutual funds that specialize in bonds.

The following section shows the valuation process of bonds and the relationship of interest rate changes to the value of bonds. I provide several easy-to-use approaches that take the mystery out of determining your bond yield.

Calculating bond values

A bond issued by a corporation is called a *debt instrument*. The bond states how the debt holder (investor) is repaid. Generally, these terms are normal debt arrangements. The borrower makes interest payments and then pays the principal at a predetermined date. Several issues make bonds complicated, such as provisions to convert the bonds to common stocks at a predetermined stock value, or terms that allow the bond issuer to retire the bond before maturity.

Treasury securities and government agency and municipal bonds are valued in the same way as corporate bonds. However, this doesn't show the entire picture. Treasury securities are subject to Federal taxes but are exempt from state and local taxes. Government agency securities are generally taxable for Federal, state, and local purposes, but some exceptions exist. Municipal bonds are generally tax-free (from Federal, state, and local taxes). Therefore, when you value corporate bonds, the calculated rate of return is somewhat overstated because it doesn't take the impact of taxes into consideration.

The value of the bond is based on the investor's assessment of the bond's value. The receipt of future interest payments, the repayment of principal, and the credit rating or riskiness of the bond usually temper these assessments. You aren't obligated to hold a bond until maturity, and bonds are traded freely in the marketplace.

Calculating the value of a bond involves determining the present value of the interest payments and the eventual recovery of the principal. *Present value* means discounting the future cash flow to calculate how much you're willing to pay today for these future receipts.

At times, calculating the yield on bonds can seem more complicated than it really is. For example, if you purchase a one-year Treasury bill for $9,500, and redeem it in 12 months at full face value ($10,000), your gain is $500 (subject to Federal income tax but exempt from state and local taxes). To determine your yield, use the following formula if your holding period is one year:

(Face Value – Price) / Price = Annual Return

($10,000 – $9,500) / $9,500 = 0.0526 or 5.26%

See the section "The easy way to value your bond returns" later in this chapter, where I show you how to calculate the yield for a bond that has a maturity term greater than one year.

Creating yield curves

A yield curve is a diagram that illustrates the relationship of bond yields to maturities on a specific day. Yield curves can be used to decide which type of bond is best for your financial objectives. Bond yields and maturities are posted daily at the Wall Street Journal Interactive Web site (www.wsj.com).

On a piece of graph paper, on the horizontal axis, plot the maturities of Treasury securities from left to right starting with the shortest maturity of 30 days to the longest maturity of 30 years. Then, on the vertical axis, plot the yield of each Treasury security. Next, connect the dots to make a yield curve. See the curve descriptions in the following list to find out what your results indicate:

- ✔ If the short-term rates are higher than the long-term rates, the yield curve becomes *inverted,* or has a downward swing to it, which tells you that this situation tends to be *bearish* for the market. In this situation, monetary policy is likely to be tight and the Federal Reserve is pushing up short-term rates.

- ✔ If the short-term rates are lower than the long-term rates, the yield curve is *positive,* or has an upward swing to it, which usually indicates that investors are willing to tie up their money in long-term commitments to reap higher rewards.

- ✔ If the short-term rates and the long-term rates are the same (or nearly the same), the yield curve appears to be flat, like a line.

The Internet provides many sources for yield curves. Here are a few examples of what you can find on the Internet:

- ✔ **Bloomberg.com: U.S. Treasuries** (www.bloomberg.com/markets/c13.html) offers yield curves and statistics on Treasury bills, notes, bonds and inflation-indexed Treasuries.

- ✔ **The Federal Reserve Board** (http://www.bog.frb.fed.us/releases) provides all the statistics and historical data you'll need to plot yield curves.

- ✔ **Silicon Investor: Tools-Bond Market** (www.siliconinvestor.com/tools/bond_mkt.gsp) has a bond market snapshot that includes statistics and a yield curve of Treasury bills, notes and bonds.

✔ **Stock Research** (www.stockresearch.com) offers a U.S. Treasury yield curve that is updated daily. The Treasury Matrix shows the spread between various maturities of Treasuries. All bonds are compared to Treasuries of similar maturities for relative value. You may be interested in the commentary that accompanies the Treasury yield curve.

The yield curve approach also works for other types of bonds, such as government agency, municipal, or corporate bonds. Remember that you only need to include bonds with the same level of risk, such as all AA-rated corporate bonds, in the curve.

The easy way to value your bond returns

Bonds are often quoted at prices that differ from their stated (or *par*) values, a situation that can be troublesome for investors who want to determine the yield of the bond. Many ways exist to calculate the yield value of a bond. In my opinion, the *approximate yield to maturity* method provides the easiest way to determine a bond's current yield.

To calculate the approximate yield to maturity (YTM), you need the following information:

✔ Annual interest payment (I)

✔ Principal payment (P)

✔ Price of the bond (B)

✔ Number of years to maturity (M)

Using these values, you calculate the approximate yield to maturity by using the following formula:

$$YTM = (I + ((P - B) \div M)) \div ((0.6 \times B) + (0.4 \times P))$$

For example, what is the yield to maturity on a 12-year, 7 percent annual coupon, $1,000 par value bond that sells at a discount for $942.21? Here are the calculations:

$$YTM = (70 + (($1,000 - $942.21) \div 12)) \div ((0.6 \times $942.21) + (0.4 \times $1,000))$$

$$YTM = (70 + (57.79 \div 12)) \div (565.33 + 400)$$

$$YTM = (70 + 4.82) \div 965.33$$

$$YTM = 74.82 \div 965.33$$

$$YTM = 0.0775$$

$$YTM = 7.75\%$$

Let the Internet do the math

FICALC (www.ficalc.com) is a free, online, fixed-income calculator. At the home page, just click Use Calculator. Select the security market by choosing from a list (U.S. Treasury Securities, U.S. Agency Securities, U.S. Municipal Securities, U.S. Corporate Securites, and so on). Click Select Market and then select the security type. For example, if you selected U.S. Treasuries, you would then select from a list that includes such items as bills, notes (fixed coupon), and bonds (fixed coupon). Make your selection and click Select Structure. Enter bond-specific data such as the price of the security, issue date, maturity, and settlement dates (if you plan to sell before maturity, enter your personal sell date). To determine the yield on your proposed investment, click Calculate.

If your required rate of return is 8 percent, you should *not* purchase the bond because the approximate yield to maturity (7.75 percent) doesn't meet your financial requirements (an 8 percent return). Conversely, if the bond has a return that is equal to or *greater* than 8 percent, the bond meets your objectives and is a "buy" candidate.

Note: If the value of the bond is discounted (that is, sells below its par value — in this case, below $1,000), the yield to maturity (YTM) is greater than the 7 percent coupon rate.

Trading Bonds Online

Of the big six online brokerages, Ameritrade (www.Ameritrade.com), Charles Schwab (www.schwab.com), E*Trade (www.etrade.com), Fidelity (www.fidelity.com), Datek (www.datek.com), and Waterhouse (www.waterhouse.com), only Datek does not trade bonds online. Many online bond brokerages are designed for professional bond traders. However, a few are beginning to cater to the needs of individual investors.

Often, investors can increase the performance of their bonds from purchasing the right securities at the lowest price by viewing a wider selection of the fixed-income investment candidates. Some online bond brokerages specialize in certain types of fixed-income products. Other online bond brokerages provide access to thousands of securities in all the major fixed product areas such as bank certificates of deposit, Treasury securities, government agency, municipal, and corporate bonds, and mortgage-backed securities.

Here are a few examples of online bond brokerages:

- ✔ **Bond Agent** (www.bondagent.com) provides thousands of bond offerings. Research tools include news, a learning center, online calculators, book suggestions, and links. Minimum initial cash deposit is $10,000. There are no commissions on Treasury, corporate, agency, or municipal bonds. However, Bond Agent may act as a principal, and markups may be included in the price paid or received on purchases or sales. There is an additional $25 charge for *odd lot orders* (orders for less than 25 bonds).

- ✔ **Bondpage.com** (www.bondpage.com) trades thousands of different types of fixed-rate securities. There is no initial minimum deposit amount, but you must have the amount of your purchase in your account before the firm will execute your trade. There is a flat $50 transaction fee for trades of less than 100 bonds. For trades of 100 bonds or greater, there is no transaction fee, but the firm may act as principal in the transaction.

- ✔ **Direct Notes** (www.direct-notes.com) offers Direct Access Notes (DANs), a straightforward, fixed-income security specifically designed to enable the investing public to purchase original issue corporate bonds directly from major U.S. corporations. DANs are sold directly to individual investors (via their brokers with no transaction fee), usually at par (or an even face value amount; typically $1,000 per note).

- ✔ **Muni Direct** (www.munidirect.com) is an online brokerage that specializes in municipal bonds. Muni Direct offers detail search capabilities, access to new issues, and a large selection of municipal bond offerings. There is even a Muni Wizard that can guide you in finding municipal bonds that meet your investment needs. This firm has no initial minimum deposit. Commissions or markups are no more than $5 per bond ($1,000 face value).

- ✔ **Trade Web** (www.tradebonds.com) offers thousands of live corporate, municipal, government, and mortgage-backed bonds as well as FDIC-insured CDs — all available for online execution. You'll also find investing tools and news, financial calculators, an independent Treasury ticker, and e-mail notification of Federal government policy actions and daily and weekly market wrap-ups. There is a $25,000 minimum initial deposit. Trade Web may act as a principal, and markups may be included in the price paid or received on purchases or sales.

You can open a Treasury Direct account (www.treasurydirect.gov/sec/secform1.htm) and trade Treasuries online without a broker.

A hot, no-fuss bond strategy

More Americans have invested in bonds than in any other security. Some of the advantages of bonds are that they offer regular interest payments that are higher than money market accounts, they can be tax-exempt, and they offer a way to stay ahead of inflation.

Some of the limitations of investing in bonds are interest rate risk (if interest rates go up, the value of your bond goes down) and credit rating risk (if your bond gets downgraded, its value goes down). Additionally, unless you own a Treasury security, your principal investment isn't guaranteed by the government the way bank deposits are protected by the Federal Deposit Insurance Corporation (FDIC).

Tucker Anthony, an investment counselor, suggests one way to reduce your exposure to interest rate risk. He suggests creating a *bond ladder*. Each rung of the bond ladder consists of a different bond maturity. For example, the first rung of the bond ladder may consist of bonds that mature in one year; the second rung may consist of bonds that mature in two years, and so on, for ten years.

The yield of the ten-year bond ladder is less than 20-year bonds, but the ladder provides diversification. As each rung matures, you can reinvest the funds in the same or better ways to conserve your principal. The benefits of this approach are some protection from declining interest rates and low maintenance on your part.

If this bond ladder scheme seems too complex, you can always invest in a bond mutual fund. But keep in mind that bond mutual funds rarely "beat the market" and tend to have more risk than individual bonds. Some aggresively managed bond funds include risky investing strategies that can be a real gamble. On the other hand, one of the advantages of a bond mutual fund is that you often get to own a share of bonds that are $50,000, $100,000, or $250,000 each — something that you may not be able to achieve as an individual investor.

Part III
Expanding Your Investment Opportunities

In this part . . .

*I*n this part, you find out how you can invest in foreign securities without leaving your computer. You also discover how to reduce the purchase costs of buying your favorite stocks by using direct purchase and dividend reinvestment plans. You see the benefits and hazards of online investing in initial public offerings (IPOs), and you find out how you can reduce your portfolio's risk by making online international investments. You also discover how you can take advantage of the latest online portfolio management tools available.

Chapter 14

Going International Online

*T*his chapter explains how international investing can assist you in diversifying your portfolio beyond the usual alternatives. You discover how you can find indexes that indicate those economies that are not moving in the same direction as the United States, and how you can use this information to reduce the risk of your personal portfolio. When you decide which market meets your investment criteria, check out the country's political, market, and inflation risks at the Web sites suggested in this chapter.

This chapter also describes the many ways you can make foreign investments. You may be surprised to discover that even though you should be a specialist in foreign securities to invest directly in an international company in its foreign market, even beginning investors can purchase American Depository Receipts (ADRs). This chapter explains how ADRs, which represent foreign equities, have the look of domestic stocks and can be purchased online through your electronic brokerage. You can even purchase ADRs online without a broker.

This chapter goes on to explore how you can make indirect purchases of international equities by buying international mutual funds or purchasing shares of multinational corporations. Keep in mind that international investments are subject to their own unique kinds of risk. This chapter explains how political risk, currency risk, and other types of risks can quickly reduce your profits or even wipe out your initial investment.

Taking Advantage of International Opportunities

Almost two-thirds of the world's investment opportunities are beyond U.S. borders. You cannot find the best investment opportunities without considering international equities. As U.S. markets have grown and international companies have prospered, the performance of many international investments has been strong.

International investing offers an opportunity to diversify your portfolio. *Diversification* is defined as the lack of concentration in any one item. In other words, a portfolio composed of many different securities is diversified. Diversification can mean spreading your personal assets among different types of investments (such as stocks, bonds, and mutual funds) so that returns do not depend on the performance of any one type of investment. Diversification also can include diversifying your assets among different sectors, such as technology and consumer products. In addition, you can diversify your portfolio by investing in international companies, either directly or indirectly, as I explain in this chapter.

The advantage of international diversification is that foreign markets often do not move in the same direction as U.S. markets at any point in time. Consequently, portfolios with stocks from many countries may have less volatility than a portfolio of just domestic stocks. Additionally, the returns on your foreign securities could be higher than those of your domestic investments.

However, investing in foreign securities is not a sure fire way to avoid investment risk. In the market crash of 1987, about 19 of 23 foreign markets declined more than 20 percent. (A crash is usually defined as a decline of 33 percent.) This decline was considered unusual because of the low degree of correlation between the historical returns of different countries.

In general, the benefits of international investing are

- ✔ **More investment opportunities:** Studying the market indexes of foreign markets may provide you with insight about new investment opportunities.

- ✔ **Greater diversification safety:** Not investing all your personal assets in one type of security or industry sector may *bullet proof* your portfolio, insulating you from domestic market volatility.

- ✔ **Higher overall returns:** Global markets frequently do not move in the same direction as the U.S. market. If the U.S. market is down, a foreign market may be up.

You may want to consider investing 10 percent of your portfolio in foreign securities. Then use dollar-cost averaging (see Chapter 3 for details) to increase your international holdings to a risk level that allows you to sleep at night. Keep in mind that international investing has its own unique risks.

Getting Started with Online International Quotes and Indexes

Stock indexes or averages are sets of stocks that are grouped to make a composite index. Stocks are selected and given a weighting relative to the other stocks in the group. Comparing stock indexes from different countries around the world is a good place to start your search for international investment candidates. By looking at the price and percentage change of an index, you can gain a good idea of which markets are moving in which direction. You can use this information to compare markets and spot investment opportunities.

Keep in mind how stocks are ranked in the different indexes. For example, the Dow Jones Industrial Average is a *price-weighted average*. The higher the sales price of a particular stock, the greater the impact on the average. In contrast, the Standard & Poor's 500 Index is a *value-weighted index*. Each company is weighted in the index by its own total market value as a percentage of the total market value of all the firms in the index. In this case, the higher the number of shares outstanding, the bigger the impact on the index. For example, if two companies have stock selling at the same price but one company has more outstanding shares, the company with the most outstanding shares has a bigger impact on the index when the price of its stock changes.

For online international quotes and indexes, visit the following Web sites:

✔ **Bloomberg.com** (www.bloomberg.com), shown in Figure 14-1, provides international coverage by geographic area (Asia, Australia, Brazil, France, Germany, Italy, Japan, Latin America, Spain, and the U.K.). At the home page, look for International Sites, scroll through the text box until you find the area you are interested in, and then click Go. At the geographic location you are interested in, click Markets for World Indices. Additionally, you can get news, currency rates, and international interest rates.

✔ **CBS MarketWatch** (cbs.marketwatch.com/data/gfa.htx) offers information on international indexes, a key rate snapshot, and non-U.S. stocks — that is, American Depository Receipts, or ADRs. (I discuss ADRs in the section "Buying ADRs Is an Easy Solution," later in this chapter.) You'll find columns on international market activity such as the ADR Report, London Calling, Euro Markets on the Move, and Work Markets, in addition to market data on foreign stocks and funds.

✔ **DataStream** (www.datastream.com) includes daily updated stock indexes for 34 countries. Get end-of-the-day quotes for 32,000 stocks at www1.datastream.com/quotes/equity1.htm.

✔ ESPIN (www.espin.net/markets) provides information about global markets, U.S. markets, a forum, chat, links, and other information. It also provides charts that can visually assist you in evaluating the trends of global markets.

✔ European Investor (www.europeaninvestor.com) requires your free registration for the following services: cost-free real-time equity prices across major European and U.S. stock exchanges, a multicurrency portfolio tracker, free daily newsletters about European markets, and coverage of the European high technology markets (Euro.NM, Neuer Markt, Nouveau Marche, and Easdaq).

✔ Morgan Stanley (www.msci.com) offers data and comparisons of different indexes. Index coverage is by sectors and industries, regions, and countries. This site also offers alternative index calculations, news about sectors and industries, real-time indexes, and style and assets class indexes.

✔ Stock Smart (www.stocksmart.com) provides stock quotes for 47 countries. You'll find continuously updated marketplace information. This site offers updates from major trading exchanges and interactive charting of the world's major indices. You'll also find real-time rates on global currencies corporate earnings, announcements, and filings. Real-time subscriptions are $19.95 per month, or $215.46 per year. Wireless real-time service with alerts is $25.59 per month, or $280.26 per year. Delayed service is $12.95 per month, or $139.86 per year.

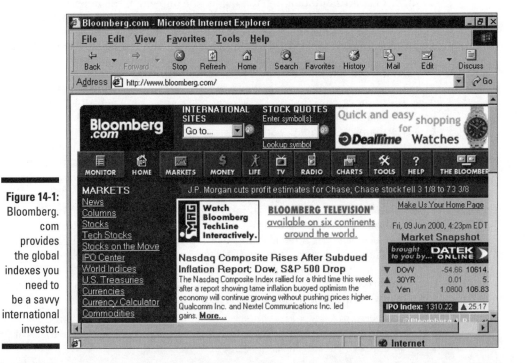

Figure 14-1: Bloomberg. com provides the global indexes you need to be a savvy international investor.

Wonder if you might be overlooking the next Cisco somewhere around the world? Intltrader.com (`www.intltrader.com/winvestor/global_co`) provides a listing of worldwide companies that are comparable to the 30 companies listed in the Dow Jones Industrial Average. Compare key financial ratios and decide whether another country has the next Home Depot or Intel.

Gathering International News and Research

The political environment of your international investment is important. The Internet can assist you in monitoring and researching your current investments and investment candidates. For example, you can track breaking international news stories through all the online major news organizations, including ABC News (`www.abcnews.com`), CNNfn (`www.cnnfn.com`), CNBC (`www.cnbc.com`), and CBS MarketWatch (`www.cbsmarketwatch.com`). Online magazines and newspapers such as *Newsweek* (`www.newsweek.com`), the *International Herald Tribune* (`www.iht.com`), and *The Economist* (`www.economist.com`) provide timely analysis of the latest international news.

The Internet even provides international investor Web sites for specific geographic locations and hard-to-locate information that can assist you in your research. Here are a few examples:

- ✔ **CentralEurope.com** (`www.centraleurope.com`) includes general and business news, stocks and currencies updates, news from Central Europe Review and BBC Monitoring, country information, discussion boards, chats, and classifieds. Get information about the Czech Republic, Hungary, Poland, Romania, Slovakia, Slovenia, and the Balkans.

- ✔ **Economist Intelligence Unit Views Wire** (`www.viewswire.com`) provides daily country analysis for decision makers. Just click the name of the country you are researching. For each country, get the following information: basic data; quarterly economic indicators; briefings on the economy, industry, and politics; and country forecasts.

- ✔ **The Emerging Markets Companion** (`www.emgmkts.com`) has an extensive research section that includes market strategies, international economic indicators, international laws and regulations, databases, country profiles, and background information. It also has asset prices, news, global markets, and a site search feature.

✔ **The International Economics Study Center** (`www.internationalecon.com`), shown in Figure 14-2, requires free registration for reports on international trade theory and policy analysis, international finance theory and policy analysis, and news from the International Center for Trade and Sustainable Development.

✔ **Investor Relations Asia** (`www.irasia.com`) has a search engine that makes finding Asian ADRs easy (you can search by symbol, name, country, or industry). At listed companies, you'll find company profiles, links to corporate home pages, and contact information. You'll find earnings releases, important announcements, and more.

✔ **LatInvestor** (`www.latinvestor.com`) provides country, industry, and company research reports, stock recommendations, and an extensive link directory. Report samples and some short reports are free. Prices for other reports range from $10 for 1–5 pages, up to $150 for 60-plus pages.

✔ **Singapore Business Times** (`business-times.asia1.com.sg`) provides Asian financial news, which includes Singapore, Malaysia, Southeast Asia, East Asia, and South Asia. You can compare companies and markets, and access regional views and opinions.

Figure 14-2:
Keep up-to-date on international economic issues at the International Economics Study Center.

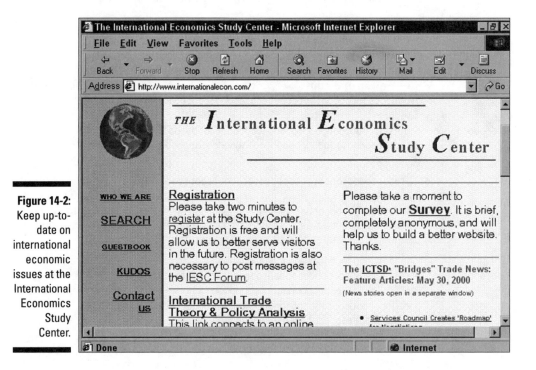

Online Trading Abroad

If you are traveling internationally, do not stop monitoring your online investment accounts. Additionally, you can trade stocks online with your current online brokerage. (If you haven't selected an online brokerage, see Chapter 4.) Before you hit the road, you have to do some preparation. You need to do three things:

1. **Make certain that your Internet service provider (ISP) has an international connection or counterpart. (Recently, when I traveled to Europe, the "international" part of my ISP was in a dispute with its U.S. partner, and I had to sign up with another ISP.)**

2. **Purchase and install an international modem card for your laptop computer.**

3. **Get telephone adapters (just like the electrical adapters you'll bring along) for each country you plan to visit.**

Test each foreign city's local dial-up number from your home. Using your travel itinerary as a guide, write down the names of the cities and countries you plan to visit. Refer to your ISP for the local dial-up telephone number for each city. Dial the number and make certain the connection to your laptop computer works. If anything doesn't work, it is easier to fix the problem before you leave home.

If for some reason you can't get your online connection to work, you may want to consider opening an account while abroad. London City Brokers (www.londoncitybrokers.com) has a prescreened list of online brokerages that provide good service, speedy order execution and reliability, good back-office administration, after-sales support, and helpfulness at the initial inquiry and account opening stage. (Don't be surprised to find the European counterparts to U.S. online brokerages such as Charles Schwab, E*Trade, and TD Waterhouse.)

E*Trade UK and E*Trade France are two different operations. E*Trade UK (www.etrade.co.uk), which specializes in U.K. and other European securities, trades in Pounds. E*Trade France (www.cpretrade.com/newhtml/index.htm), which requires your familiarity with the French language, focuses on French and other European securities and trades in Francs.

Methods of Making Foreign Investments

The most obvious, but least likely, approach to participating in foreign investments is directly purchasing shares of a firm in its own foreign market through a foreign online broker or overseas branch of an American online brokerage. This approach may be the source of numerous problems for an inexperienced online international investor. These problems can be summarized into three areas: administrative, tax, and information gathering.

Administration troubles

Sometimes, the administration rules in foreign countries differ from the rules in the United States. For example, in the Swiss and Mexican stock markets, investors must settle their accounts one day after a transaction. In London, you have a two-week settlement procedure. And in France, you may have several different settlement dates depending upon the securities you purchase. Additionally, transaction costs (fees and commissions) may be higher than in the United States. For example, mutual funds with foreign equities usually have higher fees and expenses than funds that invest in stocks of U.S. companies, in addition to difficulties with stock delivery and capital-transfers.

Tax problems

Some foreign countries levy withholding taxes of 15 to 30 percent on dividends or interest that is paid to nonresidents. You may need to hire a tax accountant to secure an exemption or rebate on part of the foreign withholding tax. This time-consuming, costly paper-shuffling may reduce your net returns.

Information difficulties

The SEC closely regulates U.S. equities. For example, American companies have to send the SEC reports of their activities every 90 days. If something extraordinary happens during this 90-day period, the publicly traded firm has to send in a report explaining what's happening. Additionally, all financial reports have to meet established accounting standards, and publicly traded companies must provide investors with audited annual reports.

Foreign investments standards may not be this rigorous. Additionally, you may encounter a language problem. Even with English-speaking countries, you may be in for a few surprises. For example, British financial statements are upside-down when compared to U.S. statements. Fixed assets are listed first, and current assets are listed last, as opposed to U.S. financial statements, which list current assets first and fixed assets last.

Buying ADRs Is an Easy Solution

Only the most sophisticated money managers tackle the problems associated with investing directly in a firm in its own foreign market. (However, with the consolidation of many of the world's exchanges, this may change in the near future.) The solution for individual investors is to purchase shares in foreign firms in the United States through American Depository Receipts (ADRs). ADRs enable American investors to acquire and trade foreign securities denominated in U.S. dollars without concern for the differing administration procedures, such as settlement time, that usually accompany trading in foreign markets.

ADRs were first introduced in 1927 in response to a law passed in Britain. Two banks are generally involved in maintaining and listing ADRs on a U.S. exchange:

- An investment bank establishes an ADR by arranging to buy the shares on a foreign market, and issuing the ADRs on the U.S. markets.

- A depository bank, such as the Bank of New York (www.bankofny.com), handles the issuance and cancellation of ADR certificates backed by shares based on investor orders, as well as other services provided to an issuer of ADRs, but is not involved in the selling of ADRs.

ADRs are U.S. dollar-denominated, negotiable instruments issued in the United States by a depository bank representing ownership in foreign securities. ADRs are generally listed with the letter 'a' after the firm's name. You can find ADRs on the New York Stock Exchange (www.nyse.com) and NASDAQ (www.nasdaq.com). You can trade ADRs online just like any other type of security. Dividends are paid in dollars, and annual company reports are in English. Online brokerage commission rates are usually the same as for any other type of security.

You can purchase ADRs without a broker. For details, see NetStock Direct at www.netstockdirect.com. At the home page, just click International, and you'll discover almost 400 ADRs you can purchase without paying a brokerage commission.

The risks of international investments

For the most part, ADRs look and feel pretty much like any other stock. However, although investing in ADRs may be convenient, it is not risk-free. Keep in mind the risk/return trade-off. Generally, the higher risks associated with ADRs include country or political risk, and changes in currency valuations.

Country and political risk

Many foreign governments operate in unstable environments. Some countries may be subject to civil wars or revolutions. The danger of nationalization (the government takes control of a company you have invested in) can limit the capital flows to foreign investors. Countries that cannot meet their foreign debt obligations are subject to political problems. Additionally, is inflation under control? Are there any trade barriers? Do rulers succeed one another without civil war or revolution?

Exchange rate risk

If the currency exchange rate changes for your investments, you may earn less or more than you expect. If the value of the U.S. dollar weakens relative to the foreign currency, the foreign currency increases in value. If the U.S. dollar gets stronger, the foreign investment decreases in value. One way to avoid this situation is to purchase financial futures that guarantee you a return if the value of the foreign currency decreases in value relative to the U.S. dollar.

Currency devaluation may be the biggest risk for international investing. Investing in a foreign equity from a country that has a strong currency is better than investing in a foreign equity that has promises of big gains but an unstable economy or a high likelihood of political upheaval.

Online ADR resources and research

The Internet can assist you in researching the company profiles of foreign companies, and provide lists of companies that offer ADRs. Here are several examples of what you can find online:

- ✔ **ADR.com** (www.adr.com) is sponsored by J.P. Morgan and offers regional, industry, and company-specific data, an economic calendar, commentary, and timely analyses.

- ✔ **The Bank of New York** (www.bankofny.com/adr) provides a complete listing of all Depository Receipts, including issuer name, exchange, ticker symbol, ratio, and effective date of issue. The list is available alphabetically, geographically, and by industry classification. You can view the directory online, or download the directory as an Excel spreadsheet.

- ✔ **Global Investor** (www.global-investor.com) provides a list of ADRs that are sorted by geographic region (Africa, America, Asia-Pacific, and Europe) and by country (Botswana, Egypt, Ghana, Morocco, South Africa, Zambia, and Zimbabwe).

- ✔ **WorldlyInvestor** (www.worldlyinvestor.com), shown in Figure 14-3, provides commentary, newsletters, information on industry sectors, mutual fund information, a data center (currencies, global indexes, stocks by industry, and U.S. stock ranking), regional information, and other resources. My favorite online tool on this Web site is the ADR screener.

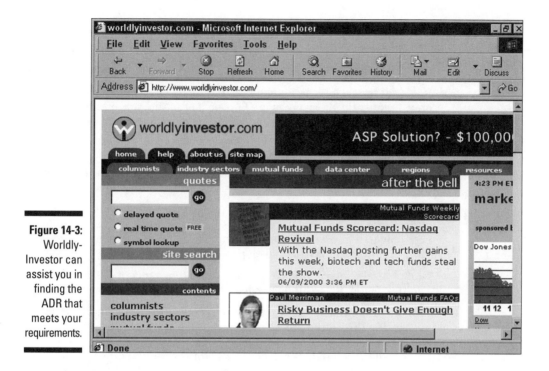

Figure 14-3:
Worldly-
Investor can
assist you in
finding the
ADR that
meets your
requirements.

Indirect Foreign Investing Is a Great Approach

ADRs are a great approach to directly purchasing foreign investments, but they have one drawback. Many ADRs aren't available on the majority of foreign corporations. If you are like many individual investors who want to participate in foreign investments, you'll check out international mutual funds. The advantages of mutual funds are the ability to vary your foreign investments, and professional management so that you don't have to hassle with the many administrative and legal barriers to online international investing.

As with all investments, you'll want to look beyond this quarter's earnings. Check the company's profits relative to competitors and industry standards. Find out if the company's market share is dominant and growing.

International mutual funds

You can choose from many types of international stock funds:

- ✔ **Regional funds:** International funds that focus on a certain geographic area. Frequently, these areas are Europe, Latin America, and the Pacific Basin. The prices of these funds tend to be more volatile than funds that cover a broader area and are more diversified.

- ✔ **Single-country funds:** International funds that are limited to just one country. The fund may include stocks, bonds, and other types of investments. These funds tend to be risky due to their narrow focus.

- ✔ **Emerging-market funds:** International funds that are moving from an agricultural to an industrial economy, or from a government-controlled economy to a free enterprise economy. These funds frequently offer more risk than funds from developed countries.

- ✔ **Global funds:** International funds that are often a mix of U.S. and foreign equities. Often, these funds are geared toward long-term growth.

- ✔ **International funds:** A mutual fund that concentrates on equities that are outside the United States.

Some mutual fund companies select stocks worldwide, and others select stocks from a certain region, country, or emerging market. Additionally, mutual fund companies may select companies that are growing quickly or are value stocks, which money managers are hoping will have a rebound.

Global funds invest in companies wherever they are located, including the United States. International funds focus solely on foreign companies. If you don't have lots of U.S. investments, a global fund may be the way to go. On the other hand, if you already have many U.S. stocks or mutual funds, you may discover that an international fund better meets your requirements for diversification.

International closed-end mutual funds

International closed-end funds provide investors with an opportunity for diversification and professional management. Often, managers have extensive international investment experience and are prepared to deal with administrative problems, which reduces the likelihood of inexperienced individual investor mistakes.

International closed-end funds have a predetermined number of shares and are listed on a major stock exchange. (The number of outstanding shares fluctuates in open-end funds; that's why they are called "open.") Closed-end funds are purchased via a stock exchange or over the counter. In contrast, open-end funds are purchased directly from the fund or fund salesperson.

Like open-end funds, the portfolios of international closed-end mutual funds can be equities, bonds, convertibles, or any combination of these securities. The holdings of the closed-end mutual funds can be geared toward income, capital gains, or a combination of these goals. For example, Korea Fund specializes in the stocks of Korean companies. In contrast, ASA Limited, another international closed-end mutual fund, specializes in the stocks of South African companies involved in gold mining.

Unlike open-end mutual funds, you won't find the closed-end mutual fund company ready to buy your shares if you decide to sell. You have to purchase or sell shares either on a national exchange or over-the-counter, as if the shares were from an individual company. Generally, the net asset value (NAV) of a closed-end fund is valued at a discount or premium. (Open-end funds shares are traded at net asset value.)

Buying shares in multinational companies

Many large U.S. corporations are multinational companies with assets and operations spread throughout the world. Purchasing shares in these companies is an easy way to indirectly participate in the international marketplace. However, some analysts warn that investing in multinationals does not provide the investment benefits that individual investors are seeking because the stock prices of multinational companies tend to move in the same direction as their own country's financial markets.

Investing in international securities is a long-term commitment. Plan on at least a five-year time horizon for your investment. International markets can be more volatile than U.S. markets. Therefore, a long-term commitment and the self-discipline to stay the course is essential to your financial well-being.

Finding International Mutual Funds Online

Investments in international mutual funds enable investors to diversify their portfolios beyond the usual choices. Foreign markets are often influenced by different factors from those that affect domestic markets. Investing in international mutual funds is one way investors can take advantage of international opportunities without having to become specialists in international securities.

Here are a few examples of online sources for international mutual fund information:

- ✔ **I Money** (www.imoney.com/funds/index.shtml) is a Canadian online marketplace for financial services information, planning, and direct online purchasing. The Mutual Fund Centre includes 2,200 mutual funds that can be screened based on your investment objectives.

- ✔ **Morningstar.com** (www.morningstar.com) provides an easy way to select international stock funds. At the home page, go to Fund Finder. In the preset criteria, select Standout Foreign-Stock Funds. You can choose how to view your results (snapshot, performance, and so on). Get the results your way by clicking the data column headings.

- ✔ **Site-by-Site** (www.site-by-site.com) provides closed-end fund profiles and articles, key decision-making performance information on the entire universe of closed-end funds, comparisons of this week's current data to historical averages, and potential buy and sell opportunities. This site also offers information on open-ended mutual funds, divided into regions and countries.

For more information about indirect international investing, check out Vanguard's Plain Talk Series: International Investing at victory.vanguard.com/educ/lib/plain/intntl_invest.html. At the home page, click Education, Planning and Advice. Next click Speeches and Interviews, then click Bogle. You find a list of the former Vanguard chairman John Bogle's speeches. Check out the speech titled, "Globalization of Mutual Funds: Perspective, Prospects, and Trust."

Chapter 15

Looking for the Next Big Thing: IPOs, DPOs, and DRIPs

. . . .

In This Chapter

▶ Evaluating initial public offerings (IPOs)

▶ Getting in early with direct public offerings (DPOs)

▶ Bypassing broker fees to buy shares directly from the company

▶ Using dividend reinvestment plans (DRIPs) to increase your personal wealth

. . . .

*E*veryone has heard stories about someone who got rich by purchasing the right stock at the right time. Looking back at these stories, the type of stock these individuals usually purchased was an initial public offering — called an IPO for short. In this chapter, I show how you can evaluate these types of stocks, determine what their limitations are, locate online sources of IPO news and research, and know which brokers specialize in IPOs or the mutual funds that include this type of financial asset.

An even grander opportunity is a direct public offering, or DPO. Even more speculative than IPOs, shares in these companies are comparable to investments by venture capitalists. This chapter explains the limitations of DPOs, how to purchase DPOs, and where to find online DPO research and information. Additionally, you find out how you can purchase your shares directly from the company, as well as participate in dividend reinvestment plans (DRIPs).

Looking for Investment Opportunities: IPOs

When a company sells stock that trades publicly for the first time, that event is called an *initial public offering* (IPO). These IPO company issuers sell shares to an underwriter. The underwriter, in turn, resells shares to investors at a prearranged offering price. Underwriters often underprice issues by 5 to 10 percent to ensure adequate demand. Generally, shares begin trading immediately on a stock exchange or *over the counter* through the NASDAQ stock market. About one week after issue, due to market efficiency, these excess returns disappear. This indicates that the best time to purchase an IPO is on initial distribution from the underwriting syndicate (which include investment bankers, dealers, and brokers).

Every year, development companies and companies just starting to generate revenues seek additional capital for business expansions. Investors purchase shares so that they can reap the short-term rewards of price swings or share in the long-term prosperity of getting in early for a new investment opportunity.

The investment in an IPO is speculative. These companies often have no proven strategies for success and no track record of marketing success or corporate earnings. Many of these companies crash and burn, and only a few endure to become big-time financial success stories. Keep in mind that for every Intel or Microsoft, 50 companies go bankrupt. (Studies show that about 50 percent of IPO firms are in business five years after their initial offerings.) In other words, the success rate of IPOs is one out of every two.

Understanding the basics of IPOs, performing fundamental research, and knowing how to be an early shareholder can increase your chances of success. Figure 15-1 shows IPO.com (`www.ipo.com`), which provides content and services to investors interested in initial public offerings, private placements, and emerging growth companies. The company provides comprehensive IPO content, including summaries, up-to-date pricing and filings, searchable EDGAR documents, daily columns and free weekly e-mail newsletters through the company's interactive portal, and links to more than 150 financial Web sites.

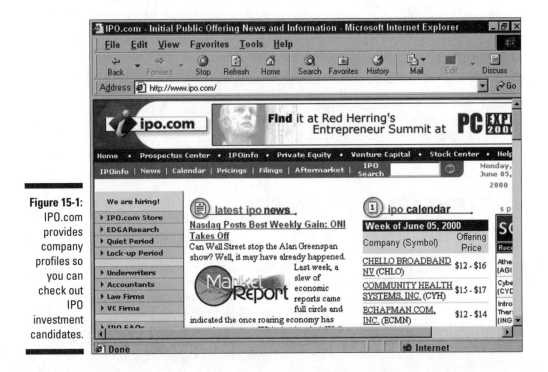

Figure 15-1:
IPO.com provides company profiles so you can check out IPO investment candidates.

Getting the scoop on IPOs

The following guidelines may help you select a winner out of the thousands of companies that have initial public offerings each year:

1. **Read the prospectus.**

   Read the preliminary prospectus *(red herring)* to find out about the company's expected growth. The red herring (a preliminary prospectus that provides information but is not an offer to sell the security and does not include any offering prices) includes a description of the issuer's business, the names and addresses of key corporate officers, the ownership amounts of the key officers, any litigation problems, the company's current capitalization, and how the company plans to use the new funds from the offering.

2. **Perform fundamental analysis.**

   Evaluate the company's financial performance by using fundamental analysis, just like you would for any other stock. (Fundamental analysis is a form of security valuation that seeks to determine the intrinsic value of a stock based on the stock's underlying economics. You then compare the intrinsic value to the asking price. For more details about how to perform a fundamental analysis, see Chapter 11.)

3. **Check out the company's management.**

   Examine the backgrounds of the firm's senior managers. What is their executive management experience and education? Do they have work experience in their current jobs?

4. **Read the mission statement.**

   Investigate the firm's strategy. Is it realistic? How large is the company's market? Who is the competition? If the company plans to gain less than 25 percent of the total market, the firm may not be a long-term success.

5. **Investigate the planned use of funds.**

   Determine why raising a certain amount of capital is so critical to the company's success. If the money is used to pay debt, the company may be headed for problems. A positive sign is using the money for expansion.

6. **Compare IPO prices.**

   Compare expected IPO prices in the red herring to the final prospectus. If the price is higher in the later prospectus, the underwriters are enthusiastic about the offering. Lower prices indicate a lack of interest by the investment community.

7. **Determine whether it's your kind of company.**

   Decide whether you want to own stock in the company you're researching. Maybe it's a great financial opportunity, but you have reservations about the product or service. (For example, do you really want to be part owner in a company that kills frogs?)

8. **Estimate your planned holding period.**

   Decide how long you plan to keep the shares. If the IPO is going to be successful, it will be a better long-term investment than short-term investment because IPO stock prices tend to move up or down with the stock market.

For more information on IPOs, see www.invest-faq.com/articles/ stock-ipo.html. This article includes educational materials about IPOs, the mechanics of IPO offerings, the underwriting process, and IPOs in the real world.

Understanding the limitations of IPOs

If your goal is to create massive wealth or enjoy a comfortable lifestyle, making the most of your money takes time and vigilance. You always need to be on the lookout for new opportunities and new ways to invest your savings. To many online investors, an IPO may seem like the perfect way to get in on the ground floor of a great opportunity for high-flying returns. If the IPO you select is going to be a good investment, then with luck, it could pay off over the long term. Your investment will grow as the company expands and becomes profitable. But a high level of risk exists. IPOs are speculative investments. Many promising firms go bust. You need to consider the limitations of IPOs — for example:

✔ Many IPOs lose much of their value after the first day of trading.

✔ Many positive-looking IPOs are offered only to the "best" clients of large brokerage firms, pension plans, and institutions. However, you can always gain access to an IPO when it starts trading on the secondary market. (The stock begins trading on the secondary market when an investor purchases it from the investment-banking firm in the primary market and begins to sell it on a stock exchange.) The performances of these stocks are similar to the performances of small cap stocks and are very volatile.

✔ After three to six months, IPOs may underperform some small cap stocks. The source of this problem may be employees selling their shares and forcing the stock price to decline.

✔ After three to six months, the popularity of a strong IPO often fades.

Before you invest in an IPO, take the time to learn the terminology, understand the risks, and research investment candidates. Here are several examples of IPO research and education sources you'll find online:

- ✔ **4anything.com** (www.4anything.com) has IPO highlights, information about aftermarket performance, resources and services (IPO education for beginning IPO investors), IPO glossary, stock quotes, and financial news. To access these IPO resources from the site's home page, click Money ☞ Market News ☞ 4IPO.

- ✔ **Hoover's IPO Central** (www.hoovers.com) has all the important facts about a new issue listed on one Web page. At the Hoover's home page, click IPO Central for the latest filings, pricing, views of IPOs, IPO scorecards and statistics, and a handy beginner's guide. Members have access to detailed company profiles and other services. Membership is $14.95 per month, or $124.95 per year.

- ✔ **IPOPros.com** (www.ipopros.com) provides opinions and commentary about the last IPOs. The Web site is divided into sections that include deals expected to price this week, IPO historical data, and answers to IPO Pros FAQs. Subscribers have access to daily updated pricing terms, possible deal pricings for tomorrow's trades, buy suggestions, buy and hold recommendations, deals to avoid, new IPO offerings, and industry search functions. Subscriptions are $25 per month.

- ✔ **Morningstar** (www.morningstar.com) has an IPO Center. At the home page, click Stocks. You'll see the IPO Center, which has links to upcoming IPOs, recent IPO news, a calendar, and IPO FAQs.

- ✔ **Red Herring** (www.redherring.com) provides leading-edge analysis and commentary about the business of technology. With analysis and insider perspective, RedHerring.com explains how technology business news and events affect you, your industry, the economy, the stock market, and your portfolio. The Web site offers news, pre-IPO and IPO company tracking, business and investing information, insight on the latest events and trends, and a free e-mail newsletter called IPO Critic.

The Securities and Exchange Commission provides information about initial public offerings to consumers. To discover more about the underwriting process, hot IPOs, eligibility requirements, and other restrictions, see www.sec.gov/consumer/keyword/tipodiff.html.

Finding IPO news, filings, and pricing on the Internet

You can access various sources for IPO-related news and information on the Internet. A few of these sources follow companies from the initial filing to their performances after the issues become public. Many of these sites provide news, commentary, and quotes. Other information includes recent Securities and Exchange Commission (SEC) filings, scheduled pricing, and registration information. Additionally, some sites include statistics on after-market performance, IPO ratings, and company performance data.

The following Internet sites provide IPO news and alerts:

- ✔ **Alert-IPO!** (www.ostman.com/alert-ipo) provides limited IPO information for free. Subscribers have access to IPO real-time alerts and a large searchable database. The Alert-IPO system searches the SEC's EDGAR database for new issues. The site includes data on more than 1,664 IPO filings and 1,364 underwriters. Search by company, industry, or underwriter. Annual subscriptions are $34.95, and $19.95 for e-mail alerts.

- ✔ **Bloomberg.com, IPO Center** (www.bloomberg.com/markets/ ipocenter.html) gives you IPO headlines and the latest IPO listings from the Bloomberg news service.

- ✔ **IPO Daily Report** (cbs.marketwatch.com/news/current/IPO_rep.htx) offers daily IPO news from CBS MarketWatch.

- ✔ **IPO Monitor** (www.ipomonitor.com) offers free information on recent IPO events. Subscribers have access to e-mailed IPO news, a searchable IPO database, company profiles, information about the IPO market, special reports, and tools. Information is available online or via e-mail to subscribers. Subscriptions are $29 per month, or $290 per year.

- ✔ **Street Fusion** (www.streetfusion.com) provides individual investors with access to publicly available live, on-demand, or special event webcasts. Registration is for investment professionals and companies. Registration is not necessary to access publicly available webcasts.

- ✔ **Yahoo! IPO News** (biz.yahoo.com/reports/ipo.html) is IPO news from Yahoo! (Yahoo! started as a type of topic-specific search engine, and has expanded into different areas such as the IPO News.)

The following Web sites provide IPO filings:

- ✔ **Edgar Online's IPO Express** (www.edgar-online.com/ipoexpress) offers a database of IPOs that is searchable by industry, state, country, and underwriters. News, recent filings, pricings, and performance information are also available.

✔ **IPO Data Systems** (`www.ipodata.com`) is a subscription service that includes an IPO calendar, company profiles, listings of top performers, IPOs by underwriter, and online information about IPOs. At the time of this writing, fees are $15 per month, or $100 per year.

✔ **NASDAQ** (`www.nasdaq.com/reference/IPOs.stm`) lists recent IPO filings with ticker symbols, pricings, and share information, a listing of IPO ceremony events and IPO summaries. At the NASDAQ home page click IPOs.

The following sites provide online IPO pricing:

✔ **Cnet Investor: Today's IPOs** (`www.cnetinvestor.com/ipos-today.asp`) offers a listing of IPOs starting to trade in the current day, plus links to upcoming offerings.

✔ **IPO.Com** (`www.ipo.com`) has IPO pricings for companies listed on the NASDAQ, AMEX, and NYSE exchanges, a review of the most recent IPO filings, an IPO calendar that provides a look at IPOs that are about to be priced and traded, news about which companies have withdrawn or postponed their offerings, research articles, reviews, and information about how to locate other online financial sources.

✔ **IPO Maven** (`www.ipomaven.com`) offers free IPO market information, pricing, SEC filings, company news, quotes, and charts. There is a free IPO e-mail alert service. If you want real time quotes, you'll have to register.

✔ **Quote.com: IPO Edge** (`www.quote.com/ipo`) provides information about upcoming IPOs, data about active IPOs, recent filings and pricings, and information about the biggest gainers.

Finding online brokers that offer IPOs

After researching IPOs, you may decide that you want a broker who specializes in this type of security. The Internet can assist you in locating the right broker. Here are a few examples:

✔ **Charles Schwab** (`www.schwab.com`) provides its best customers (those with substantial assets in their trading accounts — usually $100,000 or more) with offerings underwritten by Credit Suisse, First Boston, Hambrecht & Ouist, and J.P. Morgan Securities, Inc.

✔ **DLJ Direct** (`www.dljdirect.com`) offers IPO shares to online Preferred customers ($100,000 or more in assets in DLJ accounts) and Select customers ($1,000,000 or more in assets in DLJ accounts).

- ✔ **E*Trade** (www.etrade.com) has announced that Wit Capital, as of this writing, will acquire eOfferings. This means that Wit Capital will become the exclusive source of IPOs, follow-on offerings, and other investment banking products for E*Trade customers. Customers of E*Trade will get an expanded range of investment products and opportunities, and access to Wit Capital's proprietary research. In return, E*Trade will acquire all of Wit Capital's trading accounts.

- ✔ **Fidelity Brokerage** (www.fidelity.com) offers customers some shares in IPOs underwritten by Salomon Brothers. Fidelity uses several factors to decide who gets the limited shares. These factors include trading habits and how long the customer has had a trading account with Fidelity.

- ✔ **IPO Syndicate** (www.iposyndicate.com) sells IPO shares and private placements. Access to the Web site's features requires you to open a trading account. Make certain you do your homework before investing. Many of the IPOs offered may contain higher than normal risks.

Including IPOs in mutual funds

Several large mutual funds include IPOs. However, participation in IPOs shouldn't be the only reason you purchase a mutual fund. Before making your investment decision, you still need to carefully read the fund's prospectus and compare it to other mutual funds and your overall financial objectives.

Here are a few examples of mutual funds that include IPOs:

- ✔ Govett Smaller Companies (GSCQX)
- ✔ Janus Olympus (JAOLX)
- ✔ PBHG Emerging Growth (PBEGX)
- ✔ USAA Aggressive Growth (USAUX)
- ✔ Warburg Pincus Post-Venture (WPVCX)

For more details, use the ticker symbol lookup feature at Morningstar (www.morningstar.com).

IPOs for the serious investor

IPO Home (www.ipo-fund.com), shown in the accompanying figure, is offered by the research firm Renaissance Capital. IPO Home offers IPO research calendars, pricings, filings, and rankings. Detailed analyst reports by Renaissance's staff are available for $50 per report. The educational sections describe Wall Street, investing, and the IPO process for beginning investors. Additionally, the firm offers shares in its IPO mutual fund.

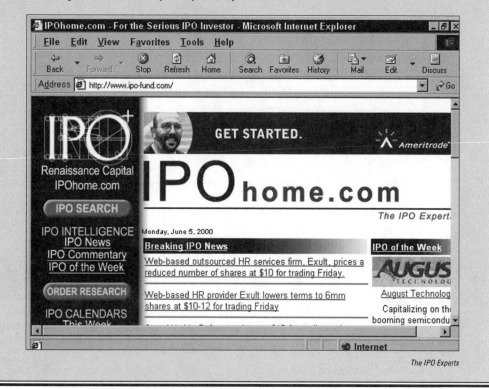

The IPO Experts

Be Your Own Broker with Direct Public Offerings (DPOs)

Historically, small companies have had a difficult time finding capital to expand their businesses. Traditional lenders are frequently unwilling to take risks with untried companies. Venture capitalists negotiate tough deals that often force company founders out of key management roles. And traditional IPOs require a minimum of $15 million in annual revenue.

If you take an initial public offering (IPO) and cut out the underwriter, what you have left is a direct public offering (DPO). DPOs have been around for more than 20 years. For example, Ben & Jerry's used a DPO to raise capital for the ice cream company. However, the offering was limited to its home state of Vermont.

In October 1995, the SEC fueled DPOs with a ruling making electronic delivery of a prospectus okay. Consequently, companies can raise needed capital by selling their shares directly to the public via the Internet. These DPOs have the following advantages for small companies:

- **Cost and time savings:** The company saves thousands of dollars in underwriting expenses.

- **Regulation of Internet IPOs:** Issuers can file faster, turnaround times are quicker, filing is less expensive, fewer restrictions exist on the sales process, and issuers can announce planned offerings.

- **Management remains focused:** Management isn't drawn away from the company's day-to-day business needs and customers.

- **Investors can get in really early:** Investors have access to venture capital-types of investments.

- **No broker commissions:** Investors don't have to pay high broker commissions.

Recognizing the limitations of DPOs

Many companies are offering DPOs instead of initial public offerings (IPOs). For many online investors, a DPO is the best way to get in on the ground floor and share in a company's success. Investors can purchase shares directly from the companies that they want to be part owners of. However, DPOs have some limitations:

- **Blue sky laws:** Issuing companies must be registered with the SEC and the states where they offer securities, but new legislation allows companies to use the Internet to present initial public offerings. This new legislation is inconsistent with regulations passed in 1911. The 1911 rule requires issuers to register in the states where they offer stocks, but the Internet has no boundaries and thus offers worldwide distribution of stock offerings. Does this mean that issuers don't have to register in each state that uses the Internet? Some issuers register in all 50 states before offering shares. However, one state, Pennsylvania, only requires companies to clearly indicate where they are registered and who may purchase securities.

✔ **Fraud and abuse:** Stock issues are highly regulated, but the Internet is an unregulated environment. The enforcement of registration issues on the Internet is keeping the SEC more than busy. The result may be fraudulent solicitations on the Internet.

Buying DPOs

DPO issues often open in a blaze of glory due to strong public interest. Then the share prices settle down to a consistent trading range. During the stock's initial period of volatility, the stock price may double or triple. Cashing in at this point can be very profitable and may compensate you for earlier investment mistakes.

DPOs are speculative and definitely for aggressive investors. In other words, if you can't afford to lose all your investment, you shouldn't be in this market. That said, even the most aggressive investors should only invest between 5 and 10 percent of their total portfolio in this type of financial asset.

To purchase shares, obtain a subscription agreement for the DPO. The subscription agreements are usually included in the last page of the prospectus. If you can't find the form, request one by e-mail or through the U.S. mail. Send the completed agreement and a check for the appropriate amount to the company. The company sends a confirmation letter within five days and the stock certificate within 30 days. (I suggest making a duplicate copy of your check and subscription agreement for your records and sending the originals by registered mail.)

The following list offers some online sources for DPOs:

✔ **Direct IPO** (`www.directipo.com`) focuses on direct equity offerings via the Internet and supporting services. Direct IPO works with technology and new-media companies in their early stages of development. At Direct IPO, you'll find investor resources such as tutorials on how IPOs work and how DPOs work, a guide to investing, a glossary of terms, an IPO contest, an industry spotlight, and the newsroom.

✔ **Virtual Wall Street** (`www.virtualwallstreet.com`) offers information on companies that are seeking $1 to $10 million in capital. Educational materials include a comparison chart of a DPO and an IPO, definition of a DPO, information about the DPO process, online resources, DPO and securities laws, and state regulations.

Small, unproven firms carry very high risks. You should do lots of homework before you invest in companies that big banks avoid.

Trading direct public offerings online

The Internet provides several sites that enable small investors to view direct public offering materials and to interact with small and medium-sized companies offering shares. These sites do not function as stock exchanges, but include many of the same elements: A great place to start your research is at the Direct Stock Market (www.dsm.com), shown in Figure 15-2. The Direct Stock Market (DSM) provides investors, entrepreneurs, and securities industry professionals with current, complete, and immediate information about public and private offerings. DSM provides companies that are issuing stock in a public offering or a private placement with a central location from which to distribute their documents and reports electronically. To become a member, complete the online form, read the suitability questionnaire, and indicate your investor status.

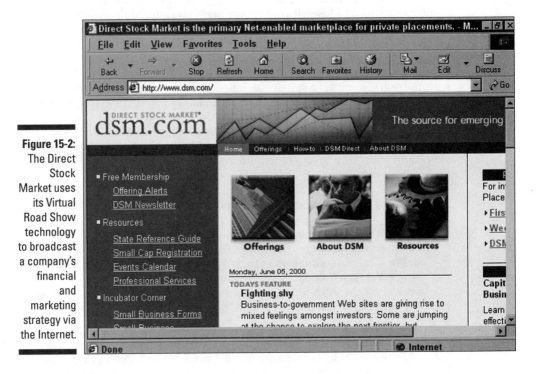

Figure 15-2:
The Direct Stock Market uses its Virtual Road Show technology to broadcast a company's financial and marketing strategy via the Internet.

Buying Stock in a Direct Purchase Plan (DPP)

The Securities and Exchange Commission eased regulations in 1994 so that companies can comfortably offer their shares directly to the public. This change has caused a small boom in the number of companies that allow investors to buy shares directly.

Sometimes, direct purchase plans (DPPs) are called *no-load* stock plans. These plans allow you to join direct purchase plans (which include dividend reinvestment features) without first purchasing shares through a broker. Some corporations with DPPs sell shares only to corporate customers, and others are open to all investors.

In the past, utilities were the main companies having DPPs. In 1996, 150 companies sold their stock directly to the public. In 1997, more than 300 companies offered DPPs. In the coming years, as many as 1,500 companies may sell their stock directly to the public.

About one million individuals purchase stocks directly. Minimum investments can be as small as $50 a month for IBM shares. Some of the DPPs include dividend reinvestment plans (DRIPs), tax-deferred IRA investments, and loans against stock holdings. A few companies even sell shares below market price. Currently, you can't purchase shares over the Internet, but that's expected to change soon.

The Internet provides many sources for DPP information and education. A few examples follow:

- ✔ **ChaseMellon Direct Purchase Services** (www.cmssonline.com/sect_buystock_faq.html) is sponsored by the trust division of Chase Manhattan Mellon Bank, and offers investors the ability to purchase certain stocks. ChaseMellon Direct Purchase services provides information about what a direct purchase plan (DPP) is, the benefits of investing in a DPP, how to enroll, and FAQs about direct purchases.

- ✔ **InvestPower** (www.investpower.com) allows you to search a firm's DPO plan by entering the ticker symbol or company name. You can search an alphabetical listing of direct purchase plans and employee stock purchase plans, check out plans ranked by investment amount, and research a company's financial and market performance. You can purchase fractional shares so you can determine the dollar amount you want to invest. To purchase shares, you determine the dollar amount of funds you want deducted from your checking account as a lump sum or automatic monthly deduction. The site offers online retrieval of your account information 24-hours a day, 7-days a week. Fees for purchasing DPOs through InvestPower start at $2.60.

✔ **Netstock Direct** (www3.netstockdirect.com), shown in Figure 15-3, allows investors to purchase common stock without a broker. You can research over 1,600 companies, buy stocks for dollars rather than shares, invest as often you want, and enroll online. Search stock plans by company name or symbol. Find stock plans for Forbes 500 and Fortune 500 companies. Find stocks with an initial investment of $100 or less. Find plans with no purchase fees. Invest directly in mutual funds as a single investment amount, or set up an automatic monthly investment plan. Learn about different mutual funds by reading the online prospectus, linking to market information or order materials for U.S. mail delivery. The site charges $2 per transaction ($1 for custodial accounts) for recurring transactions and $5 per transaction for a one-time investment. A special feature included is the ability to transfer your DRIP and DSP shares into one Netstock Account.

Figure 15-3:
Netstock Direct is a well-organized site with high-quality DPO information.

Buying That First Share

Ford, IBM, British Telecommunications, and many other companies have direct purchase plans (DPPs). All you have to do is contact the firm via the Internet, telephone, or U.S. mail. Direct your request to the Investor Relations Department and ask whether the company has a direct purchase plan and an application. Complete the application form and include a check for your initial investment. Make a copy of these items for your records. Send the signed application and check to the company by registered mail.

In more than half of the DPPs, the minimum investment is $250 or less, and as little as $10 thereafter. The plans are designed for long-term investors who plan to hold their shares for at least three to five years. Processing your order is slower than going through a broker; it usually takes about a week. You can make subsequent stock purchases with cash payments and reinvested dividends.

However, purchasing DPPs is proof that there's no such thing as a free lunch, because these so-called no-load stocks are not cost-free. You still have to pay a few fees. You often pay a one-time enrollment fee of $5 to $15, a per-transaction fee of up to $10 plus $0.01 to $0.10 per share, and higher fees when you sell. Some plans charge an annual account management fee. To reinvest your dividend, you may have to pay up to $5 per quarter.

When comparing the fees of some DPPs to the low rates that online brokers charge (between $10 and $30 per transaction), you don't appear to be saving much by buying shares directly from the company. However, the SEC is continuing to relax its regulations about DPPs. Soon, companies will be able to advertise their programs at their Web sites. As the market for DPPs heats up, fees are likely to decrease, and you may be able to charge your DPP purchase to your credit card via the Internet.

A great place to start is with ShareBuilder (www.sharebuilder.com), shown in Figure 15-4. ShareBuilder specializes in automatic investment accounts for small investors who want to avoid high brokerage fees. For example, popular investments like Microsoft and Cisco do not have direct stock purchase plans, so ShareBuilder creates its own direct stock plans for these companies and similar companies. For automatic purchases, costs are $2 per transaction ($1 per transaction for custodial accounts). A lump sum one-time transaction costs $5.

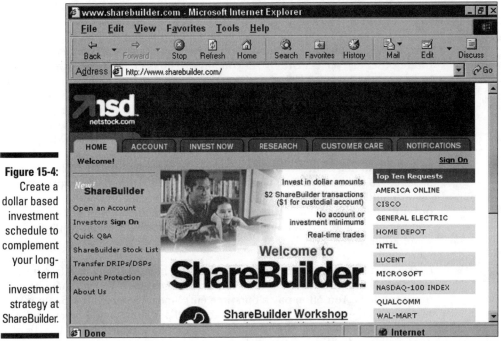

Figure 15-4:
Create a
dollar based
investment
schedule to
complement
your long-
term
investment
strategy at
ShareBuilder.

Profiting with Dividend Reinvestment Plans (DRIPs)

Dividend reinvestment plans (DRIPs) are sometimes called *shareholder investment programs* (SIPs). These plans are an easy, low-cost way to purchase stocks and reinvest your dividend income. About 1,000 companies and closed-end mutual funds sponsor DRIPs.

Most plans require you to purchase your first share through a broker, the National Association of Investors Corporation (NAIC) buying club, or some other method. A share purchased in a DRIP is like any other stock share. You have voting rights and stock splits, and your uninvested dividends are taxed when you sell your shares.

Shares must be registered in your name. You can purchase subsequent shares directly from the company, often at discounted prices and with no broker commissions. Most plans allow investors to make voluntary payments to the DRIP to purchase more shares. In other words, the advantages of DRIPs include:

✔ No brokerage commissions and few fees for purchasing stock through the DRIP.

✔ Frequent discounts of 3 to 5 percent off the current stock price.

✔ Optional cash payment plans (OCPs). These plans are often part of DRIPs. Usually after the first dividend has been reinvested, the investor can send voluntary cash payments directly to the company to purchase more shares. Amounts can be as small as $10 to $25. (This option enables investors to own fractions of stocks.) For example, General Electric allows OCPs of $10 to $10,000 every month.

Many of the nation's premier corporations have DRIPs, including most of the companies in the Dow Jones Industrial Average. The InvestorGuide page on DRIPs and DPPs (www.investorguide.com) has a public directory with links to the corporate home pages of many companies that have dividend reinvestment plans. For more information, contact each company you're interested in and ask for a DRIP prospectus. At the corporate home page, you can e-mail your request. If the company doesn't have a Web site, use Stock Smart, at www.stocksmart.com, to locate the corporation's address and telephone number.

Additional features of DRIPs

One of the benefits of DRIPs is their (often free) certificate safekeeping service. This service eliminates the need for paying for a safe-deposit box and the possibility of your stock certificates becoming lost or stolen.

DRIPs often have gift-giving programs. For example, Texaco lets you open an investor services plan in another person's name, and the company provides you with a gift certificate to give to the recipient.

Not all DRIPs are alike

Each company has its own plan. With some firms, you can pay for additional shares with cash; some allow partial redemption of shares; and some have termination fees. However, the plan may only purchase shares once a month, and if you want to sell your shares, completing the transaction may take five to ten days.

Some plans allow you to buy shares one at a time. However, some companies have a minimum purchase amount. For example, Bristol-Myers Squibb requires a minimum purchase of 50 shares. Bristol-Myers Squibb also charges a fee of 4 percent of the dollar amount of dividends being reinvested (a maximum of $5 per share). In general, plans differ from one another in the following ways:

✔ Some companies allow (and some companies don't allow) the reinvestment of preferred dividends for common shares.

✔ Some companies allow partial reinvestment of dividends.

✔ The amount of optional cash payments (OCPs) varies from company to company.

✔ Fees for participating in the DRIP vary from company to company.

How to get your first DRIP share

Sometimes, getting started is the hardest part of investing. Many ways exist to go about getting your first share for a DRIP. Here are five different approaches — one of these methods may be right for you:

✔ **Find a brokerage that charges special rates for single shares:** Several brokerages charge special commission rates to current accountholders for the purchase of single shares. A.G. Edwards charges a flat 16 percent of the share price. Dean Witter charges a flat 10 percent of the share price.

✔ **Join a special investment club:** First Share Buying Club can assist you in getting your first share so that you can participate in a DRIP. Annual membership is $18 a year ($30 for two years). Members receive a handbook about DPPs and DRIPs, transferring shares, and the registration of shares.

For individuals who don't want to join the club, you can buy one share in one company for a flat fee of $20. If you want to purchase more than one share, becoming a member is more cost-effective. You can request any number of shares in any number of companies. For more information, call 800-683-0743.

✔ **Share the cost with a friend:** You can use a buddy system to reduce the cost of purchasing your first share. You and a friend pay the brokerage to purchase two shares. Have both shares registered to one person and join the company's DRIP. After you've joined, transfer one share to your friend and split the cost of the fees.

✔ **Join the NAIC:** The National Association of Investors Corporation (NAIC) enrolls people in any of more than 100 DRIPs via its Low Cost Investment Plan. The NAIC enrolls its members in a company for a $7 per company fee. Membership in the NAIC is $39 for individuals, or $35 for an investment club plus $14 per member of the club. See the NAIC Web site at www.better-investing.org or telephone 801-583-6242 for details.

✔ **Use a deep-discount online broker:** Sometimes, the simplest way to purchase your first share is to go through a deep-discount broker. Online brokerage costs vary from free to $40. To participate in the DRIP, you need the stock registered in your name. To get the stock registered in your name (rather than in the brokerage's default street name), you may have to pay an additional fee.

Investment FAQ (`invest-faq.com/articles/trade-drips.html`) provides a useful article that shows how investors can use buying clubs to purchase their first share.

Selecting the right DRIP

DRIPs have many advantages, but you shouldn't let one characteristic be your sole criterion for purchasing the stock. Regardless of how attractive the DRIP program is, you still need to make certain that the stock fits in with your overall investment strategy. In other words, don't select a stock just because it has a DRIP.

Here are online resources for finding out more about dividend reinvestment plans:

✔ **DRP Central** (`www.dripcentral.com`) offers DRIP information for beginning investors. The Web site provides links to useful online articles, newsletters, directories, and other DRIP Web sites.

✔ **DRIP Investor** (`www.dripinvestor.com`) is a guide to buying stocks without a broker by using dividend reinvestment plans. DRIP Investor offers FAQ answers, a DRIP message board, a list of DRIP stocks, links to DRIP Web sites, and a sample DRIP. Subscriptions to the DRIP Investor newsletter are $233 annually.

✔ **NAIC Low Cost Plan Overview** (`www.betterinvesting.org/store/lcp.html`) offers a terrific plan to get your first share without going through a broker. For a one-time set-up charge of $7 plus the price of one share of stock in any of the participating companies listed, you can get started with a new holding in your personal portfolio. However, transactions take between 8 to 12 weeks for investing in monthly companies. Companies investing quarterly require even more time.

✔ **One Share of Stock, Inc.: Own a Piece of Your Favorite Company** (`www.oneshare.com`) offers a program called DRP Plus because not only do you qualify for companies with DRP programs, you can also have the original first share framed to display and keep as a collectible, unlike other firms that only enroll you on a book entry basis and maintenance service. The service averages $29, exclusive of the stock price. This is often lower than brokerages that charge additional fees for the physical delivery, and special handling of stock certificates. Frames cost between $49 and $85.

Chapter 16

The Internet and Managing Your Portfolio

*P*ortfolio management may sound like busywork, but knowing how much you own in cash, stocks, bonds, and other investments is important. Without portfolio management, how can you determine whether your returns are meeting your financial requirements? Are you missing opportunities by not buying or selling securities at the right time?

This chapter covers three Internet-based approaches to managing your portfolio. The first approach is to use free and fee Web-based portfolio tracking tools that can be customized and often provide e-mail alerts on price changes and end-of-the-day quotes. The second approach to portfolio management is to use PC-based tools that are free, offer free trials, or cost only a few dollars. These programs use your Internet connection to automatically update portfolio quotes. (If you already have Money 2000 Financial Suite or Quicken Deluxe 2000, you can use the portfolio feature and update price quotes in just a few clicks, as I explain in this chapter.) The third portfolio management approach is to use your online broker's free portfolio management program. Your broker knows all about your buying and selling habits. Your broker can automatically update your portfolio, and you don't have to wait until the end of the month to determine the value of your investment decisions. Also in this chapter, I describe the difficulties of measuring portfolio performance and risk.

Why Manage Your Investments?

You may select the best investments, but if you don't have a way to track your gains and losses, you can lose time and money. Good record keeping is invaluable for calculating your taxes, preparing for retirement, estate planning, and taking advantage of opportunities to increase your personal wealth.

Sources on the Internet can assist you in keeping careful records of every stock, mutual fund, bond, and money market security you own. Setup time can be as little as ten minutes. You can update and monitor your portfolio once a week or once a month. Your investments can be in one portfolio (for example, your retirement fund) or many (say, your retirement fund, an emergency fund, and your children's college fund). You can also track investments that you wish you owned or that you're considering for investment.

The Internet offers programs that automatically update your portfolio with daily price changes and then re-tally your portfolio's value. To sum up, many portfolio management programs can

- Help you determine how much you own in cash, stocks, and bonds.

- Show you how these investments line up with your asset allocation targets.

- Indicate what returns (capital gains or losses) you're receiving.

- Compare returns to your financial requirements.

- Alert you that securities are at the prices at which you want to buy (or sell).

Tracking the Right Information

If you own more than one investment, you probably want to compare the performances of your investments. The more investments you have, the harder this task is. Many novice investors find it difficult to determine whether they're making money, losing money, or just breaking even. To determine how your investments are performing, you need to look at the following data:

- **52-week high and low:** The highest and lowest selling prices in the previous 365 days.

- **Dividend:** The annual per-share amount of cash payments made to stockholders of the corporations.

- **Dividend yield percent:** The total amount of the dividend paid in the last 12 months divided by the closing price (the price at which the last trade of the day was made).

- ✔ **Growth rate:** How much the dividend increases from one fiscal year to the next.

- ✔ **P/E ratio:** The ratio of the closing price to the last 12 months' earnings per share.

- ✔ **Volume:** The number of shares traded in one day.

- ✔ **High, low, close:** Highest selling price of the day, lowest selling price of the day, and closing selling price.

- ✔ **Net change:** The difference between the day's closing price and the previous day's closing price.

You can compare these amounts and ratios to the performance of your other investments, the firm's previous performance, the industry, and the market indexes (for example, the S&P 500).

If you own several securities, how do you keep track of all this data? Once again, the Internet provides an answer. The Internet has hundreds of Web- and PC-based portfolio management programs that are just waiting to assist you. Some of them are free, others are fee-based, and some are automatically set up for you by your online broker.

Stock Trigger (www.stocktrigger.com) provides a free service that will notify you via your computer, pager, or telephone when any stock you are tracking has hit an important price point. You can program the service to notify you when your stock hits a stop level, breaks out to a new 52-week high, or moves a certain percentage or dollar amount. Then verify the accuracy of the stock prices before you make any investments or other financial decisions such as taking your profits or buying more stocks.

Your Portfolio Management Options

The Internet offers three types of portfolio management programs:

- ✔ **Web-based portfolio management programs:** Investor supersites, Internet portals, and large news organizations generally sponsor online portfolio management programs for free, or free with your subscription. These programs usually don't require any software downloading, and they constantly update your portfolio. However, these programs don't offer many features, such as customized graphs or charts, fundamental analysis, or tax planning tools.

✔ **PC-based portfolio management programs:** These programs present portfolio tracking as a feature of a personal software program like Quicken (www.intuit.com) or MS Money (www.microsoft.com/money). PC-based portfolio management involves tracking with a software program downloaded from the Internet. These programs can be very inexpensive, or even free. PC-based portfolio tracking programs usually have more choices and functions than Web-based portfolio management programs. However, you must download the proprietary software and you may have to *import* (transfer data from one source to another) stock quotes.

✔ **Portfolio management with your online broker:** Portfolio management with your online broker is automatic. Your online broker knows what you traded, so the brokerage can automatically update your portfolio. This is a terrific way to track distributions from mutual funds and stock splits. Overall, the advantages of using your broker's portfolio management system are that you don't have to manually add transactions and your portfolio always reflects the current value of your investments.

You don't have to limit your portfolio tracking to just one approach. For example, you may want to use an online tool to determine your percentage rate of return for the current year, and use your PC portfolio software to track your annualized returns. When traveling, you may want to use your online brokerage's portfolio services to verify the completion of investment transactions, dividend reinvestments, or stock splits.

In the following sections, I offer examples that detail the features and functions of these three types of portfolio management programs.

Using Web-Based Portfolio Management Programs

Many Web sites provide online portfolio tracking services. Some of these services are free and others are fee-based. The aim of Web-based portfolio management tools is to help you make better investment decisions and thus increase your capital gains. Each Web-based portfolio management program offers something different. In the following sections, I describe just a few examples.

Don't let the fascination of having your portfolio online tempt you into over-trading (buying or selling) your investments.

Investor compilation or supersites provide, among other things, free and fee-based portfolio tracking. Some investor supersites require your free registration, and are supported by advertisers. Other compilation sites provide different levels of services, costing up to $8 to $10 per month.

The benefits of tracking your portfolio at one of these sites is access to the vast repositories of investor information, data, and tools that they offer. If you want to research or analyze something in connection with your portfolio, you don't have to go to several investor sites to get the job done, which can save you time and money if you need to make a quick investment decision. In the following sections, I profile several of these investor compilation sites.

CNBC.com Account Tracker

CNBC.com (cnbc.com) offers Account Tracker, which brings together all your personal accounts on one page under one security key. Your Portfolio Accounts Page provides current quotes, information about insider trading, a current valuation of your portfolio, today's events, portfolio tracker alerts, valuation ratios, analysts' ratings, and technical rankings.

Account Tracker provides a wide variety of analyses. For example, the portfolio, and each stock, is rated on a scale of Strong Sell to Strong Buy, based on the recommendations of analysts who follow the company. Over- and undervaluation are based on the price/sales ratio, with individual statistics on different fundamental factors.

In addition to access to quotes, message boards, and charts, the account logon feature enables you to authorize Account Tracker to retrieve information from your personal finance program (such as Quicken or Microsoft Money), bank, or brokerage. This feature provides you with a single point to view up-to-date information on all your personal accounts. It's free and safe. According to CNBC, Account Tracker security exceeds industry standards used by banks and brokerages. Additionally, your privacy is secure because only you know your Account Tracker's security key, and you are identified only by the information you provide. Account Tracker is also available at Wall Street City (www.wallstreetcity.com).

ClearStation

ClearStation (www.clearstation.com) is a free service that sends end-of-the-day e-mail notifications outlining the events affecting individual portfolios. ClearStation users can open their portfolios to public scrutiny if they so desire. If a ClearStation's user's portfolio is an all-star winner, you can "subscribe" to that portfolio and get an e-mail message every time that person makes a transaction (buys, sells, or shorts a stock). You can track watch-list stocks and three types of general recommendations: highlighted member lists you have subscribed to, lists compiled by ClearStation experts, and lists constructed by the top 20 ClearStation members (members whose portfolios and recommendations have proven to provide the best returns). ClearStation is not an intuitive Web site, but it has lots of educational and tutorial materials to help you get started.

Morningstar X-Ray Reports

Morningstar (www.morningstar.com) has one of the better online portfolio management programs for mutual funds. First, set up the free portfolio at the Web site; then, click the tab for X-Ray Reports. X-Ray Reports includes information on fees and expenses for each of your mutual funds, indicates how all your assets (cash, stocks, bonds, and others) are allocated in your personal portfolio, and shows the fundamental statistics for each of your holdings (P/E ratio, price-to-book ratio, and earnings growth).

If you want Premium Portfolio X-Rays, you have to become a member. Membership is $9.95 per month, or $99 per year, with a free 30-day free trial. With Premium Portfolio X-Rays, you can check for your Stock Stats. With this feature, the portfolio management program looks into the equities you own individually and those held by your mutual funds. The program tallies up the total percentage that is invested in each company. For example, assume that 10 percent of your portfolio is invested in individual shares of Cisco, and you have two mutual funds that recently invested in Cisco. The total percentage of Cisco holding in your portfolio is now 17 percent. That's *stock overlap*.

How about X-raying your portfolio's asset allocations? Premium Portfolio X-Rays looks into the holdings of your mutual funds and then analyzes the total of all your portfolio's assets. For example, assume that your entire portfolio is invested in equities and mutual funds. With this X-ray feature, you may learn that about four percent of your portfolio is in bonds held by mutual fund companies. Overall, Premium Portfolio X-Rays enable you to gain better control of your personal finances.

MSN MoneyCentral Portfolio Manager

MSN MoneyCentral Portfolio Manager (moneycentral.msn.com/investor/home.asp), shown in Figure 16-1, uses MSN Investor software that you can download in about 5 minutes using a 28.8K modem. This one-time download enables you to automatically track up to 5,000 securities in one or several portfolios. You can enter transactions manually, import personal finance software programs from Money or Quicken, or download accounts directly from your brokerage or other Web-based portfolios. You can personalize the portfolio management program to show your annualized gain, current P/E, and market value. You can even display and track investments in multiple currencies.

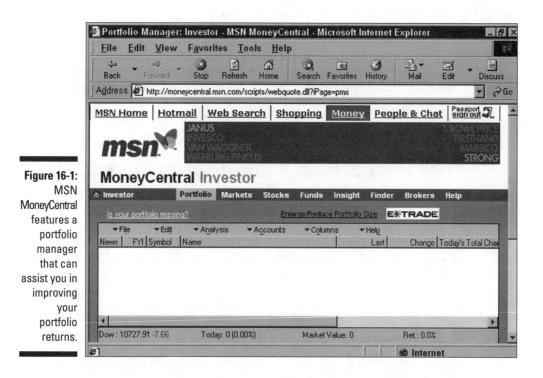

Reuters Money Network Portfolio Tracker

Moneynet (www.moneynet.com), a Reuters-sponsored investment supersite, features a free, easy-to-use Web-based portfolio management program called Portfolio Tracker. This program can create up to ten customized portfolios for as many as 40 stocks, mutual funds, and options in each portfolio. The easy-to-read grid includes a security symbol, company name, price or NAV (Net Asset Value of a mutual fund), volume, high, low, and date/time stamp. You can connect to Portfolio Tracker whenever you want for your latest portfolio update (quotes are delayed at least 20 minutes). All times are Eastern U.S.

At the Reuters Moneynet home page, click Portfolio Tracker. To create a portfolio, click Add Securities, enter a portfolio name or multiple portfolio names, and then add investments and the number of shares (optional). After you build a portfolio, the program automatically monitors the market for you.

You can include the index (Dow Jones Industrials, S&P 500, or NASDAQ Composite) that matches your portfolio best as a watch item. In this way, you can compare your portfolio's performance to a benchmark.

The summary indicates market value of your portfolio. The day's change is in dollars and as a percentage, and the portfolio's total profit or loss is in dollars and as a percentage. Alerts you can receive include e-mail messages about current market value and market information. You can select notifications for twice a day, weekly, monthly, or quarterly. Click the investment name and a Quote Detail Report appears that includes 52-week high/low, P/E ratio, and EPS (earnings per share) information.

The Wall Street Journal Interactive Edition

The Wall Street Journal Interactive Edition (www.wsj.com) offers easy access to your portfolio. Click the top-right corner of almost any page of the Interactive Edition to access the portfolio program, shown in Figure 16-2. You can establish five portfolios with as many as 30 securities in each one. Delayed stock prices constantly update the portfolio, which also shows percentage change and gain/loss information.

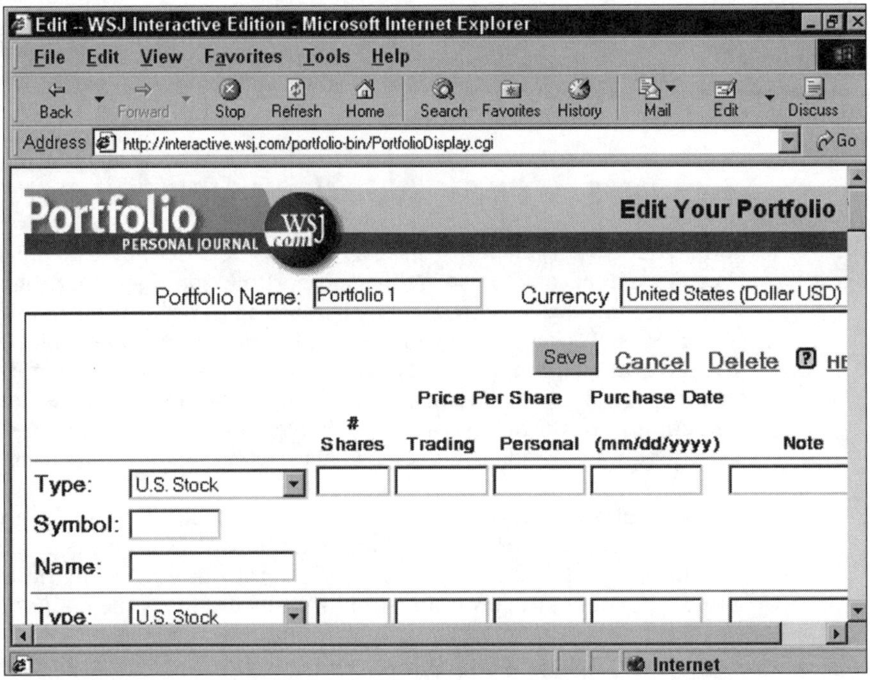

Figure 16-2: You can access your portfolio on almost any page at the Wall Street Journal Web site.

The grid displays an issue-by-issue breakdown of your investments. Total value (along with your portfolio's current gain/loss and percentage of change) is included at the top of the grid, along with the current value of the Dow Jones Industrial Average. You can download investment information to your favorite spreadsheet program.

If news is available for any company in your portfolio, a flag appears next to the company's name. To access the news, click the flag. Links to detailed quotes and mutual fund snapshots are also available. These links provide additional performance and background information. Annual subscriptions cost $59.

Thomson Investors Network Portfolio Tracker

Thomson Investors Network (www.thomsoninvest.net) has free and fee-based services. Registered guests have free use of the portfolio-tracking services with end-of-the-day quotes sent to your e-mailbox, and have limited access to other site services. The Web site is a subsidiary of Thomson Financial Services and includes a wide variety of high-quality investment research, screening tools, and news services (S&P Comstock, CDA/Wiesenberger, First Call, and Institutional Shareholder Services).

Guests are allowed one portfolio with 10 securities. Members are allowed up to 25 portfolios with as many as 25 securities each.

Figure 16-3 shows the Thomson Investors Network Portfolio Tracker, which displays account history, tax liability, and commissions (with values in fractions or decimals). Stock splits are automatically accounted for. Micro-icons indicate charts. Alerts or breaking news about your investment are available. For example, click the News icon, and the news page appears. Articles include company news, changes in credit ratings, and other pertinent information about your investment. Basic membership is $34.95 per year, with a free 30-day trial.

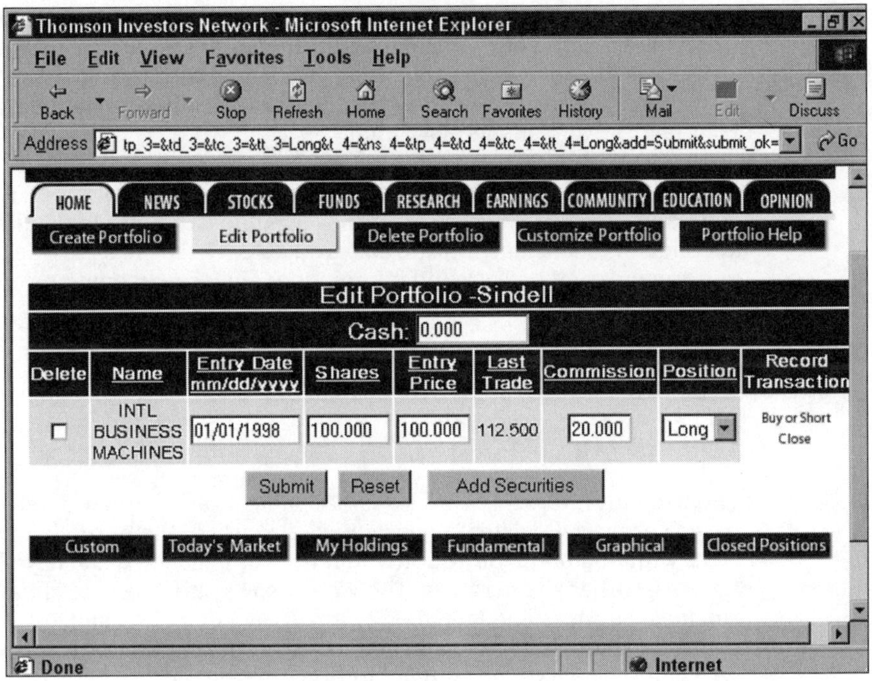

Figure 16-3:
Thomson
Investors
Network
Portfolio
Tracker
provides
daily
portfolio
updates and
more.

With Thomson's Portfolio Tracker, you can create a customized view by follow-ing a few online instructions and adjust for stock splits. Additionally, Portfolio Tracker includes *flash mail,* which notifies you by e-mail at the end of the busi-ness day with news and other information affecting your portfolio. Specifically, the portfolio management function includes the following features:

✔ **The Today's market view** shows the price for the last trade, change, high and low prices, volume, position, and value. Positions are either long or short. Long positions are the traditional buy-and-hold strategies. A short position is where the investor borrows stock from a broker and then sells it. When the stock price drops, the investor purchases the original amount of shares and returns them to the broker. The difference between the sales price and the repurchase price is the investor's profit, less broker fees.

✔ **The fundamental view** shows last traded price (delayed 20 minutes), P/E ratio, EPS, dividend rate, market capitalization, 52-week highs and lows, price/book ratio, and value.

✔ **The graphical view** compares the best and worst performers in the portfolio. If this view shows that a stock is dragging your returns to a lower than acceptable level over a period of time, you may want to con-sider selling.

✔ **The closed position view** indicates your tax liabilities, which are helpful when tax season rolls around.

Want to keep a close eye on your investments? Want to track the price of an investment candidate? With your free registration, CNBC (www.cnbc.com) has a personalized ticker that can help you. Customize the ticker with your portfolio information and the stocks you want to follow.

Following Online News with Portfolio Tracking

With online portfolio tracking tools, investors can see exactly how their investments are prospering. Many large news organizations provide portfolio-tracking services that can make your portfolio tracking very convenient if you already use one or more of these news sources. The portfolio tracking functions of online news organizations generally require the security's ticker symbol, quantity you purchased, purchase price, and date of purchase. In return, your portfolio tracker shows today's delayed market price, today's change, market value of your shares, the value of your investment, your gain or loss, and the percentage of the return. The following sections profile a few examples of online news organizations' portfolio trackers.

Business news

Many online business news organizations provide portfolio tracking. Getting your investment news and tracking your investments at the same site is like one-stop shopping and can be a real time-saver. You can read the news and check on your securities at the same time. For a few examples, check out the following sites:

- **ABC News Moneyscope** (www.moneyscope.com) features a sophisticated, free portfolio-tracking program that tracks, organizes, and graphs individual stocks, indexes, and mutual funds data on one screen. Prices and corporate news are continuously updated. (You need to download this program.)

- **CBS MarketWatch** (portfolio.marketwatch.com), a free program, enables you to create an unlimited number of portfolios and track up to 200 ticker symbols for options, mutual funds, and stocks on all the major exchanges in each portfolio. You can also customize price and value views to display the data. Prices are automatically updated every five minutes.

✔ **New York Times** (www.nytimes.com) enables you to set up or see the status of your portfolio. Go to the Business Section and click Your Portfolio. To set up your portfolio, just enter the securities you own or want to own by inputting the ticker symbol, amount of shares, commission paid, and date of purchase. The portfolio program does the rest. PC Quote (www.pcquote.com) provides the quotes, and the *New York Times* provides the free service.

Portal portfolio management

Portals are Web sites that are designed to be the Internet user's first window onto the Web — the first page that comes up when the user accesses the Web. Often, portals can be personalized so that the user can get news, sports, current portfolio data, or interest rate information before moving on to other sites. The following sections profile examples of portals with free portfolio tracking.

Yahoo! portfolio management

Figure 16-4 shows the My Yahoo! personalized portfolio program (my.yahoo.com). To use the free portfolio, you need to set up an account with My Yahoo!. Click the Log In link that appears on the Portfolio line, and then click Create an Account. Click the Edit link that appears, and enter a portfolio name. Add the ticker symbols of your investments, separated by commas where indicated. You can also enter indexes like the S&P 500 (SPX) for comparison purposes. You can use the same ticker symbol to record separate purchases. Enter or edit the number of shares or purchase prices by clicking the Enter More Info button at the bottom of the page.

Quotes are delayed by 15 minutes for NASDAQ and 20 minutes for other exchanges. Portfolio management information includes company ticker symbol, price at the last trade, amount of price change at last trade, trading volume, number of shares held, the total value of the issue, dollar and percentage of change between the purchase price and the current value, amount paid per share, dollar capital gain or loss, and percentage of capital gain or loss.

The program provides charts, news, research, SEC filings data, and related information. Recent headlines that link to news stories about your portfolio investments appear at the bottom of the page. You can get your information by signing in on any computer (and use the sign-out feature to make certain that others can't pry).

You can select a non-table version of the portfolio's data, choose to have all portfolio data downloaded to a spreadsheet, and retrieve detailed quotes for each investment. You can customize the portfolio by deciding to sort information alphabetically, use a small font, or display the portfolio by using detailed quote information rather than basic quote data.

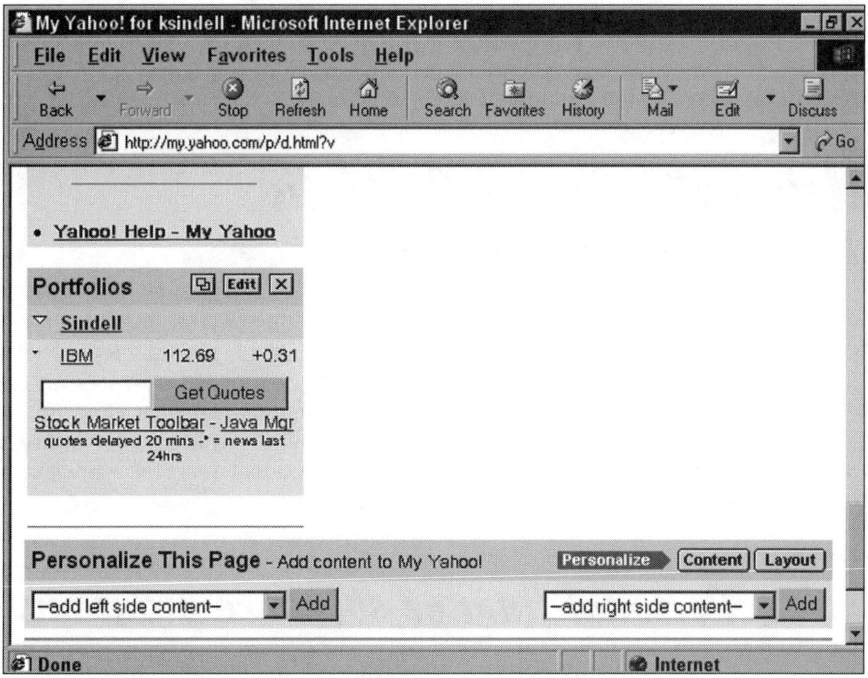

Figure 16-4:
My Yahoo!
provides
portfolio
management
with charts
and data
you can
download to
your
spreadsheet.

Detailed quote information includes last trade (date and time), change (dollars and percent), previous closing price, volume, the day's price range, 52-week range, and bid, ask, and open prices. Also included are ex-dividend dates, earnings per share, P/E ratio, last dividend per share amount, and yield. Charts of the security's price for the last three months, year, two years, five years, and maximum number of years are available.

You can view your portfolio in a floating window, which lets you track your portfolio even when you leave My Yahoo!. Just click the stacked pages icon in the top right-hand corner of the portfolio module. If you get tired of seeing your portfolio, click the X to close the floating window.

Excite

Excite (www.excite.com) is a portal that lets you customize more than any other portal Web site, after you enter your zip code and e-mail address. You can decide how the page looks, which news stories you want to have listed first, select reminders, choose your favorite links, and more. You can select stocks to track and create multiple portfolios.

The first portfolio view shows only the ticker symbol, current price, and percentage of change since the last closing price. The portfolio tracker provides alerts, information on the most active stocks, and a market update. The full portfolio screen shows the ticker symbol, current price, today's change, percentage of change, volume, shares you own, gains or losses, and links to company news and chats. If you need to look up a company's ticker symbol or find a delayed quote, Excite includes the service.

Using PC-Based Portfolio Management Software

If you want more analysis, including graphs of your investments' performance, tax data, and price and volume alerts, you may want to consider a PC-based portfolio manager (a software program that operates on your PC). For example, you can select Money 2000 Financial Suite or Quicken Deluxe 2000 (which you may already use for your online banking), shareware, or free Internet programs. In the following sections, I describe a few examples of PC-based portfolio management programs.

Personal finance software programs

Personal finance software programs often offer much more than what you pay for. These programs provide a way to access online banking, organize your personal finances, understand what you have and what you owe, and organize your financial accounts for the tax collector. Additionally, portfolio management programs track and analyze your portfolio's performance. Most personal finance software programs automatically use your portfolio's gains and losses for your net-worth calculations. With many personal finance programs, if you are connected to the Internet, you can automatically update securities prices. In the following sections, I describe the two most popular personal finance software programs: Microsoft Money 2000 and Quicken 2000.

 The NAIC portfolio management program and other portfolio management programs enable investors to sort investments by type of industry or company size, and then print the reports. In this way, investors can make comparisons within their own portfolios. In other words, it's a convenient way to sort out the winners and losers. A limitation of some personal finance software programs is that they do not include this feature. Additionally, personal finance software programs often have trouble with dividend reinvestment plans.

Microsoft Money 2000

Microsoft Money 2000 (www.microsoft.com/money) is a personal finance software program that can help you stay organized by tracking activities in your savings and checking accounts, and do your banking and bill-paying online. Manage your investments by downloading quotes and brokerage statements from the Internet. Plan your retirement and more. Three types of Microsoft Money 2000 products are available:

✔ **Money 2000 Standard** ($34.95) can assist you in balancing your checkbook, paying bills, banking online, creating a budget, and reducing your debt.

✔ **Money 2000 Deluxe** ($64.95) includes everything in Money 2000 Standard, plus investing, financial planning, and tax-saving tools. You can get a free trial at `www.microsoft.com/money/dlxtrial/dlxtrial.htm`. You can download the software but must have Internet Explorer 5.0 or higher on your computer. The 90-day trial begins the day you install the program. If you decide to purchase the program, you can open and view all the data you entered during the trial.

✔ **Money 2000 Business & Personal** ($94.59) is designed for sole proprietorships to help them easily manage both business and personal finances.

With each type of product, you can track your portfolio's investment positions, and update price or quantity held of your investments without having to enter all purchase and sales data. You get a detailed analysis of your investments by risk, performance, and asset allocation. The capital gains estimator calculates your capital gains taxes and alerts you of taxes owed if a specific investment is sold. The portfolio management program tracks stocks, CD, and bond capital gains throughout the year. The asset allocation feature analyzes the allocation of the assets in your current portfolio and suggests ways to improve it, based on the historic returns for the investment classes you hold.

Quicken 2000 Financial Suite

Quicken Deluxe 2000 (`www.quicken2000.com`) is a personal finance software program that can assist you with your home finances, and can help you prepare for retirement and educational costs. The Quicken 2000 portfolio's table-style format is easy to read and can be organized into customized views. It also tracks tricky financial transactions like stock splits and corporate takeovers. You can download up to five years of stock quotes for trend analysis and record keeping. Quicken can also help you calculate your capital gains taxes (not an easy task with today's tax laws).

Quicken 2000 has a feature called Online Investment Tracking. This feature connects individuals to financial institutions for online banking, online bill paying, and online investment tracking through the Open Financial Exchange Server. Microsoft, Intuit, and CheckFree developed the Open Financial Exchange Server software. You can choose from four types of Quicken 2000 products:

✔ **Quicken Basic 2000** ($34.95) is the easiest way to start managing your finances with software. This package provides the software to balance your checkbook, pay your bills, and create reports and graphs.

✔ **Quicken Deluxe 2000** ($59.95) includes Quicken Basic 2000, plus software to track investments online, help you reduce your tax liability, and plan for the future.

✔ **Quicken Suite 2000** ($89.95) includes four complete Intuit products: Quicken Deluxe 2000, Turbo Tax Deluxe 1999, Turbo Tax State 1999, and Quicken Family Lawyer 2000.

✔ **Quicken Home & Business** ($79.95) includes Quicken Deluxe 2000, plus the software to create invoices, simplify business taxes, and track accounts payable.

As shown in Table 16-1, both Microsoft Money and Quicken allow participating brokerages to download current account statements directly to individuals. With this feature, investors can maintain error-free portfolios and increase the level of investment decision-making. For example, each day, investors can download their brokerage statements to their Microsoft Money or Quicken personal finance program. This enables investors to see recent transactions, holdings, and balances. In other words, investors don't have to wait until the end of the month to see exactly what they own. Table 16-1 shows a few examples of online brokerages that provide downloadable statements.

Table 16-1   Online Brokerages with Downloadable Statements

Brokerage	*MS Money*	*Quicken*
Ameritrade (www.ameritrade.com)	X	X
Charles Schwab (www.schwab.com)	X	X
Datek (www.datek.com)	X	X
DLJ Direct (www.dljdirect.com)	—	X
E*Trade (www.etrade.com)	X	X
Fidelity (personal100.fidelity.com)	X	X
My Discount Broker (www.mydiscountbroker.com)	X	—
NBD Online (www.nbd.com)	X	—
Waterhouse (www.waterhouse.com)	X	X

Portfolio management software programs

Several hundred portfolio management programs are available for your investment tracking. The programs vary in price from free to $500. Many of the freeware and shareware portfolio management programs include an amazing amount of features but are somewhat cumbersome to use.

Some brokers give free portfolio management programs to customers who open an account. Financial data providers frequently give free portfolio management programs with a subscription to their services. Other portfolio management programs are components of larger investment analysis applications.

To discover what works for you, try some of the free demonstrations or trials that vendors offer. They require no obligations, and after sampling several programs, you can get a good idea of which features you need. Following, I list a few examples of PC-based portfolio management programs.

Captool Individual Investor for Windows (www.wallstreetsoftware.com) includes a portfolio management tool for all types of securities and transactions. You can define security types and groups. You can account for reinvestments, short sales, splits, mergers, and return on capital. The program contains over 70 transaction codes to facilitate modeling all situations. It also calculates returns on investments, estimates your tax liabilities, and performs batch valuations (for multiple portfolios). Captool Individual Investor automatically updates security prices with your Internet access. You can also make manual entries. Reports can be customized and graphical reports include valuation versus time, ROI versus time, and portfolio growth versus indices. The program runs under Windows 3.x, 95/98, or NT. It costs $249, plus shipping and handling.

Fund Manager (for Windows 95/98/NT; downloadable at rocketdownload. com or www.zdnet.co.uk/software/) is a top-rated portfolio management program for stocks and mutual funds for the average individual investor. It takes a short time to get the hang of it, but samples help shorten the learning curve. Fund Manager provides many easy-to-read graphs, charts, and reports that are printable. You can update prices by clicking Internet. Fund Manager imports from Prodigy, MSN, Quicken, and other sources. Retrieve the latest quotes from AOL, CompuServe, or many international Internet sites. Fund Manager tracks your investment performance quickly and easily. The program runs under Windows 95, 98, or NT. It's free to try, $39 to own, and $5 to upgrade.

NAIC Personal Record Keeper (www.quantixsoftware.com) is the official software offered by the National Association of Investors Corporation (www.better-investing.org) for personal portfolio management. The program tracks investment transactions (buy, sell, income, and reinvestment) for a variety of investments. It also automatically updates prices from online services. Reports can be printed recording the full history of your portfolio or for a specified time period, including industry and company size break-downs and return calculations. The program generates more than 35 reports and graphs, keeps tax records, indicates diversification, compares portfolio performance to the market, and automatically notifies you if a price alert has been reached. The program runs on PCs with Windows 3.1 or Windows 95/98. Pricing is $69 for NAIC Computer Group members, $79 for NAIC members, $99 for nonmembers, and $35 for the upgrade from DOS or Windows previous versions. A free demo is available for download.

Personal Stock Monitor (www.dtlink.com), shown in Figure 16-5, is an investment tool that uses the Internet to assist you in making better financial decisions by providing continuously updated quotes and charts on your desktop computer for free. Personal Stock Monitor collects quotes from 15 markets worldwide and includes a portfolio manager that works in the back-ground, recalculating the value of your holdings. You get links to news, research, and charts. You also get configurable intraday, end of day, and asset allocation charts, and import and export capabilities from Quicken, Microsoft Money, MetaStock, and similar software programs, giving you a consolidated view of your accounts. In other words, Personal Stock Monitor retrieves raw data from the Internet and organizes it according to your preferences. Your portfolio information is stored on your hard drive instead of the Internet. Overall, Personal Stock Monitor combines online finance Web sites with the convenience, automation, and privacy of a desktop application. Personal Stock Monitor Gold is $49.95, and Personal Stock Monitor is $29.95. A free 30-day trial is available.

Check out the 30-day trial version of Personal Stock Monitor now by using the *Investing Online For Dummies* companion CD-ROM.

StockTracker is free, downloadable software available at www.stockcenter.com. You need to register and download the software to use this program (downloading takes about five minutes).

StockTracker can automatically update security prices, value the portfolio, and provide price alerts that you predetermine. The program can be con-nected to the Internet and have access to all the principal U.S. and Canadian markets. You can create up to 12 portfolios. You can also save pricing data and build charts while the program constantly updates your portfolio.

Wall Street Access offers StockTracker free to the investment community in hopes that users will enjoy the product and open an account. The minimum order amount to open an account is $10,000. Placing an order with a trader averages $45. Trades placed electronically average $25.

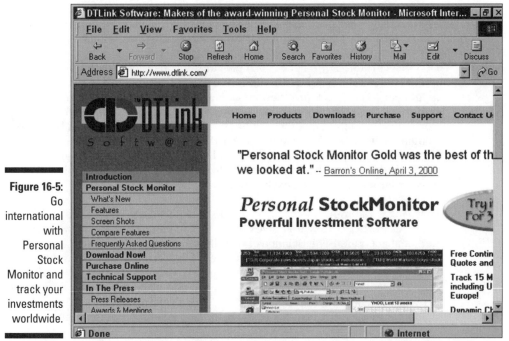

Personal Stock Monitor is a trademark of DTLink Software. Web page contents copyright 1998-2000, DTLink Software.

WinStock Pro (`www.download.com` or `www.zdnet.com/downloads/`) is a stock market tracking and portfolio management program that uses your Internet connection. You can set up several portfolios that use the Internet to update prices. The program converts foreign currencies, and features a ticker toolbar and printed reports. You can import or export to Quicken. The program includes e-mail, automatic dial-up, paging, audible alarms, and flexible reporting. WinStock Pro requires Windows 95 or 98. It is free to try, and $30 if you decide to keep it.

Using Online Brokerage-Based Portfolio Tracking

As a general rule, you have to manually update Web-based portfolio management programs when you buy or sell securities, pay a commission, or receive a dividend or stock split. This manual updating is time consuming, and the possibility exists that you may make an error. These inconveniences can be especially troublesome for active traders. Using the portfolio management function of your online brokerage is one way to avoid the problem of manually updating your portfolio. In this section, I offer several examples of electronic brokerages that provide portfolio management programs.

DLJ Direct (www.dljdirect.com) provides its customers with up-to-the-minute personal portfolio information to assist them in making better investment decisions. This information enables you to stay on top of your portfolio performance so that you can react quickly to changing market conditions. Portfolio information includes order status, execution report, cash balances, margin balance, portfolio values, and a 120-day account history. Each night, the portfolio is updated with the day's closing prices. A portfolio demo is available that shows how the firm handles alerts, balances, portfolio holdings, order status, history, cash withdrawals, and profits.

Discover Brokerage (www.online.msdw.com) provides customers with a Balances Portfolio View that gives the real-time value of all the customer's personal accounts. The Balances Portfolio View shows the total net worth of the account, long and short market values, cash, margin calls, and buying power and margin information. Other portfolio screens include views of holdings, the portfolio's asset allocation, activity, and orders. Discover Brokerage provides a demo of its portfolio-tracking program. If you want a figure defined, just click the heading to bring up an explanation of that figure.

E*Trade (www.etrade.com) provides a portfolio management tool with your free registration. Click Log-In, and the program requests data. Click Portfolios and Markets, which automatically updates your portfolio to include trading activity. To create your portfolio, simply enter the name of your portfolio and a description (for example, Retirement Account). Enter the ticker symbol, type of security, quantity, cost, date acquired, and position (long or short) of the securities you own. The portfolio management program displays your portfolio performance. You can manually edit, add, or split investments into multiple portfolios (the college account, the retirement account, and so on).

Charles Schwab (www.schwab.com) with your free registration provides visitors with the portfolio management feature shown in Figure 16-6. At the home page, click MySchwab to personalize and start using the portfolio management tool. The portfolio shows the ticker symbol of the security, the quantity owned, the name of the security, and the current market value. For company news or charts of the security's performance, just click the appropriate links. Charles Schwab also provides online tools and information for beginning investors, retirement planning, online stock analysis and more.

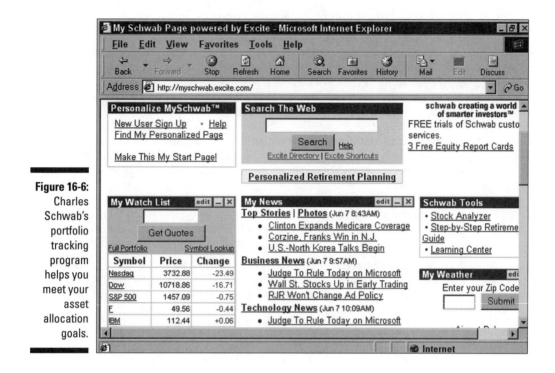

Figure 16-6:
Charles
Schwab's
portfolio
tracking
program
helps you
meet your
asset
allocation
goals.

Keeping the Winners and Selling the Losers: Measuring Performance

Measuring portfolio performance is often difficult. For example, suppose that you invest $2,000 in a mutual fund that returns 15 percent in the first quarter of the year. In each of the next three quarters, you invest $2,000, but the fund doesn't provide any returns during those months. Your return on the first $2,000 is 15 percent. Your return on $6,000 for nine months is zero. The fund reports an annual gain of 15 percent, not counting dividends and gains distributions. However, these percentages don't mean that you should measure performance on a short-term basis. Market prices vary and returns fluctuate for many reasons. What really counts is the true rate of return, which can't be measured from quarter to quarter.

Another problem in measuring portfolio performance is risk. Risk is defined as the variability of returns. In other words, the more the returns vary, the greater the risk. One of the disadvantages of using standard deviation (a measurement of the variability of historical returns around the average return) is that it doesn't take into consideration *good variability*. Good variability means that returns are exceeding expectations. This event increases the stock's volatility and standard deviation. The stock is now considered more *risky* because returns are higher than expected. What this shows is that standard deviation isn't always a good way to judge risk. In other words, standard deviation is just a measurement of volatility. Risk only enters the picture if volatility is *below* the investor's return target.

You can utilize many ways to measure the performance of your portfolio. One way to measure performance is to use *benchmarks* — that is, comparing the performance of your various investments to top performances and indices. For example:

- ✔ Divide your stocks into capitalization groups (small cap, mid cap, and large cap) and rank each group by P/E ratio. Compare your investments to top-performing stocks in each capitalization group daily and weekly.

- ✔ Divide your fixed-income investments (bonds and Treasury securities) by quality rating and then rank each group by yield. Compare your investments to the top-performing bonds in each asset allocation class.

Part IV

The Part of Tens

"HERE'S YOUR PROBLEM. SOME BOZO JAMMED YOUR KEYBOARD WITH A 4-LEAF CLOVER."

In this part . . .

In The Part of Tens, I offer some timely advice about how you can tell a good deal from a scam. I also tell you about the ten signals that it's time to sell and how to spot the green flags for buying.

Chapter 17

Almost Ten Warnings about Cyberfraud

● ●

In This Chapter

▶ Recognizing potential online investment scams

▶ Identifying pyramid schemes

▶ Requiring real financial disclosures

▶ Unmasking dishonest brokers by asking the right questions

▶ Knowing where to complain online if you receive an unscrupulous investment offer

▶ Evaluating the security of Internet transactions

● ●

The Securities and Exchange Commission receives over 200 complaints of online investment fraud a day despite many consumer warnings and a Federal crackdown. Don't get taken for a ride on the Information Superhighway. In the past, swindlers used the U.S. mail and telemarketing boiler rooms to exploit unsuspecting investors. Fraudsters have now invaded cyberspace. Cyber scam artists have taken online investor fraud to a more sophisticated level with look-alike portals of legitimate brokerages complete with hyperlinks to fabricated press releases and fake news stories that look almost like the real thing.

Investigating investments is difficult. The terms of the deal may be hard to understand, and the investment literature and salespeople may omit key facts. However, you can observe warning signs of potential scams, schemes, and deceptions. Doing so involves a little effort, homework, and investigating, but isn't that what investing is all about?

In this chapter, I provide almost ten warnings about online investment information and offers that may be too good to be true. I provide guidelines for checking out brokers and investments, and tips for identifying a pyramid scheme. I show you how to read financial disclosures to get the facts, and I explain how to complain online. I also offer a few thoughts about the online security of your personal and financial information.

Don't Believe Everything You Read

Every investor dreams of being an early stockowner in a Microsoft or Intel Corp. Dishonest brokers and stock promoters prey upon this greed and offer unsuspecting investors low-priced stocks in companies with new products or technologies (like the self-chilling soda can). Often, these companies have lots of sizzle and no steak — for example:

- On April 1, 1999, the Australian Securities and Investments Commission (ASIC) launched its own fake investment site that invited investment in Millennium Bug Insurance (www.smbi.com.au). On May 4, 1999, the commission revealed that its own fake investment site persuaded 233 people to part with more than $2.64 million U.S. dollars ($4 million Australian).

- Pairgain, a California company, was touted by scam artists on Internet message boards as being poised for a takeover by an Israeli company. The "takeover" announcement was hyperlinked to a bogus news release that looked like it was written by a legitimate financial reporting service. (This is a classic "pump and dump" scam. Fraudsters artificially drive up the stock price and unload it on unsuspecting investors who believe the stock is on the rise.)

- Cybersmears are also common. For example, a fraudster borrows 100 shares of a certain company's stock from a broker and immediately sells them at $10 a share. Then the fraudster starts an illegal negative message board campaign with fabricated news stories. The stock price drops to $8 a share. The fraudster purchases 100 shares at $8 a share and returns them to the broker. He then pockets the $2 a share difference, less interest.

Online frauds mirror the types of frauds that are perpetrated over the phone or through the mail. Many Internet messages are about general stock-picking advice or mention other investment possibilities. However, some messages tout specific stocks, moneymaking ventures, and service providers. Investment chat rooms now have sales pitches that offer more details by private e-mail and toll-free telephone numbers.

Investment swindlers can work anywhere, from dingy telemarketing offices to expensive hotel suites to cyberspace. They may be friends of friends, and they may wear natty suits or hard hats. They may be so-called "recognized experts" or have no connection to the investment community. However, they all have one goal — to get your money into their pockets.

If an Offer Seems Too Good to Be True, It Usually Is

As the popularity of the Internet grows, millions of people flock to the new Global Village. Inevitably, individuals with criminal intent are following the crowd. They seek to deceive the innocent, the hopeful, the naive, the poor, and the greedy. Consider the case of a New Jersey man who agreed to pay $5,000 in penalties after being charged with using the Internet to illegally promote himself as an investment adviser and sales broker. He also claimed his investment strategies were conservative when they were very risky, and stated that the investments were guaranteed when they weren't.

Online investor fraud often starts when you receive an e-mail message describing an appealing offer. Offers that seem too good to be true usually are. Here are a few of the warning signs to help you identify potential scams:

- **Exceptional profits:** Usually, the profits are large enough to get your interest but not large enough to make you suspicious.

- **Low risk — high return:** All investments involve some risk. If a fraudster advertises "no-risk," this should be an immediate red flag that something is wrong. Don't invest if you don't know exactly what the risks are. (Remember, fraudsters don't honor money-back guarantees.)

- **Urgency:** Fraudsters usually offer a reason why you must invest as quickly as possible. They may tell you that delays may mean losses of big profits or that they're limiting the offer to just a few individuals. Fraudsters often play on new technological advances that create a brief market that you must get into right away. However, if you feel that the posting is valid, wait before you respond. Others won't be shy about posting their opinions.

- **High-pressure tactics:** Fraudsters often act like they're doing you a favor by letting you get in on the investment opportunity. Don't be afraid to ask questions publicly. Post a follow-up message. If the original post is valid, the person who sent it will be happy to post a public response.

Although you can find plenty of helpful investment-related postings online (after all, that's what this book is all about), the Internet, like other places, has its share of fraudsters. The National Association of Securities Dealers Web site at `www.nasd.com` provides investor education about different types of investment scams, including pyramid schemes, precious metal frauds, and stock swindles. (See the section, "Determining Whether an Investment Is a Pyramid Scheme," later in this chapter, to find out about pyramid schemes.)

Checking It Out Before You Put Your Money Down

The explosion of the Internet has created new opportunities and new dangers for investors. If you're an online investment victim, the chances of getting your money back are slim. Even in cases where government agencies recover money, the consumer usually gets back less than 10 cents on the dollar. The best defense is to thoroughly investigate an online investment *before* you put your money down.

The Federal Trade Commission (FTC) inspects investment swindles and provides summaries that document recent allegations of corporate fraud and misconduct in relation to securities investors. The Alexander Law Firm sponsors a Web site (www.defrauded.com) that names these fraudulent organizations and provides links to the summary reports. New companies are added on a regular basis. I suggest bookmarking this page and including it as part of your investment candidate analysis. (I think of this approach as being similar to a cashier checking to see if someone's name is on the bad check list before accepting his or her check.)

Here are some suggestions about how to investigate that "once in a lifetime offer:"

- ✔ Check with your city or state consumer protection agency; it may have information about the firm you're considering investing in. Additionally, a consumer protection agency can direct you to other organizations that may have information about the investment.

- ✔ Contact regulators. Organizations that you can contact include the Federal Trade Commission, the Securities and Exchange Commission, and the National Association of Securities Dealers.

- ✔ For the name, address, telephone number, and other contact information of your securities regulator, go to NASAA at www.nasaa.org, and click Find Your Securities Regulator.

- ✔ Write or telephone law enforcement agencies. Fraud is illegal in every state in the nation. You can contact the local public prosecutor, the state attorney general, and the state securities administrator.

The Better Business Bureau Web page at www.bbb.org provides helpful reliability reports on firms. You need to read reliability reports before you purchase the firm's securities. Each report indicates how long the firm has been in business, how long the Better Business Bureau has known about the company, complaint patterns (if any), and whether any government agencies — for example, the Federal Trade Commission (FTC) or the State Attorney General — have taken any enforcement actions in the last three years.

Determining Whether an Investment Is a Pyramid Scheme

Pyramid schemes, sometimes called *multilevel marketing plans,* are sure ways to lose money. One person recruits six friends; those six people recruit six more friends — and so on, in a relentless search for new recruits. If everyone cooperates, then by level 15, the scheme needs 7.6 billion participants — more than the Earth's population.

Profits from these schemes don't come from selling products or distributorships but from recruiting new participants. The endless recruiting of more participants eventually leads to an oversupply of sellers. Investors are left with garages full of products and the loss of their investment.

Three elements characterize pyramid schemes:

- A reliance on funds from new investors (recruits) to pay returns, commissions, or bonuses to old investors.
- The need for an inexhaustible supply of new recruits.
- The promise of earning profits without providing goods or services.

Understanding What Real Financial Disclosures Include

If you're considering investing in a company, you may want to download and print a copy of the investment offer. If the sales literature doesn't include a prospectus with financial statements, ask for one. If you're told that the company doesn't have a prospectus, request a written financial disclosure about the company. All in all, you should have the following information:

- **Offering circular:** Sales literature that presents the investment.
- **Prospectus:** A formal written statement that discloses the terms of a public offering of a security or a mutual fund. The prospectus is required to divulge both positive and negative information to investors about the proposed offering.

✔ **Annual report:** A written report that includes a statement by the chief executive officer, a narrative about last year's performance, and a forecast for next year's performance. Financial statements include a balance sheet, income statement, a statement of cash flows, and retained earnings.

✔ **Audited financial statements:** Financial statements audited by a certified public accounting firm.

The Securities and Exchange Commission (SEC), located at www.sec.gov, doesn't require companies that are seeking less than $1 million to be "registered," but it does require these firms to file a *Form D*. Form D doesn't include an audited financial statement but it does state the names and addresses of the owners and promoters of the firm. Other information is limited. If a Form D isn't available, the SEC suggests that you call its Investor Education and Assistance Department at 202-942-7040.

Tell-Tale Signs of Dishonest Brokers

Dishonest brokers often ask their victims a steady stream of questions designed to derail honest investors from asking the right questions. Dishonest brokers don't want curious customers. In contrast, honest brokers encourage you to ask questions, provide you with additional educational materials, and make certain that you understand the risks involved in your investment decision. And if you decide not to spend your money, they are untroubled by your investment decision.

The National Futures Association has collected 16 questions that are turn-offs for dishonest brokers (www.pueblo.gsa.gov/cic_text/money/swindles/swindles.txt). In the following list, I've tailored those questions to meet the needs of online investors:

✔ **Where did you get my name?** The dishonest broker may say "a select list of investors," but your name was probably obtained from a Usenet newsgroup question you asked, a bulk e-mail response, or from a mailing list subscription list. Individuals who have been duped in the past may be on the "select list." They were conned before and probably can be conned again.

✔ **What risks are involved in the investment?** All investments except U.S. Treasury securities have some default risk. (U.S. Treasury securities are considered *risk free*. The Federal government backs these securities just as it does the *legal tender* — that is, the money — in your pocket. The government isn't likely to fail, so the securities — and your money — are risk free.) Some investments have more risk than others do. A salesperson who really has a sure thing won't be on the telephone talking with you.

✔ **Can you send me a written explanation of the investment, so I can consider it at my leisure?** This question provides two turn-offs to dishonest brokers. First, swindlers are reluctant to put in writing anything that may become evidence in a fraud trial. Second, swindlers are impatient; they want your money right now.

✔ **Would you explain your investment proposal to my attorney, financial planner or investment advisor, or banker?** You know the investment is a scam if the salesperson says something like "Normally, I would be glad to, but . . ." or "Unfortunately, we don't have enough time," or "Can't you make your own decisions?"

✔ **Can you give me references and the names of your principal investors and officers?** Swindlers often change their names so you can't check their histories. Make certain that the reference list contains the names of well-known banks and reputable brokerage firms that you can easily contact. The Investor Protection Trust page (www.investorprotection. org) includes links to various resources you can use to check out a broker or other financial professional.

✔ **Which exchanges are the securities traded on? Can I have copies of the prospectus, the risk disclosure statement, or the audited financial statements?** For legitimate, registered investments, these documents are normal. A legitimate investment may or may not be traded on an exchange. However, fraudulent investments never are. Exchanges have extensive rules for competitive pricing and fair dealing. Those that don't follow the rules are subject to severe sanctions.

✔ **What regulatory agency is the investment subject to?** Tell the broker that you want to check the investment's good standing with its regulatory agency before going forward. The possibility of having to talk to a representative of a regulatory agency is a real turn-off to a swindler.

✔ **How long has your company been in business, and what is your track record? Can I meet another representative of your firm?** If the broker or the investment doesn't seem to have a past, the deal may be a scam. Many swindlers have been running scams for years and aren't anxious to talk about it.

✔ **When and where can I meet you to further discuss this investment?** Legitimate brokers can tell you how much of a return investors have enjoyed in the past. Even if you do get this information in writing, keep in mind that past performance doesn't indicate future performance. However, dishonest brokers often won't take the time to meet with you, and they don't want you in their place of business. Legitimate registered brokers are happy to sit down and discuss your financial goals.

✔ **Where will my money be? What type of accounting can I expect?** Often, funds for certain investments are required to stay in separate accounts, at all times. Find out which accounting firm does the firm's auditing and what type of external audits the firm is subject to. (Make certain that the well-known accounting firm is actually the auditor.)

✔ **How much of my money will go to management fees, commissions, and similar expenses?** Legitimate investments often have restrictions on the amount of management fees the firm can charge. Getting what the firm charges in writing is important. Compare the firm's fees to charges for similar investments.

✔ **How can I get my money if I want to liquidate my investment?** You may discover that your investment can't be sold or that selling your investment involves substantial costs. If you're unable to get a solid answer in writing, the investment may be a scam.

✔ **If a dispute arises, how will it be resolved?** No one wants to go to court and sue. The investment should be subject to a regulatory agency's guidelines so that disputes are resolved inexpensively through arbitration, mediation, or a reparation procedure.

Is your broker dishonest or just incompetent? The Stock Detective at `www.stockdetective.com/states.asp` can help. This Web site provides a list of state investment watchdog agencies. It includes the names, addresses, telephone numbers, names of directors, and contact people of each state's securities commission.

Where to Complain Online

The Internet provides many ways to complain about online investor fraud. Here are three good resources:

✔ **Better Business Bureau** (`www.bbb.org`) has an online complaint form and promises to follow up within two weeks of your complaint.

✔ **Securities and Exchange Commission** (`www.sec.gov`) has an excellent online complaint process.

✔ **National Fraud Information Center** (`www.fraud.org`) forwards your complaint to the appropriate organizations and includes it in the center's Internet fraud statistics (which may not help you get your money back but may be helpful to other online investors).

Your Bank Account Number, Security, and the Internet

Just as you take various precautions to protect your home and its contents, you must prevent online thieves from accessing your personal and financial assets via the Internet. Locked doors, alarm systems, and nosy neighbors can help you safeguard your home. Precautions on the Internet take such forms as firewalls, passwords, and encryption of important information.

Online financial institutions use a distributed security system. Security is on your computer during the transmission of information and in the bank's own computer system. Online banks use several types of security systems simultaneously:

- ✔ **Encryption:** *Encryption* is a high-tech word for encoding and is used by more people than spies. It is used so that your banking information is gibberish to unauthorized individuals.

- ✔ **Passwords:** Personal passwords are necessary to access your account information.

- ✔ **Automatic sign-off protection:** When you sign off, your session terminates so that no one can continue in your absence.

- ✔ **Browser security:** Your browser isn't allowed to save any of your bank information.

- ✔ **Monitoring:** The system constantly scans for unauthorized intrusions.

At banks, the Federal Deposit Insurance Corporation (FDIC) insures your money, but online securities firms don't have similar insurance for consumers. To date, electronic theft has been slight, but as more money flows over the Internet, the need for insurance is certain to change.

Chapter 18

Ten Signals to Sell

- -

In This Chapter

▶ Getting a grip on when to hold and when to fold

▶ Setting profit goals and maintaining them

▶ Facing your disappointments

▶ Moving out mediocre performers

▶ Watching what the insiders are doing

▶ Keeping an eye on the right economic indicators

- -

*I*ndividual investors routinely sell winners too early and ride losers too long. Knowing which stocks to sell and when to sell them is the hallmark of a savvy investor. From the time that you purchase a stock, you want to be considering the right time to sell and reap your rewards.

If you're pondering a sale, don't focus on only the sale price. Take the time to ask several questions, and to research the Internet for answers about the security's future.

When you purchase a security, you anticipate a certain rate of return. To examine your investment selection's performance, calculate what you have gained by holding the security:

✔ **For bonds,** measure the current yield by taking the annual interest payment and dividing it by the current price of the bond. (For details, see Chapter 13.)

✔ **For stocks and mutual funds,** calculate the investment's total return (ending value less beginning value plus income divided by beginning value). (See Chapter3 for more information.)

To check the quality rating of all bonds, read the appropriate annual reports and fund statements for your stocks and mutual funds. Remember that no scientific formulas exist to guide your selling decisions. Knowing some general rules and the kinds of questions to ask, however, can help you become a more successful investor.

The selling system that's best is the one that locks in gains and protects you if the value of your assets drops. Your personal selling system needs to work well with your investment time frame, investment style, and risk-tolerance level.

Know When to Fold

In this section, I describe some general examples of selling rules that beginning investors may find valuable. Veteran investors may have the same selling rules or quite different ones. Regardless of which category you fall into, both new and experienced investors need to choose a personal system and stick to it.

A sure way to lose big money is to hang on to an investment that's losing money. Try not to emotionally involve yourself with your investment selections. One way to lower the likelihood of holding on to an investment for too long is to develop a few personal selling rules. Write your personal selling rules in your investment plan and store the plan on your computer's hard disk. Your personal selling rules may state, for example, that you're to sell the stock if any of the following conditions occur:

- The stock drops below your predetermined trading range.

- Market experts call the company "steady," or dividend increases are behind the general market.

- You discover that the company's sales growth, profitability, or financial health is in trouble.

- You discover that the industry is in a serious decline.

- The company loses its competitive edge, and market share is declining.

- The stock's trading volume increases, but the stock price doesn't rise.

Don't hold on to any securities that you don't believe are investment candidates.

FundAlarm (www.fundalarm.com) is a free, noncommercial Web site that provides objective information to help individual investors make mutual fund selling decisions. FundAlarm compares your mutual fund to an appropriate benchmark and tracks its performance. If the fund consistently underperforms, you should consider selling.

Set Profit-Taking Goals

Realizing your profit is what investing is all about. Paper profits may look good, but money in the bank is what pays for your child's education or enables you to retire early. If your stock is selling for a high price and is now a large part of your portfolio, you may want to sell.

What's more, if you're contemplating selling the stock, you don't want to sell before the stock reaches its peak. In other words, you want to sell at the best price and before the stock starts to decline. What should you do? The following list gives you some ideas:

- ✔ Say that your stock is currently selling for 50 percent more than your purchase price. Take the money and run if the stock is not likely to go any higher.

- ✔ Set a target price that may not be your sell price but a benchmark. If your stock reaches the benchmark price, reevaluate your investment plan. Make certain that you check similar companies to see whether they're selling at the same level or higher. If so, you may want to raise your target price.

- ✔ Consider selling if a stock starts showing up on brokerage buy lists, gets included in many mutual funds, or receives lots of favorable press.

- ✔ If a winner now represents more than 10 percent of your portfolio, you may want to sell part of your holdings. That way, you lock in part of the profit and still benefit if the stock keeps rising.

- ✔ Don't try to sell at the stock's top price. You didn't buy at the bottom, so don't expect to sell at the very top. Even after all your analyses, you still need to rely on your gut feelings about the right time to sell.

Remember that you must pay taxes on your capital gains. To get a handle on your tax liability, see the Wells Fargo Securities Special Report on the Web at `wellsfargo.com/investing/srtra/`.

You Can't Be Right All the Time

Selling a loser is often harder than selling a winner. If you purchase a stock with a certain expectation, but the company never lives up to your expectations, you should sell. The following list provides a few examples of such situations:

> ✔ Sell a stock if it declines 20 percent in a down market and 10 percent in an up market. If a stock drops 15 percent in a flat market, reevaluate.
>
> ✔ The company's growth rate and earnings trends peak and then fall.
>
> ✔ The company cuts its dividend or stops dividend payments entirely.

If you sell a loser, note exactly why it didn't turn out as expected and include these notes in your investment plan. Such documentation helps you avoid making similar mistakes in the future.

Everyone expects strong performers to keep up the pace. Past performance however, doesn't guarantee future performance. For more information, see the article "Do Past Winners Repeat?" at the Investor Home Web site (www.investorhome.com/mutual.htm#do).

If the Stock Is Going Nowhere, Get Going

If the stock or fund in which you invested is a mediocre performer, you need to replace it. You may not want to rush to judgment, however. Give the company about a year to make any needed changes to bring its performance up to speed. Then sell it if you don't see any improvement at all.

You can tell whether you have a nowhere stock by comparing it to the appropriate index. (See the section, "What Does the S&P 500 Have to Do with Anything?" in Chapter 8.) If the index is consistently matching your nowhere stock, you may want to consider selling. Doing so frees up funds for you to use in purchasing better performers. If you don't have any great investment candidates, think about spreading the proceeds among your portfolio's best existing ideas. Or, better yet, just hang in there — a good investment opportunity is likely to appear sooner or later.

Get some help to beat the crowd from The Online Investor at www.investhelp.com.

Don't Be Fooled by P/E Spurts

Be suspicious of sudden jumps in the P/E (price/earnings) ratio. Such spurts may mean that it's headed for a fall. Soaring P/E ratios and depressed dividend yields can be signs that market prices are unstable. Consider selling if the P/E ratio rises more than 30 percent higher than its annual average for the last ten years. Say that the P/E ratio for the last ten years is 20, for example, and then it suddenly climbs to 26. Consider selling the stock. (On the other hand, don't sell stocks that are in a temporary sinking spell.)

Watch Interest Rates

Bond investors must anticipate the turns and directions of interest rates. If interest rates increase, bonds and bond fund prices decrease because buyers are less willing to purchase investments with lower rates than those stated on new bond issues. Bonds with longer maturity terms lose more value if interest rates continue to climb. Bonds are subject to inflationary expectations, monetary demand, and changes in short-term interest rate expectations. Thirty-year bonds purchased in the '70s, for example, lost approximately 45 percent of their value after interest rates increased in the '80s (for details, see Chapter 13). Keep in mind the following principles for a personal selling system:

- ✔ Rising interest rates tend to divert money from the stock market and depress stock prices.

- ✔ Low interest rates usually indicate a good time to own stocks, because the economy grows as a result, and stock prices are sure to increase.

- ✔ Declining interest rates indicate less fear of inflation.

- ✔ Income stocks often are more sensitive to changes in interest rates than are other types of stocks.

Keep an Eye on Economic Indicators

Until recently, inflation has averaged 3 percent a year since 1926. Investments like certificates of deposit, Treasury securities, agency bonds, and corporate bonds are fixed-income investments. Their yields don't vary regardless of the inflation rate. Over the long term, therefore, low-yielding fixed-income securities can lose out to inflation.

Stock market declines often precede economic recessions. Indications of an economic slump may suggest to you that you want to get out of the market. Stock prices often rebound at the end of a recession, however, which argues against selling during a recession.

For more information about what to look for in economic data, see the CBS MarketWatch Web site (cbs.marketwatch.com/news/primer/stocks/econ_primer.htx?source=htx/http2_mw).

Watch What the Insiders Are Doing

Do you want an inside tip? Watch what insiders do with the stocks for their own companies. The SEC requires that officers, directors, and shareholders owning 10 percent or more of the company's stock report their trades. These reports are readily accessible on the Internet.

Insiders trade shares so that they can purchase shares by using the options that they receive as part of their employment contracts. Additionally, if the stock's value is significantly different from its selling price (either higher or lower), you see lots of insider trading activity. High sales activity by insiders may foreshadow a financial debacle. Consider selling your own shares if such trading occurs (especially if the sale price is decreasing).

For a daily report of insider trading, see CNET Investor (`www.investor.cnet.com`). Bloomberg powers this handy daily report.

If the Company or Fund Changes

The company in which you own stock may have changed its core business since your purchase, or the fund changed its objectives or increased fees. You need to think about the original reasons you purchased a company's stock or a mutual fund. If the investments no longer meet these criteria, you're best off to move on.

Similarly, if your own financial situation changes, you may want to sell some or all of your investments. A good reason to do so is if your risk-tolerance level changes; for example, you're getting close to retirement, or your child is about ready to start college.

Have you witnessed a material change in the company? For the latest news, see CBS MarketWatch (`cbs.marketwatch.com`) or Yahoo! Finance (`quote.yahoo.com`).

Chapter 19

Ten Green Flags for Buying

The exit poll for the 1994 election indicated that 24 percent of all Americans have investments. More recent studies by the National Association of Investors Corporation (www.better-investing.org) show that more than 51 million individuals invest in the New York Stock Exchange. Furthermore, if you have a pension, you're likely to have at least half your pension funds currently invested in the stock market. Despite all this popularity, however, equities (stocks) have a serious drawback: They don't offer the security of interest-bearing investments (market funds, CDs, and fixed-income securities).

Interest-bearing securities offer consistent returns. In contrast, stock price fluctuations just "happen." Every stock investor can count on market increases and decreases. These fluctuations aren't company specific, but that fact doesn't offer much comfort. Over time, stock investments tend to reward patient investors with good, inflation-beating returns that are greater than those of any other type of investment. For many individuals, investing is the only way that they can reach their financial goals.

Over the years, avid investors have developed many methods to help others decide which stocks to buy and when to purchase them. No hard-and-fast rules exist. The approach that's best is the one that works for you. The following sections offer a collection of investor wisdom that can assist you in maximizing your personal wealth.

Buy If the Stock Is at Its Lowest Price

"Buy low" is simpler said than done. Excellent investment candidates are stocks that are selling at their lowest price in three to five years (assuming that the company's financial position hasn't deteriorated). Wait for the price to stop declining and the company to show some strength, however, before you put your money down.

You must condition yourself to work against the crowd. The time to sell your stock is whenever it's "hot," its prices are high, and everyone wants to own it. For free, delayed quotes and online company reports, see Zacks Investment Research at www.zacks.com.

Check Out the Earnings Forecast

People use *earnings forecasts* in fundamental analyses to determine the fair value of a stock. If this fair value is less than the stock's current price, the stock is overpriced. If the fair value is more than the current price, the stock may be underpriced and a bargain.

Financial software developers and most brokerages have analysts that develop earnings forecast for companies. Prices for these reports vary from free to several hundred dollars. The Internet provides many sources for earnings forecast reports. Here are a few examples.

- ✔ **Financial Web** (www.financialweb.com/research) provides free earnings upgrade and downgrade information in addition to other related information.

- ✔ **Stock Wiz Links** (www.i-soft.com) provides a links page for company information. Just enter the ticker symbol of the company you're researching, and you have your choice of hyperlinks to quotes, news, broker recommendations, research analysts' earning estimates (and actuals), company profiles and fundamentals, SEC filings, and intraday charts.

- ✔ **Thomson Investors Network** (www.thomsoninvest.net) offers free access to First Call Snapshots of earnings data, including current quarter and current fiscal year estimates, recommendations, and price to earnings ratios. (From the home page, click Earnings.) Get estimate revisions, earnings surprises, and a report listing the 10 most heavily followed companies expected to report earnings the next day. For full access to the First Call Earnings Center, subscriptions are $19.95 per month, or $199 for the year. There is a free 30-day trial.

Watch for Stocks That Are Trading under Book Value

Book value is the company's net-asset value — that is, assets minus liabilities divided by the number of outstanding shares. This amount appears in the company's annual report. See the Securities and Exchange Commission (www.sec.gov) and Zacks Company Reports (www.zacks.com). Companies that sell below their book value (if they don't have serious problems) are often bargains.

Beware of Firms with High Long-Term Debt

Usually, the lower the debt ratio is, the safer the company is. Beware of companies that aggressively borrow but never earn a high return on their new capital. Compare the company you're researching to similar firms. Companies that have paid down their debt over the last two or three years, however, may be worth your serious consideration.

Get an industry report from Hoover's (www.hoovers.com), and discover the average debt ratio for the industry. Compare this average to the debt ratio of the firm you're researching. To discover which firms have low debt ratios, use the online stock screens at Quicken (www.quicken.com) or Morningstar (www.morningstar.com).

Invest in Entrepreneurial Companies

Locate a rising company in a rising market. Small and midsized companies tend to be hungrier and more innovative than their older and bigger siblings. A company needs something new to create a startling increase in stock price, and these companies may have that something.

Successes in American industry come from a major new product or service, new management, or an important change for the better in the conditions of a particular industry.

Select companies with entrepreneurial management — rather than caretakers who discourage innovation — that takes risks and keeps up with the times. Companies with managing executives who own a meaningful share of the outstanding stock are generally good investment candidates.

Bigger is not always better. If you're choosing between two stocks, and one has 10 million shares outstanding and the other has 60 million shares outstanding, select the smaller company. All things being equal (that well-used economics expression), the smaller company is going to be a better performer.

To find out where the entrepreneurial companies are, see *The Wall Street Journal* (www.wsj.com), annual subscription, $59; *CNN Financial Network* (www.cnnfn.com), free; the *Investor's Business Daily* (www.investors.com), which requires your free registration for most of its content; or the ABC News business section (abcnews.go.com/sections/business).

Invest in Industry Leaders

If you investigate a company in a specific industry, determine which companies are growing the fastest in that industry and which are the industry leaders. By focusing on just these two elements, you're likely to reduce the number of investment candidates for your consideration in this industry by 80 percent. You also discover the following information:

- ✔ Many companies in the industry have no growth or display lackluster growth.
- ✔ Older companies have slower growth rates than do younger companies.

Remember that investing in industry laggards seldom pays, even if they're amazingly cheap. Look for the market leader and make certain that you have a good reason to invest in the industry in the first place. Additionally, be aware that all industries have their own cycles of growth, and you want to invest in an industry that's in an upswing. For industry surveys and reports, see Value Line Investment Surveys (www.valueline.com).

Buy Good Performers

Try to buy for value and not for price. Select companies that regularly outperformed their competition in the last three to five years. Invest in companies that have consistent rather than flashy returns. Take into consideration the following guidelines:

✔ Check the company's stability and examine its five-year earnings record.

✔ Keep in mind that an annual percentage increase is desirable but so is stability and consistency over the past five-year's earnings.

✔ You may want to consider not including a company's one-time extraordinary gains in your calculations.

✔ Determine whether the company's annual growth rate is between 25 percent and 50 percent for the last four or five years. If so, it may be a winner.

Don't try to chase after last year's high performer; it could be this year's loser. For company reports, see Standard & Poor's Wealthbuilder (`www.wealthbuilder.com`).

Select Your P/E Ratio Strategy

Any analysis of investment candidates generally includes P/E (price/earnings) ratios. The importance of these ratios varies from analyst to analyst. The following subsections describe two strategies that are worthwhile to consider. Select the one that works best for you. (See Chapter 12 for additional information about P/E ratios.)

Low P/E and high dividend approach

Long-term investors often employ the "7 and 7" approach — that is, they purchase stock in companies with a P/E ratio of 7 or less and a dividend yield greater than 7. Additionally, if the company's P/E ratio is lower than 10, and the earnings are rising, you may have found a winner. Make certain, however, that no major long-term problems exist that can drive the P/E to 4 or lower by investigating the security. (See Chapter 11 for details.)

High P/E ratios are worth the price

The following example shows that you often get what you pay for. From 1953 to 1985, the average P/E ratio for the best-performing emerging stocks was 20. The Dow Jones Industrial's P/E at the same time averaged 15. If you weren't willing to pay for the stocks that were trading over the average, you eliminated most of the best investments available.

For more information about how to use P/E ratios in your stock buying analyses, visit the Investor Home Web site (`www.investorhome.com`).

Look for Strong Dividend Pay-Out Records

If you're risk-averse, your time horizon for investments is shorter than that of many investors, or you believe that the market is heading for a downturn, you may want to invest in companies with consistent records of paying generous dividends. These *income stocks* tend to hold their value in volatile markets because investors are confident that they're going to continue to receive sizable dividends. The disadvantage of these companies is that, because they pay out such a large proportion of earnings, they may not retain enough capital to grow the company. This failure to invest in their own growth may cause the stock prices of these companies to drag. Additionally, income stocks are more sensitive to changes in interest rates than are other stock types. To find companies that investors categorize as income stocks, see Vector Vest (a software developer), at www.vectorvest.com/safegro.htm, for a weekly report.

Appendix

About the CD

_H_ ere's some of what you can find on the _Investing Online For Dummies,_ 3rd Edition, CD-ROM:

- ✔ An easy-to-navigate, electronic version of the book's Investing Online Directory so you can quickly jump to the Internet sites you need for selecting, buying, selling, and tracking your investments online.

- ✔ Free, high-quality software programs to assist you with a variety of investor tasks.

- ✔ Shareware and freeware programs for financial planning and analysis, portfolio management, and other essential investor activities.

- ✔ Demonstration versions and free trials of invaluable software tools for online investors.

System Requirements

Make sure that your computer meets the following minimum system requirements:

- ✔ A PC with a Pentium or faster processor or a Mac OS computer with a PowerPC processor.

- ✔ Microsoft Windows 95/98/NT/2000 or Mac OS system software 7.5 or later.

- ✔ At least 16MB of total RAM installed on your computer. For best performance, I recommend that Windows 95-equipped PCs have at least 32MB of RAM installed.

- ✔ At least 100MB of hard drive space available to install all the software from this CD. (You need less space if you don't install every program.)

- ✔ A CD-ROM drive — double-speed (2x) or faster.

- ✔ A sound card for PCs. (Mac OS computers have built-in sound support.)

- ✔ A monitor capable of displaying at least 256 colors or grayscale.

- ✔ A modem with a speed of at least 28,800 bps.

If your computer doesn't match up to most of the requirements, you may have problems using the contents of the CD.

If you need more information on the basics, check out *PCs For Dummies*, 7th Edition, by Dan Gookin.

How to Use the CD Using Microsoft Windows

To install the programs from the CD to your hard drive, follow these steps:

1. **Insert the CD into your computer's CD-ROM drive.**

2. **Open your browser.**

   Just in case you do not have a browser, we have included Microsoft Internet Explorer as well as Netscape Communicator. You can find them in the Programs folders at the root of the CD.

3. **Click Start⇨Run.**

4. **In the dialog box that appears, type** D:\START.HTM.

   Replace *D* with the proper drive letter if your CD-ROM drive uses a different letter. (If you don't know the letter, see how your CD-ROM drive is listed under My Computer.)

5. **Read through the license agreement, nod your head, and then click the Accept button if you want to use the CD — after you click Accept, you'll jump to the Main Menu.**

   This action displays the file that will walk you through the content of the CD.

6. **To navigate within the interface, simply click any topic of interest to take you to an explanation of the files on the CD and how to use or install them.**

7. **To install the software from the CD, simply click the software name.**

   You'll see two options: You can run or open the file from the current location, or you can save the file to your hard drive. Choose to run or open the file from its current location, and the installation procedure continues. After you are done with the interface, simply close your browser as usual.

To run some of the programs, you may need to keep the CD inside your CD-ROM drive. This is a Good Thing. Otherwise, the installed program would have required you to install a very large chunk of the program to your hard drive space, which would have kept you from installing other software.

How to Use the CD Using the Mac OS

To install the programs from the CD to your hard drive, follow these steps:

1. **Insert the CD into your computer's CD-ROM drive.**

   An icon representing the CD appears on your Mac desktop. Chances are, the icon looks like a CD-ROM.

2. **Double-click the CD icon to show the CD's contents.**

3. **Double-click the Read Me First icon.**

   This text file contains information about the CD's programs and any last-minute instructions you need to know about installing the programs on the CD that I don't cover in this appendix.

4. **Open your browser.**

   In case you don't have a browser, we have included the two most popular ones for your convenience — Microsoft Internet Explorer and Netscape Communicator.

5. **To install the software on this CD, just drag the program's folder from the CD window and drop it on your hard drive icon.**

   After you install the programs that you want, you can eject the CD. Carefully place it back in the plastic jacket of the book for safekeeping.

   After you click an install button, the CD interface drops to the background while the CD begins installation of the program you choose.

MindSpring Internet Service Provider

For Mac and Windows. Commercial version.

In case you don't have a connection to the information superhighway, the CD includes sign-on software for MindSpring Internet Access, an Internet service provider.

If you already have an Internet service provider, be forewarned that downloading the MindSpring Internet Access software may cause you to lose your Internet access with your current provider. The software makes changes to your computer's current Internet configuration and may replace the current settings.

When you install MindSpring on the Mac, the installation program asks you for a key code. Enter **DUMY8579** into the dialog box. Be sure to use all capital letters, just as it's shown here.

After you are signed on, one of the first places you can check out is the MindSpring Web site at `www.mindspring.com`. (You do need a credit card to sign up with MindSpring Internet Access.)

An Electronic Version of the Directory

The *Investing Online For Dummies,* 3rd Edition, companion CD-ROM includes a listing of the book's Investing Online Directory, which lets you quickly go to the Internet sites you want. You can access these links from the HTML interface.

What Investor Software You'll Find

This section is a summary of the software on this book's companion CD-ROM. The CD interface can help you install the software easily. (If you have no idea what I'm talking about when I say "CD Interface," see the section, "How to Use the CD Using Microsoft Windows," earlier in this appendix.) This summary is divided into four parts.

- ✔ The first section includes short descriptions of all the free software programs you'll find on the companion CD-ROM.

- ✔ The second section discusses the shareware and freeware programs that are included on the CD-ROM. I know these programs are available on the Internet, but if you download them from the CD-ROM you'll be certain they are virus free, and you won't have to pay for your Internet connection or tie up your telephone connection while the programs are downloading.

 The second section is divided into five subcategories. That is, investor shareware and freeware programs that focus on: stocks, bonds, mutual funds, options, and other types of investments.

- ✔ The third section of the summary describes the investor demonstration programs you'll find on the companion CD-ROM.

- ✔ The last section of the summary presents the investor simulation programs you'll find on the companion CD-ROM.

Free software programs that every investor can use

If you love getting something for free, these programs are just what you're looking for. The following sections describe the free software you can find on the *Investing Online For Dummies* companion CD-ROM.

Adobe Acrobat Reader

For Mac and Windows. Freeware.

Web pages may be great looking, but some publishers aren't happy with having to change the original page layout to an HTML design. (HTML is the computer language that Web pages are written in.) To avoid having to use HTML, some publishers use the Adobe portable document format (PDF), which preserves the page layout and lets you see pages in their original glory. With Acrobat Reader, you can view and print PDF files. For details about Acrobat Reader, see www.adobe.com/prodindex/acrobat/readstep.html.

Internet Explorer

For Mac and Windows. Commercial product.

Internet Explorer 5.01 brings you Web browsing features that provide an easy, consistent, and organized way to explore the Web. The integration into Windows makes it easy to find the information you need, whether it's on your computer's hard drive, a local area network, or the Internet. For more on Internet Explorer 5.01, refer to microsoft.com/windows/ie/default.htm.

Netscape Communicator

For Mac and Windows. Commercial product.

While the Netscape folks are working on Netscape Communicator 5.0, others in the organization have been improving the 4.0 version. Netscape Communicator 4.72 adds several new features to satisfy corporate customers, brings its mail and graphics capabilities up-to-date, and makes it easier for you to stay in touch with your friends. For details, see home.netscape.com/comprod/mirror/index.html.

Options Toolbox for Windows

For Windows. Commercial product.

Designed for both beginners and experts, this software can help you with the fundamentals of options trading. The program includes an options position-modeling feature that simulates the performance of your planned strategy under a variety of conditions. Use this software to test before you invest. For more information, see www.cboe.com/education/software.htm.

(**Note:** Before you use the Options Toolbox software, you have to accept the terms of the License Agreement that appears on the screen. If you don't accept the terms of the License Agreement, you can't use the software.)

Shareware and freeware financial management programs

Shareware programs are not free. Shareware programs are free to try but cost a few dollars to keep, which allows software developers to distribute their programs inexpensively. Shareware programs use an honor system. If you don't like the program, you delete it from your computer. If you keep the program, you pay by registering the program, which entitles you to upgrades, information, and other goodies from the software developer. In contrast, freeware programs are yours to keep at no charge.

The Internet provides many downloadable financial shareware and freeware programs for PC and Macintosh computers. The book's companion CD-ROM includes some of the best shareware and freeware programs available. The following sections outline what you'll find on the CD-ROM for personal financial management.

Shareware and freeware for stocks

Byte into the Market
For Windows. Shareware.

This technical analysis and charting software emphasizes mechanical-system oriented trading approaches. Develop and try stock trading systems. For additional information, see www.tarnsoft.com.

Capital Gainz for Windows
For Windows. Shareware.

This popular shareware program is terrific for handling stocks, bonds, and mutual funds. Record your purchases, sales, dividends, capital gains, and other transactions. Calculate your gains or losses, and print reports and tax forms. Visit www.localweb.com/alleycatsw for details.

DLJ Direct Market Speed 3.0

For Windows. Freeware.

Market Speed allows self-directed investors to trade stocks, options, fixed-income securities, and mutual funds online with unprecedented convenience and ease, delivering up-to-the-minute news and quotes. You can get more information from `www.dljdirect.com`.

Financial Authority for Windows

For Windows. Shareware.

Designed for financial planning, this program tracks loans, annuities, retirement savings, series EEE bond appreciation, mutual fund performance, and more. Visit `www.halcyon.com/cbutton/welcome` for details.

MarketWatch

For Mac. Shareware.

MarketWatch is a utility that allows you to monitor the progress of your stocks and mutual funds while you continue to do word processing, search the Internet, or do other work on the computer. The MarketWatch ticker continues to move across your screen as you work in other application programs. For details, see `www.nearside.com/EkimSW/MarketWatch`.

NetStock

For Windows. Freeware.

NetStock is a fast, easy way to keep track of your stocks and mutual fund investments via the Internet. Fundamentally, the software is a simple stock and mutual fund quote-retrieval program. For a set of stocks, NetStock displays a variety of data, including the current price, P/E ratio, yield, value, daily high, daily low, 52-week high, 52-week low, and more. Quotes can be imported into the Intuit Quicken program. For details, see `www.splitcycle.com/pages/netstock.html`.

Personal Stock Monitor

For Windows. Shareware.

Personal Stock Monitor is a portfolio management program that retrieves stock quotes from a variety of free online quote servers. For details, see `www.personaltools.com/psm`.

QuickChart

For Windows. Shareware.

QuickChart is a great tool for viewing for financial data stored in MetaStock/CompuTrac format. User-configurable charts for stocks display up to three years of data with high/low bars, closes, trends, and averaging curves in your choice of colors. You can print selected charts or run all data in a slide-show presentation. Paul Gerhart publishes QuickChart.

Quote Ticker Bar for Windows

For Windows. Demo.

This shareware program can access stocks, mutual funds, or index prices from any of nine different online quote servers. You can even set an audio alarm to notify you if your preset price is reached. Check it out at Starfire Software (www.starfire-inc.com).

QuotesNow!

For Windows. 30-day trial.

QuotesNow! for Windows 95/98/NT retrieves stock, option, mutual fund, index, and other quotes, as well as news, graphs, and other information for all your investment needs. For details, see www.quotesnow.com.

QuoTracker

For Windows. Shareware.

QuoTracker collects and connects information (chart, quote, news, profile, and so on) from different free Internet services, puts everything in an easy-to-glance Explorer-like interface and lets you access all the information with a mouse click. QuoTracker has customization options, and lots of features and utilities. This handy program should make your investment tracking easier and help you keep abreast of market changes. For more information, see www.quotracker.com.

SpeedResearch Browser

For Windows. Shareware.

The SpeedResearch Browser is a Web browser with a collection of stock data links that may save you hours researching your stocks online. SpeedResearch Browser is highly customizable and easy to learn. For details, see www.speedresearch.com/stockwatch.

Spredz

For Windows. Shareware.

Spredz is an options analysis, stock/options/volatility database, and risk management software application that lets you evaluate profit/loss potentials of each of over 20 different options/stock strategies, using data (if you want), from your own previously created speculations. For more information, see www.spreadsystems.com.

Stock Tracker

For Mac. Shareware.

Stock Tracker is a database that keeps a record of all your equity purchases and sell transactions. It enables you to see which shares of stock you own that are available to sell, as well as how much you paid for them. Stock Tracker is designed to keep you organized. Stock Tracker is published by Jeff Russell at www.stocktrader.com.

Stock Vue 2000

For Windows. Freeware.

Track financial information on the Internet with Stock Vue. For details, see www.stockvue.com.

Stock Wiz Pro 2000

For Windows. Lite Version.

This investment-tracking program uses historical data from over 8,000 public companies (one-day delayed). Check it out at www.stockwiz.com for more information.

Talking Stocks

For Windows. Shareware.

Using nothing more than your Internet connection and sound card, an animated character called StockMan reads aloud the latest stock prices. In addition, the Stock Strip(tm) continually displays the latest stock information on your screen, allowing you to track your investments with one glance. For details see, www.4developers.com/ts/index.htm.

TickerPage

For Windows. 30-day trial.

TickerPage is a simple-to-use stock data retrieval and paging program designed to track your stock/option portfolio and keep you informed while you're on the move. TickerPage acts as your broker, notifying you of news alerts, e-mail, stock prices, and stock limits at any time interval. For more information, see www.breezesoft.com/breezeindex.html.

Tradex

For Mac. Shareware.

Tradex is a software package for the Macintosh (no, there isn't a Windows version, and there's not likely to be one in the near future) that analyses stock market data using the techniques of technical analysis. Additionally, some simple portfolio management capabilities are included to allow the tracking of securities, computation of gains, and so on. Check it out at www.serv.net/ilanga/tradex.html.

Valuation Accountant

For Windows. Shareware.

Valuation Accountant is an application for performing the bookkeeping chores for an investment club. Being able to easily account for each member's share (which is often uneven) is important. For more information, see www.cnotc.com/~cnc/valact/index.html.

Shareware and freeware for mutual funds

Fund Manager

For Windows. Shareware.

Fund Manager is a full-featured portfolio management application for individual investors. Fund Manager is designed to help investors monitor and analyze their stocks, mutual funds, and other investments with a wide variety of easy-to-use graphs and reports. This shareware program is ideal for stocks but is especially well suited for managing your mutual funds portfolio. For more information, see www.beiley.com/fundman.

Shareware and freeware for bonds

EEBond

For Windows. Shareware.

This savings bond analysis shareware can help you determine what your savings bonds are worth at any point in time. For details, see MMR Software at www.mmrsoft.com.

Shareware and freeware for options

OptionBook

For Windows. Shareware.

OptionBook is designed to assist you in understanding the implied volatility of your investments. OptionBook seeks to make this complex calculation with just one mouse click. The program also calculates market sensitivities. Often, these numbers show how fast option prices change and may be valuable tools in tracking risk. For more information, see www.appliedresearch.com/index_content.htm.

Option Insight

For Windows. Trial Version.

Option Insight© takes a different approach from other option software programs that expect you to understand delta, gamma, theta, and vega, implied volatility, statistical volatility, and so on. Option Insight just suggests the best trades. For more information, see www.optioninsight.com.

Investor demonstration programs

The Internet provides many downloadable demonstration programs for PCs. These demonstration programs are often just like the full editions, but they have a limited life. The *Investing Online For Dummies* companion CD-ROM includes the best of these investor demonstration programs. This section outlines what you can find.

EZStock

For Windows. 30-day trial.

EZStock aims to take the hassle out of searching and managing online investment information from various sources. EZStock is designed to reduce your surfing and having to log on to different accounts. EZStock is designed to provide you with a consolidated picture of all your investment portfolios, including mutual funds, stocks, bonds, or derivatives (whether the trading account is with one or ten institutions). For details, see www.datacow.com/ezstock.htm.

First Finance

For Windows. Demo.

First Finance is demonstration software for financial planning and financial management calculations. Visit `www.what.com/firstfin` for details.

Investor's Advantage

For Windows. Limited demo.

Investor's Advantage lets you chart your favorite stocks and general market trends on your computer using technical market indicators. Investor's Advantage for Windows also provides a weekly report of all the stocks you are tracking, sorted from the strongest to weakest by a strength rating. This rating is calculated based on the price performance of each individual stock. (Sometimes, the more stocks you track, the better your chances of including the strongest stocks in your portfolio.) For more information, see `www.sacc.com/iawin/iawin.htm`.

MacTicker

For Mac. Shareware.

MacTicker is an Internet application that gathers information from financial Web sites around the world and displays the stock information on a continually updating ticker on your desktop. Without launching your browser, MacTicker can track your stock portfolio, mutual funds, and leading indexes automatically. You can watch any number of your stocks roll by on the ticker, or retrieve a detailed report for each of your favorites. For more information, see `www.aladdinsys.com/macticker/index.html`.

Market Watcher for Windows

For Windows. 30-day trial.

Market Watcher for Windows is an Internet interactive software program for tracking your portfolio. Visit `www.marketwatcher.com` for more information.

myTrack

For Windows. Demo.

myTrack, from Track Data, is an Internet-based personal investment tool with free basic service. Check out myTrack for continually updated quotes, breaking company news, trade-by-trade log, charting, and a proprietary library of intraday market statistics. Real-time quotes are free. The Track Data Web site is at `www.mytrack.com`.

OptionVue5
For Windows. Non-interactive presentation demo.

Gain a unique understanding of the special qualities of options and why traders love 'em. This 10-minute demo presentation gives you an overview of the OptionVue5 software features. OptionVue offers a fully functional 30-day trial version of the software for $49. For details, go to www.optionvue.com.

Power Optimizer, Ramcap, Xpress, ScanData, and Analytics
For Windows. Demo.

These downloadable demonstration copies of asset allocations programs help you get organized and get going. Here's a brief description of each. (For more details, see Wilson International at www.wilsonintl.com.)

- ✔ The **Power Optimizer** program provides interactive computer models to analyze the risk and return characteristics of existing or proposed investments.

- ✔ **Ramcap** is an entry-level asset allocation package that offers an easy-to-use alternative to the Power Center programs. If you're restrained by budget limitations, Ramcap may be the program for you.

- ✔ The **Xpress** program is an entry-level asset allocation package designed primarily for point-of-sales presentations. The program includes an internal questionnaire to establish your risk/return parameters and limited asset allocation (optimization) capabilities.

- ✔ **ScanData** is a tool for sorting and reviewing information on asset classes, mutual funds, stocks, variable annuities, and closed-end funds.

- ✔ The **Analytics** program permits users to review and analyze asset classes, mutual funds, stocks, variable annuities, and closed-end funds.

Investor simulation programs

Space King
For Windows. Shareware.

Space King is a futuristic stock market simulation. Discover how you can make lots of money by trading within a unique solar system in this economic strategy game set in outer space. This stock market simulation game has music, sounds, animation, and full color graphics. With Space King, you'll travel from planet to planet, buying and selling stocks, bonds, and commodities. For details, see eternityzone.hypermart.net/spacekng.htm.

If You've Got Problems (Of the CD Kind)

I tried my best to compile programs that work on most computers with the minimum system requirements. Alas, your computer may differ, and some programs may not work properly for some reason.

The two likeliest problems causing these programs not to work on your computer are that you don't have enough memory (RAM) for the programs you want to use or you have other programs running that are affecting installation or running of a program. If you get error messages such as Not enough memory or Setup cannot continue, try one or more of these methods and then try using the software again:

- Turn off any antivirus software that you have on your computer. Installers sometimes mimic virus activity and may make your computer believe incorrectly that a virus is infecting it.

- Close all running programs. The more programs you're running, the less memory is available to other programs. Installers also typically update files and programs. So if you keep other programs running, installation may not work properly. (This may include closing the CD interface and running a product's installation program from Windows Explorer.)

- Have your local computer store add more RAM to your computer, which is, admittedly, a drastic and somewhat expensive step. However, if you have a Windows 95/98 PC or a Macintosh with a PowerPC chip, adding more memory can really help the speed of your computer and allow more programs to run at the same time.

If you still have trouble installing the programs from the CD, please call the IDG Books Worldwide Customer Service phone number: 800-762-2974 (outside the United States: 317-572-3342).

The Investing Online For Dummies, 3rd Edition Directory

The 5th Wave — By Rich Tennant

ORIGINAL VAN-GOGH-OF-THE-MONTH CLUB

"SINCE WE BEGAN ON-LINE SHOPPING, I JUST DON'T KNOW WHERE THE MONEY'S GOING."

In this directory . . .

The Internet has a wide variety of resources for online investors, and this directory provides a sampling of some of the latest and greatest online investing sites available at this time. I don't claim that this guide is comprehensive. With the constant growth and change that characterize the Internet, it is almost impossible for anyone to create a directory that lives up to such a claim.

The Internet is a constantly changing resource. Some sites listed in this directory (and elsewhere in this book) may have changed or gone away due to mergers with larger sites. Some Web sites just vanish for no reason. If a site has moved, you may find a link to the new location. If not, try a search engine (like AltaVista or Infoseek) to locate the resource you need.

About This Directory

To give you as much information as possible, this directory uses these *micons* (mini icons) — small graphics that point out some of the special features of a Web site:

This micon identifies sites that offer chat rooms where you interact with other visitors or an investment expert. Participating in chat rooms (and sometimes, message boards) often requires registering at the site.

This site has software that you can download.

$ This site charges an access fee. I use this micon if most of the site's content — or the most important content — is available only to paying subscribers.

The site has interactive message boards that you can use for communicating with other online investors.

You need a special piece of software — a *plug-in,* such as Shockwave or Real Audio — to get the most out of this site.

This site features shopping opportunities.

An increasing number of sites on the Internet require your free registration.

Analyst Evaluations

Finding out what the experts are saying about your investment selection is often useful. Here are a few of my favorite sources for analysts' evaluations.

Financial Web
www.financialweb.com

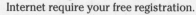

Find out what the experts are saying about your investment selections: Financial Web offers one of the Internet's best Web sites for discovering what brokerages are recommending. You may discover a large number of brokerage evaluations and a wide range of opinions.

S&P Advisor Insight
www.advisorinsight.com

$

For the pros: More of a professional resource than S&P Personal Wealth, this site enables you to buy full S&P research reports. You can also find market commentaries and some information on foreign-owned public companies.

S&P Personal Wealth
www.personalwealth.com

$

Reports for the individual investor: To get a quote on a public company's shares, just enter its ticker symbol and click Go. If you subscribe, you can get advice from S&P's analysts. Plus, the welcome page has free news and market status information.

W3OTC.com Research Reports
www.w3otc.com/discover/research.htm

For the small cap investor: This site offers reports on selected small cap issues with analyst ratings and initiations coverage.

Zacks Investment Research
www.zacks.com

$

Compilations of experts' knowledge: Zacks reports on what hundreds of expert analysts around the world are saying about stocks you can invest in. Some of these reports are free; others require you to pay a fee. All of them are top-quality reports.

Annual Reports

Annual reports are the yearly audited statements required by the SEC for publicly traded and mutual fund companies. Annual reports cover the company's financial results and include forecasts for future results.

The Annual Reports Library
www.zpub.com/sf/arl/index.html

For easy access to annual reports: The Annual Reports Library includes more than 1.5 million original annual reports from corporations, foundations, banks, mutual funds, and public institutions located throughout the world.

Disclosure
www.disclosure-investor.com

Annual reports you can download to your spreadsheet program for additional analysis: This site provides SEC filings, financial information on over 12,000 U.S. public companies, financial data on over 13,000 global companies, and company press releases.

Financials.com
www.financials.com

For easy access to annual reports: This Web site provides quotes, company data, charts, portfolio tracking, educational resources, research, and annual reports on over 3,000 companies.

Global Securities Information
www.gsionline.com/websites.htm
For company information: This index provides Internet users with easy access to information provided by public companies. Information provided by public companies includes 10-Ks, A/RS, 10-Qs, proxy, and press releases.

Hoover's Online
www.hoovers.com

For in-depth company information: This site includes company profiles and annual report information on more than 25,000 publicly traded, private, and international firms.

Investor's Relations Information Network
www.irin.com

Get the picture with annual reports in the original format: The Network offers over 32,500 free company annual reports in their original formats. Annual reports may include photographs, graphs, and text.

Just Quotes
www.justquotes.com

For in-depth company information: For annual reports, and just about anything else you want to know about a company, Just Quotes will build a customized page of hundreds of direct links for corporate news, information, and charts.

Public Register's Annual Report Service
www.prars.com

For online and offline annual reports: This service is free and provides both online annual reports and hard copies on over 3,000 company annual reports.

Report Gallery
www.reportgallery.com

For domestic and international annual reports: Report Gallery offers 2,200 annual reports that cover the majority of Fortune 500 companies. Report Gallery also offers international annual reports, financial links, and a link to Finance Wise, a financial search engine.

SEC's EDGAR
www.sec.gov

For primary information: Reports are entered into a government-sponsored database called The SEC's EDGAR service, providing downloadable data that can be accessed by individual investors.

Web100
metamoney.com/w100
Got the biggest companies on the Internet: Web100 provides links to the 100 largest U.S. and international businesses on the Internet.

Zacks Investment Research
my.zacks.com

$

For easy access to online annual reports: This database includes more than 7,000 U.S. and Canadian companies. The site also tracks 200 industry groups.

Basics of Investing

If you're looking for good investor starting places, try the Web sites I list in this section.

Accutrade Asset Allocation Worksheet
www.Accutrade.com/fhtml/asset allocation.fhtml
For allocating your personal wealth: This free, easy-to-use worksheet can immediately assist you in matching your risk-tolerance levels to your financial goals.

College Investors
www.collegeinvestors.com

For beginning investors: College students have College Investors as a venue for research and education.

DowJones.com World of Stocks
www.dowjones.com

 $

For beginning investors: DowJones.com can assist you in gaining an understanding of the different types of stocks you can purchase.

Eldernet
www.eldernet.com

For beginning investors: Eldernet is the seniors' guide to health, housing, legal, financial, retirement, lifestyles, news, and entertainment information. Eldernet has financial tutorials, including those for mutual funds, insurance, and 401(k) plans.

Green Pages Online
www.greenpages.org

For beginning investors: Green Pages is a directory of thousands of socially and environmentally responsible businesses, products and services.

Invest Wisely
www.sec.gov/consumer/inws.htm

For beginning investors: This is a feature article for beginning investors from the Securities and Exchange Commission (SEC), a government regulatory agency. The SEC Web site (www.sec.gov) provides this and many other feature articles to inform and protect first-time investors.

Investing Basics
www.aaii.com/invbas

For beginning investors: Articles at this site show individuals how to start successful investment programs, pick winning investments, and evaluate their choices.

Investing Online Resource Center
www.investingonline.org

For beginning investors: The Investing Online Resource center is a noncommercial organization dedicated solely to serving the individual consumer who invests online or is considering doing so.

Investment Basics
www300.fidelity.com

For beginning investors: This a site where Peter Lynch, a successful investor, former fund manager, and author, freely offers his expertise.

Invest-O-Rama
www.investorama.com

Lots of good stuff: Put together by Douglas Gerlach, Invest-O-Rama is a collection of links to online sources, such as electronic brokers, mutual funds, financial reports, and related investor sources.

Investor FAQ
invest-faq.com/articles/stock-a-basics.html

For beginning investors: Visit this site for answers to questions like "What is stock?", "Why does a company issue stock?", "Why do investors pay good money for little pieces of paper called stock certificates?", "What do investors look for?", and "What about ratings and what about dividends?"

InvestorGuide
www.investorguide.com

Start here: InvestorGuide features newsletters, articles, stock analyses, and links to thousands of investment sites. Plus, the site features loads of educational materials that can help you figure out what you want to do with your money, and why. Much of this educational information is goal-oriented, so it contains information about saving for college, in addition to investments in general.

InvestorMap
www.investormap.com

For beginning investors: InvestorMap has over 100 categories and more than 3,000 links for financial evaluation, analysis, and news.

Learning to Invest
www.learningtoinvest.com

Online education for beginning investors: Designed for novice investors, this Web site provides step-by-step guides to the world of high finance.

Money.com
www.money.com

For beginning and veteran investors: News, articles, and analysis of the stock market and related economics are here in the online version of *Money Magazine.* The site has 24 interactive lessons on the basics of savings, budgeting, and investment.

Moneyminded
www.moneyminded.com

For women investors: Moneyminded is dedicated to women's financial goals and helping women achieve those goals.

News Radio
stream.internet.com

For online news you can use: News Radio is a streaming audio provider of global real-time news and information resources.

Online Investor
www.investhelp.com

For a great place to start: Online Investor points out sources of information, explains the information, and then advises ways to use it.

S&P Personal Wealth
www.personalwealth.com

$

Reports for the individual investor: To get a quote on a public company's shares, just enter its ticker symbol and click Go. If you subscribe, you can get advice from S&P's analysts. Plus, the welcome page has free news and market status information.

StockJungle.com
www.stockjungle.com

For online education: StockJungle operates funds with full disclosure each and every day to educate about mutual fund investment.

Stock Trigger
www.stocktrigger.com

For staying well informed: Stock Trigger lets you know what is happening to your stock, commodity, and option while you are at a meeting, watching a baseball game, working on a job site, or having lunch, via e-mail, pager, or digital cell-phone.

Women's Financial Network
www.wfn.com

For women investors: The Women's Financial Network (WFN) is designed to provide women access to the information and tools they need to better understand and manage their finances. In addition to presenting financial information from a woman's perspective, WFN helps women take action: At WFN, women buy competitive financial products and services and find a prescreened advisor committed to women via the WFN Advisor Network.

Young Investor
www.younginvestor.com

For beginning investors: Young Investor is geared toward children, teaching investment through educational games. There are also forums for parents.

Other Stuff to Check Out
www.financialweb.com
www.laughingstockbroker.com
www.quicken.com/investments
www.wsdinc.com

Bonds

Bonds (sometimes called fixed-income investments) can be short-term or long-term, high-risk (like junk bonds) or low-risk (like Treasury bonds). If you own mutual fund shares, you may already be a bond investor. Check out the following sites for bond-related information.

Bank of America Investment Services Inc.
www.bankofamerica.com/investments

For your investor profile: Bank of America Investment Services can assist you in determining which type of bonds are right for you.

The Bond Market
www.bondcan.com

News you can use: The Bond Market is the best online resource for those investing in Canadian bonds. It lists all the news about the Bank of Canada, dispatches from all the provincial banks, and government statistics. The site also features a message board. Add quotes and a joke page, and you've got a valuable site.

D-8 Bonds: Historical Data

Bondsonline
www.bondsonline.com

$

News and more: Bondsonline provides charts and historical data that compare various bond market sectors. For example, this site offers a comparison of 30-year Treasury bonds, 10-year Treasury notes, and the Dow Jones Industrial Average. You can also find news of the goings-on at the Fed and elsewhere in debt circles.

DowJones.com
dowjones.wsj.com/d/perfin-guide-bonds-future.html

 🛒 $

For online education: DowJones.com provides an overview of the different types of bonds, who issues bonds, how to make money with bonds, and how bonds are sold. At the Home page click Personal Finance, next click WSJ Guide. In the left margin click Bonds.

Duff & Phelps Credit Rating Co.
www.dcrco.com

For bond ratings: Duff & Phelps apply local financial, economic, and social developments to rate and monitor credits around the world.

Federally Insured Savings Network
www.fisn.com

For the best rates: This firm researches across the nation for the safest and highest CD rates.

IBC's Money Fund Selector
www.ibcdata.com/basics.htm
For the best rates: IBC provides information about what a money fund is, the difference between taxable and tax-free money funds, a discussion about how safe money funds are, and how to read a money fund prospectus.

Investing In Bonds.com
www.investinginbonds.com/investing-2col.shtml
For online education: Investing In Bonds.com can help you get educated about investing in

bonds. There is even a yield calculator so you can compare your returns to other types of investments.

The Investment FAQ
invest-faq.com/articles/bonds-a-basics.html
For online education: The Investment FAQ provides investors with a good idea of what bonds are all about. If you want to start your bond education with something that doesn't have lots of finance jargon, this is a good place to begin.

money-rates.com
www.money-rates.com

For the best rates: Money-rates.com has market updates; information about the economy; consumer interest rates; and investment rates for money market funds, certificates of deposit, Treasury securities, and special bank offerings.

Rate.Net
www.rate.net

For the best rates: Rate.Net provides information on the best 30-, 60-, 180- day, and one-year jumbo CDs in the United States. (*Note:* A jumbo CD is $100,000.)

Other Stuff to Check Out
www.stls.frb.org/fred/data/irates.html
www.moodys.com

Bonds: Historical Data

To determine the yield curve of the bond market you are wise to look at the historical data of the bond type you are researching. For example, an upward yield curve indicates that rates are expected to be higher in the future. If the yield curve is flat, there is no discernible pattern for future rates. If the curve is downward, it is often predictive of lower rates.

Bondsonline
www.bondsonline.com/bcgraphs.htm

$

For easy online access to the bond data and charts: Bondsonline provides charts and historical data that compare various bond market sectors and stock market indexes.

Federal Reserve Bank of St. Louis
www.stls.frb.org

For easy online access to all Treasury bond data: This site lists the monthly interest rate for each type of Treasury security. Files for specific Treasuries and a downloadable zipped file that contains all the Interest Rate Series (historical archives of interest rate data) are available.

Moody's Investor Services
www.moodys.com

For easy online access to corporate bond data: Moody's provides long-term corporate bond yield averages based on bonds with maturities of 20 years and above.

Bonds: New Offerings

New bonds are frequently "priced to sell." The Internet provides a wide variety of sources that can assist you in getting the latest bond offering information. The following Web sites are a sampling of the best online sources for this type of information.

A. G. Edwards
www.agedwards.com/bondpub/
　　curr_mbi.shtml

For a general idea of what's happening with new bond issues: A. G. Edwards provides a sampling of the bonds it offers. Additionally, you can access a sample of several upcoming new issues that A. G. Edward expects to underwrite.

The Bond Buyer
www.bondbuyer.com

↘ $

For new municipal bond issues: This online edition of *The Bond Buyer* covers new municipal bond offerings, city and state officials involved in issuing debt, underwriters and underwriting, brokerages, and bond lawyers.

Fidelity Brokerage Service
personal100.fidelity.com/news/calendars

↘

Get a listing of new bond issues from the brokerage that specialized in bonds: Fidelity provides a list of new fixed-income offerings. You'll find everything from CDs to municipal bonds.

Salomon Smith Barney Municipal New Issues Calendar
www.smithbarney.com/prod_svc/bonds/mu
　　nical.html

For new municipal bond issues: This site provides a free listing of new municipal free issues and bond issues that Smith Barney is involved in, intends to bid on its own, or is part of a syndicate. The bonds listed at the Web site are updated weekly but are subject to prior sale (and may not be available).

Broker Fraud and Complaints

If you suspect that your broker is not as honest as you once thought, you can voice your complaint to the right people using the Internet. Many of these organizations follow up on your complaint and keep you informed of its status.

Better Business Bureau
www.bbb.org

Your complaint will be heard: The Better Business Bureau has an online complaint form. The bureau promises to follow up within two weeks of your complaint.

National Fraud Information Center
www.fraud.org

↘

Help others by reporting fraud: The National Fraud Information Center forwards your complaint to the appropriate organizations and includes it in the Center's Internet fraud statistics (which may not help you get your money back, but may be helpful to other online investors).

Securities and Exchange Commission
www.sec.gov

Check up on your broker: The Securities and Exchange Commission (SEC) has an excellent online complaint process. You can use this site to request any registered broker's disciplinary history, too, free of charge.

Brokerage Ratings

Not all online brokerages are alike. Find out which electronic brokerage meets your individual needs.

American Association of Individual Investors
www.aaii.org/survey

For comparisons of online brokerages: Discover who are the top ten vote-getters, see how discount brokers rate, and see how your online brokerage compares.

Forrester Research Power Ratings
powerrankings.forrester.com/ER/Power Rankings/Industry/0,2142,3,FF.html

For expert ratings: Power Ratings is based on interactive consumer surveys and unbiased expert analysis. The goal of Forrester's brokerage ratings is to provide consumers with objective research to assist them in selecting an online brokerage.

Gomez.com
www.gomezadvisors.com

For expert ratings: Whether it's autos, auctions, personal finance, travel, health, home and garden, computers and office, or shopping, consumers get all the information they need from Gomez Advisors to plan, research, and execute their online service selection.

Keynote Web Broker Trading Index
www.keynote.com/measures/brokers

For comparisons of online brokerages: The Keynote Web Broker Trading Index shows the average response time in seconds and the success rate for creating a standard stock-order transaction on selected brokerage Web sites.

Money.com
www.money.com/money/broker/
    index.html

For expert ratings: Money.com ranks the top 15 online brokerages based on their ease of use, customer service, system responsiveness, products and tools, and total cost.

Company Profiles

If you're thinking about investing in a company, you can do much of your research online. For example, you can read the company's profile or develop your own company profile based on your online research and analysis.

Company Sleuth
www.company.sleuth.com

For comprehensive company research: Company Sleuth is a covert information specialist providing free, legal, inside information on publicly traded companies. Company Sleuth scours the Internet for hard-to-find business information on investments, competitors, partners, and clients.

Corporate Information
www.corporateinformation.com

For domestic and international company research: Corporate Information includes 15,000 research reports, 20,000 corporate profiles, 1,700 profiles in French, 600 profiles in Spanish, and other resources.

Corptech
www.corptech.com

For public and private company research: The database includes over one million global public and private companies from more than 25 information providers drawing upon over 2,500 sources of content.

CyberInvest.com
www.cyberinvest.com

For locating the best Web sites with company research: CyberInvest does a feature-by-feature comparison of hundreds of the best investing resources on the Internet. CyberInvest also features particularly useful or helpful investment tools and Web sites.

Hoover's Online
www.hoovers.com

Good freebies — great, if you pay the fee: Hoover's Online has free and fee-based information on 8,500 companies. You can search company ticker symbols, locations, and sales at this Web site. Company profiles include the firm's address, phone numbers, executive names, recent sales figures, and company status.

Individual.com
finance.individual.com/ticker_lookup.asp

For snapshots of company research: Information includes a snapshot of companies, charts, news, earnings, financials, and SEC filings.

SiliconValley.com
www.sv.com

For nontraditional company research: Silicon Valley company profiles include information on benefits, corporate culture, and financial history for the three most recent years.

Direct Public Offerings

In a direct public offering (DPO), a company bypasses an underwriter and offers its shares directly to the public. This procedure has both good points and drawbacks. The Internet provides information and materials about many DPOs.

Direct IPO
www.directipo.com

Buy and sell shares directly: Direct IPO provides investor resources, information about traditional IPOs and DPOs, an industry spotlight, an IPO contest, a newsroom, and more. The site is a good place to visit whether you want to buy shares or sell equity in your own company to others.

The Direct Stock Market
www.dsm.com

Companies for sale, info for free: The Direct Stock Market provides information about companies that are issuing direct public offerings. It provides a central online location for the distribution of these companies' prospectuses and documents. You can also find an exchange for over-the-counter and Bulletin Board shares, and regular webcasts disseminating investment information.

Netstock Direct
www.netstockdirect.com

Buy and sell shares directly: Netstock Direct is an online source for purchasing shares directly from a company (and not paying brokerage fees). The Web site includes online education about direct investing and company materials about direct stock purchase plans. Additionally, many of these companies have dividend reinvestment plans that can help you defer taxes and purchase more shares with your dividends.

Other Stuff to Check Out
www.virtualwallstreet.com

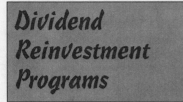

Dividend Reinvestment Programs

Dividend Reinvestment Programs (DRIPs) enable shareholders to purchase additional shares directly from the company (bypassing brokerage fees) and sometimes at reduced prices. Direct Stock Purchase plans (DSPs), sometimes called Direct Purchase Plans (DPPs), enable you to use cash to buy shares directly from issuing companies.

DRIP Advisor
www.dripadvisor.com

It's the DRIPpiest: This site is useful for its apparently complete list of all U.S. companies offering DRIPs and DSPs, plus lots of general information on DRIP investing and some advice on assembling a portfolio of DRIPs.

Netstock Direct
www.netstockdirect.com

A great starting point: Here, Netstock's managers have assembled a great list of online DRIP and DSP resources. A superb search engine enables you to winnow out the plans that don't fit your plans, based on industry, minimum investment, and other criteria.

Other Stuff to Check Out
www.natcorp.com/direct.html
www.aaii.com
www.better-investing.org/store/
    store.html

Dollar-Cost Averaging

Dollar-cost averaging is a sensible way to invest in the market. You invest the same amount each month, buying more shares when prices are low and fewer shares when prices are high.

Institute of Systematic Investing Research
www.isir.com
Get online education: ISIR provides education and related links to help investors understand the benefits of dollar-cost averaging. Check out the dollar-cost-averaging site of the week.

Montgomery Funds
**www.montgomeryfunds.com/
    Fundamentals**
Get online education: Montgomery Funds includes dollar-cost averaging in its basics of investing. Discover how to determine your goals, manage different types of investment risk, and get ahead with dollar-cost averaging.

The Armchair Millionaire
www.armchairmillionaire.com

Get online education: The Armchair Millionaire features investing basics and how dollar-cost averaging can help you build a strong financial plan.

Earnings Estimates

When determining the value of a stock, you often need to estimate the company's earnings. Compare your earnings estimates with the experts' estimates at the following Web sites.

CBS MarketWatch: Analyst Rating Revisions

cbs.marketwatch.com/news/current/
ratings.htx?source=htx/http2_mx

For earnings forecasts from the experts: CBS MarketWatch is updated throughout the trading day. The revised analyst reports show the name of the company, the broker, the new and old ratings, and comments.

InvestorNet

www.investornet.com

For earnings forecasts from many experts: InvestorNet offers earnings news, announcements, surprises, and movers. Links to earnings alerts provided by CBS, Zacks, IBES, First Call, Upside Sectors, and TechWeb are also available.

Reuters moneynet

www.moneynet.com

A money/news portal, and more: Reuters Moneynet provides an S&P evaluation of the company and dividends rank, average quality opinion, fiscal year ending month, and date of the next expected earnings report. The consensus earnings per share forecast for the next year and statistics about past earnings are included.

Thomson Investors Network

www.thomsoninvest.net/FirstCall/
intro.sht

Online investor supersite: Free First Call Snapshot reports offer earnings data, including current quarter and current fiscal year estimates, recommendations, and price to earnings ratios.

Zacks Investment Research

www.zacks.com

A long-standing favorite: Zacks provides estimated earnings reports that are based on broker opinions. The site includes a listing of current earnings surprises, recommendations,

and the company's annual balance sheet and income statement.

Other Stuff to Check Out

www.nrmcapital.com
www.stocksmart.com

Before you invest, checking out the big picture is always a wise idea. Find out how the economy is doing, both nationally and regionally. For example, if the economy weakens, how will this change affect your investment selections?

Census Bureau

www.census.gov

How many, exactly: The Census Bureau provides information about industry, statistics, and general business. *Current Industrial Reports* provide production, shipment, and inventory statistics. *Census of Manufacturers Industry Series* includes industry statistics (some of this information may be outdated). *The Census of Wholesale Trade* contains data about organizations that sell merchandise to retailers, institutions, and other types of wholesalers. The *Survey* provides updates about current and past statistics of monthly sales, inventories, and stock/sales ratios.

Dismal Scientist

www.dismal.com

For a look at the future: The Dismal Scientist presents real-time analysis of major economic events around the globe — from monetary and fiscal policy changes in the United States, to the maturation of the corporate bond market in Europe, to the burgeoning recovery of the Asian economies.

The Economic Statistics Briefing Room
www.whitehouse.gov/fsbr/esbr.html

For the latest statistics: The Economic Statistics Briefing Room is designed to provide easy access to current Federal economic indicators. Links are to Federal agencies that maintain and update information.

GSA Government Information Locator Service
www.gsa.gov

Government Central: The GSA Government Information Locator Service includes many U.S. Federal agency reports in either full-text or abstract forms. Most information resources are cataloged and searchable. Searches can include more than one agency.

Internet Federal Reserve sites
www.bog.frb.fed.us/otherfrb.htm

For the latest statistics: This site provides links to all the Fed home pages. Publications by this organization include high-quality statistics, analyses, and forecasts of regional, national, and international economic and financial conditions.

Glossaries

The Internet provides many online financial glossaries. A glossary contains a set of extended definitions of technical terms that you will likely find useful.

Investor Words
www.investorwords.com

For an extensive glossary with links to investor Web sites: Over 5,000 definitions of financial terms and 15,000 links between related terms.

Prudential's Glossary of Terms
www.prusec.com/glossary/glos_txt.htm

For an extensive glossary: This site provides an online glossary for finding the definitions of financial and investment terms. This extensive glossary offers helpful examples of how investment terms are used.

Silicon Investor: Glossary
www.siliconinvestor.com/misc/glossary/alist.html

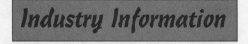

For an extensive glossary: This glossary provides a fast and easy way to find out investment terms and concepts. Definitions include links to related online sources.

Yahoo! Financial Glossary
biz.yahoo.com/f/g/g.html

For an extensive glossary: Yahoo! offers a convenient glossary that includes hyperlinks that define words used in the text.

Industry Information

Compare the performance of your investment candidate to the industry standard. How is the company performing? Is the company an industry leader or fighting for market share? Find out by researching the company's industry at the following Internet sites.

American Society of Association Executives
www.asaenet.org

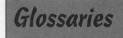

For online information about industry trends: The American Society of Association Executives provides links to Web sites for various industries. The Web sites are generally high-quality industry overviews that often include briefings of industry trends, geographic profiles, and statistics for financial performance analysis.

Fuld & Company
www.fuld.com/i3/index.html

For online information about industry trends and links to useful Web sties: Fuld & Company provides a free listing of industry-specific Internet resources. The firm divides industries into 27 categories.

Hoover's Online
www.hoovers.com

For identifying a company's industry: Lists of companies that are part of a certain industry or sector are listed. Hoover's has researched and written over 45 in-depth overviews of various industry groups, archived at `www.hoovers.com/industry/archive/0,2048,169,00.html`.

Lexis-Nexis
www.lexis-nexis.com

$ 🔌 🛒

Where talk-show hosts get their background info: Lexis-Nexis has a wide variety of business and legal databases and recently added a new database of 10- to 20-page market summaries of particular industry sectors or demographic markets. Additionally, the Lexis-Nexis database includes the *Market Share Reporter* (from 1991 to the present) and *Computer Industry Forecasts*.

Michigan Electronic Library
mel.lib.mi.us/business/BU-IPmenu.html
For online information about industries and links to useful Web site: This site lists 30 basic industries and provides links to industry publications.

STAT-USA
www.stat-usa.gov

$

Statistics for all occasions: STAT-USA is sponsored by the U.S. Department of Commerce and provides financial information about economic indicators, statistics, and news. STAT-USA is a relatively friendly way to access deep troves of U.S. government research.

Yahoo! Industry News
biz.yahoo.com/industry

For online information about industries: Yahoo! categorizes business into 10 major industries which have subcategories. Click the appropriate subcategory for industry press releases and current news.

Other Stuff to Check Out
www.fedstats.gov
www.technometrica.com
www.trainingforum.com

Initial Public Offerings (IPOs)

Usually, in an initial public offering (IPO), a company offers shares to the public for the first time. Purchasing shares in an IPO may be one way to get in on the ground floor of a new investment opportunity. Investing in an IPO is also an excellent way to lose your shirt. Take your pick.

Equity Analytics
www.e-analytics.com/ipo/bplandi.htm}

🛒 ↘

Equity Analytics provides research and analysis such as: portfolio modeling advisement, IPO assistance, individual company profiles, sector analysis, and hedging strategies with derivatives for institutions.

Everything About IPOs
www.moneypages.com/syndicate/stocks/ipo.html

🛒 ↘ 🗋

An IPO primer: This Web page contains an informative article about the advantages and limitations of initial public offerings. Start here.

IPO Central
www.ipocentral.com

📓 🛒

News of a turbulent field: IPO Central provides the most recent IPO filings, weekly pricing, commentary, and informative articles. This resource is part of the Hoover's empire, so it's reliable.

IPO Maven
www.IPOmaven.com

The best site for the knowledgeable IPO investor: IPO Maven is a portal into online resources for IPO investors. Here, you can find the latest pricing information and news in an attractive, frequently updated format that you can refer to easily.

Other Stuff to Check Out
biz.yahoo.com/reports/ipo.html
cbs.marketwatch.com/news/current/
  IPO_rep.htx
www.ostman.com/alert-ipo
www.investhelp.com
www.ipodata.com
www.ipomonitor.com
www.techweb.com/wire/finance/

Interest Rates

The Internet can help you find the best savings rate in the United States. Some Web sites even include instructions about how to open out-of-state savings accounts.

Bank Rate Monitor
www.bankrate.com

All-purpose loan shopper: Bank Rate Monitor shows the interest rates offered throughout the United States on home mortgages, car loans, small business loans, and more. The Web site even includes a listing of financial institutions that offer special deals to Internet shoppers.

Bank-CD Rate Scanner
www.bankcd.com

$

Rating the rates: This site provides, for $9.95, a list of the top CD rates in the United States, complete with minimum-investment and term information. Bank-CD Rate Scanner guarantees its service; if you can find a lower rate at an FDIC-insured institution that accepts nationwide deposits, you don't have to pay. Besides, if you're investing enough, this service pays for itself.

BanxQuote
banx.com

Rate quotes, by region: BanxQuote is a good online source for the best rates for money market deposit accounts and various kinds of loans. BanxQuote allows searches by location or terms. Data includes the financial institution's name and contact information and the money market account's rate of return.

International

International online investing provides opportunities to diversify your portfolio and to hedge against major shifts in the domestic market.

ADR.com
www.adr.com

For online analysis of international offerings: Analysis and statistics on American depository receipts are provided by ADR.com and JP Morgan.

CIA World Factbook
www.odci.gov/cia/publications/factbook/
  index.html

For online analysis of different countries: The CIA World Factbook provides geographic, economic, demographic, political, and military data about every country in the world.

Depositary Receipt Services
www.bankofny.com/adr/
For online analysis of international offerings: Depositary Receipt Services, from the Bank of New York, is a source for international ADR and GDR market intelligence and investor information.

Emerging Markets Companies
www.emgmkts.com

For online analysis of world markets: Emerging Markets Companies compiles news, quotes, and financial data on the emerging markets.

The Globe and Mail
www.globeandmail.ca

For online analysis of international offerings: The Globe and Mail is a Canadian news source including coverage of stock and mutual data and screening.

Institute of Finance & Banking, University of Göttingen
www.wiso.gwdg.de/ifbg/ifbghome.html

For online analysis of world markets: Data and links for the international market provided in both English and German.

Morgan Stanley Capital International
www.msci.com

For global indexes: MSCI has a variety of indices on countries and regions, including sector, industry, and fixed income.

Nekkei Net Interactive
www.nni.nikkei.co.jp/

$

For analysis of international offerings: On Nikkei Net, detailed news and data for Japanese listed companies may be found.

Worldlyinvestor.com
www.worldlyinvestor.com

For analysis of world markets: Worldlyinvestor.com provides timely, proprietary, and investable stories about financial markets, stocks, bonds, and mutual funds.

Investment Clubs

If you want build up your confidence before you start investing on your own, you may want to consider an investment club. Investment clubs pool their money, talk about their investment decisions, and divide up the profits (or losses).

National Association of Investors Corporation (NAIC)
www.better-investing.org

For online education: This Web site shows how to join or start an investment club.

Investorama
www.investorama.com

For online education: Find out what people are saying about the advantages and limitations of joining an investment club. Investorama also has a directory of investment club Web sites listed by state at www.investorama.com/directory/Investment_Clubs/Club_Web_Sites.

Investor Compilation Sites

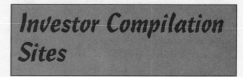

Investor compilation sites are excellent sources for beginning investors. These investor-starting points are also good sources for finding new investor Web sites.

BuckInvestor
www.buckinvestor.com

An investor supersite: BuckInvestor offers tips and advice on investing and stock profiling for long-term investment.

Investorama
www.investorama.com

One-stop research: Investorama includes more than 2,000 investor-related links sorted into categories. The site has a directory that covers bonds, brokerages, dividend reinvestment plans, futures, mutual funds, and more.

Investing Online Resource Center
www.investingonline.org

An investor supersite: The Investing Online Resource center is a noncommercial organization dedicated solely to serving the individual consumer who invests online or is considering doing so.

InvestorGuide
www.investorguide.com

A good place to start: InvestorGuide is a well-organized directory with links to thousands of investor-related sites. InvestorGuide includes site reviews, summaries, and an extensive section on initial pubic offerings (IPOs).

Morningstar
www.morningstar.com

Fund research from a leader: Morningstar is a Chicago-based, independent rating company that specializes in mutual funds. The site includes information about both stocks and mutual funds, easy-to-use screening tools, and research sources. Plus, it offers advice to newcomers, reviews of investing books, financial celebrity interviews, and a lot more.

Silicon Investor
www.siliconinvestor.com

An investor supersite: The Silicon Investor includes research reports, portfolio tracking, company profiles, historical data, and news.

The Syndicate
www.moneypages.com/syndicate

Ask questions, get answers: The Syndicate includes informative articles on investor topics, more than 2,000 links to related investor sites, and information on brokers, bonds, and more.

Wall Street Research Net
www.wsrn.com

Share and share alike: Wall Street Research Net focuses on stock market research. The site includes more than 65,000 links to company information, the economy, market news, investor reports, quotes, mutual fund indexes, and more. Some of it is free, too, including a handy stock-of-the-week feature.

Zacks Investment Research
www.zacks.com

$

An investor supersite: Zacks specializes in free and fee-based investment research. Get company reports, broker recommendations, analysts' forecasts, earnings announcements, and more.

ZDNet Interactive Investor
www.zdii.com

An investor supersite: Interactive Investor is a source of financial news and commentary within the ZDNet online community.

Other Stuff to Check Out
www.ragingbull.com

Investor Databases

When researching an investment candidate, investors often use specialized databases to find that elusive piece of data. Here are a few free and fee-based online databases.

Free Databases

Federal Reserve Bank of St Louis
www.stls.frb.org/research/index.html

For free research from the government: This site provides links to high-quality economic research such as FRED, a historical database of economic and financial statistics.

FINweb
www.finweb.com

Free advice from an academic expert: FINweb is from the University of Texas at Austin.

FINweb has links to the finance and economics departments of many universities, commercial sources, and financial institutions. This financial supersite includes high-quality recommendations, and all links are screened for content.

GovBot
ciir.cs.umass.edu/Govbot/
An all-purpose search tool with financial applications: Govbot is sponsored by the Center for Intelligent Information Retrieval (CIIR). The free database allows you to search more than 1,000,000 government and military Web pages, lots of which contain information of interest to investors.

Government Information Locator Service
www.gsa.gov
For free research from the government: This site includes many U.S. government agency reports in both full-text and abstract forms. Sources are cataloged and searchable.

Securities and Exchange Commission
www.sec.gov

Check up on your broker: The Securities and Exchange Commission (SEC) has an excellent online complaint process. You can use this site to request any registered broker's disciplinary history, too, free of charge.

STAT-USA
www.stat-usa.gov
$

For free research from the government: This site includes economic indicators, statistics, and news. It also offers data about state and local bond rates, foreign exchange rates, and daily economic news. Statistics include interest rates, employment, income, prices, productivity, new construction, and home sales.

Fee-Based Databases

Lexis-Nexis
www.lexis-nexis.com
$ 🔌 🛒

For research that is worth the fee: Lexis-Nexis includes information from major regional and national newspaper, news sources, company information, and financial information, including SEC reports and proxy statements.

The Electric Library
www.elibrary.com
$

For research that is worth the fee: The Electric Library has, among other things, many newspapers, periodicals, and journals. Searches can be by keyword. The Electric Library is a good source for background or academic financial research.

Investor Profiles

How much risk can you take? The Internet provides a variety of online questionnaires that can assist you in determining your investor profile.

Bank of America Investment Services
www.bankofamerica.com/investments/ index.cfm?template=inv_tools_profile. cfm&from=eba

For an easy to use online investor questionnaire: Bank of America offers a survey of 11 questions. Enter your answers, and the online calculator suggests an investment allocation strategy that suits your current needs and situation.

Bank of Hawaii
www.boh.com/invest/paccen/invest/ calculator/index.asp
🛒 $

D-20 Magazines

For an easy to use online investor questionnaire: Bank of Hawaii offers a seven- question worksheet to assist you in identifying your investor profile and risk tolerance.

PrudentialSecurities.com
www.prudentialsecurities.com/financial_ concerns/quiz.htm

For an easy to use online investor questionnaire: This site provides a helpful investment personality quiz. For each statement, just choose the response that most accurately reflects your feelings or behavior.

Safeco Mutual Funds
www.safecofunds.com/safecofunds/ investor

For an easy to use online investor questionnaire: At the Safeco Investor Services page, click Risk Tolerance for a questionnaire that can help you determine your personal comfort zone with regard to risk.

UMB Bank
www.umb.com/invest/retirement/ investor.html

For an easy to use online investor questionnaire: UMB Bank helps you determine your investor type with ten questions. Results indicate whether you are a conservative, balanced, or aggressive investor, and which investment offered by your retirement plan best suits your needs.

Magazines

Many investor magazines are available online. Some online editions are free and others cost less than the paper-based publications.

Barrons Online
interactive.wsj.com/barrons

For helpful free commentary, insights, and advice: Barrons Online includes This Week's Barrons, Weekday Extra, Market Lab, and a searchable archive.

Business Week
www.businessweek.com

$

For helpful free commentary, insights, and advice: Free registrants get a daily briefing, special reports, the searchable archive, banking centers, quotes, and portfolio tracking.

The Economist
www.economist.com

For helpful commentary, insights, and advice: Subscriptions to the Web edition only are $48 a year and include a searchable archive. When you register, you receive five free retrievals, a downloadable The Economist's World Data Screensaver, and *Politics This Week* and *Business This Week* sent to your e-mailbox.

Forbes
www.forbes.com

For free helpful commentary, insights, and advice: Forbes is available in an online version. Departments include technology, personal finance, startups, and e-business.

Kiplinger Online
www.kiplinger.com

For free helpful commentary, insights, and advice: Kiplinger presents news, stock quotes, listings of the top-performing funds, mutual fund analyses, online calculators, yield and rate information, retirement advice, Web site recommendations, personal finance information, advice, and a FAQs section.

Money
www.money.com/money

For free helpful commentary, insights, and advice: This is the online version of Time Warner's *Money* magazine. You can access market information, stock and fund quotes, and charts. Additionally, you can track your portfolio and receive business and finance news.

Mutual Funds Online
www.mfmag.com

For helpful free commentary, insights, and advice: Registrants have access to fund family guides and brokers, fund services, a load performance calculator, and related links.

Newsweek Online
www.newsweek.com

For free helpful commentary, insights, and advice: This Web site edition includes breaking news from its sister publication, the *Washington Post,* daily updates from *Newsweek,* narrated photo essays, quotes, company look-ups, market data, and personal portfolio tracking.

Mailing Lists

Mailing lists are special e-mail programs that re-mail all incoming mail to a list of subscribers. Get new insights and advice from savvy investors by joining a topic-specific mailing list.

CataList
www.lsoft.com/lists/listref.html
A list of lists: CataList lists more than 21,000 mailing lists and is searchable by site, country, and number of list subscribers. Note that the listed lists aren't all about financial matters — they're about all different subjects.

Liszt Home Page
www.liszt.com
For a large mailing list database: Liszt is a searchable index of listservers (mailing list programs) arranged alphabetically, by description, name, and subject.

PAML — Publicly Accessible Mailing Lists
paml.alastra.com
For a mail list database: PAML is a directory of 7,500 mailing lists.

Market Information

Companies react to market changes differently. The Internet provides many resources for discovering the latest changes in the market and pinpointing market trends that can assist you in determining whether you should buy more shares, hold your investments, or sell now.

Clearstation
www.clearstation.com

For market data, analyst evaluations, and discussions: ClearStation enables you to personalize the market data you want, and to get information about the major indexes, analyst's upgrades and downgrades, and earnings surprises, as well as market updates and stock investment ideas.

FreeRealTime.com
www.freerealtime.com

For real-time market information: You can get news, real-time streaming quotes, analysis, earnings reports, information on what's hot and what's not, and start a watch list.

Holt Stock Report
metro.turnpike.net/holt
For market data and indexes: This online resource provides indexes; averages; information about foreign markets; issues trades; new highs and lows; currency rates; gold prices; interest rates; most active issues on the NYSE, NASDAQ, and AMEX; stocks whose trading volume was up by more than 50 percent that day; and stocks that reached new highs or lows.

Prophet Finance
www.prophetfinance.com

For market data and discussions: Prophet provides market information and charts for stocks, funds, futures, options, and indices; market data such as end-of-day updates and historical data on CD-ROM; online portfolio tracking; and investment discussions.

Quote.com
www.quote.com

For real-time market information: This site provides free, unlimited, delayed security quotes from U.S. and Canadian exchanges; limited balance-sheet data; some company profile information; an unlimited number of updates for a portfolio of up to seven securities; daily, weekly, and monthly stock price charts; daily market index charts; daily information for major industry groups; and foreign exchange rates.

Wall Street City
www.wallstreetcity.com

For domestic and international market data: Wall Street City provides free market data about U.S. stocks, the Dow Jones Averages, U.S. futures, bonds, Canada, Latin America, Europe, Asia, Australia, and Africa.

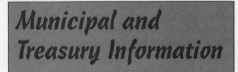

Municipal and Treasury Information

State or local units of the government often issue municipal bonds (sometimes called *munis*). Treasury securities (sometimes called *Treasuries*) are issued by the U.S. Federal government. Both types of investments can help you diversify your portfolio, providing some tax protection and predictability in the process.

Bond Agent
www.bondagent.com

For bond news you can use: Bond Agent is an online bond brokerage firm where investors can search for corporate and municipal new issues and breaking bond news.

The Bond Market Association / Bloomberg National Municipal Bonds Yields
www.bloomberg.com/markets/psamuni.html

For bond yield data information: This site provides investors with an overview of the national municipal bonds yields for triple A rated, tax-exempt, insured revenue bonds.

Bond Resources
www.bondresources.com

For bond news and analysis you can use: Bond Resources includes news, analysis, charts, rates, and education for Treasuries, municipal, agency, and corporate bonds.

Bondtrac
www.bondtrac.com

For bond information: Investors can view a descriptive list (no ratings, issuer or yield information) of around 8,000 government agency, municipal, and corporate bonds that can be purchased from brokerages.

Bureau of the Public Debt
www.publicdebt.treas.gov/servlet/
    OFAnnce

For bond news you can use: Check here for information about Treasury auction dates. For information about the different types of savings bonds and notes that are available, see www.publicdebt.treas.gov/sav/sav.htm.

Capital Markets Commentary
www.intdata.com/capital.htm

Informed commentary: Capital Markets Commentary is a weekly fixed-income (bond) market review provided by Interactive Data Corporation, a Financial Times company. The Capital Markets Commentary includes market information about U.S. government agency bonds, U.S. corporate bonds, international bonds, U.S. municipals, and commercial mortgage-backed bonds.

CBS Bellwether Bonds Report
www.cbsmarketwatch.com

For bond news you can use: This site provides constantly updated bond market news and data about corporate bonds.

Fannie Mae
www.fanniemae.com/financilinfo.
  index.html

For Fannie Mae bond information: Fannie Mae provides investors with background information about the bonds it issues.

Financial Forecast Center
www.neatideas.com

For forecasting bond yields: Forecasts are based on data from the last ten years and a forecasting methodology. You may find this information useful for spotting market trends.

First Miami Securities
www.firstmiami.com/yields.html
For bond information: First Miami Securities is a financial institution that provides tables and charts of investment grade municipal bond yields, among other things.

Ginnie Mae
www.ginniemae.gov

For Ginnie Mae bond information: Ginnie Mae is a government agency that specializes in nonconforming home loans. Consequently, this agency is always issuing to fund its activities. For investor information, click Guides.

GovPX
www.govpx.com
For bond news you can use: GovPX provides some quotations and statistics on trading volume of U.S. government securities, and is updated several times a day in the Daily Treasury Report.

The Investment FAQ
www.invest-faq.com/articles/bonds-treas.
  html
For bond information: The Investment FAQ has a useful article about the difference between Treasury bills, notes, and bonds. The article also includes a discussion of zero-coupon bonds. Check out www.invest-faq.com/articles/bonds-treas-direct.html for useful information about how to open a Treasury Direct account so you can purchase Treasuries directly from the Federal government.

J. C. Bradford Municipal Bonds
www.jcbradford.com/personal/bonds.htm
For bond news you can use: J. C. Bradford provides a state-by-state listing of its current municipal bond inventory and selected Municipal Research reports.

Lebenthal & Company
www.lebenthal.com

For beginning bond investors: The Bond Kit covers general obligation and revenue bonds, bond insurance, coupons, taxes, and how to sell your bonds.

MCM Watch
www.mcmwatch.com

For international bond news you can use: This site offers real-time direct Internet access to MCM's global fixed-income, equity, and foreign exchange analyses.

PC Trader
www.pctrader.com

For bond information you can use: PC Trader offers a GovPX full-feed package that includes U.S. Treasury and government markets.

Quote.com Street Pricing
www.quote.com

For Treasuries information: This site provides quotes for Treasury securities and government agency securities. Specific information includes interest rates and spreads, quotes on active Treasuries, and quotes on government agency securities.

Smart Money
www.smartmoney.com

For bond news you can use: Smart Money provides key interest rates, bond market updates, a bond calculator, educational articles on bonds, and glossary.

The Standard & Poor's Blue List
www.bluelist.com/bltsdemo.dem

$

For municipal bond information: The Blue List shows current municipal and corporate bond offerings. You can search the database for state issuers, maturity dates, lot size of the issue, coupon, and CUSIP.

Stone & Youngberg
www.styo.com

For mortgage-backed securities information and more: Stone & Youngberg offers weekly listings of mortgage-backed securities, corporate bonds, and municipal bonds.

The Syndicate
www.moneypages.com/syndiate/bnds/
    tauction.html

For beginning bond investors: The Syndicate provides an overview of how to purchase Treasury securities.

Treasury Direct
www.publicdebt.treas.gov/sec/
    sectrdir.htm

Government instruments on the cheap: Avoid brokerage fees by purchasing Treasury bills, notes, and bonds directly from the Federal government. Find out all about it from the Federal Reserve Bank of San Francisco.

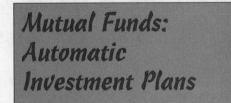

Mutual Funds: Automatic Investment Plans

Even if you have only $50 to invest, you can purchase shares in a mutual fund. Automatic Investment Plans (AIPs) enable you to avoid hefty initial minimum investment requirements.

Strong Automatic Investment Plan
www.strong-funds.com/strong/Learning
    Center/aipbroch.htm

How Strong's program works: Strong has an automatic investment plan for 36 of its no-load funds. The program enables you to invest at predetermined intervals for as low as $50. No charges are required to establish or maintain this service.

T. Rowe Price
www.troweprice.com

Load up on no-loads: T. Rowe Price has two no-load funds in its automatic investment plan that allow monthly, bimonthly, quarterly, semi-annual, and annual automatic payments. Minimum payments can be as little as $25.

Vanguard Fund Express
www.vanguard.com/catalog/service/
    5_3_1_2.html

A disciplined savings plan: The Vanguard Fund Express plan allows monthly, bimonthly, quarterly, semi-annual, and annual automatic payment to be transferred to your Vanguard account. The maximum amount of investment is $100,000, and the minimum amount is $25.

Mutual Funds: Companies and Funds

In this section, I list mutual fund companies that manage many mutual funds. Purchasing a mutual fund from a company that manages many mutual funds has some advantages. One such advantage is that some mutual fund companies allow you to swap your investment in one of their funds for another of their mutual funds at no charge.

Fidelity
www.fidelity.com

A titan on the Web: Fidelity is the largest mutual fund house around, with 35 percent of the total market. This Web site has news about Fidelity investments, a mutual fund library, online prospectuses, online investment and retirement planning advice, and more.

Invesco
www.invesco.com

A good corporate site: If you're a beginning investor, you'll appreciate Invesco's useful advice. This Web site includes online prospectuses, charts to compare rates of return, and a list of the firm's financial services. If you register with this service, you can access your investment account balances through this site.

Janus
www.janus.com

Two faces: Janus has a family of no-load funds. The site provides account access, brief overviews of fund performance, application forms, investor chats, and articles.

T. Rowe Price
www.troweprice.com

Price quotes and more: T. Rowe Price provides daily mutual fund prices, brief updates of fund performance, and more. You have the option of downloading a prospectus or having one sent to you by mail.

Vanguard
www.vanguard.com

On the cutting edge: Vanguard has about 90 funds that do not charge sales fees. Vanguard is one of the larger mutual fund companies. The site includes fund descriptions, downloadable prospectuses, an education center for investors, and more. You can also sign up to receive your statements by e-mail.

Mutual Funds: Information Services

Uncertain about which mutual fund is best for you? The Internet provides lots of mutual fund information sources.

Brill Funds 101
www.brill.com/newbie

For beginning investors: Mutual funds for first-time investors.

CBS MarketWatch — Super Star Funds
cbs.marketwatch.com

Eye on funds: CBS MarketWatch provides articles, news, market data, fund research, links to fund sites, mutual fund tutorials for new investors, market data, portfolios, and a stock chat room. Click the Super Star Funds box to see the fund information.

Charles Schwab & Co., Inc.
www.schwab.com

For beginning investors and the pros: Charles Schwab provides the mutual funds marketplace with a comprehensive list of mutual funds with Morningstar ratings.

Fund Focus
www.fundfocus.com
For mutual fund investors only: This site provides free quotes, performance reports, and investment kits for more the 10,000 U.S. mutual funds.

Mutual Funds INVESTOR'S CENTER
www.mfea.com

For mutual fund investors only: This site provides a news center, information about the new tax rules, links to mutual funds, and a research center that allows you to track from a list of more than 1,000 funds.

Mutual Fund Magazine
www.mfmag.com

A complete toolkit, for a price: Mutual Fund Magazine offers two levels of membership: You can be a registered user (it's free) and get some service, or you can be a charter member (it costs $9.95 a month) and get full access to a wide variety of features, departments, screens, reports, online calculators, and tools to assist you in making your mutual fund selections.

Mutual Funds Interactive
www.fundsinteractive.com/profiles.html

An excellent center of information: Mutual Funds Interactive has recommendations, analysis tools, and links to other useful sites. Plus, you can find profiles of many top money managers.

Other Stuff to Check Out
www.fundalarm.com
www.stocksmart.com

Mutual Funds: Performance

Check out how your mutual fund stacks up against the competition with these Internet sources.

Find a Fund
www.findafund.com

For mutual fund investors only: Find-a-Fund features quotes, top mutual fund performers, and lists of mutual funds by name, category, and ticker symbol.

InvestorSquare
www.investorsquare.com
News, graphs, and commentary: InvestorSquare ranks more than 9,500 funds on 100 different variables. This Web site also includes a detailed profile of each fund. The site covers stocks, too.

Morningstar
quicktake.morningstar.com/Funds/
    Ratings/_RPMGX.html

For everything you want to know about a mutual fund: Morningstar calculates such statistics as the standard deviation of a fund's return.

Mutual Funds Interactive (The Mutual Funds Homepage)
www.brill.com

For beginning mutual fund investors: This site offers tutorials for beginning mutual fund investors, interviews, descriptions of fund strategies with top mutual fund managers, analyses of the mutual funds market, and links to mutual fund home pages.

Standard & Poor's Micropal
www.micropal.com
For domestic and international mutual fund investors: Micropal provides fund information and monitoring for over 38,000 funds across

the globe on a daily, weekly, and monthly basis. Additionally, Micropal supplies summaries on the funds it monitors.

The Street.com
www.thestreet.com

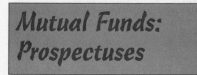

Search by symbol: The Street provides fund profiles and scorecards. You can search free and fee-based areas. One free area is Lipper Analytical's latest top performers for the week.

The Wall Street Journal
interactive.wsj.com

For high quality mutual fund information: The *Wall Street Journal* provides information on mutual funds as part of its Money & Investing section.

Other Stuff to Check Out
www.investorama.com
www.stockmaster.com

Mutual Funds: Prospectuses

The first rule in purchasing mutual funds is to read the prospectus before you buy any shares. Here are a few great online sources for mutual fund prospectuses. Don't forget to look at the fund companies' sites, too.

EDGAR Online
www.edgar-online.com

Quick and dirty (and free) searching: EDGAR Online is a Web site that provides prospectuses for more than 7,000 mutual funds. If you know the name of the fund you are interested in, you can investigate the fund's activities at this site.

Morningstar
www.morningstar.com

For everything you always wanted to know about a mutual fund: Morningstar provides a mutual fund search engine.

Mutual Fund Resource Center
www.fundmaster.com

❯

Education and data: The Mutual Fund Resource Center provides free information, prospectuses, and applications for more than 75 mutual funds.

Mutual Funds: Screens

Out of the 9,500 available mutual funds, which one meets your financial objectives? Use a mutual fund screen to help you find likely candidates. Mutual fund screens are on the Internet, easy to use, and often free.

Forbes Mutual Fund Tool
www.forbes.com/tool/toolbox/lipper/screen.asp

For finding mutual fund winners: Forbes Mutual Fund Tool lets you screen the Lipper database of more than 6,000 mutual funds. You select the criteria that match your investment objectives by choosing screening fields.

Investor Square
www.InvestorSquare.com

Limit by criteria: The Investor Square mutual fund screen is particularly useful for beginning investors. The screen is designed to help you find the best 25 performers by category, detailed objective, and specific category (such as short-term or long-term bond fund).

Morningstar
www.morningstar.com

Take it from the experts: Morningstar uses a few sensible preselected variables in its screen of 6,500 mutual funds. Each broad fund category contains narrower categories.

For example, if you're interested in the technology sector funds that have the highest Morningstar ratings, you can first check out the screen on U.S. Stock Funds with the highest Morningstar rating. After you get your results, you get a new pull-down list of narrower fund-category choices, and Technology becomes one of your new options. Choose it, and click View Results to view more choices on-screen.

MSN MoneyCentral Investor
investor.msn.com

Investment wizardry: Now free, MSN MoneyCentral Investor includes the Fund Research Wizard, which can help you identify mutual funds that meet your needs. The Wizard provides several options. First, you can select one of almost a dozen prebuilt screens. Second, you can build a mutual fund screen that includes all the variables you feel are important. Each type of mutual fund screen is easy to use, and you can copy the results to your spreadsheet.

Quicken.com
www.quicken.com

The online presence of a personal finance software leader: Quicken provides three types of mutual fund screens free of charge. Each screen is more complex than the one before it. If you're a beginning investor, this site may be the place to start. The screen's values are updated on a monthly basis.

Smart Money Interactive
www.smartmoney.com

For find the mutual fund that's right for you: Smart Money Interactive has a do-it-yourself mutual fund finder that searches a database of over 6,000 mutual funds.

Other Stuff to Check Out
www.researchmag.com
www.thomsoninvest.net

Mutual Funds: Ratings

There are many independent organizations that rate mutual funds. Some of this information is free and online.

Morningstar
www.morningstar.com

For a comprehensive rating system: Morningstar uses historical data to develop its ratings. The unique feature of the rating system is that it penalizes mutual funds for excess risk that doesn't result in excess returns. Morningstar rates funds for consistently giving the highest returns and adjusts for risk as compared to funds in the same category.

Value Line
www.valueline.com

For a comprehensive rating system: Value Line uses a dual rating system that includes overall rank and measures various performance criteria, including risk.

Other Stuff to Check Out
www.barrons.com
www.businessweek.com
www.forbes.com
www.stockinfo.standardpoor.com
www.wsj.com

News

The Internet offers online news from many large news organizations. Often these organizations will send brief versions of the daily business and investor news or breaking news directly to your e-mailbox free of charge.

ABCNews.com
www.abcnews.com

Features business and industry news, market commentary, and personal finance articles: Catch up on the latest investment issues with the Laughing Stockbroker, The Street, and S&P's Personal Wealth.

Bloomberg Personal Finance
www.bloomberg.com

$ ▨

Bloomberg Personal Finance is loaded with timely news, data, and analyses of financial markets and businesses: Find data on securities, statistics, indices, and research for free. As of this writing, access to the member area of the Web site is $49 per year. Additional levels of service are available, including portfolio tracking, online stock quotes, company news, mutual fund information, and at-home delivery of the monthly magazine.

CBS MarketWatch
cbs.marketwatch.com

▨ ▧ ▥ 🛒

CBS MarketWatch combines the resources of CBS News and Data Broadcasting Corporation: This Web site has many free and fee-based services. The free edition offers delayed stock quotes, feature articles, and breaking news targeted for individual investors. CBS MarketWatch RT is a $34.95/month service offering real-time quotes, company snapshots, deeper historical and fundamental data, and research tools for active investors. CBS MarketWatch LIVE is a branded version of DBC's new StockEdge Online ($79/month). This service gives you a virtual trading desk on any or all of your computers. Using proprietary *active push* software, CBS MarketWatch LIVE allows the user to set up dynamically updated charts, tickers, and quote screens. (Push technology "pushes" the information you preselect to your desktop computer, as opposed to the usual "pulling" of information from different search engines and other sources.)

CNNfn
www.cnnfn.com

▨

CNNfn offers news, articles on investment topics, and professional advice on money management: Major global stock indices, stock quotes, currency rates, commodities, and interest information are also available. CNNfn offers links to official company Web sites, a glossary of business terms, general references, and government resources. At your request, free daily news briefings are sent to your e-mailbox.

Dow Jones
www.dowjones.com

▨ $ 🛒

An old standby: Dow Jones information technology has been on the Internet forever with a wide variety of products and services designed for individual investors who want to manage their own portfolios and make their own investment decisions. A few examples of its products are Smart Money (`www.smartmoney.com`), CNBC (`www.cnbc.com`) Far Eastern Economic Review (`www.feer.com`), Barron's Online (`www.barrons.com`), and The Wall Street Journal (`www.wsj.com`).

NASDAQ
www.nasdaq.com

▨

News you can use: The official site of The NASDAQ Stock Market. By providing an environment for raising capital, NASDAQ has helped thousands of companies achieve growth and make the leap into public ownership.

Reuters moneynet.com
www.moneynet.com/home/moneynet/
　　homepage/homepage.asp

▨ $

Moneynet.com is sponsored by Reuters and specializes in financial data: moneynet.com is a convenient Web site for quotes, financial and company news, charts, research, and market snapshots. If you're looking for free online portfolio management, this site has Portfolio Tracker, one of the better portfolio management programs on the Web.

Newsgroups

Newsgroups contain discussions about different subject areas. The content of these discussions ranges from the ridiculous to the sublime. By using the search engines I list in this section, you may find a newsgroup that's a good source for opinions on different investments.

Beginners Central at Northern Webs
www.northernwebs.com/bc/index.html

For beginning investors: Discover how to navigate your browser's newsreader, select a newsgroup, and post to newsgroups.

Deja
www.deja.com

Usenet without the hassle: You can use this site to search more than 25,000 Usenet newsgroups (including those directly, indirectly, and not at all related to investments) for the information you are seeking. Searches can be by group, author, subject, or dates.

Infinite Ink Finding News Group
www.ii.com/internet

For beginning investors: This user-friendly site can assist you in finding the perfect newsgroup.

netINS's List of Recently Created Newsgroups
www.netins.net/usenet/hyperactive/
   recent-newsgroups.html
For beginning investors: Find out what the new newsgroups are all about.

Usenet Info Center Launch Pad
sunsite.unc.edu/usenet-i
Newsgroup information for beginners: If you're new to Usenet, the resources here can help you get up to speed.

Newsletters

If you subscribe to an online newsletter, you may receive issues several times a day, daily, weekly, biweekly, monthly, or quarterly. Investor newsletters may be free or costly, and they may have hard facts and breaking news or chatty items about the market's latest events. Or they may be completely full of hot air. These are some of the better ones.

GS Research on Demand
www.gsnews.com

Good information, for a price: GS Research on Demand is a high-end service from Goldman Sachs. Research on Demand offers *Research Headlines,* a daily update of rating and estimate changes, and *U.S. Research Viewpoint,* a weekly review of the impact of earnings and rating changes.

Holt Stock Report
metro.turnpike.net/holt
All-encompassing news and comment: The Holt Stock Report can be delivered to your e-mailbox daily. This newsletter provides all the market statistics you need for your investment decision-making.

InvestorGuide Weekly
www.investorguide.com/weekly.htm

Internet for fun and profit: InvestorGuide Weekly is designed to keep you informed of new Web-related developments in the areas of investing and personal finance. It includes links to articles on how to use the Internet for investing, new and improved Web sites, investing in Internet companies, and electronic commerce.

Kiplinger Online
www.kiplinger.com

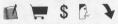

The electronic version of a popular print mag: Kiplinger Online provides news of the day, business forecasts, personal finance, stock quotes, lists of top funds, online calculators, retirement advice, listings of great Internet sites, and financial FAQs.

Newsletter Access: Investments
**www.newsletteraccess.com/subject/
 invest.html**
For locating the right investor newsletter: Newsletter Access has an extensive searchable directory of investment newsletters.

Other Stuff to Check Out
 www.wsj.com
 www.zdnet.com/zdnn

Newspapers

Get the news in quick summaries and then read the full story at your leisure, all-online. Many online newspapers let you customize your paper so you get just the news that interests you.

Newsdirectory.com
www.newsdirectory.com
Newspaper central: Newsdirectory.com contains links to more than 1,500 Web sites for published material from local and specialty papers, magazines, and major news services. You can search titles by keyword.

Individual NewsPage
www.individual.com

News you care about: Individual NewsPage provides free and fee-based information. You can set a personal profile that makes this online newspaper your personal clipping service. Its home page provides breaking news, company links, news searches, and quotes.

InfoBeat
www.infobeat.com

Tailored news: InfoBeat enables you to select user profiles that highlight finance, news, weather, sports, entertainment, or snow. To subscribe, just go to the Web site and enroll. You can also get updates sent to you by e-mail.

Newspaper Association of America
www.naa.org/hotlinks/index.asp
All online papers: The Newspaper Association of America offers comprehensive indexes to the online versions of major newspapers, searchable and browsable.

Other Stuff to Check Out
 www.nyt.com
 www.wsj.com

Night Trading

The following is a list of some of the online brokerages that offer extended-hours trading.

Ameritrade
www.ameritrade.com

$

Join the after-hours club: Ameritrade uses Island, Market XT, Knight/Trimark ECNs for after-hours trading.

Datek
www.daytek.com

Join the after-hours club: Has the longest after-hours club of any online brokerage and uses Island ECN.

E*Trade
www.etrade.com

$

Join the after-hours club: E*Trade uses Instinet for after-hours trading.

Fidelity
www.fidelity.com

Join the after-hours club: Fidelity uses REDIBook ECN for after-hours trading.

Schwab
www.schwab.com

$ ↓ ▢

Join the after-hours club Schwab's Internet trading site (sometimes called eSchwab) uses REDI book for after-hours trading.

Pre-market Information

CBS MarketWatch
www.cbsmarketwatch.com

▢ 🛒 📓 🔖

For after-hours trading news: CBS MarketWatch provides summaries of pre-market trading, and Instinet quotes for actively traded stocks and companies that have released important news.

MarketXT
www.marketxt.com

For after-hours trading news: MarketXT provides investors with access to in-depth financial information. Through the affiliate Web sites of subscribing brokerage firms and the MarketXT Web site, investors can receive breaking news, closing results, market data, and charts.

Other Stuff to Check Out
www.zacks.com
www.reuters.com

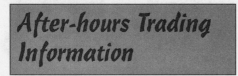

After-hours Trading Information

Nite Traders Online
www.nitetradersonline.com
For after-hours trading news: Nite Traders Online provides after-hours news from CBS MarketWatch, WorldlyInvestor.com, Bridge News, Business Wire: Financial, Internet Wire: Financial News, and more.

Quote.com
www.quote.com

📓 $ ↓ 🛒 🔖 🗒

For after-hours trading news: Quote.com provides after-hours market updates.

Reuters After the Bell by Yahoo!
search.news.yahoo.com/search/news?p=after+the+bell&n=10

📓

For after-hours trading news: Reuters After the Bell by Yahoo! and Reuters After the Bell by DLJ Direct (www.dljdirect.com/dljd/qnnewsab.htm) are highlights of significant after-hours trading activity.

Stockwinners
www.stockwinners.com

📓 $

For after-hours trading news: Stockwinners provides pre-market and after-hours market prices.

Online Brokerages

Electronic brokerages often charge the lowest commissions available. Each commercial enterprise charges a different fee and has its own unique features. Online brokerages are generally as accurate as their full-service counterparts.

Ameritrade
www.ameritrade.com

$

Do-it-yourself, online: Ameritrade features equity and option trading, retirement accounts, and trading on margin.

DLJ Direct
www.dljdirect.com

The online version of a well-known company: Donaldson, Lufkin and Jenrette offers a wide variety of brokerage services, downloadable software, and investment information.

E*Trade
www.etrade.com

Fast and competent: E*Trade charges a flat rate for online trades. One of the more popular online brokerages.

Fidelity
www.fidelity.com

A titan on the Web: Fidelity is the largest mutual fund house around, with 35 percent of the total market. This Web site has news about Fidelity investments, a mutual fund library, online prospectuses, online investment and retirement planning advice, and more.

Invest FAQ
invest-faq.com/links/trading.html
For broker information: For a good alphabetical list of licensed brokers, you can easily look here.

Morgan Stanley Dean Witter
www.online.msdw.com

$ ↘

For reliability: Morgan Stanley Dean Witter offers a breadth of investment products including stocks, bonds, options, and thousands of mutual funds.

Mydiscountbroker.com
www.mydiscountbroker.com

$

For experience and reliability: Mydiscountbroker.com provides a personal broker to aid in investments.

National Association of Securities Dealers
www.nasdr.com/2000.htm

↘

For broker information: Check the background of a brokerage firm before investing.

National Discount Brokers
www.ndb.com

$

Trading plus information: National Discount Brokers is a Chicago-based firm that charges a flat fee for basic transactions. The firm offers portfolio accounting, technical analysis, and more.

New York Stock Exchange
www.nyse.com

For broker information: Each month a brokerage disciplinary action list is published at NYSE.

Schwab
www.schwab.com

$ ↘

For the largest online brokerage: Schwab's Internet trading site (sometimes called eSchwab) offers downloadable trading software, online trading, account information, quotes, and more.

Other Stuff to Check Out
www.abwatley.com
www.accutrade.com
www.computel.com
www.datek.com
www.discover.com
www.jboxford.com
www.money.com/broker
www.msiebert.com
www.mytrack.com
www.protrade.com
www.quick-reilly.com
www.suretrade.com
www.waterhouse.com

Online Calculators

If you have a hard time with the math of personal finance, the Internet can help you. The Net provides many online financial calculators that can do all the math you require.

Bank of America Investment Services
www.bankofamerica.com/investments/
index_tools.cfm?template=inv_tools_
future.cfm

Get a grip: This page from the Bank of America Web site provides a survey of 5 questions. Enter your answers and the online calculator suggests an investment allocation strategy that suits your current needs and situation.

FinanCenter
www.financenter.com

Calculators by the bagful: The FinanCenter provides many online calculators that can help you with your personal finances and investment decision-making. Just click an icon (budget, investments, retirement, and so on) and select the appropriate calculator.

Star Strategic Asset Allocation
www.io.org/~nobid/star.html
Investment by Q&A: Answer the questions, and the online calculator suggests the types of investments that are good matches to your risk-tolerance level.

Portfolio Management: Online Tools

Many online portfolio management programs exist that can monitor your investments, track their performance, and send you end-of-the-day messages to notify you of major changes. This section lists just a few examples.

Stockpoint Portfolio Management
www.stockpoint.com

A favorite of Barron's: Stockpoint provides a free personal portfolio-tracking program. Other Web site offerings include quotes, analysis, stock news, and end-of-the-day e-mail portfolio updates. You can also download this information to your Quicken personal finance program.

Thomson Investors Network
www.thomsoninvest.net

Tracking, by e-mail and on the Web: Thomson Investors Network provides free and fee-based services. Subscribers and registered guests can use the Web site's portfolio tracking services (which include end-of-the-day quotes sent to your e-mailbox).

Yahoo!
edit.my.yahoo.com/config

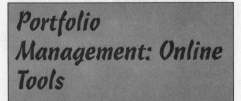

You can Yahoo!, too: Yahoo! has a personalized portfolio program. To create portfolios, just enter a portfolio name and then add the ticker symbols of your investments separated by commas.

Other Stuff to Check Out
www.moneynet.com
my.excite.com
www.quicken.com
www.wsj.com

Quote Servers

The Internet provides many quote servers that provide real-time and delayed stock, mutual fund, bond, option, and Treasury security prices. Here are a few examples of online quote services and their features.

BigCharts
www.bigcharts.com

For delayed quotes: BigCharts is an investment research Web site providing access to research tools like interactive charts, quotes, news, industry analysis, and intraday stock screeners.

Briefing.com
www.briefing.com

For real-time and delayed quotes: Briefing.com features live analysis updates throughout the day covering, stocks, bonds, and foreign markets.

ClearStation
www.clearstation.com

For delayed quotes: ClearStation integrates portfolio management with investment education and the essentials of technical analysis.

Data Broadcasting Online
www.dbc.com

Quickie quotes: Data Broadcasting Online retrieves up to seven ticker symbols at one time. Quotes include last price, change, currency, percent change, opening price, today's low, today's high, previous day's closing price, and volume.

FreeRealTime.com
www.freerealtime.com

For real-time quotes: This site offers free access to real-time stock quotes, financial news, and corporate profiles.

InfoSpace
www.infospace.com/info/rtq/index.htm

For real-time quotes: Infospace offers free real-time stock quotes. Each user is allowed 50 free quotes per day.

Interquote
www.interquote.com

For real-time quotes: Interquote provides real-time, continuously updated quotes with the help of a special Windows program.

MSN Mobile
mobile.msn.com

For real-time wireless quotes: MSN Mobile has a free wireless service that provides alerts on stock quotes based on dozens of preset options from MSN MoneyCentral delivered to wireless devices.

PC Quote
www.pcquote.com

Quotes, now: PC Quote offers many free services and five levels of fee-based service. Free services include ticker symbol lookup, current stock prices, portfolio tracker, company profiles, and Zacks Investment Research broker recommendations.

Yahoo! Mobile
mobile.yahoo.com

For free wireless alerts: Yahoo! Mobile provides stock alerts via your mobile device. The service is free for registered Yahoo! members.

Other Stuff to Check Out
www.cnnfn.com
www.stocksmart.com
www.thomsoninvest.net
www.quote.com

Retirement Planning

Can you retire early? Check out the helpful guidance that the Internet offers, and maybe you can say good-bye to your day job earlier than you think.

Deloitte & Touche LLP

www.dtonline.com/

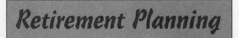

Tax law, translated: Deloitte & Touche LLP provides help interpreting the IRS tax language with a summary of new tax laws and Individual Retirement Accounts (IRAs). Following each tax law change, this site offers suggested action steps that you may want to consider.

Independence Life and Annuity Company FAQ

www.websaver.com/WSfaq.html

Annuity how and why: Independence Life and Annuity Company answers the most frequently asked questions about annuities, costs, and income options.

Social Security Online

www.ssa.gov

For information about your Social Security benefits: The official Social Security Association site speaks to issues regarding Social Security, be it current news or help with Social Security hearings and appeals to tax benefits.

Financial Engines Investment Advisor

www.financialengines.com

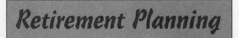

For calculating your retirement needs: Financial forecasting for long-term investments and retirement savings like Roth IRA and 401(k) plans is featured at Financial Engines.

Retirement Planning: Online Worksheets

Need to do a few calculations for your retirement planning? The following Web sites can do the math for you.

BYG Publishing

www.bygpub.com/finance/
    RetirementCalc.htm

High-level planning: This site's retirement planning calculator can assist you in determining what sort of lifestyle you can expect during retirement by showing your 401(k) account balance before and after retirement. You can experiment with different savings amounts so that you can see the effect these amounts will have on your retirement lifestyle.

Fidelity Investments

personal.fidelity.com/toolbox

Retirement calculators, among others: Click the toolbox icon and go to a page with lots of links to online calculators. One of these calculators is for retirement planning. Use the calculator to determine the value of your nest egg at retirement, estimated savings surplus or shortfall, and estimated additional annual savings needed.

Other Stuff to Check Out

www.troweprice.com/retirement/
    retire.html
www.waddell.com

Savings Bonds

You can purchase savings bonds at banks, thrifts, or credit unions. Also, many employers offer payroll deduction plans that allow you to purchase savings bonds. For many people, purchasing savings bonds is the only way they can save money.

The Bureau of the Public Debt
www.publicdebt.treas.gov/sav/
savbene.htm

The government promotes its bonds: The Bureau of the Public Debt provides information on the benefits of savings bonds and covers interest rates and maturity periods. You can either purchase (for the cost of the shipping and handling) or download Bond Wizard, a software program that calculates the value of your savings bonds.

Market Analysis of Savings Bonds
www.bondinformer.com

Easy for anyone to understand: One expert provides a market analysis of short- and long-term interest rates for savings bonds.

Search Engines

Search engines are commercial enterprises that assist Internet users in finding the information they need online.

AltaVista
altavista.digital.com
For locating that last piece of investor information: AltaVista has the largest database on the Internet.

Ask Jeeves
www.ask.com
For locating that last piece of investor information: Ask Jeeves is designed for individuals who are new to the Internet. Write your question in plain English to focus your search.

Dogpile
www.dogpile.com
For locating that last piece of investor information: Dogpile is a metasearch engine that searches the Web, Usenet, FTP, weather, stock quotes, business news, and other news wires, and includes a Web catalog.

Excite
www.excite.com
For locating that last piece of investor information: Excite uses a combination of concept (a general idea) and keyword (a specific word in the Web page) searches. Excite also offers helpful reviews (editor evaluations of Web sites) and Boolean advanced searches.

HotBot
www.hotbot.com
For locating that last piece of investor information: HotBot is ranked as the Internet's best search engine for ease of use, accuracy, and advanced search functionality.

Infoseek
infoseek.go.com
For locating that last piece of investor information: Infoseek is easy to use and accurate. Results are fast. It also has Web site reviews, company profiles, stock prices, and other investor information for one-stop shopping.

LookSmart
www.looksmart.com
For locating that last piece of investor information: LookSmart is a human-compiled directory including more than 1.5 million Web sites.

Lycos
www.lycos.com
For locating that last piece of investor information: It searches its subject categories, and provides editor reviews and a listing of its top 5 percent of the search results.

Netscape
www.netscape.com
For locating that last piece of investor information: The Netscape search engine is powered by Excite but the site allows the option of using other company search engines.

Northern Light
www.northernlight.com
For locating that last piece of investor information: Northern Light has over 230 million sites in its database, makes this search engine major even if it is not a popular as others.

SavvySearch
www.savvysearch.com
For locating that last piece of investor information: SavvySearch uses over 200 search engines, guides, auctions, Usenet archives news archives, shareware libraries, and other Web resources. SavvySearch integrates and lists results by relevancy.

Search.com
www.search.com
For locating that last piece of investor information: Search.com taps into Infoseek for a general database and uses its own database for more subject searches.

Webcrawler
www.metacrawler.com
For locating that last piece of investor information: Webcrawler works like Dogpile but is doesn't search Usenet newsgroups and FTP (file transfer protocol) sites. Search results are not annotated.

Yahoo!
www.yahoo.com
For locating that last piece of investor information: Yahoo! is a popular starting point. This directory search engine includes a vast array of subject directories, categories, and special services.

Search Engine Help

Not all search engines are alike. To get better results, use the search engine that meets your needs. The following Web sites are a few examples of the help you can find online.

About.com
**websearch.about.com/internet/
websearch/msub21.htm**
For getting better search engine results: Discover how to choose the best general-purpose search engine and get advanced search technique tips and tricks.

Gelman Library Search Engine Guide
gwis.circ.gwu.edu/~gelman/websearch
For getting better search engine results: This guide can assist you in understanding education how to search the Web using search engines. Get a description of what search engines do, types of search engines, and basic search techniques.

Nueva School Library Help
**nuevaschool.org/~debbie/library/
research/adviceengine.html**
For getting better search engine results: This handy guide lists examples of information needs and the matching search strategy.

UC Berkeley Tutorial
**www.lib.berkeley.edu/treachinglib/
guides/internet/findinfo.html**
For getting better search engine results: This tutorial has step-by-step directions on how to get the best search results on the Internet.

ZDNet
**www.zdnet.com/pccomp/features/
fea1096/sub2.html**
For getting better search engine results: ZDNet provides an online publication about how to unlock the secrets of search engines and how to search online like a pro.

Stock Market Simulations

Stock market simulation games give online investors the opportunity to practice online investing and try new investment strategies without risking a dime.

Final Bell Play the Market Game
**www.sandbox.net/finalbell/pub-doc/
home.html**

For stock market games for beginning investors: You can explore new investing strategies while you master online trading in this risk-free stock market simulation.

MarketPlayer
www.marketplayer.com

For stock market games for beginning and advanced investors: MarketPlayer teaches how to build an investment strategy by creating a long-term game based on the stock market, pitting players against each other with prizes given to the players that do the best.

Money.com Stock Tournament
www.stocktournament.money.com

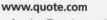

For stock market games for beginning investors: Money.com provides an investment simulation game that puts your stock-picking skills to the test. If you want a few ideas, check out what the game's leaders hypothetically own.

Stocks2Games
www.stocks2games.com
For locating stock market games: Stocks2Games is a list of links to stock market games and simulations.

Virtual Stock Exchange
www.virtualstockexchange.com

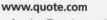

For stock market games for beginning and advanced investors: This stock simulation game allows you to trade shares like a real brokerage account.

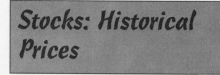

Stocks: Historical Prices

As part of your investment research of equities, you likely want to know the historical stock prices. This information is valuable for your forecasts of future stock prices.

Big Charts
www.bigcharts.com/historical

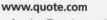

For a blast from the past and more: Big Charts provides graphs of historical stock prices, and will allow you to look up a security's exact closing price.

Historical Stock Data for S&P 500 Stocks
kumo.swcp.com/stocks/

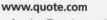

For hard-core analysts: Here, you can download files containing historical information for the stocks that make up the S&P 500 stock index (as well as those that were part of it in the past). The files can be used with analysis software.

Quote.com
www.quote.com

Not just current quotes: Quote.Com provides historical data files as an additional service ($1.95) for current subscribers.

SLS Reference Service
www.sls.lib.il.us/reference/por/features/
    99/stock.html
For a blast from the past: SLS assists local libraries in gathering information and educating staff. The organization supports three key functions: reference, consultation, and continuing education. With these goals in mind, the site provides a great online article titled, "Stock Answers: Finding Historical Stock Prices."

Stockmaster
www.stockmaster.com

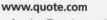

For a blast from the past: Stockmaster charts historical stock prices for one month, two months, three months, six months, and year-to-date, in addition to one year, two years, three years, five years, and ten years.

Yahoo! Finance
chart.yahoo.com

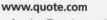

For a blast from the past: Yahoo! offers historical quotes.

Other Stuff to Check Out
    www.prophetfinance.com/
    www.stockwiz.com/stockwiz.html

Stock Screens: Online

Stock screens can help you whittle down your list of investment candidates. Your creative searches can reveal stocks that have just the characteristics you're looking for.

Daily Stocks
www.dailystocks.com

For beginning and advanced investors: The basic stock screens are prebuilt. The advanced stock screens allow you to enter the industry and criteria that you feel are important. You can then query the database for fundamental and historical stock information by using your own investment criteria.

Financial Web
www.financialweb.com

For beginning investors: Financial Web has Super Screener, an online stock-screening tool.

Hoover's StockScreener
www.hoovers.com

For beginning investors: You can use the original stock screen, which uses up to 22 variables and sorts the results alphabetically, or you can use any of Hoover's three prebuilt stock screens to analyze growth, value, and high-yield stocks Each stock screen's results are hyperlinked to a Hoover's *company capsule* (a snapshot of the company), as well as the company's home page, stock quotes and charts, SEC filings, and investment news.

Market Guide's NetScreen
www.marketguide.com/MGI/screen/
AScreen.asp?rt=screen&rn=

Do your own sifting: Market Guide's NetScreen allows you to screen for stocks using any of 20 variables. The database is updated weekly.

MSN Investor
moneycentral.msn.com/investor/
home.asp

Loads of data: MSN Investor has a stock screen called Investment Finder that searches 8,000 companies to find securities that meet your specific criteria. The program uses dozens of variable combinations. You'll have better luck with this site (surprise, surprise) when you use the latest version of Microsoft Internet Explorer.

Nasdaq-Amex Stock Screening
www.amex.com/sitemap/tour_
screening.stm

For beginning and advanced investors: In one search, you can find up to 100 NASDAQ, Amex, and NYSE stocks that meet your criteria.

ResearchMag
www.researchmag.com

Applied research: The stock screen has 12 basic variables that screen more than 9,000 stocks. To use the advanced stock screen, you must be a subscriber. The subscription cost is based on the number of reports you use per year.

Stock Selector
www.stockselector.com

For beginning and advanced investors: Stock Selector has basic and advanced stock screens.

Wall Street City
www.wallstreetcity.com

For beginning and advanced investors: Wall Street City is a comprehensive investment site for beginners and advanced investors. Search capabilities, technical analysis, market commentary, and educational tools are just a small sampling of the information available.

Wall Street Research Net
www.wsrn.com

 $ ⬇

For beginning and advanced investors: This stock screen is designed for beginning and advanced investors who want an easy-to-use quick search tool that focuses on price and yield, growth and size.

Yahoo!
screen.yahoo.com

For beginning investors: Yahoo! offers a stock screener that sorts companies by industry, average analyst recommendation, market capitalization, price earnings ratio, daily volume, estimated earnings growth and stock price performance.

Stock Screens: Prebuilt

Online prebuilt stock screens can assist you in finding the stocks that are worthy of your additional analysis. (Remember, the best pre-built screen is the one that screens for the things that you believe are important.)

MarketPlayer
www.marketplayer.com

Power tools: Market Player provides a relatively advanced stock-screening engine. Instructions about how to use the engine are easy to understand, but you should allow some time for figuring out the program. Market Player has many prebuilt screens that you may find useful. You can also play stock-picking games here.

The Motley Fool
www.fool.com

The original stock chat site: The Motley Fool offers a weekly discussion of its stock screens. The Motley Fool provides screen results that pick out companies that missed

or beat analysts' consensus estimates by 9 percent or more. Stocks are listed alphabetically as well as by descending percentages.

MSN MoneyCentral
moneycentral.msn.com/investor/finder/
   welcome.asp

For many online prebuilt stock screens: MoneyCentral offers the Investment Finder, which identifies stocks and mutual funds that best match your investing strategy. The 17 prebuilt stock screens are based on criteria favored by MoneyCentral Investor editors and well-known professionals.

Quicken.com — Popular Stock Searches
www.quicken.excite.com/investments/
   stocks/search/

For many online prebuilt stock screens: Quicken.com uses a large database that's owned by an independent financial information company, Disclosure.

Other Stuff to Check Out
www.accutrade.com
www.ameritrade.com
www.dljdirect.com

Stock-Screening Software

There are many standalone stock-screening programs that you can use to find investment candidates.

American Association of Individual Investors
www.aaii.org

For stock screening software: In addition to in-depth company fundamentals of over 8,000 stocks and a powerful screening/navigation tool to narrow your choices to the handful matching your investment criteria, Stock Investor Pro provides deeper data and monthly updates. With the enhanced Stock Investor Pro version, more timely data is combined with more in-depth data (over 1,500 data fields per company) to help you keep abreast of the market.

Equis International — MetaStock Professional 7.0
www.equis.com

For stock screening software: MetaStock Professional analyzes stocks, bonds, commodities, futures, indices, mutual funds, and options to assist investors in making better-informed decisions. You can even generate your own buy and sell signals and test your investment strategies to see how much you would have made before using real money. MetaStock for Windows is designed for beginning and experienced investors.

STB Prospector II
www.better-investing.org/computer/
   stbpro.html

For stock screening software: Prospector II examines all the companies and helps beginning and experienced investors find the best stocks in any category they choose. The program displays each company easily and quickly, and graphs up to 20 different financial items to help visualize historical information. Prospector II is a Windows-based program that is fully menu-driven, has a Screening Wizard to search for investor preferences (Growth, Quality, Safety, and so on), and provides fully customizable criteria setup and reports.

Telescan's Investor's Platform (TIP)
www.telescan.com

For stock screening software: The program includes ProSearch 5.0 screening module and Analyzer, Telescan's charting and research program. The database contains historical price and volume information dating back to 1973, and the latest online quotes on securities listed on the New York, American, NASDAQ, and Canadian exchanges as well as the Futures and Options markets.

Stock Valuations

There are several ways you can evaluate the fair value of a stock. Business schools recommend fundamental analysis.

Fundamental Analysis

The Leuthold Group at T. Rowe Price
www.troweprice.com

For online stock evaluations: At the T. Rowe Price home page, enter **Value Investing** in the Search Function box and click Go. At the search results screen, click Value Investing.

Money.com's Fair Value Calculator
www.money.com/money/value

For letting the Internet do the math for you: This online fundamental analysis calculator can assist you in determining the fair value of a stock.

Technical Analysis

Decision Point
decisionpoint.com/TAcourse/
   TAcourseMenu.html

$

For online education: Visit Decision Point for a more detailed explanation of technical analysis techniques.

E-Analytics
www.e-analytics.com/f13.htm

For online education: Find information on the Dow theory to analyze stocks.

Index

IDG Books Worldwide, Inc., End-User License Agreement

READ THIS. You should carefully read these terms and conditions before opening the software packet(s) included with this book ("Book"). This is a license agreement ("Agreement") between you and IDG Books Worldwide, Inc. ("IDGB"). By opening the accompanying software packet(s), you acknowledge that you have read and accept the following terms and conditions. If you do not agree and do not want to be bound by such terms and conditions, promptly return the Book and the unopened software packet(s) to the place you obtained them for a full refund.

1. **License Grant.** IDGB grants to you (either an individual or entity) a nonexclusive license to use one copy of the enclosed software program(s) (collectively, the "Software") solely for your own personal or business purposes on a single computer (whether a standard computer or a workstation component of a multiuser network). The Software is in use on a computer when it is loaded into temporary memory (RAM) or installed into permanent memory (hard disk, CD-ROM, or other storage device). IDGB reserves all rights not expressly granted herein.

2. **Ownership.** IDGB is the owner of all right, title, and interest, including copyright, in and to the compilation of the Software recorded on the disk(s) or CD-ROM ("Software Media"). Copyright to the individual programs recorded on the Software Media is owned by the author or other authorized copyright owner of each program. Ownership of the Software and all proprietary rights relating thereto remain with IDGB and its licensers.

3. **Restrictions on Use and Transfer.**

   (a) You may only (i) make one copy of the Software for backup or archival purposes, or (ii) transfer the Software to a single hard disk, provided that you keep the original for backup or archival purposes. You may not (i) rent or lease the Software, (ii) copy or reproduce the Software through a LAN or other network system or through any computer subscriber system or bulletin-board system, or (iii) modify, adapt, or create derivative works based on the Software.

   (b) You may not reverse engineer, decompile, or disassemble the Software. You may transfer the Software and user documentation on a permanent basis, provided that the transferee agrees to accept the terms and conditions of this Agreement and you retain no copies. If the Software is an update or has been updated, any transfer must include the most recent update and all prior versions.

4. **Restrictions on Use of Individual Programs.** You must follow the individual requirements and restrictions detailed for each individual program in the "About the CD" appendix of this Book. These limitations are also contained in the individual license agreements recorded on the Software Media. These limitations may include a requirement that after using the program for a specified period of time, the user must pay a registration fee or discontinue use. By opening the Software packet(s), you will be agreeing to abide by the licenses and restrictions for these individual programs that are detailed in the "About the CD" appendix and on the Software Media. None of the material on this Software Media or listed in this Book may ever be redistributed, in original or modified form, for commercial purposes.

5. **Limited Warranty.**

   (a) IDGB warrants that the Software and Software Media are free from defects in materials and workmanship under normal use for a period of sixty (60) days from the date of purchase of this Book. If IDGB receives notification within the warranty period of defects in materials or workmanship, IDGB will replace the defective Software Media.

   (b) IDGB AND THE AUTHOR OF THE BOOK DISCLAIM ALL OTHER WARRANTIES, EXPRESS OR IMPLIED, INCLUDING WITHOUT LIMITATION IMPLIED WARRANTIES OF MERCHANTABILITY AND FITNESS FOR A PARTICULAR PURPOSE, WITH RESPECT TO THE SOFTWARE, THE PROGRAMS, THE SOURCE CODE CONTAINED THEREIN, AND/OR THE TECHNIQUES DESCRIBED IN THIS BOOK. IDGB DOES NOT WARRANT THAT THE FUNCTIONS CONTAINED IN THE SOFTWARE WILL MEET YOUR REQUIREMENTS OR THAT THE OPERATION OF THE SOFTWARE WILL BE ERROR FREE.

   (c) This limited warranty gives you specific legal rights, and you may have other rights that vary from jurisdiction to jurisdiction.

6. **Remedies.**

   (a) IDGB's entire liability and your exclusive remedy for defects in materials and workmanship shall be limited to replacement of the Software Media, which may be returned to IDGB with a copy of your receipt at the following address: Software Media Fulfillment Department, Attn.: *Investing Online For Dummies,* 3rd Edition, IDG Books Worldwide, Inc., 10475 Crosspoint Blvd., Indianapolis, IN 46256, or call 800-762-2974. Please allow three to four weeks for delivery. This Limited Warranty is void if failure of the Software Media has resulted from accident, abuse, or misapplication. Any replacement Software Media will be warranted for the remainder of the original warranty period or thirty (30) days, whichever is longer.

   (b) In no event shall IDGB or the author be liable for any damages whatsoever (including without limitation damages for loss of business profits, business interruption, loss of business information, or any other pecuniary loss) arising from the use of or inability to use the Book or the Software, even if IDGB has been advised of the possibility of such damages.

   (c) Because some jurisdictions do not allow the exclusion or limitation of liability for consequential or incidental damages, the above limitation or exclusion may not apply to you.

7. **U.S. Government Restricted Rights.** Use, duplication, or disclosure of the Software by the U.S. Government is subject to restrictions stated in paragraph (c)(1)(ii) of the Rights in Technical Data and Computer Software clause of DFARS 252.227-7013, and in subparagraphs (a) through (d) of the Commercial Computer–Restricted Rights clause at FAR 52.227-19, and in similar clauses in the NASA FAR supplement, when applicable.

8. **General.** This Agreement constitutes the entire understanding of the parties and revokes and supersedes all prior agreements, oral or written, between them and may not be modified or amended except in a writing signed by both parties hereto that specifically refers to this Agreement. This Agreement shall take precedence over any other documents that may be in conflict herewith. If any one or more provisions contained in this Agreement are held by any court or tribunal to be invalid, illegal, or otherwise unenforceable, each and every other provision shall remain in full force and effect.

Installation Instructions

Here's some of what you can find on the *Investing Online For Dummies,* 3rd Edition, CD-ROM:

- ✔ An easy-to-navigate, electronic version of the book's Investing Online Directory, so that you can quickly jump to the Internet sites you need for selecting, buying, selling, and tracking your investments online.
- ✔ Free, high-quality software to assist you with a variety of investor tasks.
- ✔ Shareware and freeware programs for financial planning and analysis, portfolio management, and other essential investor activities.
- ✔ Demonstration versions and free trials of invaluable software tools for online investors.

For details about the contents of the CD and instructions for installing the software from the CD, see the "About the CD" appendix in this book.

YOUR ONLINE RESOURCE

WWW.DUMMIES.COM

Discover Dummies Online!

The Dummies Web Site is your fun and friendly online resource for the latest information about *For Dummies* books and your favorite topics. The Web site is the place to communicate with us, exchange ideas with other *For Dummies* readers, chat with authors, and have fun!

Ten Fun and Useful Things You Can Do at www.dummies.com

1. Win free *For Dummies* books and more!

2. Register your book and be entered in a prize drawing.

3. Meet your favorite authors through the IDG Books Worldwide Author Chat Series.

4. Exchange helpful information with other *For Dummies* readers.

5. Discover other great *For Dummies* books you must have!

6. Purchase Dummieswear® exclusively from our Web site.

7. Buy *For Dummies* books online.

8. Talk to us. Make comments, ask questions, get answers!

9. Download free software.

10. Find additional useful resources from authors.

Link directly to these ten fun and useful things at
http://www.dummies.com/10useful

WWW.DUMMIES.COM

For other technology titles from IDG Books Worldwide, go to
www.idgbooks.com

Not on the Web yet? It's easy to get started with *Dummies 101*®: *The Internet For Windows*® *98* or *The Internet For Dummies*® at local retailers everywhere.

IDG BOOKS WORLDWIDE

Find other *For Dummies* books on these topics:

Business • Career • Databases • Food & Beverage • Games • Gardening • Graphics • Hardware
Health & Fitness • Internet and the World Wide Web • Networking • Office Suites
Operating Systems • Personal Finance • Pets • Programming • Recreation • Sports
Spreadsheets • Teacher Resources • Test Prep • Word Processing

IDG BOOKS WORLDWIDE
BOOK REGISTRATION

Register This Book and Win!

We want to hear from you!

Visit **http://my2cents.dummies.com** to register this book and tell us how you liked it!

- ✔ Get entered in our monthly prize giveaway.

- ✔ Give us feedback about this book — tell us what you like best, what you like least, or maybe what you'd like to ask the author and us to change!

- ✔ Let us know any other *For Dummies®* topics that interest you.

Your feedback helps us determine what books to publish, tells us what coverage to add as we revise our books, and lets us know whether we're meeting your needs as a *For Dummies* reader. You're our most valuable resource, and what you have to say is important to us!

Not on the Web yet? It's easy to get started with *Dummies 101®: The Internet For Windows® 98* or *The Internet For Dummies®* at local retailers everywhere.

Or let us know what you think by sending us a letter at the following address:

For Dummies Book Registration
Dummies Press
10475 Crosspoint Blvd.
Indianapolis, IN 46256

FOR DUMMIES ™

BESTSELLING BOOK SERIES